RINGO
STARR

ENCYCLOPEDIA

THE

RINGO STARR

ENCYCLOPEDIA

BILL HARRY

First published in Great Britain in 2004 by
Virgin Books Ltd
Thames Wharf Studios
Rainville Road
London
W6 9HA

ISBN 07535 08435

Typeset by Phoenix Photosetting, Chatham, Kent
Printed and bound in Great Britain by Mackays of Chatham,
Chatham, Kent

INTRODUCTION

In those heady days in Liverpool when the music that became known as the Liverpool Sound (or the Mersey Sound) was still confined to the Merseyside conurbation, I spent most waking hours with the aspiring young hopefuls in the cellars and dancehalls of the city, where they created a type of music that was to reverberate around the world.

Coining the name Mersey Beat and founding a newspaper of that name, I was rubbing shoulders with the musicians who I looked upon as friends. Apart from the Beatles, one of my favourite groups was Rory Storm and the Hurricanes, and we used to sit around together in places like the Jacaranda, the Grapes, the Blue Angel and backstage at gigs and parties. Rory's drummer Ritchie was a nice bloke; he had a good heart, a person you felt comfortable with. He also used to drop in to see us at the *Mersey Beat* office regularly when he was visiting the dole office in Renshaw Street.

I liked Pete Best a lot, but when Ritchie joined the Beatles, I didn't have divided loyalties. There wasn't much between them as far as musical ability was concerned. After spending months in Hamburg developing their sound (in what I called their 'baptism of fire'), they returned to Liverpool and blew everyone's mind. They were brilliant. I'd been involved with them since 1958 in my art school days and before their trip to Hamburg had enjoyed their role as the 'college band' when we booked them for our art college dances.

But after Hamburg they were giants. The few people who had actually been aware of them before they went to Germany could hardly believe how much they had progressed in every way. A quantum improvement! And Pete Best had improved too, giving them a fantastic sound with his 'atom beat'. When he left the Beatles, joined Lee Curtis and the All Stars and then led his own groups, I gave him lots of promotion in *Mersey Beat* – covers, write-ups, and his new group were voted No. 2 to the Beatles in the *Mersey Beat* poll. I thought he'd achieve a profile as a drummer/group leader in the way Dave Clark had, but it wasn't to be.

But Ritchie was great, no doubt about it. Not only a fantastic musician who fitted neatly into the group, but someone who everyone seemed to take to because of his good nature and kind character. Once the Beatles began to achieve success I continued to meet them for drinks in the Blue Angel and attended their concerts and TV shows, visiting them backstage. I'd go and visit Ritchie's lovely mum Elsie at Admiral Grove, where she'd proudly relate to me stories about her son over hot cups of tea.

When the Lennon and McCartney songwriting team began to domi-
nate, I suggested to George that he write songs with Ritchie and create
a balance with a Harrison/Starkey songwriting partnership. He told me
he did try it and they did write a song together. I mentioned it in *Mersey
Beat* but never knew the title of the song and it was one they never
recorded. It seemed a songwriting partnership wouldn't work,
although George tried his hand and came up with 'Don't Bother Me',
the beginning of a talent which ended up producing some of the
strongest tracks on the *Abbey Road* album with 'Something' and 'Here
Comes The Sun'.

Since Ritchie wasn't too keen on the songwriting aspect, I noticed he
now sported a Pentax camera and asked if he could take photographs
for *Mersey Beat*. He agreed, but I never received any. I heard he did
come out with a book of photographs, but I've never seen it.

I was to learn of his early nervousness with the group: the feeling
that he wasn't initially accepted by John Lennon, that Brian Epstein
hadn't really wanted him, and the attitude of fans who were still gaga
about Pete Best.

George was the one who was Ritchie's friend from the start and the
one, I suspect, who did the most to persuade the others to accept him
in the group. John and Paul gradually came to respect his talent,
although I was aware of the comments they made at times which
seemed to regard him as some sort of comic or clown. Perhaps it was
good-natured humour – I'll have to give them the benefit of the doubt.

I remember one time when the media accused John of calling Ringo
ugly. John wrote me a letter to explain. He said that a fan had sent
them drawings of each of them. He looked at the picture of Ringo,
which was almost a caricature and said, 'Isn't he ugly?' and was actually referring to the bad drawing and not to Ringo himself.

I'm surprised that there have been shoals of books on John and Paul,
hardly any about George until after his death, but only one about
Ringo until this encyclopedia. With almost 2,000 books about the
Beatles having appeared in print, and a new book about the Beatles
currently running at one new publication every two weeks, it's incredible that the Beatle who travelled the farthest has attracted the least
attention among writers.

I think American fans got it right when he became the most popular
Beatle on the group's initial American trips, with Brian Epstein
remarking that 'America discovered Ringo'.

Why do I say that he was the one who travelled farthest? Because
Ritchie had the most remarkable journey of them all on his way to
becoming one of the most famous men in the world. He was born in
extreme poverty, deserted by a father when he was three and reared by
a single parent who lavished love on him, but had to struggle to make
ends meet on a job as a barmaid.

Born into one of the poorest and most run-down areas of Liverpool, already a city with few prospects for its young citizens, he suffered extreme ill-health, nearly died, spent literally years in hospitals, had barely any schooling and seemed likely to live his whole life mired in poverty. He didn't have conventional looks at a time when pretty faces were in vogue, particularly in show business, and was often the butt of jokes. What he did have, despite all that had happened to him, was a gentle nature, one that wasn't poisoned by anger at his apparent early poor fortune. He was someone whose cup was half full rather than half empty. He had a ready sense of humour and his Ringoisms were to inspire the Beatles in years to come.

So this young person from the direst of backgrounds did, as far as I am concerned, spark off the most remarkable rags-to-riches story of his time. A small youth plagued by poor health, and apparently with no prospects, rose above it all and became one of the most famous individuals on the planet, mixing with the elite, with two loving sons and a daughter, married to a beautiful film star, with mansions and houses in Monte Carlo, England and Los Angeles, successfully performing the music he loves with musicians he respects.

I can well understand how, despite not having the conventional good looks, he had the personality, humour and warmth that were probably far more appealing to women. His name has been associated with a number of glamorous women. The American scandal magazine *Confidential* even hinted that Ringo and film actress Ann Margret were having a romance, and commented that Ringo had 'bent her shell-like pink ears with an hour of long-distance oogly-googling, all in a special Teddy Boy lingo that left little Annie limp'. His name was also linked with actresses Shelley Duvall and Nancy Andrews, singer Lynsey De Paul and finally, Barbara Bach.

But when he found love, it was constant, particularly in the relationship with his second wife Barbara, who sees, like a lot of people before her, that the inner Ritchie is a unique and loving person who has found a deserved place in the scheme of things.

ACKNOWLEDGMENTS

Many thanks to Virginia Harry, Bill King, Erich Weber, Carmen Salmon, Rene van Harlem, Mal Jefferson, Spencer Leigh, Alan Clayson, David Maggin, *Beatlefan*, *Beatles Unlimited*, *Daydreaming* and Beatle fans who continue to provide me with support and information. I would also like to thank Carolyn Thorne and Barbara Phelan for their editorial support and everyone at Virgin Books for making my book a reality.

Please feel free to contact me via my website:
www.triumphpc.com/mersey-beat

Act Naturally

A number originally penned by Johnny Russell and Voni Morrison that the Beatles recorded in 1965, with Ringo on lead vocals. The track was included on the *Help!* album, on the American LP *Yesterday ... And Today* and on the EP 'Yesterday'. It was also used on the B side of the American single of 'Yesterday' released on 13 September 1965, which reached No. 47 in the American charts.

Ringo also performed it on the Beatles' 1965 American tour, on a 1965 appearance on *The Ed Sullivan Show*, on the Beatles' 1965 British tour, on the 1965 TV show *Cilla* and on the 1978 'Ringo' television special.

It had been a No. 1 country and western hit for Buck Owens in March 1963, and on Monday 27 March 1989 Ringo joined Owens at Abbey Road Studios to record a new version of the number, lasting 2 minutes and 59 seconds.

This single was produced by Jerry Crutchfield and Jim Shaw and issued in America on Capitol B-44409 on 29 July 1989, although it didn't enter the charts. The flipside featured Buck Owens performing the Harlon Howard number 'The Key's In The Mailbox'.

10 Admiral Grove

The house in the Liverpool 8 district of Dingle where Elsie Starkey moved with her son in 1944. Her husband had left her but had moved further up Madryn Street and Elsie didn't want to keep bumping into him. She also had to move to a house where the rent was cheaper, as she only earned her living as a barmaid at the Empress pub at the time. Ringo was to live there until the beginning of 1963.

Ringo's mother Elsie and stepfather Harry moved out of the terraced house in 1965 when Ringo bought them a bungalow.

After All These Years

A track from the 1992 *Time Takes Time* album, written by Ringo Starr and Johnny Warman. It was produced by Jeff Lynne and engineered by Richard Dodd. Ringo was on lead vocals, drums and percussion and Jeff Lynne on guitar, bass, piano, keyboards and backing vocals. The number is 3 minutes and 11 seconds in length.

Akustic Studio

A tiny recording booth at Kirchenalle 57 in Hamburg, Germany, where John, Paul, George and Ringo played together on record for the very first time on Saturday 16 October 1960.

Ringo was a member of Rory Storm and the Hurricanes at the time, a group who were topping the bill over the Beatles at the Kaiserkeller club in the Grosse Freiheit.

Liverpool agent Allan Williams, who had booked the Hurricanes and the Beatles into the club, was very impressed with Lu Walters, the singer with the Hurricanes. He decided to make a recording of Walters and took him along to the Akustic, which was on the fifth floor of a building at the rear of Hamburg's main railway station. Members of the Hurricanes and John, Paul and George accompanied him – Pete Best went into the city to buy some new drumsticks and Stu Sutcliffe didn't bother coming along as Walters was also a bass guitarist. Williams then had John, Paul and George back Lu on the number 'Summertime'. Hurricanes drummer Ringo also played on the track. Lu then recorded two further numbers, 'Fever' and 'September Song', this time backed by Ty Brien, Johnny Guitar and Ringo from the Hurricanes.

John, Paul and George then asked Williams if he'd let them record some numbers, presumably with Ringo on drums, but Williams refused, not willing to pay the small fee, around £5, for them to record.

Alibi

A track from the 1983 *Old Wave* album, written by Richard Starkey and Joe Walsh and produced by Walsh. Ringo is on lead vocals, drums and percussion, Joe Walsh on guitar and backing vocals, Mo Foster on bass and Gary Brooker and Chris Stainton on keyboards. It is 4 minutes and 2 seconds in length.

Alice In Wonderland

A CBS TV adaptation of the Lewis Carroll tale, screened in two parts on 9 and 10 December 1985. Ringo appeared as the Mock Turtle and sang the Steve Allen song 'Nonsense'. It was recorded in May 1985 and later issued on Warner Home Video VHS PEV 34099.

All By Myself

The opening track of side two of Ringo's 1974 album *Goodnight Vienna*. The number was co-penned by Ringo and Vini Poncia and features John Lennon and Alvin Robinson on guitars and Dr John on piano, with vocal backing by Richard Perry, Vini Poncia, Clydie King, Linda Lawrence and Joe Greene. It is 3 minutes and 18 seconds in length.

All In The Name Of Love
A track from the 1992 *Time Takes Time* album, written by Lynn Williams. It was produced by Phil Ramone and engineered by Bill Drescher. Ringo was on lead vocals, drums and percussion, Jeffrey Vanson on keyboards and song arrangements, Michael Thompson and Jeff Baxter on guitars, Neil Stubenhaus on bass, Mark Hudson on additional percussion and backing vocals, Mark Hart on additional synth keyboards, guitar and backing vocals, and Craig Copeland, Naomi Star and Darlene Koldenhoven on backing vocals. The number is 3 minutes and 42 seconds in length.

All-Starr Band, The
When David Fishof approached Ringo to tour again, the concept was an innovative one, to gather together artists who had enjoyed major hits in the charts in one group to tour and play their various hits.

Ringo was to say, 'I love to play with people who shine – that's what it's always been about for me. We're all playing together, but the fact that you're singing the song is a bonus.'

He was also to say, 'I'm not bothered about making records. I just love playing live, it's what I do – I'm not a plumber, I'm not an electrician. I'm a drummer.'

It's interesting to note that Ringo also liked to have other drummers in the All-Starr Band to play alongside him and support him on his solo vocals.

When he appeared with the first All-Starr Band, it was his debut public appearance since his battle against his drink problem. The band comprised Levon Helm and Rick Danko of the Band, Billy Preston, Dr John, former Eagle Joe Walsh, Clarence 'Big Man' Clemons (Bruce Springsteen's saxophone player), Nils Lofgren and Jim Keltner on drums. The band was active between 23 July and 3 September 1989.

The second All-Starr Band existed from 2 June to 6 September 1992 and comprised Dave Edmunds, Todd Rundgren, Timmy Cappello, Zak Starkey, Burton Cummings, Nils Lofgren, Timothy B. Schmit and Joe Walsh.

The third All-Starr Band ran from 2 July to 28 August 1995 and comprised Mark Rivera, Randy Bachman, Felix Cavaliere, John Entwistle, Mark Farner, Billy Preston and Zak Starkey.

The fourth All-Starr Band was almost an all-British line-up and lasted from 28 April to 7 June 1997, comprising Peter Frampton on guitar, Jack Bruce on bass, Gary Brooker on keyboards and Simon Kirke on drums. The only American musician in the band was saxophonist and percussionist Mark Rivera, who also acted as the tour's musical director.

The fifth All-Starr Band ran from 12 February to 29 March 1999 and comprised Simon Kirke, Jack Bruce, Gary Brooker, Todd Rundgren and Timmy Cappello.

The sixth All-Starr Band existed from 1 May to 29 June 2000 and comprised Mark Rivera, Simon Kirke, Dave Edmunds, Eric Carmen and Jack Bruce.

The seventh All-Starr Band in the summer of 2001 comprised Howard Jones, Ian Hunter, Sheila E, Greg Lake, Roger Hodgson and Mark Rivera.

The eighth All-Starr Band in 2003 comprised Paul Carrack, former member of Squeeze and Mike and the Mechanics on keyboards and vocals, Colin Hay of Men At Work on guitar and vocals, Sheila E on drums and percussion and John Waite from the Babys and Bad English on bass and vocals.

Although Ringo gathered together past and present members of the All-Starr Band for a live concert at the Bottom Line club in New York on 12 June 1998 – as a rehearsal and warm-up for the appearance on VH-1 *Storytellers* the following night – he dubbed the group Ringo and the Roundheads.

For the first time he performed two numbers of his own with the group that he'd never played with the All-Starr Band on tour, 'Octopus's Garden' and 'Don't Pass Me By'.

After the performance it was suggested that the time might be right for Ringo to go on tour as a 100% Ringo Starr show. He commented, 'I don't really ever want to do the two hours where it's just me. I like the mixture of the All-Starrs because it's so much fun. I get down in front and do the entertaining thing, and then I'm back behind the drums. It can't be bad backing Jack Bruce and Peter Frampton, and having all the fun while they take the weight.'

Alpha Band, The

A trio comprising T-Bone Burnette, Steven Soles and David Mansfield. Ringo first met them on 25 January 1976 when he appeared on the Rolling Thunder Revue at the Houston Astrodome. He played drums on the tracks 'Born In Captivity' and 'You Angel You' on the trio's 1977 album *Spark In The Dark*.

Andrews, Nancy Lee

Ringo's live-in lover from 1974 to 1980.

In January 1974, when she was 24, he took her visiting sites around London on her first visit to Europe and then the couple flew back to California on Friday 7 February. In December 1974 the two moved to Monte Carlo for tax reasons, although they returned to spend Christmas at Tittenhurst Park.

In 1975 Nancy was cited in Maureen's divorce action.

In July 1978 Ringo and Nancy began work on a 30-minute film to promote Ringo's album *Bad Boy*. Christian Topps was director, but the special was never completed. All that has been seen is an excerpt for *Tonight* which features Ringo and Nancy dancing together.

Nancy co-wrote 'Las Brisas' with Ringo, a number that appeared on his *Ringo's Rotogravure* album. She also took the photographs that appeared in the inner sleeve of his *Bad Boy* album.

When Ringo was filming *Caveman* he fell in love with his co-star Barbara Bach and dropped Nancy, who was to say, 'I was furious at being abruptly dropped by Ringo for Barbara. He had already proposed to me and I wanted to settle down with him and raise a family. I was very hurt and angry at the way he treated me. He did not behave at all like a gentleman. I had been his "wife" for the best part of a decade and he suddenly dropped me without warning. It was like being slapped in the face. I considered Barbara as a close friend and I felt humiliated that their love affair had started behind my back.'

On 1 April 1981 she filed a lawsuit against Ringo at the Los Angeles Superior Court, claiming damages of $5 million as her right to half of the assets bought while they were still together. In filing for a share of Ringo's income for the six years that they had lived together, Nancy claimed that Ringo breached an oral contract in which he'd promised that he'd support her for life in exchange for her abandoning her acting career to look after him. Ringo said that he would eventually marry Nancy, but invariably kept postponing the actual day the event would take place.

She was unsuccessful in her suit.

Angel In Disguise

Paul McCartney wrote 'Angel In Disguise' especially for Ringo's *Time Takes Time* album. Paul had sent Ringo an incomplete piano/drum-machine demo of the number that Ringo completed by adding the final verse, with the backing tracks being recorded on 9 September 1991. Peter Asher produced the recording at Conway Studios in Los Angeles, but it was not included on the album.

Angelus, Paul

A Liverpool actor who dubbed Ringo's voice for the animated feature *Yellow Submarine*.

Art Of Dying, The

A book that includes George Harrison's account of how he wrote the song 'The Art Of Dying', which became a companion book to the film *Walking After Midnight*. It was published in January 1991 with a preface by Ringo.

As Far As We Can Go

A track from the 1983 *Old Wave* album, written by Russ Ballard and produced by Joe Walsh. Ringo was on lead vocals, Joe Walsh on synthesizers and backing vocals and Joe Vitale on piano and backing vocals. It is 3 minutes and 51 seconds in length.

Asher, Peter

A British singer/record producer, born in London on 22 June 1944. He was the brother of Jane Asher, Paul McCartney's long-time girlfriend, and also one half of the duo Peter and Gordon. McCartney gave the duo a number of songs to record, beginning with their first hit 'A World Without Love'. When Peter and Gordon disbanded, Asher became A&R man at Apple Records, signing up artists such as James Taylor. When Allen Klein arrived to take over management of the company, James Taylor left and Asher followed him to America where he became Taylor's manager. He then forged a successful career producing and managing other artists such as Linda Ronstadt, Carole King, Diana Ross, Little Feat, Bonnie Raitt, Cher and Joni Mitchell.

Ringo commissioned him to be one of the producers of the 1992 *Time Takes Time* album and he produced 'Golden Blunders', 'Everyone Wins' and 'Angel In Disguise'.

Aspel And Company

A London Weekend Television chat show hosted by Michael Aspel. Ringo and George appeared together on the programme, recording it on Thursday 3 March 1988 at LWT's South Bank Studios in London. The show was transmitted two days later.

George appeared first and recalled his days with the Beatles and the making of the 'When We Was Fab' promo. Then Aspel introduced Ringo, who turned to George and said, 'I've met you before.' When Aspel persuaded Ringo to take off his dark glasses, George said, 'He's got the bluest eyes in the world.'

Describing the individual members of the Beatles, Ringo said, 'I had the mothers and the children. Always have. George had the Mystics. John had the –'

'Intellectuals,' interjected George.

Ringo continued, 'And Paul had the teenies. That was part of our strength. We were a band that was appealing to the children, to grand-parents.'

Commenting on the Beatles visit to Rishikesh over twenty years previously, Ringo said, 'I still thank Maharishi for what he said, but in the end I felt he was telling stories, but that's my problem.' When Ringo mentioned that he left after ten days, George said, 'He ran out of beans.'

Among other topics the two commented on were media claims that there was bad blood between George and Paul, which George and

Ringo denied, the possibility of a reunion between the three of them, Apple and *Thomas The Tank Engine*.

George and Ringo's appearance lasted for 35 minutes and Thelma Barlow of the TV soap *Coronation Street* was also on the show.

Attention

A track from the 1981 album *Stop And Smell The Roses,* lasting 3 minutes and 19 seconds. It was written by Paul McCartney, who also produced the track.

B.B. King In London
An album issued in America on 11 October 1971 and in Britain on 19 November 1971. Recording began on 8 June and ended on 16 June 1971. Ringo performed on three of the album tracks. Other artists appearing as guests on the album included Peter Green, Gary Wright, Bobby Keys, Jim Keltner and Alexis Korner. The BBC was also at the recording, filming for a television documentary.

Bach, Barbara
See Starkey, Barbara Bach

Bachman, Randy
A Canadian musician, born on 27 September 1943 in Winnipeg, Manitoba. He was a founder member of the band Guess Who. After leaving them in 1970, he made a solo album, *Axe*, and then founded the band Brave Belt in 1971, which was renamed Bachman-Turner Overdrive the following year.

He became a member of Ringo's third All-Starr Band in 1995 and recalled, 'When my phone rang and the voice said, "Hello, this is Ringo calling from Monaco – welcome to the band," I was speechless. It was a dream come true. It was the ultimate rock'n'roll bar band led by the world's greatest rock drummer.'

In the band Bachman performed the Bachman-Turner Overdrive hits 'Takin' Care Of Business' and 'You Ain't Seen Nothin' Yet', as well as Guess Who's 'No Sugar Tonight' and is included on the CD *Ringo Starr And His Third All-Starr Band Volume 1*.

He said, 'Playing guitar on Ringo's songs every night and looking back over my shoulder and hearing and seeing him playing drums on my songs was the highlight of my musical career. Every show was memorable. I would have done it for nothing. It was a privilege. For his birthday my wife and I had a newly discovered star named after him called "The Ringo Starr".'

Back Off Boogaloo

The single was released in Britain on Apple R 5944 on Friday 19 March 1972 and reached No. 2 in the *New Musical Express* charts. It was issued in America on Apple 1849 on Saturday 20 March and reached No. 9 in the charts. George Harrison produced the A side and also played guitar on it. The other musicians were Gary Wright on keyboards, Klaus Voormann on bass and Ringo on drums and vocals. The backing vocalists were Madeline Bell, Lesley Duncan and Jean Gilbert. It is 3 minutes and 18 seconds in length.

Ringo and Klaus Voormann produced the flipside 'Blindman', from Ringo's western movie of the same name.

Ringo related how the title 'Back Off Boogaloo' came about during an interview on VH-1's *Storytellers* programme in May 1998. He revealed that Marc Bolan influenced it. It occurred when Ringo invited Bolan for dinner. Ringo recalled, 'He was an energised guy. He used to speak: "Back off, boogaloo ... ooh you, boogaloo ... do you want some potatoes? Ooh you, boogaloo."'

Ringo recorded a new version of 'Back Off Boogaloo' for his 1981 album *Stop And Smell The Roses*. Harry Nilsson produced the track and the arrangement was by Van Dyke Parks. The new recording included Ringo singing parts of his own numbers and those by the Beatles such as 'With A Little Help From My Friends', 'Help!', 'Lady Madonna', 'Good Day Sunshine', 'It Don't Come Easy' and 'Baby You're A Rich Man'.

Bad Boy (album)

This album was recorded in 1977, released on the Polydor label and issued in Britain on Polydor 2310 599 in June 1978. Three years were to pass before his next album release.

Although Ringo remained with Polydor in Britain, he'd switched to Atlantic in America and now changed to the small label Portrait with this album (it was later issued on CD in March 1991 by Sony on Epic EK 35378). It was issued in America on Portrait JR-353778 on 21 April 1978 and was Ringo's only album on the Portrait label, reaching No. 129 in the American charts.

Most of Ringo's previous albums had been recorded in Los Angeles, but this album was recorded at the Elite Recording Studio in the Bahamas and the Can-Base Studio in Canada. Vini Poncia produced it.

The backing musicians are anonymous and are credited as: Push-a-lone on lead guitar, Git-tar on rhythm guitar, Hamish Bissonette on synthesizers and Die-sel on bass guitar, with Vini Poncia's Peaking Duck Orchestra and Chorus.

John Kosh designed the sleeve; the photographs on the cover and inside sleeve were by Nancy Andrews and the back-cover photograph by Ringo.

The tracks were: Side One: 'Who Needs A Heart', 'Bad Boy', 'Lipstick Traces (On A Cigarette)', 'Heart On My Sleeve' and 'Where Did Our Love Go'. Side Two: 'Hard Times', 'Tonight', 'Monkey See – Monkey Do', 'Old Time Relovin'' and 'A Man Like Me'.

Bad Boy (song)

A track on the 1978 *Bad Boy* album lasting 3 minutes and 13 seconds. The number was originally penned by Louis Armstrong and Avon Long. The Jive Brothers featuring Clarence Palmer recorded it and their version was a chart hit in the States in 1957. Sha Na Na and Mink De Ville also recorded the number.

Band, The

A Canadian group with one American member. They were Eric Hudson, Robbie Robertson, Richard Manuel and Rick Danko, all from Ontario, and Levon Helm, who was born in Arkansas.

The group had originally formed as Ronnie Hawkins' backing band, the Hawks, but changed their name to the Band and became backing group for Bob Dylan. They had success with their own album *Music From Big Pink*. When they appeared backing Dylan at the Isle of Wight Festival on 20 August 1969, Ringo, John Lennon and George Harrison were in attendance.

The group gave their farewell concert at the Winterland Ballroom in San Francisco on Thanksgiving Day 1976 and several guest artists were to join them on stage, including Ringo, Eric Clapton, Bob Dylan, Ronnie Hawkins, Ron Wood and Dr John. The event was recorded for posterity by Martin Scorsese, who directed a film of it called *The Last Waltz*, acclaimed as one of the best concert films ever made.

However, there were various reunion concerts over succeeding years and the Band made some further recordings. Among their records was 'Sunshine Life For Me (Sail Away Raymond)' a George Harrison composition that Ringo had recorded for his *Ringo* album. Richard Manuel wasn't on the single, having committed suicide on 4 March 1986.

Robbie Robertson played on Ringo's album *Goodnight Vienna*, and both Rick Danko and Levon Helm were members of Ringo's first All-Starr Band in 1989.

Barbara Walters Special

Barbara Walters has been a major American television interviewer for many years and she interviewed Ringo and Barbara for her 'Barbara Walters Special', which was transmitted at 10 p.m. on 31 March 1981. This was during the American promotion for Ringo's *Caveman* film.

Here is a basic transcript:

Barbara W (to Barbara Bach): Barbara, is it difficult to be with a man who is part legend as well as part man?

Ringo: All legend! All man!

Barbara B: I don't live with the legend, I live with my Ritchie. Every once in a while Ringo comes popping out at me.

Barbara W: What's the difference?

Barbara B: Well, Ringo is the performer.

Ringo: He's the brat.

Barbara B: Ringo is the loudmouth sometimes. Ringo's the shades and the drinks and the cigarettes when you prefer him not to. And, uh, his Ringo is the deep voice, you know. And Ritchie is my Ritchie.

Barbara W: Very different?

Barbara B: No. Yes! I'd say different enough.

Ringo: It's attitude!

Barbara B: It's the attitude.

Ringo: They like the shades and the drugs and the drinking.

Barbara W: Do you drink too much?

Ringo: No. She just thinks I do. It's just our little joke you see and when it goes over TV it'll be in all the national papers. Oh, he's a drunk and did you see him on the Barbara Walters show ... and he had his shades on ... it must mean he was on drugs. So, you know, they laugh at all the crap that goes down but, you see, you also learn that there's no controlling them. So you live your life and you have a good time or whatever ... it's not always good.

Barbara W: Do you see yourselves acting together? Do you want to do more films?

Ringo: We're doing it now.

Barbara W: At this very moment? Is this how you see your life?

Barbara B: We just want to be together. We don't care, either one of us, which one is working.

Ringo: We will get married. We never actually said that before.

Barbara W: You're getting married soon?

Ringo: We're getting married this year. So that's the end of that. Like, we'll never get married again.

On the Beatles, Ringo said:

Ringo: Well, laughingly, we used to call John the wit, Paul pleasantly insincere, and George the mystic.

Barbara W: ... and Ringo?

Ringo: Loveable chap.

Barbara W: What was it like for you, when you were on that stage and there were the masses and the screaming and the cheering?

Ringo: It was fabulous.

Barbara W: Not frightening?

Ringo: Never frightening. It was fabulous and people used to get crazy because they say, 'they never listen to you'. When we were around, the point was not to listen; it was just to have a good time. Why we gave up touring was between ourselves as musicians, and human beings. We realised that it didn't matter what show we did ... good or bad show, we would get the same reaction. And so everyone had their own idea of what they wanted to do. Now you can't do that when the band is trying to do *one* thing, so you have to split up by now. And the three of us would have played on John's album to do what he wanted of us, and the three of us would have played on Paul's album, and the three of us would have played on George's album, and the three on mine. But that would have made it separate albums, you know. We weren't then interested in –

Barbara W: Four people as one unit no longer existed.

Ringo: That's right. We all had definite ideas of what we wanted to do individually.

Barbara W: And that's why it broke up?

Ringo: That's why it broke up.

Barbara W: But this last year, now ... the four of you ... were close, were brothers, as you used to say.

Ringo: Ahhh, I've never *not* been a brother. I've always felt close to each one. Though, like brothers, we've had terrible rows. But it was never ... all the things you read in the press like Paul suing us and us fighting, went on, but it never stopped the love between us all. And the music was always more important than anything else ... to me personally ... you'd have to ask the other two. You sound funny when you say that now, you know, it's not new to me – that I always thought ... it clogs you up a bit. You know, because you're so glib when you say, 'Oh well, ask the other three.' Now we can only ask two, which is a drag in its way, but I'm sure he's OK. I'm really sad. I still miss John a great deal. I'll always miss him, but it's still brand new.

Barbara W: When you heard about it, how *did* you hear about it?

Ringo: Barbara's daughter called us up saying John had been shot and so that drove me crazy. But you think if he's been shot, he's been shot in the arm or shot in the leg. And then they came back and said he was dead.

Ringo (to camera crew): Do you want to stop that now, cause it doesn't help, but it always gets me upset.

Barbara W: But it would be amazing if it didn't.

Ringo: No. We were so ... he was a great friend.

Barbara W: Tell us about the good time. When did you see him last? What was it like?

Ringo: I saw him on the fifteenth of November and we, uh, I was staying at the Plaza and we went over to New York for a while because, you know, we see each other wherever we are and he came over with Yoko for an hour. And we had such a great time 'cause they stayed *five* hours. And it didn't matter if it was a year between we didn't see each other, it was always fine when we did, but it was a particularly great time . . . that I had, anyway.

Barbara W: When you were talking a moment or two ago, and we know how the country was affected by John Lennon's death –

Ringo: Not only this country . . . the world!

Barbara W: The world. But for you, I mean for people who grew up with him and cared about him, all of you cared about him, but for you it must have just been blind.

Ringo: It blew me away. I keep quoting this line because it's still an amazing line – I phoned Yoko before, no, in fact I went into the Dakota.

Barbara W: You went to see her right after his death?

Ringo: Yes. I was in the Bahamas and as soon as we heard we rented a plane as early as we could and we flew up to New York. There's nothing you can do, but you just have to go and say hello and if there's anything . . . but there's nothing you can do . . . except saying we're here and, you know, you want some ice cream, or whatever you say. Because, you know, your brain is rattled at the time. I said to her, 'You know, I know how you feel,' and the woman, straight as a dime, in all honesty, said, 'No, you don't.' Because no matter how close I was to him, it was not half as close as she was to him. And *that* blew me away more than anything.

Barbara W: And he was happy?

Ringo: Oh, man, they were happy. But you've seen. They were two people in one.

Barbara W: When you went back to New York to see Yoko, *you* were so surrounded. It was almost like –

Ringo: I wasn't surrounded. I was not surrounded.

Barbara W: When the crowds and the people used to –

Ringo: They were waiting at the Dakota and there were people while we were there shouting up to Yoko, 'Come to the window!' or to Sean. In fact, it would've been better if they'd all left her alone because they're not going to bring him back and it didn't help her with this whole crowd outside playing his music which is, you know, fine if they want to do that but then why don't they play it at home? And then when we came out I didn't need to hear people telling me how much they loved the Beatles. I was there to see my friend, not relating to this band.

Barbara W: Do you feel that you're in touch with John at times?

Ringo: No. Not right now.

Barbara W: Because every once in a while with love you look up and say, 'OK up there, fella?'

Ringo: Oh, well, I believe he's OK. I mean, I believe he's got a good place up there and he's just waiting for me to come up and play the kit . . . in that big band up in the sky. And I believe he's up there with Jimi Hendrix and Elvis and all the rest of them, 'cause they're probably the ones who stay out all night. The rest are probably just flying around in the day saying, 'Isn't it nice here?' The rockers are saying, 'Hey, it's nine o'clock at night, let's get out there!'

Barbara W: Are they playing together? Is Elvis singing with John?

Ringo: Well, I mean . . . it's got to be a great band up there . . . 'cause we've lost a lot of great people.

Barbara W: You said once that when you're number one it's hard to accept anything else. Is it?

Ringo: Yes, as an individual. Notoriety and the publicity and everything else will never be as big as the Beatles.

Barbara W: And you don't say, 'Someday, by myself . . .'

Ringo: No. Not any more.

Barbara W: What can you do, maybe you can't, so that finally you can be you and not the Beatle?

Ringo: I'll never be able to be . . .

Barbara W: Do you ever think about, because everybody's saying there'll be the lines and the history books: 'And he is remembered as . . .' How would you like them to write it?

Ringo: How would they write it? Man who lived and died. I've never been called a man – that also upsets me, we might as well get it all out in the open now, folks.

Barbara W: OK.

Ringo: Always been one of the lads. They've never said, 'He's a man' or whatever . . . 'one of the boys'.

Barbara W: So if you could say to people, 'OK, here I am, Ringo Starr or Richard Starkey – and this is what I am today,' what would it be?

Ringo: People will very seldom say hello to me unless they relate to the past. So I would just like to say, 'Well, here I am as a human being now. Let's start from here.'

Basie On The Beatles

A 1970 album of Beatle covers by the legendary jazz artist Count Basie. Ringo provided the sleeve notes to the album in which he related how on 1 October 1969 he asked Count Basie if he could write him an arrangement for the number 'Night And Day' for inclusion on the *Sentimental Journey* album. The complete score arrived five days later. Strangely, the *Sentimental Journey* album credits Chico O'Farrell as the arranger of 'Night And Day'.

Baxter, Jeff 'Skunk'

A musician born in Washington DC on 13 December 1948. He was originally a member of the pop group Ultimate Spinach and then played with a number of notable bands, including Steely Dan and the Doobie Brothers. As a producer he has recorded several bands including Scottish group Nazareth. He is the recipient of 17 gold and 8 platinum album awards and has received two Grammies. He played on Ringo's 1992 album *Time Takes Time*.

Be My Baby

A track from the 1983 *Old Wave* album, written and produced by Joe Walsh. Ringo is on lead vocals, drums and percussion, Joe Walsh on guitar and backing vocals, Mo Foster on bass and Gary Brooker and Chris Stainton on keyboards. It is 3 minutes and 38 seconds in length.

Beach Boys, The

An American group formed in 1961. The original line-up comprised Brian Wilson on bass, Dennis Wilson on drums, Carl Wilson on lead guitar, Mike Love on lead vocals and Al Jardine on rhythm guitar. Initially associated with the 'surf sound', they soon developed a reputation as one of America's major bands thanks to classic numbers such as 'Good Vibrations' and 'God Only Knows'. Dennis Wilson was drowned in 1983 and Carl died of cancer in 1998.

The 1980s saw the Beach Boys producing special concert events each Fourth of July and Ringo made a guest appearance with the group on 4 July 1984 in concerts in Washington DC (during which he played drums on 'Back In The USSR', 'You Can't Do That' and 'Day Tripper') and Miami (where he played drums on 'Dizzy Miss Lizzie' and 'Slow Down'). The live version of 'Back In The USSR' appeared on a mail-order-only album release – *Fourth Of July – A Rockin' Celebration Of America* – in 1985. Ringo was due to appear with them again at the celebration in the same year, but he cancelled at the last minute. He did play on the number 'California Calling' released on the 1985 album *The Beach Boys*.

Brian Wilson dropped into the Whatinthewhatthe? Studios in Los Angeles during the recording of Ringo's 1992 album *Time Takes Time*, and contributed backing vocals to the number 'Without Understanding', which contained the words 'no good vibrations'.

Beatles, The

While a pupil at Quarry Bank High School in Liverpool, John Lennon formed a skiffle group in the autumn of 1956. Skiffle was a form of music popularised in Britain by Lonnie Donegan, who had a major chart hit on both sides of the Atlantic with 'Rock Island Line'. He was to become a seminal influence on John Lennon, Paul McCartney and George Harrison.

John was born at 6.30 p.m. on 9 October 1940 at Oxford Street Maternity Hospital, Liverpool, the son of Julia and Alfred Lennon.

Contrary to the numerous claims in biographies of John, there were no bombing raids on the city that night.

John's father was away at sea during the war and his mother fell in love with another man, John Dykins. Alfred and Julia parted, although they were never divorced, which meant that Julia and Dykins couldn't get married, despite the fact that they had two daughters, Julia and Jacquie.

In the meantime, John went to live with his Aunt Mimi and Uncle George in the leafy middle-class suburb of Woolton (John could never describe himself as working class).

He enjoyed a happy upbringing among the close family group of the five Stanley sisters (Mary Elizabeth, known as Mimi, Elizabeth, known as Mater, Anne Georgina, known as Nanny, Julia, also known as Judy, and Harriet, known as Harrie), their husbands and children.

Sadly, his Uncle George died and his mother was killed in a tragic accident while crossing Menlove Avenue after visiting her sister Mimi.

John had developed a love of music from his mother and grandfather, who both played banjo, and he initially learned banjo chords rather than guitar chords.

It was John's Aunt Mimi who bought him a guitar for £15 at the local musician's store, Frank Hessy. John immediately enrolled his best friend Pete Shotton to play washboard and another classmate, Bill Smith, to play tea-chest bass. Bill only lasted with the group for a few weeks and the tea-chest bass duties were shared over a period of time by Ivan Vaughan, Len Garry and Nigel Wally.

John decided to call the outfit the Quarry Men, after the school song, which included the words 'Quarry men strong before our birth'.

Other members of the group were Rod Davis on banjo, Eric Griffiths on guitar and Colin Hanton on drums.

Initially they rehearsed in the houses of the group members, appeared in local skiffle group competitions and even performed in a Carroll Levis Discovery competition on 9 June 1957 without success.

The most important event in the lives of the Quarry Men occurred on Saturday 6 July 1957 when the group were booked to appear at Woolton parish church's garden fete. Ivan Vaughan, a close friend of John's, brought along a schoolmate from Liverpool Institute to watch the group. His name was Paul McCartney.

The Quarry Men's repertoire comprised skiffle numbers such as 'Baby Let's Play House', 'Maggie May', 'Cumberland Gap', 'Railroad Bill' and 'Putting On The Style'.

After Paul was introduced to John he wrote down the words of 'Twenty Flight Rock' and 'Be-Bop-A-Lula' for him, borrowed a guitar and began to play Little Richard numbers such as 'Long Tall Sally' and 'Tutti Frutti'.

John was impressed. Skiffle was on the wane and every red-blooded Liverpool youngster now seemed to be itching to play rock'n'roll.

Paul had been born at Walton Road Hospital, Liverpool, on 18 June 1942 to Jim and Mary McCartney. His brother Michael was born eighteen months later. His mother was a midwife, which at the time meant that the family were given a council house at a nominal rent. They moved on a number of occasions until they finally settled in Forthlin Road, Allerton in 1955.

Sadly, Paul's mother died of breast cancer in October 1956.

His father had formed a swing band at the end of the First World War called the Masked Melody Makers, but finished performing in the band at the onset of the Second World War when he began to work in a munitions factory and acted as a fireman. He was exempted from joining the army because of a hearing disability.

Paul was to recall, 'Dad used to play the cornet a lot, just for fun, at home. This was my earliest musical influence at, say, the age of five. This and the radio, listening to Luxembourg under the bedclothes, the *Top Twenty Show* on a Sunday night.'

His father bought Paul his first musical instrument, a trumpet, which he later exchanged for a guitar.

Paul entered Liverpool Institute when he passed his eleven-plus exam. While at the grammar school he became friends with Ivan Vaughan and George Harrison. It was Ivan who took him along to see John Lennon's Quarry Men in July 1957, which resulted in Paul becoming a member.

In the meantime, John asked Nigel Wally to become the group's manager, and he had professional cards printed reading: 'Country. Western. Rock 'n' Roll. Skiffle. The Quarry Men. Open For Engagements.' (Incidentally, the name Quarry Men was always two words, never one.)

Nigel placed cards in shop windows and took out classified advertisements in the *Liverpool Echo*. He also decided to attempt to book them into the Cavern. He knew that Alan Sytner, who owned the club, had a father who was a member of the Lee Park golf club and asked him if he could persuade his son to book the group. Dr Sytner suggested that they audition at the golf club, which they did. As a result they were booked to make their Cavern debut on 7 August 1957.

Paul McCartney had been asked to join the group by that time, but wasn't present at the Cavern gig, being away on a scout trip. John caused problems during the appearance by playing 'Hound Dog' and 'Blue Suede Shoes'. Rock'n'roll was banned at the Cavern then and a furious Alan Sytner sent a note to the Quarry Men on stage – 'Cut out the bloody rock!'

Paul actually made his debut with the group on 18 October of that year when they were booked to appear at the New Clubmoor Hall in Broadway, Liverpool, before an audience of about a hundred youngsters. Paul was to be the lead guitarist but he made a hash of it. Possibly because of nerves, he made a poor attempt at a solo during the performance of the Arthur Smith number 'Guitar Boogie', and was never to play lead with them again. The poor performance could also be a result of Paul having to play the guitar upside down and backwards, as he still didn't know how to restring a guitar for a left-handed person. For the gigs in the immediate future he had to play rhythm guitar, the same as John.

At Liverpool Institute, Paul had developed a friendship with George Harrison, who shared the same No. 86 bus to school each morning as he did, and when George told him about an appearance he'd made with a band he'd formed called the Rebels, Paul began to see if he could interest John Lennon in offering him a job with the group. This happened during a bus ride following a Wilson Hall, Garston, gig in February 1958.

George Harrison was born on 25 February 1943 in the bedroom of his parents' home at 12 Arnold Grove in the Wavertree area of Liverpool. His parents were Louise and Harold Harrison, and he had a sister Louise and two brothers, Peter and Harry.

He attended Liverpool Institute where he first met Paul McCartney and his interest in music was aroused by the skiffle boom that had been sweeping the country at the time.

George's mother helped him to obtain a guitar and he formed a group called the Rebels with his friend Arthur Kelly and his brother Peter.

The outfit only ever performed a single gig and this took place at a local British Legion club in Speke. This was the performance George mentioned to Paul on the bus ride to school.

On 12 July 1958 the Quarry Men recorded two numbers at Percy Philips's studio at 53 Kensington. One was the Buddy Holly number 'That'll Be The Day', the other was 'In Spite Of All The Danger', which sported the composing credit Harrison/McCartney and on which Paul sang lead vocal.

George remained with the Quarry Men until January 1959, when it seemed that the group had disbanded. There were no further gigs for the Quarry Men and the members had gone their separate ways, although John and Paul still met at Paul's house in Forthlin Road to write songs together. George decided to join a group called the Les Stewart Quartet.

Later that year, when group leader Les Stewart refused to take up the offer of a residency at a new club, the Casbah, opening in the West Derby district, it was George who contacted Paul and John to ask them to rejoin him for a residency at the Casbah club, along with a fourth member, Ken Brown. The Quarry Men were revived. It's interesting to note that but for the Casbah, George might have remained in the Les Stewart Quartet and John and Paul might have just remained a songwriting team with dreams of writing for stars such as Frank Sinatra. Apart from providing them with their first residency, the Casbah was also the first club the Beatles played at when they returned from Germany as a dynamic, transformed outfit. It could well be called 'the birthplace of the Beatles' (and one could well ask: 'which Liverpool club with six letters beginning with 'C' was the birthplace of the Beatles?').

On 10 October 1959 there was a dispute over Ken Brown being paid a fee for a Casbah appearance when he was too ill to play with the band and they sacked him, gave up their residency and became a trio. They also abandoned the name the Quarry Men. When they entered a Carroll Levis talent show at Liverpool's Empire Theatre, they called themselves Johnny and the Moondogs. They became a quartet again in November of that year when John Lennon's art school friend, Stuart Sutcliffe, became their bass guitarist. He'd won the annual John Moore's exhibition at the Walker Art Gallery, and used the money to put down a deposit on a Hofner guitar with local music store Frank Hessy (he didn't buy it outright with the money as some people have suggested).

John had felt that the group needed a bass guitarist and he actually asked Stuart and his flatmate Rod Murray to fill the post, without revealing to either that he'd asked the other. Whoever came up with the bass guitar would become a member of the band. As neither had any money, Rod began making a guitar by hand (which he retains to this day), but Stuart won because of the sale of his painting.

By May 1960 they were disenchanted with the name the Moondogs and spurned suggestions such as Long John and the Silver Men, put forward by local group leader Casey Jones of Cass and the Cassanovas.

The name the Beatles had its origin when John and Stuart were trying to think of suitable names one night at a flat they shared in Gambier Terrace. Buddy Holly was a firm favourite of theirs and Holly's songs had been quite prominent in the Quarry Men's repertoire. Stuart suggested that they pick a name like Holly's backing band the Crickets. All they had to do was think of names of insects. He suggested Beetles.

The name went through a few changes until August – the Beatals, the Silver Beats, the Silver Beetles and the Silver Beatles. John is generally considered to be the one who placed the 'a' to change Beetles to Beatles.

In the Beatles *Anthology* book George came up with a very misplaced story. He suggested that Stuart really liked the film *The Wild One* with Marlon Brando in which there is a scene with Lee Marvin as the leader of a motorcycle gang called 'the Beetles'.

As neither George nor Paul was present when John and Stuart devised the name, he is completely off the mark. *The Wild One* was banned in Britain for fourteen years (it was first screened in London on 15 February 1968) so no member of the group had even seen it when they thought up the name in 1960. It's one of those ridiculous myths that are repeated so often that even those concerned get mixed up between truth and reality.

It was coincidental that all four members were in close proximity during the school day. George and Paul attended Liverpool Institute and John and Stuart attended Liverpool College of Art. The schools were attached, as they were originally one building. The four rehearsed at the art college and played at the art school dances.

Stuart and Bill Harry, as members of the Student's Union, proposed and seconded the motion that the union pay for a PA system, which the group could use. The group took it and never returned it, which is possibly why Stuart's application to enrol on the Art Teachers' training course was later turned down.

John, Stuart, Bill Harry and Rod Murray used to hang around various pubs and coffee bars such as Ye Cracke in Rice Street and the Jacaranda in Slater Street. The Jacaranda was run by Allan Williams, a local entrepreneur, who asked Stu and Rod to paint some murals in his club. Then he asked them to design displays for his Mardi Gras Arts Ball at St George's Hall in December 1959.

Although he was aware that Stuart was in a group, he didn't include them among the Liverpool bands he featured on a joint promotion with Larry Parnes at Liverpool Stadium on 3 May 1960. Parnes, one of the leading British manager/promoters, was impressed by the Liverpool groups who appeared at the stadium and asked Williams to set up some auditions, as he was seeking bands to back his solo artists. Stu heard of this and asked Williams if they could be included on the auditions. At the time they had just found themselves a drummer, Tommy Moore, a fork-lift truck operator from Garston Bottle Works.

The audition took place at the Wyvern Social Club in Seel Street, a club that Allan Williams was about to turn into a nightclub called the Blue Angel. At this time the group were calling themselves the Silver Beetles (although several days later they called themselves the Silver Beats for a dance by local promoter Brian Kelly at Alexandra Hall).

Johnny Hutchinson, drummer with the Big Three, occupied their drum seat when it came their time to audition, as Moore was late turning up. Parnes didn't like the fact that the drummer was late and he noted that he dressed differently to the other members and was a lot older. Despite this, he booked them on a short tour of Scotland to back one of his singers, another Merseyside lad called Johnny Gentle.

Despite claims by Williams that Parnes complained about Stuart's ability on the guitar, Parnes himself denied this. As a result, Stuart has been traduced down the years by numerous writers, who never heard him play, as a terrible guitarist who performed with his back to the audience. This is untrue.

Contemporary reports indicate that there were no complaints about Stuart. Paul McCartney was to say, 'I believe that playing an ordinary guitar first and then transferring to bass has made me a better bass player because it loosened up my fingers. Not that I'm suggesting that every bass player should learn on ordinary guitar. Stuart Sutcliffe certainly didn't, and he was a great bass man.' When Stuart remained in Hamburg following their first trip, George wrote to him pleading for him to return.

Rick Hardy (a.k.a. Richards), who was a member of the Jets, the first British rock band to appear in Hamburg, recalled, 'Stu never turned his back on stage ... He certainly played to the audience and he certainly played bass. If you have someone who can't play the instrument properly, you have no bass sound. There were two rhythm guitarists with the Beatles and if one of them couldn't play, you wouldn't have noticed it – but it's different with a bass guitar. I was there and I can say quite definitely, Stuart never did a show in which he wasn't facing the audience.'

Klaus Voormann, who was considered as a replacement for Paul when he left the Beatles and played on records by George, John and Paul, said that Stu 'was a really great bass player ... you could say he was at the time my favourite bass player, but primitive. But of all the people or groups, and when we saw groups later, he was my favourite bass player.'

The Silver Beetles were booked to back Johnny Gentle on a tour of Scotland from 20 to 28 May 1960, and three of them decided to adopt pseudonyms. Paul became Paul Ramon, Stu became Stuart de Stael (after his favourite painter) and George became Carl Harrison (after his favourite guitarist, Carl Perkins). John didn't adopt a pseudonym – and they were superfluous anyway, as their individual names were never used in publicity during the course of the tour.

Following the tour, George recalled, 'That tour was our first faint hope of actually making it one day. But unfortunately it didn't really do much for us back home in Liverpool. After hanging out for weeks the only gig that came along was backing up a stripper named Janice in a club on Upper Parliament Street. It was work, I suppose, but definitely not what any of us had in mind when we got together. As for me, I was just about convinced it was never going to happen, which gave me great reason for concern. After all, the only other reasonable alternative was to just go out and find a real job. Frankly, that was something all of us dreaded.'

On their return they hung around the Jacaranda coffee bar once more. As Williams' resident Steel Band had left for Germany and he hadn't found a replacement, he booked the group into the Jacaranda for a handful of gigs. At the time Williams ran an agency, Jacaranda Enterprises, booking some of the local groups into a couple of venues on the Wirral: the Grosvenor Ballroom, Birkenhead, and the Institute, Neston. He booked the Silver Beetles into the two venues over the following months.

Tommy Moore had left the group by then and they had a short-term temporary replacement in Norman Chapman. However, after three gigs with them he was called up for National Service (a compulsory two-year stint in the armed forces) and they were left without a drummer once more.

(Tommy Moore later worked for Liverpool Corporation, played in a jazz band in the evenings and sadly died following an apoplectic fit at the age of 47. Norman Chapman became a teacher and continued playing drums and was a member of a trio when he died in 1995 at the age of 58.)

In the meantime, Parnes had booked local group Howie Casey and the Seniors to back one of his local singers on a tour with Duffy Power and, as a result, they'd given up their day jobs. When Parnes cancelled the tour they were furious, and Howie Casey and Derry Wilkie went to see Williams, who they considered partly responsible. He told them that as a consolation he would take them down to London and arrange for them to appear at the 2 I's coffee bar (a leading showcase for aspiring musicians in Old Compton Street, where artists such as Tommy Steele and Cliff Richard had played).

While they were performing, a German club owner, Bruno Koschmider, was in the 2 I's looking for a replacement for the Jets, a group he had booked after visiting the 2 I's some months earlier. He liked the Seniors and booked them to appear at his Kaiserkeller club in Germany.

Koschmider was so impressed with the Seniors that he contacted Williams to ask for another Liverpool band. Williams initially asked Rory Storm and the Hurricanes, but they were already booked for a season at Butlin's holiday camp. He next asked Gerry and the Pacemakers, but Gerry Marsden didn't want to give up his day job at that time (incidentally, Gerry once asked Ringo to join the Pacemakers as bass guitarist). In desperation, he turned to the Silver Beetles.

The group were still without a drummer. They were due to appear at the Grosvenor Ballroom on 6 August, but the gig was called off as Wallasey Corporation had told the promoter Les Dodd to cancel the dances due to complaints from local residents. So George, John and Paul drifted down to the Casbah club. Pete Best, Mona Best's son, was playing there with his band the Blackjacks. His brand-new drum kit particularly impressed them and Paul phoned him to ask if he'd like to join them in Germany. As the Blackjacks were on the point of breaking up, he agreed and, following an audition with them, he was accepted into the group, who now shortened their name to the Beatles for their Hamburg appearance from 17 August 1960.

They had expected to appear at the Kaiserkeller, but when they arrived they were told they were to play at a smaller club, the Indra.

The group were to play for long hours and gradually found themselves transforming their music, becoming a tighter band and gaining a new sound, with Best developing a loud drum style that was tagged 'the atom beat'.

George was later to say, 'Our peak for playing live was in Hamburg. At the time, we weren't famous and people came to see us simply because of our music and the atmosphere we created. We got very tight as a band in those clubs. Playing such long hours we developed a big repertoire of our own songs but still played mainly rock'n'roll tunes.'

The group were placed in terrible accommodation, cramped quarters in a cinema, the Bambi Kino. It was here that George lost his virginity and he recalled, 'My first shag was in Hamburg with John, Paul and Pete watching. We were in bunk beds and they really couldn't see anything because I was under the covers. But after I finished, they all applauded and cheered. At least they kept quiet while I was doing it.'

George referred to his days in Hamburg as his 'higher education'.

Due to complaints about the noise, the police ordered the Indra to close and the Beatles were moved down to the Kaiserkeller. Rory Storm and the Hurricanes then arrived from Liverpool to top the bill over the Beatles.

The Hurricanes were not only the bill-toppers; they were paid more money and provided with better accommodation than the Beatles. They were currently well known in Liverpool, while the Beatles were virtually unknown in their home city at the time.

The Hurricanes were led by Rory Storm (vocals), with Johnny Guitar (lead), Ty Brien (guitar), Lu Walters (bass/vocals) and Ringo Starr (drums).

Ringo, real name Richard Starkey (the name Starkey dates back to 1260 and means 'dry and unyielding'), had been born in the front bedroom of a tiny terraced house in Madryn Street in Liverpool's Dingle area, a fairly run-down working-class section of the city. He was one month late and had to be induced with forceps.

His father was originally a Liverpool dockworker and member of a large family. He had two brothers, Billy and George, and three sisters, Angie, Lily and May. He later changed jobs and began to work in a bakery where he met Elsie Gleave. They were married in 1936 and initially moved in with his parents prior to moving into the small two-storey terrace house in Madryn Street.

When their son was born in 1940 he was named Richard after his father, a working-class tradition at the time. Although Richard senior was called Dickie, it was decided to call Richard junior Ritchie.

His father left the family home when Ritchie was only three years old. His mother Elsie, a plucky woman, lavished lots of love and care on a young son who was prone to numerous illnesses.

There were only a few brief occasions when Ritchie saw his father again, twice when he was a young child. Dickie had remained in Liverpool, still working at the bakery, and visited his son during one of Ritchie's regular hospital confinements. Ritchie recalled, 'He came once to see me in hospital with a little notebook and asked me if I wanted anything. I wouldn't speak to him. I suppose my mother filled me up with all the things about him.'

Dickie remarried and moved away from Liverpool. He met his son for the very last time in 1965, escorted by his second wife, but commented, 'I got the feeling we weren't wanted. He never paid our train fare.'

A newspaper traced Dickie in 1980. He was now a window cleaner, living up north, and talked about his son, saying, 'He's done well, the lad, and good luck to him, but he owes me nothing.'

Ringo was to say about his upbringing, 'We were a poor working-class family. My mother's mother was really very poor. She had four-teen kids.'

Describing the area he lived in, Ringo said, 'There's a lot of tene-ments in the Dingle. A lot of people in boxes trying to get out. We've always been ordinary working class on both sides of the family.'

At first Dickie had sent support payments of thirty shillings a week, but when these dried up after a few months, Elsie and Ritchie had to move to smaller and cheaper accommodation in nearby Admiral Grove, with Elsie working as a barmaid in the Empress pub to make ends meet.

She was to say, 'Sometimes he used to wish there was more than just the two of us. He used to look out of the window and say, "I wish I had brothers and sisters. There's nobody to talk to when it's raining." I never thought of putting Ritchie away in a home. He was my child. With the bar job I was just able to manage.'

Then, while at St Silas Infants School, Ritchie began to suffer the first of the numerous illnesses that were to have such a detrimental effect on his education.

He began to suffer severe abdominal pains and was rushed to the Royal Children's Infirmary in Myrtle Street. He recalled, 'I felt an awful stab of pain. I remember sweating and being frightened for a while.' He also said, 'I remember going out of the house on a stretcher to the ambu-lance. In hospital, this nurse started smashing me stomach. That's how it felt anyway. She probably just touched it. I was wheeled in to the operation. I went into a coma and didn't come round for ten weeks.'

A ruptured appendix was diagnosed and this had led to an inflamed peritoneum. As a result, the first of what were to become several oper-ations took place. While still in his ten-week coma there were further operations. When he did emerge from the coma he was so ill he was required to remain in hospital for several further months.

Ritchie was then able to return to St Silas, where his classmates included Billy Fury, who was to become Liverpool's first pop superstar, and Billy Hatton, a talented guitarist who was to find chart success as a member of the Fourmost.

On his return to school, due to his near-fatal brush with death, some of the other pupils began to refer to him as Lazarus.

At the age of eleven, the youngsters moved on to Dingle Vale Secondary Modern. However, Ritchie wasn't allowed to take the eleven-plus examination, as his primary teachers believed that he wouldn't pass it. Thus, Ritchie became the only member of the Beatles who never attended a grammar school.

Elsie's neighbours, the Maguire's, had introduced her to Harry Graves, a Romford-born painter and decorator who now worked for Liverpool Corporation. Ritchie was over the moon when they got married on 18 April 1953 and was to refer to Harry as his 'stepladder'.

Ritchie was due to attend the Dingle Vale School between the ages of eleven and fifteen, but in 1953, at the age of thirteen, he caught a cold which turned into chronic pleurisy and was taken to Myrtle Street Hospital once again. He developed complications in his lungs and was to spend his final two school years at Heswall Children's Hospital.

As a result of his hospitalisation he finished his education without any qualifications. After leaving Dingle Vale School he had to return to collect a certificate to prove he'd been educated there. The certificate was required in order to obtain a job. He recalled, 'They didn't even remember I'd been there.'

He summed up his time in the hospital, saying, 'I was given lots of things to keep my mind occupied, like knitting. I made a big island out of papier-mâché and a farm full of animals.'

It was while he was in hospital that he took an interest in drumming. He recalled, 'We had a ward band in the hospital. There were four kids on cymbals and two on triangles. I would never play unless I had a drum.'

He was also to say, 'We always had a piano, but not in the house. I wasn't interested. My grandparents also had a banjo and mandolin, but it was of no interest. From the age of thirteen I just wanted to be a drummer.'

Ringo also recalled that his grandmother forced him to write right-handed when he was actually a southpaw. Many years later he was to say, 'I play a right-handed kit with a left-handed heart.'

It was his stepfather Harry who actually bought Ritchie his first drum kit. During a visit to Romford he noticed one for sale, purchased it for £10, and lugged it all the way to Liverpool on the train.

Remembering that first kit, Ringo was to comment, 'I banged me thumbs the very first day. I became a drummer because it was the only thing I could do.'

Without any qualifications and due to his inadequate education, job options for Ritchie were limited. He applied for a position as a British Rail messenger boy, but says, 'I went for a uniform, but all they gave me was a hat. You had to do twenty years to get the rest. Anyway, I failed their medical and left after a couple of months.'

His next job was also a brief one, as a barman on a Mersey ferry ploughing between Liverpool and New Brighton.

It was his stepfather who then arranged a job for him at a local engineering firm, Henry Hunt's, where he became an apprentice to a joiner.

Initially, Ritchie had no ambitions about becoming a musician, but he recalls, 'I couldn't play a note at the time. I just used to bash around in the house until I got some idea. One night my mum came in and said a neighbour's husband was in a band, and why didn't I go along and join. I think she thought they played jazz.

'Anyway, I went along to rehearsals and there was this crowd of blokes playing in a silver band. They were all working out the numbers they were going to do in the park that Sunday. It wasn't for me. I left the same night.'

With skiffle such a huge craze in Liverpool, it was inevitable that Ritchie would succumb. Together with his friend and neighbour Eddie Miles (who called himself Eddie Clayton when the group was formed) on guitar and vocals, and three other workmates from Hunt's – Roy Trafford on tea-chest bass, John Dougherty on washboard and Frank Walsh on guitar – the group, calling themselves the Eddie Clayton Skiffle Group, made their debut at the Peel Street Labour Club. By that time Ritchie's grandfather had lent him £50 to buy a new drum kit.

Ringo's mum was to recall, 'He was in hospital so much that he didn't have the chance to do all the usual things that young boys get up to.' She commented that the first time he took an interest in drumming was in 1957.

In 1957 Ringo fell in love. He met his girlfriend Geraldine McGovern, who he called 'Gerry', at a local gig that year. She worked for an upholsterer. They became engaged and Ringo's grandfather gave Ringo his own gold wedding ring, which he gave to Gerry.

They were due to get married, the reception hall was booked, as were the wedding cars, and Ringo was to say, 'I was engaged and I did love her and she loved me, and we'd got our bottom drawer started and made all the preparations that go into marriage.'

The crisis came when she forced him to make a decision about the direction of his future, siding with his mother and stepfather in pleading with him to remain at his job at Hunt's and give up playing drums.

She was to recall, 'His music always came first. He was playing most nights and if I wanted to see him I had to trail along with him to a dance. We were never able to have much time together.'

The crunch came when Rory Storm and the Hurricanes, who Ringo was now playing for, were due to appear at another season at Butlin's and she gave him an ultimatum: her or playing the drums. She was later to say, 'When he went off to Butlin's I told him I didn't want him to go. We talked it over – there was no shouting or slagging. But that was the end.'

Ringo was to say, 'That was a very poignant moment in my life. I left her one night and I got on the bus and thought, "Well, what happens if

I don't go back?" and I never went back. I just wanted to play. It was more important to me.'

To get over the break-up of the relationship, Gerry left Liverpool to live with relations in America, although she returned in 1964. She said, 'Ritchie was shy in a way, but he was determined to be famous. He wasn't at all flamboyant; his humour was quiet and witty without being offensive or cynical.'

The Eddie Clayton Skiffle Group disbanded in 1958 and Ritchie went on to join another outfit, the Darktown Skiffle Group. It was while he was performing with the Darktown (although he also sat in with other bands) that he was approached by Alan Caldwell with an offer to join his band, Al Caldwell's Texans. Ritchie made his debut with them at the Mardi Gras club in Mount Pleasant on 25 March 1959.

Al Caldwell's Texans had various name changes as they transformed themselves into a rock'n'roll band. First it was the Raving Texans, then Al Storm and the Hurricanes, followed by Jett Storm and the Hurricanes and finally, Rory Storm and the Hurricanes.

In 1960 the group secured a summer season at Butlin's holiday camp in Pwllheli for which they were to be paid the princely sum of £25 each. Yet Ringo was reluctant to go.

Rory Storm had a lot to do with Ringo's final decision.

Ringo recalled, 'Elsie and Harry tried everything to persuade me to stay. "Get your trade," they told me, "and you'll never be stuck for a job."'

Ringo was undecided about what to do. Rory came round to his house to put the pressure on and Johnny 'Guitar' Byrne was to say, 'If Rory hadn't twisted his arm, I don't think he'd have done half the things he did.'

Both Rory and Johnny kept enticing him with tales of the 'easy' girls at Butlin's, telling him that he'd be able to enjoy lots of sexual experiences there.

The group set off for a summer season at Butlin's in Pwllheli where they were to appear at the Rock and Calypso Ballroom from July to September.

It was during this period that Rory decided on some changes. At the time there were numerous Western television shows on British television and Rory decided that his group should have Western-sounding names. Johnny Byrne became 'Johnny Guitar', named after the Joan Crawford Western movie, Charlie O'Brien became Ty Brien, in deference to Ty Hardin, star of a number of Western shows, while Wally Eymond became Lu Walters and Ritchie Starkey became Ringo Starr. Rory also decided that Ringo should have his own spot in the show called 'Ringo Starrtime' in which he performed numbers such as 'Boys' and 'You're Sixteen' (numbers which he continues to perform today).

The group was performing for sixteen hours a week, a regimen that was to tighten up their sound and performance and hurl them into the front ranks of the Liverpool groups.

Ringo's position in the group was also to result in a write-up in the *South Liverpool Weekly News*.

The issue of 25 August 1960 carried a story headed 'RICHARD REALISES A BOYHOOD AMBITION'.

It read:

Richard Starkey always wanted to be a drummer. From when he was a small boy he was always tapping his fingers.

He has been in hospital twice, and has had twelve operations, several of them major ones.

When he came out last time after two years spent mostly in bed, he looked around for something to do – and started his fingers tapping again.

So he saved up and spent £10 on a second-hand drum kit and set about teaching himself to play.

After two months' hard practice he joined a group. And now, with a new drum kit costing £125, he is entertaining hundreds of teenagers at Pwllheli (North Wales) holiday camp as a member of Rory Storm's Hurricanes.

All five of them Liverpool lads are packing the camp's Rock and Calypso Ballroom each evening for three-hour jive sessions.

Working a 16-hour week they spend their spare time joining in all the fun of the camp, swimming, sport and sunbathing.

'It's as good as a holiday – and we get paid for it,' said 20-year-old Richard – who lives in Admiral Grove, Dingle – during a break in the rock session.

His suntanned face broke into a smile as he added: 'It's fabulous.'

Richard – he plays under the name Ringo Starr – is the second ex-pupil of St Silas C of E School, Dingle, to make a professional career in rock and roll.

The first – Ronnie Wycherley, now carving a niche for himself as Billy Fury.

It is the group's biggest contract so far: before they filled dates at Liverpool jazz clubs and had a spot in a rock show at Liverpool Stadium in May, which starred Gene Vincent and was to have featured Eddie Cochran. But he was killed a few days before.

Led by ex-cotton sampleman Rory Storm (his real name is Alan Caldwell), whose home is at 54 Broadgreen Road, Stoneycroft, the group has been playing together for just ten months.

The other members – Lou Walters, 22 (bass guitar and vocal), Ty Brien, 19 (lead guitarist), Johnny Guitar, 20 (rhythm guitar and vocal), and Richard, all belonged to other groups before that.

When they finish their 13-week engagement at Pwllheli in a few days, the lads plan a holiday in London.

Said Richard: 'There is too much competition here. Rock and roll is beginning to wane.'

He added: 'But I like the life. I certainly don't want to give it up.'

Following their summer season the group travelled to Hamburg in October 1960, replacing Derry and the Seniors at the Kaiserkeller, where they alternated with the Beatles on the daily twelve-hour stretch that the groups had to play. Each band did ninety minutes on and ninety minutes off.

Allan Williams also arrived from Liverpool and was so impressed by the voice of Lu Walters, the Hurricanes' second vocalist, that he arranged to record him at the Akustic Studio, a small recording booth near Hamburg railway station. The event took place on 15 October 1960, and on one of the tracks Williams invited George, John and Paul to provide harmony vocals. Pete Best was in Hamburg buying drumsticks and the Hurricanes drummer Ringo Starr played with them. It was the first time John, Paul, George and Ringo played together.

John, Paul and George backed the two Hurricanes, vocalist Lu and drummer Ringo on 'Summertime'. Then the other members of the Hurricanes backed Lu on 'Fever' and 'September Song'. (Williams had a copy of this historic disc, but left it behind in a London pub some years later.)

The Beatles asked Williams if they could record some numbers, but he refused to pay for them to do so.

George Harrison was to recall, 'I didn't like the look of Rory's drummer myself. He looked the nasty one, with his little grey streak of hair. But the nastier one turned out to be Ringo, the nicest of them all.'

The Beatles began to attract the attention of a group of students who they called 'the Exis', because they were like the French existentialists. Klaus Voormann, a student, had initially been attracted by the sound of Rory Storm and the Hurricanes and entered the Kaiserkeller to watch them. He was even more impressed by the Beatles and began to bring along his other student friends, including Jurgen Vollmer and his own girlfriend Astrid Kirchherr.

Both Astrid and Jurgen began to take photographs of the group, which are among the best photographs ever taken of the Beatles. A romance also began to develop between Stuart and Klaus's girlfriend Astrid. Astrid then left Klaus to 'go steady' with Stu.

The Beatles remained in Hamburg for four months. They might have remained even longer, but for a series of circumstances. With their season at the Kaiserkeller coming to an end, they had an offer to appear at a nearby rival club, the Top Ten. However, their contract with Koschmider forbade them from appearing at any club within a 25-mile radius.

Koschmider was furious when he heard that the Beatles were playing the Top Ten and on 1 November 1960 he sent them a letter:

> I, the undersigned, hereby give notice to Mr George Harrison and to Beatles Band to leave on November 30 1960.
> The notice is given to the above by order of the Public authorities who have discovered that Mr George Harrison is only 17 (seventeen) years of age.
> Bruno Koschmider.

Stuart and his German girlfriend Astrid took George to the railway station.

Pete Best and Paul were the next to be removed from Hamburg. They had moved their gear into the Top Ten club and were then arrested by the police who accused them of trying to burn down the Bambi Kino. When trying to collect their belongings, since there was no proper light, they had attached some condoms to the wall and lit them to provide illumination. There was some slight singeing, which resulted in them being put into a cell and then deported from the city. The next to leave was John, but Stuart decided to stay behind with his girlfriend.

Their first gig on their return to Liverpool was at the Casbah club, home of their first residency. As Stuart had remained behind, Pete Best managed to contact Chas Newby, the former bass guitarist with the Blackjacks, who was in Liverpool during a college break. He played with them for three appearances. John Lennon offered him the permanent job as bass player with the Beatles, but he turned him down, as he wanted to complete his college course. George invited his friend Arthur Kelly to take Stuart's place, but he also turned the position down. George then wrote to Stuart asking him to return.

As the Beatles were hardly known on the Liverpool rock circuit, with hand-painted posters announcing them as 'direct from Hamburg', some members of the audiences thought they were a German group.

Their turning point came with a booking at Litherland Town Hall on 27 December 1960.

Promoter Brian Kelly remembered the occasion in an article in *Mersey Beat*: 'I was organising a dance at Litherland Town Hall to be held on Boxing Day 1960, but I was short of a group. On Christmas Day I received a phone call from Bob Wooler who said, "I've found a group for you at the Jacaranda and they're free. They want eight pounds. Will they do?"

'"Not at that price they won't," I said. "A group just won't increase my attendance enough to warrant that." We finally agreed to pay them six pounds.

'In their first appearance I was completely knocked out by them. They had a pounding, pulsating beat which I knew would be big box office. When they finished playing, I posted some bouncers on the door of their dressing room to prevent other promoters who were in the hall entering. I went inside and booked them solidly for months ahead.'

In his prophetic article in the third issue of *Mersey Beat*, Cavern compere Bob Wooler was to write: 'Why do you think the Beatles are so popular? Many people many times have asked me this question since that fantastic night (Tuesday 27 December 1960) at Litherland Town Hall when the impact of the act was first felt on this side of the river.' He ended the feature writing, 'Such are the fantastic Beatles. I don't think anything like them will happen again.'

The group's next important date took place on 21 February 1961 when they appeared at a lunchtime session at the Cavern. Most Liverpool groups were semi-professional, working at normal jobs during the day, and when Ray McFall introduced lunchtime sessions at the club, there were few groups who were able to appear. The Beatles were able to do so as none of them had a full-time job (Because some of the Hurricanes worked during the day, Rory Storm used some other musicians to back him at lunchtime sessions under the name Rory Storm and the Wild Ones).

Stuart had returned to Liverpool to appear with them on a couple of gigs. He then returned to Hamburg. They followed him on 27 March for a fourteen-week engagement at the Top Ten club.

The group had no further association with Allan Williams. They had secured their own booking at the Top Ten, and since their return from Hamburg he'd only got them a single gig at the Grosvenor Ballroom on 10 March. Williams had only acted as their unofficial agent during several months in 1960, but now he demanded a percentage of their Top Ten fee. Since they had secured the booking themselves, they refused. He wrote a letter to them stating, 'I will also submit a full report of your behaviour to the Agency Members Association, of which I am a full member, and every Agent in England is a member, to protect Agents from Artistes who misbehave and welsh out of agreements.'

Peter Eckhorn of the Top Ten club extended the Beatles contract twice and they were required to play between 7.00 p.m. and 2.00 a.m. with a fifteen-minute break each hour.

George commented, 'We performed like a gang of fanatics. It was all right once we got the hang of it all and it was great fun. The boss would send up cups of coffee on stage and we'd take turns to take a nip.'

While they were at the Top Ten they backed Tony Sheridan, the former lead guitarist with the Jets. Sheridan was a great influence on the band, but because he played lead, there was a surfeit of guitarists, so Paul played piano until Stuart decided to leave the band – then Paul took over on bass guitar.

German A&R (Artistes and Repertoire) man Bert Kaempfert entered the club one night with music publisher Alfred Schacht. He'd come to see Tony Sheridan on the recommendation of singer Tommy Kent. Kaempfert decided to record Sheridan, who suggested that he hire the Beatles to back him on the session.

They began a three-day recording stint from 22 June 1961 at the Harburg Friedrich Ebert Halle. Kaempfert decided to rename the Beatles 'the Beat Brothers' for recording purposes and he chose two numbers for them to record, 'My Bonnie Lies Over The Ocean' and 'When The Saints Go Marching In'. Sheridan sang a further number, 'Why (Can't You Love Me Again)'. When the Beatles asked Kaempfert if they could record some of their own compositions he listened to their material and decided on George's 'Cry For A Shadow'. Although credited to Harrison/Lennon, being an instrumental it is mainly George's number (it's interesting that the first original composition they ever recorded, 'In Spite Of All The Danger', was a Harrison/McCartney number).

They returned to Liverpool in July, sans Sutcliffe, with Paul now established as their permanent bass guitarist.

On 6 July the first issue of *Mersey Beat* was published. This was the creation of Bill Harry and his girlfriend Virginia and the first issue contained John Lennon's own version of the Beatles origin, which Harry had captioned 'Being A Short Diversion Of The Origin Of Beatles, Translated From The John Lennon'.

Harry took copies of the initial edition round to all the clubs and record stores in Liverpool and at NEMS (North End Music Stores) requested to see the manager. He was introduced to Brian Epstein, who ordered a dozen copies. They sold out immediately and Epstein was on the phone to request more – and more. With issue No. 2 he placed an advance order of twelve dozen copies. More than any other person on the local scene, he must have anticipated the potential of the publication – for a provincial record store to order 144 copies of a music paper was unprecedented.

The entire front cover of issue No. 2 was devoted to the Beatles' recording session in Hamburg under the caption 'Beatles Sign Recording Contract!' and was illustrated with a photograph of the group taken by Astrid Kirchherr, her first published work.

The full story read: 'Bert Kaempfert, who may be remembered for his golden record "Wonderland By Night", which reached the top of the American hit parade, contracted the Beatles for Polydor, Germany's top recording company. Under the contract they will make four records per year for the company.

'At a recording session, the Beatles provided vocals and backing for three numbers for Tony Sheridan. Tony, a first-class songwriter, penned "Why", a number familiar to readers through Gerry Marsden's excellent rendering. Apart from waxing "Why", the Beatles recorded "My Bonnie Lies Over The Ocean", opening in waltz-time, then breaking into a rock beat. Finally, the group provided good bass and drum backing to Sheridan for 'The Saints Go Marching In', a very popular number in Germany.

'The Beatles recorded two further numbers for Kaempfert on their own. One side, an instrumental written by George Harrison, has not yet been named – probable titles include "Cry For A Shadow" and "Beatle Bop". The other side, "Ain't She Sweet", featured a vocal by John Lennon. The boys weren't quite satisfied with these two numbers, so they sold the rights to Polydor. Thus, in fact, under the contract the Beatles still have four more records to make this year.

'Bass-guitarist Stuart Sutcliffe has remained in Hamburg and will shortly be marrying a German girl. At present he is studying at Hamburg Art College and has an English tutor. The group have no plans for taking on another guitarist, but have decided to remain a quartet.'

Epstein was so enthusiastic about *Mersey Beat* that he invited Harry into his office and asked if he could become the paper's record reviewer. His first reviews appeared in issue No. 3 on 3 August, along with advertisements for NEMS record store. In fact, the NEMS advert appeared on the full-page feature by Bob Wooler lauding the Beatles.

Brian Epstein was avid for information on the local bands, which he'd been entirely unaware of, and took Harry for lunch at the Basnett Bar on a couple of occasions to ask all about this exciting music scene on his own doorstep. He was particularly interested in the Beatles and asked Harry if he could arrange for him to see them at the Cavern. Harry phoned Ray McFall at the Cavern and arranged for Epstein and his personal assistant to visit a Cavern lunchtime session to watch the Beatles on 9 November.

In his biography *A Cellarful Of Noise*, for some reason Epstein said that he'd never heard of the Beatles until a boy named Raymond Jones came into his shop on 28 October and asked for the record. Why he chose to begin his book with this untrue fact is puzzling, although the apocryphal story probably makes a neat little anecdote. Raymond Jones did ask for the record, as did several other customers who had read about it in *Mersey Beat* and heard Bob Wooler playing the single at local venues – but the Beatles were regulars in Epstein's own NEMS store, round the corner from the Cavern club, and always dropped in there following lunchtime sessions, still dressed in their black leather. They would listen to singles in the record booths, and witnesses say that Brian Epstein noticed them and asked who they were.

At Brian's invitation, the Beatles visited him at his NEMS office in Whitechapel, accompanied by Bob Wooler, who John introduced as his father. Paul was half an hour late, having first gone home to have a bath, leading to George's deadpan comment about him being late but very clean.

Epstein asked them if they had a manager and they said no, that Pete Best looked after their affairs. In fact, since their return from Hamburg,

Pete and his mother Mona had effectively managed the group. They arranged all the bookings and had Neil Aspinall, Pete's friend and Mona's lover, act as the group's road manager. Mona had originally written to Ray McFall at the Cavern requesting that he book the group and she'd also written to Granada Television inviting them to watch the group perform.

The Beatles had another meeting with Epstein on 6 December, this time at the Casbah club, and they all came to an agreement that he was to be their manager.

In the *Mersey Beat* poll the Beatles were voted No. 1 group and Epstein began advertising them as '*Mersey Beat* Poll Winners and Polydor Recording Artists'.

Brian contacted numerous record companies seeking a recording audition and invited Mike Smith of Decca to watch the group at the Cavern on 13 December, after wining and dining him first. A few days later Brian received a letter from EMI Records saying that three of the company's four A&R men had heard the record and turned the group down. The details hadn't been given to the fourth A&R man, Parlophone's George Martin, as his label wasn't a pop label.

Smith arranged a recording session for the group at Decca's West Hampstead Studio and the group had a ten-hour journey by road during inclement weather, while Brian travelled down by train.

Prior to the session, Brian discussed their repertoire with them. While John had wanted them to perform their strong rock'n'roll repertoire with some of their own numbers such as 'One After 909', Brian vetoed this and said they must concentrate on standards such as 'Till There Was You'.

The group performed fifteen songs, with Paul taking lead on 'Like Dreamers Do', 'Till There Was You', 'Sure To Fall', 'Love Of The Loved', 'September In The Rain', 'Besame Mucho' and 'Searchin''. John was lead vocalist on 'Money', 'To Know Him Is To Love Him', 'Memphis' and 'Hello Little Girl'. George sang 'The Sheik Of Araby', 'Take Good Care Of My Baby', 'Three Cool Cats' and 'Crying, Waiting, Hoping'.

Smith auditioned another group that day, Brian Poole and the Tremeloes from nearby Aldershot. As it turned out, the Beatles were rejected and the Tremeloes accepted.

Brian Epstein claimed that Decca's head of A&R, Dick Rowe, had made the decision. In *A Cellarful Of Noise* Epstein said that Rowe had told him, 'Not to mince words, Mr Epstein, we don't like your boys' sound. Groups are out: four-piece groups with guitars particularly are finished.'

Rowe has denied that he said this and the situation at the time seemed to bear Rowe's word out. That month Rowe had been appointed to head a new Decca team spearheading the search for new talent, and he was to sign up several guitar groups who became hit artists.

Mike Smith was new to the team and, according to Rowe, when Smith approached him he said he'd like to sign up both groups. Rowe told him that since he was new and relatively inexperienced, he could only sign up one of them, the choice was his. Smith chose the Tremeloes.

The reason could well be due to the fact that in those days there was no motorway and the trip from Liverpool to London took several hours, as the Beatles' experience had already proved. It was more convenient to have a group literally on Decca's doorstep and Aldershot was not far away. Therefore, the decision could well have been because of convenience and not because of the music.

Every other major recording company, including Pye, Philips and Oriole, turned the Beatles down. People in Liverpool were saying that Epstein would end up approaching the Woolworth's label!

Then a stroke of luck happened – and luck was to be a continuing factor in their rise to fame. Decca had generously given Brian the Beatles' audition tapes. Paul Murphy, a former member of Rory Storm and the Hurricanes, bumped into Brian in London and when Brian explained what he was doing, Murphy pointed out that A&R men wouldn't listen to the tapes in their present state, he'd have to have acetates made, and he took Epstein to EMI's HMV Shop in Oxford Street. Ted Huntley, the engineer who was transferring the tapes, noticed that a number of the songs were originals and told his boss Kenneth Boast. Boast then asked Brian if he would be interested in meeting Syd Coleman of EMI's music arm Ardmore & Beechwood, who had an office on the top floor of the HMV Shop.

Coleman listened to the tapes and said he'd like to publish the songs 'Love Of The Loved' and 'Hello Little Girl', but Brian demurred and said he'd like to get a recording contract first. Coleman then called George Martin's office, talked to Martin's secretary Judy Lockhart-Smith and arranged an appointment. Even then, the situation wasn't exactly straightforward. Alistair Taylor, Epstein's assistant, said that Parlophone began to play around with him and he became so angry he threatened to withdraw all EMI's business from his record stores if they didn't give the Beatles a recording contract.

Taylor commented, 'EMI took them on sufferance because Brian was one of their top customers. I saw Brian in tears, literally, because Martin promised to phone back, and day after day went by and George Martin was never available, always "in a meeting". I saw Brian thumping the desk and in tears because George Martin hadn't phoned back.'

The pressure Brian was exerting on EMI paid off and an audition was arranged for 6 June 1962. The recording manager for the session was Ron Richards, Martin's assistant, who dealt with all of Parlophone's pop-style artists. He was officially down as their recording manager and would have remained so but for another stroke of luck. After they'd played four of their numbers, the recording engineer was impressed by their original material and went down to the EMI canteen and brought George Martin to the studio. Martin then took over the rest of the session. When it was finished he told them, 'You must listen to it, and if there's anything you don't like, tell me, and we'll try and do something about it.'

George replied, 'Well, for a start, I don't like your tie.'

It's said that this sample of George's humour endeared the group to Martin, although the A&R man still had to decide whether to sign them up. He arranged for them to come for another recording session and told Epstein that although he didn't have a problem with vocals and guitars, for a recording studio session he preferred to use a session drummer and would be hiring one for their next session. This remark was used as an excuse to sack Pete Best, who at that time was probably the most popular member of the Beatles in Liverpool. In fact, A&R men generally used session drummers such as Clem Cattini and Andy Smith as a matter of course due to their familiarity with the studios and the type of drum sound required.

In January 1962 Ringo left the Hurricanes to join Tony Sheridan at the Top Ten club in Hamburg. Club owner Peter Eckhorn had been in Liverpool attempting to book a return season by the Beatles for his club, but was unsuccessful. While in Liverpool he offered Ringo £30 a week plus the use of a car and a flat if he would become part of Sheridan's band at the Top Ten.

Ringo joined the Star Combo, as Sheridan called the outfit (much to the annoyance of Eckhorn – as Sheridan had named it in honour of a new club about to open, the Star Club, where he intended playing next), which also featured Roy Young, a musician friend of the Beatles.

However, Ringo found that Sheridan was a difficult and frustrating artist to back, as he'd often change to another number in the middle of the one he was performing, or begin playing a number without informing the band. Ringo soon tired of the eccentricities and returned to Liverpool and the Hurricanes.

In the meantime, the Beatles returned to Hamburg to make their debut at the Star Club when it first opened on 13 April 1962, where they were to appear for a seven-week season. The Star Club is a Hamburg legend and the German equivalent of the Cavern in terms of rock-music history. It was launched in 1962 by Manfred Weissleder and was to provide a home for numerous Liverpool groups, in addition to rock legends such as Ray Charles, Little Richard, Jerry Lee Lewis, Bo Diddley and the Everly Brothers.

When the Beatles arrived at Hamburg airport a tear-stricken Astrid met them and told them the devastating news – Stuart had just died of a brain haemorrhage. There have been all sorts of speculation as to what led to his death, one of which was Stuart being beaten up outside Litherland Town Hall. Philip Norman in *Shout!* says the incident happened three years prior – but, of course, the Beatles had never appeared at Litherland Town Hall three years earlier, plus Stuart had never been involved in a fight there – the only fight involved an incident at Lathom Hall in which John and Pete Best intervened and Stuart was unharmed and never kicked in the head. Besides, the type of bleeding into the brain that Stuart experienced could not have occurred so far in the past. Albert Goldman came up with the fantasy that John had kicked Stuart in the head in Hamburg. Mrs Sutcliffe herself said that Stuart's headaches began after he fell down the attic stairs at Astrid's house in Altona. Astrid's mother Neilsa, an actual witness, also confirmed this.

On 15 August Pete Best was asked to meet Epstein in his office. This wasn't unusual as it was Pete who usually dealt with arrangements such as organising their transport with Neil Aspinall and making sure everyone knew about the gigs. He was completely unprepared for the news that he'd been sacked and Ringo Starr was to replace him.

Mona Best attempted to contact Epstein by phone for an explanation, but he remained elusive. She did succeed in contacting George Martin and asked him what was going on. He was surprised at the news and told her, 'I never suggested that Pete Best must go. All I said was that for the purposes of the Beatles first record I would rather use a session man. I never thought that Brian Epstein would let him go. He seemed to be the most saleable commodity as far as looks went. It was a surprise when I learned that they had dropped Pete. The drums were important to me for a record, but they didn't matter much otherwise. Fans don't pay particular attention to the quality of the drumming.'

Johnny Hutchinson deputised on the drum seat until Ringo made his debut with them at Hulme Hall on 18 August 1962. He was told to shave off his beard and rid himself of the silver streak in his hair.

Hutchinson, in fact, had been Epstein's initial choice as a replacement, but Hutch turned the offer down. Ringo had already accepted an offer to join Kingsize Taylor and the Dominoes in Germany, but the Beatles offered him £5 a week more than Taylor.

Later, Brian Epstein was to admit, 'Ringo, the last to become a Beatle, came into the group not because I wanted him, but because the boys did. To be completely honest, I was not at all keen to have him. I thought his drumming rather loud, his appearance unimpressive, and I could not see why he was important to the Beatles. But again, I trusted their instincts and I am grateful now. He has become an excellent Beatle and a devoted friend. Ringo is warm and wry-witted, a good drummer, and I like him enormously. He is a very uncomplicated, very nice young man.

'We rarely fall out because he, probably more than the others, is amenable to most of my suggestions.'

The Beatles arrived at Hulme Hall in the afternoon of 18 August 1962, as they needed to rehearse with Ringo for two hours before he joined them on their first gig together.

Beryl Adams, Brian Epstein's secretary, recalled, 'When we got to the gig that night, it was absolutely amazing. Some of the girls were crying. They wanted Pete back. "Who's Ringo?" they asked. It was really sad.'

When Ringo appeared with the Beatles at the Cavern on 19 August there was all hell to pay. Brian Epstein was frightened at being jostled by angry fans and had to have bodyguards, the audience were shouting, 'Pete forever, Ringo never,' and George received a black eye from a Best fan called Bruno from Norris Green.

George was possibly picked on because a *Mersey Beat* report said that he'd gone to Ringo's house to make enquiries about Ringo joining them and it was known that he was a good friend of the Hurricanes' drummer.

However, by the end of the performance the animosity seemed to have faded away and the fans apparently accepted the new member.

Ringo wasn't invited to John's wedding to Cynthia Powell a few days later on 23 August.

It's interesting to note that how John presented his views to the media and how he acted in reality were often different. John hadn't taken much part in the sacking of Pete Best as he thought it was a dishonourable thing to do. He also initially wasn't totally supportive of Ringo and didn't invite him to his wedding with Cynthia because he wasn't sure he could trust him to keep the marriage a secret. Ringo recalled, 'It was kept from me because I wasn't considered a real member at the beginning.'

John was also initially patronising to Ringo, asking him to get him drinks, saying, 'Hey, Ritchie, get us a beer. There's a good mate,' as if he were a road manager. Yet in public he said, 'Ringo was a star in his own right before we even met. His talents would have come out one way or another. Whatever that spark is in Ringo, we all know it but we can't put our finger on it. There's something in him that's projectable and he would have surfaced as an individual.'

On another occasion, he said, 'Ringo is not like the rest of us. If everything sounds all right, nobody says it is because of Ringo's great drumming. But if anything goes wrong, we can all blame Ringo, That's what he's here for.'

The Beatles' next session at Abbey Road Studios took place on 4 September. The Beatles recorded 'Love Me Do' and 'How Do You Do It'. Norman Smith, who was present at the session, said, 'I've a feeling that Paul wasn't too happy with Ringo's drumming, and felt it could be better.' Both George Martin and Ron Richards were also unhappy about Ringo's drumming and decided to book Andy White as session drummer for their next session on 11 September. Richards was to say, 'We weren't happy with the original drum sound on "Love Me Do" so I booked Andy White for the remake. I used him a lot at the time – he was very good.'

When the group arrived, Ringo was visibly shaken to see the session drummer and thought, 'They're doing a Pete Best on me.' Richards felt sorry for him and asked him to play maracas on 'P.S. I Love You' and tambourine on 'Love Me Do'.

Ringo mentioned the occasion at a later date, although he mixed Richards up with Martin: 'I walked into the studio and saw a drum set that wasn't mine and sitting behind it a drummer that definitely wasn't this baby. George Martin said he wanted me to play tambourine. You can imagine how I felt. He obviously thought that first record wasn't good enough because of my drumming.'

This situation has led to some confusion and even Ringo didn't realise that it was his version of 'Love Me Do' that was released as the single on Friday 5 October 1962. It was discovered that there wasn't much difference between Ringo's drumming and White's, so the 4 September recording with Ringo was issued as the official single. It was only later on, following the release of the EP 'The Beatles Hits' that the Andy White 11 September version replaced the earlier recording as a single.

It's interesting to note opinions from those concerned regarding Ringo's ability as a drummer.

George Martin was to say, 'Ringo hit good and hard and used the tom-tom well, even though he couldn't do a roll to save his life.' At a later stage he was also to say, 'He's got tremendous feel. He always helped us to hit the right tempo for a song, and gave it that support – that rock-solid backbeat – that made the recording of all the Beatles' songs that much easier. He was sympathetic. His tempos used to go up and down, but up and down in the right way to help the song.'

In 1987 George Harrison said, 'He could be the best rock'n'roll drummer – or at least one of the best rock'n'roll drummers. He does fills which crack up people like Jim Keltner. He's just amazed because Ringo starts them in the wrong place and all that, but that is brilliant. That's pure feel. You know, he does everything back to front.'

Paul McCartney noted in 1980, 'We always gave Ringo direction – on every single number. It was usually very controlled. Whoever had written the song, John for instance, would say, "I want this." Obviously, a lot of the stuff came out of what Ringo was playing, but we would always control it.'

John Lennon, also in 1980, said, 'Ringo's a damn good drummer. He was always a good drummer. He's not technically good, but I think Ringo's drumming is underrated the same way as Paul's bass playing is underrated.'

At one time Ringo commented, 'Whenever I hear another drummer I know I'm no good. I'm no good on the technical things but I'm good with all the motions, swinging my head, like. That's because I love to dance but you can't do that on drums.'

He also said, 'I'm your basic offbeat drummer with funny fills. The fills were funny because I'm really left-handed playing a right-handed kit. I can't roll around the drums because of that. I have to start with my left hand. If I come off the snare onto the tom-tom, I can't go onto the other tom, to the floor tom. That's why we used to call them funny fills.'

It might be interesting here to document Ringo's vocal and composing contributions to the entire Beatles canon. John and Paul weren't all that supportive of George regarding George's original material. They were also too focused on their own compositions to really give Ringo any consideration. Because it's said that Ringo was given his own spot on each album, it's assumed that this was part of the Lennon and McCartney canon giving 'a little help' to their friend, Ringo.

In fact, Ringo was given a token song every now and then. Here is a rundown of the vocal contributions of Ringo to the Beatles recordings, which indicate that Lennon and McCartney songs didn't have that much of a role to play in Ringo's case.

On the *Please Please Me* album Ringo sang 'Boys'. But this had been a part of the Beatles repertoire anyway and had previously been sung by Pete Best when he was the group's drummer. The flipside of the Shirelles 'Will You Love Me Tomorrow', it had also been one of the numbers Ringo sang with Rory Storm and the Hurricanes as part of 'Ringo Starrtime'.

The *With The Beatles* album saw Ringo sing his first Lennon and McCartney composition, 'I Wanna Be Your Man'. John and Paul had originally given this number to the Rolling Stones. John was to say, 'It was a throwaway. The only two versions of the song were Ringo and the Rolling Stones. That shows how much importance we put on it. We weren't going to give them anything great, right?'

Their EP 'Long Tall Sally' included Ringo's vocal on the Carl Perkins number 'Matchbox'. It was another number from the Beatles repertoire that Pete Best had originally sung.

There was no Ringo vocal on the *A Hard Day's Night* album, proving that Ringo wasn't given a vocal contribution on each of the Beatles' albums.

On *Beatles For Sale*, Ringo sang 'Honey Don't', a Carl Perkins number, which had been the flipside of Perkins' 'Blue Suede Shoes', another song from the Beatles' stage repertoire.

The *Help!* album included Ringo's vocal on the country number 'Act Naturally', a hit for Buck Owens – and Ringo was to record a duet of the number with Owens decades later.

Rubber Soul presented Ringo with the first song he received a composer credit for, 'What Goes On'. It was credited to Lennon/McCartney/Starr. John Lennon was to say, 'It was a very early song of mine. Ringo and Paul wrote a new middle-eight together when we recorded it.'

At the time, Ringo was to say, 'I used to wish that I could write songs like the others – and I've tried, but I just can't. I can get the words all right, but whenever I think of a tune and sing it to the others they always say, "Yeah, it sounds like such a thing, and when they point it out I see what they mean."'

The number was left off the American release of the *Rubber Soul* album, but used as the B side of the 'Nowhere Man' single.

The *Revolver* album saw Ringo being given another Lennon and McCartney composition, 'Yellow Submarine', a number actually written by Paul as a children's song.

The *Sergeant Pepper's Lonely Hearts Club Band* album gave Ringo 'With A Little Help From My Friends', a number also given to Joe Cocker who took it to No. 1 in the British charts. It was another Lennon and McCartney number mainly written by Paul.

Ringo was to say, 'With *Sgt Pepper* I felt more like a session man because we were interested in making it an album with strings and brass parts. Everyone says that record is a classic, but it's not my favourite album.

On the *Magical Mystery Tour* double EP (an album release in the States), all four members of the Beatles are given a composer credit on 'Flying', the only instrumental they recorded for Parlophone.

The album *The Beatles*, more familiarly known as the White Album, saw Ringo give voice to his own composition, 'Don't Pass Me By', which he wrote during his short sojourn in the Maharishi's ashram in India. The original title of the song had been 'Some Kind Of Friendly'. Perhaps due to it being a double album, Ringo was given lead vocal on another number, the John Lennon composition 'Good Night'. Some years later, John was to say, '"Good Night" was written for Julian the way "Beautiful Boy" was written for Sean, but given to Ringo and possibly overlush.'

Ringo had no lead vocal track on the *Let It Be* album.

On *Abbey Road* Ringo had another of his own compositions, 'Octopus's Garden'. George Harrison was to comment, '"Octopus's Garden" is Ringo's song. It's only the second song Ringo has written, mind you, and it's lovely. Ringo gets bored with just playing drums all the time, so at home he sometimes plays a bit of piano, but unfortunately he only knows about three chords. He knows about the same on guitar, too. This song gets very deep into your consciousness, though, because it's so peaceful. I suppose Ringo is writing cosmic songs these days without even noticing it.'

'Octopus's Garden' had actually been written when Ringo had walked out of the White Album sessions.

Beatles associate Peter Brown commented, 'Most of the time Ringo spent in the studio he sat in a corner playing cards with Neil and Mal. It was a poorly kept secret among Beatles intimates that after Ringo left the studios, Paul would often dub in the drum tracks himself.

'When Ringo returned to the studio the next day, he would pretend not to notice that it was not his playing.'

Ringo actually walked out after one session during which Paul criticised his drumming; although he didn't refer to this when he later gave an explanation for his walkout: 'I felt I was playing like shit. And those three were really getting on. I had this feeling that nobody loved me; I felt horrible. So I said to myself, "What am I doing here? Those three are getting along so well, and I'm not even playing well." That was madness, so I went away on a holiday to sort things out. I don't know, maybe I was just paranoid. You know that to play in a band you have to trust each other.'

Yet it was a fact that Ringo must have felt humiliated when Paul criticised his drumming – and it was a similar incident which caused George Harrison to walk out after Paul had rubbished his ability on guitar.

As a final comment on *The Beatles* double album, Ringo said, 'As a band member, I've always felt the White Album was better than *Sgt Pepper* because by the end it was more like a real group again. There weren't so many overdubs like on *Pepper*. With all those orchestras and whatnot, we were virtually a session group on our own album.'

To return to the Beatles' story, the official contract with Brian Epstein was signed on 1 October 1962 and Brian had now increased his percentage to 25% of their gross earnings. A few days later, on 5 October 1962, their first British single 'Love Me Do' c/w 'P.S. I Love You' was released.

When it first entered the charts on 26 October Paul was to say, 'If you want to know when we knew we'd arrived, it was getting in the charts with "Love Me Do".'

The highest position it reached was No. 17 in one London music-paper chart. In fact, it made its presence felt in the charts of all four London music papers, reaching No. 24 in *Disc* and No. 32 in *Record Mirror*. It went straight to No.1 in *Mersey Beat*. Rumours abounded in Liverpool, first that Brian Epstein had bought a thousand copies of the disc, then the figure leaped to ten thousand. He denied this and he was correct – the way the charts were compiled in those days meant that it would have been impossible to influence the charts by the bulk purchase of records for one outlet.

The Beatles then returned to Hamburg for their third and last season (their second engagement had taken place from 1 to 14 November).

During their final season, they were recorded on stage by Adrian Barber, former member of the Big Three, and these tapes were to surface many years later as *The Beatles Live! At the Star Club In Hamburg, Germany: 1962*. George was to give evidence to prevent their release as a CD a few decades later.

1963 was the year of Beatlemania in Britain and the year they began touring seriously.

A small Scottish tour took place between 3 and 6 January and the group were then booked as a support to Helen Shapiro on her nation-wide tour between 2 February and 3 March. Their next tour was in support of American hit-paraders Tommy Roe and Chris Montez between 9 and 31 March, followed by a tour with Roy Orbison between 18 May and 9 June, during which they came to share top billing. They were now topping the bill in their own right and undertook another mini-Scottish tour from 5 to 7 October, toured Sweden from 25 to 29 October and ended the year with an autumn tour of Britain from 1 November to 13 December.

The group were now regularly appearing on the radio and their record success became phenomenal. By 19 February their single 'Please Please Me' had topped the *New Musical Express* charts. Their other singles successes that year all reached the No. 1 position: 'From Me To You', 'She Loves You' and 'I Want To Hold Your Hand'. Their EPs 'Twist And Shout' and 'The Beatles Hits' also topped the charts and 'The Beatles No. 1' reached No. 2. Their albums *Please Please Me* and *With The Beatles* topped the album charts.

John Lennon's son Julian was born on 8 April. Sadly, John seemed to neglect his first-born son and, in a *Playboy* interview decades later, he was to say, rather ungenerously, 'Julian was born out of a bottle of whisky on a Saturday night,' which hurt his son immensely.

Paul was also making the headlines with his romance with actress Jane Asher. The first story about the Beatles to appear in a national newspaper occurred when Don Short of the *Daily Mirror* wrote about an incident at Paul's 21st birthday party on 18 June, when John Lennon beat up Cavern disc jockey Bob Wooler because he implied John had had a homosexual relationship with Brian Epstein following a brief holiday the two of them had recently enjoyed in Barcelona.

The Beatles also made their final appearance at the Cavern club on 3 August 1963. They had appeared at the venue 292 times.

They were also to help the career of the Rolling Stones. George Harrison had initially recommended them to Decca A&R man Dick Rowe during a Beat competition at the Philharmonic Hall, Liverpool, and John and Paul were to give them the song 'I Wanna Be Your Man', which became the Stones' biggest hit.

There has always been an interesting clash of images here. While the Beatles were a rough, tough, savage rock'n'roll and R&B band in the seedy St Pauli area of Hamburg, taking drugs and mixing with prostitutes and gangsters, the Stones were in middle-class areas such as Cheltenham and Mick Jagger was at the London School of Economics. It was a far cry from the basic working-class rough-looking crew the Beatles were.

Then Brian Epstein changed their image, made them dispense with their leathers and fitted them out in mohair suits. He took them to the Empire Theatre, Liverpool, to see the Shadows and asked them to emulate them, bowing to the audience at the end of their act. This smoothing out didn't go down too well with John and Pete Best, who didn't want to get rid of their leathers.

When they began to appear on tours, they only had a twenty-minute or half-hour spot, simply playing their latest recordings. John and George in particular disliked this. John was to say that the best music they played was in Hamburg and Liverpool – and that they sold out after that. George was to concur, saying, 'I was disappointed that we got so famous, because as musicians, we were a really good band in the early days. The more fame that we got, the more the audience screamed and the more that we did just twenty or thirty-minute sets of our latest singles, the musicianship kind of went out the window. We pigeonholed ourselves by the mania that was going on and the inability to perform for longer periods of time, because of the way it was.'

It's also interesting to note that, due to the small amount of time the Beatles now spent on stage – in contrast to the lengthy hours in Hamburg and Liverpool – Pete Best actually spent more hours in live performance with the group than Ringo did.

Rolling Stones manager Andrew Loog Oldham was to watch a performance by the Beatles. He said, 'I sat there with a lump in my throat. In one night you knew they were going to be very big. It was just an instinctive thing. From that night on, it registered subconsciously that when they made it, another section of the public was going to want the opposite.'

So he created an image for the Rolling Stones, which was close to what the Beatles had originally been like before Brian Epstein smoothed them out – and John Lennon always resented it, claiming that the Stones had stolen the original Beatles image.

Writers who regard the Stones as a rough-and-ready band and the Beatles as loveable moptops, never saw their original act in Liverpool and Hamburg.

The first major television documentary on the group was 'The Mersey Sound', directed for BBC by Don Howarth, which was first broadcast on BBC1 on 9 October 1963 and repeated on 13 November.

Earlier that year Ringo had been asked what his ambition was. He said he would open a chain of women's hairdressing salons. 'I figure it would be a good business move. Girls will always want their hair doing, and if the Beatles ever fell through I'd have a good sideline. I could go round from time to time saying, "Is everything all right, Madam? A cup of coffee, perhaps?"'

Don Howarth took this quote literally and 'The Mersey Sound' documentary ended with a scene in which a smartly dressed Ringo, his dream come true, walks past a bank of hairdryers at a hairdressing salon declaring that his ambition was to make enough money to open his own chain of salons.

On 13 October 1963 the Beatles topped the bill on *Sunday Night At The London Palladium*, the leading television show with the highest ratings, drawing an audience of 15 million to watch the group. The following day the *Daily Mirror* was published with the headline 'Beatlemania!' It was a new word to be added to the English language.

An even more prestigious event took place on 4 November when they were added to the bill of the *Royal Variety Show* at the Prince of Wales Theatre, during which John made his famous quote, 'Those in the cheaper seats, you clap your hands. The rest of you just rattle your jewellery,' which endeared him to the nation.

Around that time another coincidence happened, which was another example of the strokes of luck that were to boost their career. On 31 October Ed Sullivan, host of America's biggest television show, happened to be passing through Heathrow Airport. The Beatles were returning from their short tour of Sweden.

Sullivan recalled, 'My wife Sylvia and I were in London at Heathrow Airport. There was the biggest crowd I've ever seen in my life! I asked someone what was going on and he said, "The Beatles". "Who the hell are the Beatles?" I asked. But I went back to my hotel, got the name of their manager, and arranged for them to do three shows.'

Other strands of luck were also coming together to aid the destiny of the Beatles. EMI Records owned the American company Capitol Records and always offered their US arm first choice of British releases. Capitol continually turned the Beatles' records down. Alan Livingstone, the Capitol President, had sent a memo from his Hollywood office: 'We don't think the Beatles will do anything in this market.'

EMI then put pressure on Brown Meggs, Director of Eastern Operations of Capitol and he agreed to release 'I Want To Hold Your Hand', which they intended to issue in late January 1964 to tie in with the *Ed Sullivan Show* appearance.

Carroll James, a disc jockey at WWDC-AM in Washington DC, obtained a copy of the British single and began playing it on his programme on 17 December. There was such a reaction that he continued to play it. One of his friends taped it and sent it to a disc jockey in Chicago and he had such a response he sent a tape to a disc jockey in St Louis. Capitol had no choice but to advance the release date and issue the single on 27 December 1963.

Another piece or luck (or pure coincidence) concerned Sid Bernstein, who'd worked for General Artists Corporation, the largest theatrical agency in America. He'd been taking an evening course in social research, part of which required him to read English newspapers each week. He noticed the rise of 'Beatlemania' in Britain and on a hunch contacted Brian Epstein and asked if he could book the Beatles for a Carnegie Hall concert to take place on 14 February 1964. Epstein agreed on condition that the deal would become null and void if they didn't have a hit in the American charts.

All these strands came together. The alteration of the release date meant that 'I Want To Hold Your Hand' would reach the No. 1 position prior to the *Ed Sullivan Show* and create a huge interest in America.

In the meantime, the Beatles ended the year with their own Christmas Show at the Astoria, Finsbury Park, in London. On 14 January 1964 they left for Paris where they were to appear at the Olympia on a bill with Trini Lopez and Sylvie Vartan. On 17 January they received a telephone call with the news that 'I Want To Hold You Hand' had topped the American charts three weeks after its initial release. Their road manager Mal Evans described their glee at the news. 'They always act this way when anything big happens – just a bunch of kids, jumping up and down with sheer delight. Paul climbed on my back demanding a piggyback. They felt this was the biggest thing that could have happened. And who could blame them? Gradually they quietened down, ordered some more drinks and sat down to appreciate fully what happened. It was a wonderful, marvellous night for all of them. I was knocked out.'

The Beatles flew to New York on 7 February, were greeted by 3,000 fans at JFK airport and endeared themselves to the media during a much-quoted press conference in which their Scouse humour came to the fore. It must also be remembered that America had been in mourning over the death of President Kennedy the previous November, and the appearance of the Beatles was able to put a smile on America's face again.

When he was asked, 'Ringo, why do you wear two rings on each hand?' he answered, 'Because I can't fit them through my nose.'

When asked, 'How did you find America?' he replied, 'We went to Greenland and made a left turn,' and when asked, 'What is the biggest threat to your careers, the atom bomb or dandruff?' he said, 'The atom bomb. We've already got dandruff.'

When John Lennon was asked, 'Does all the adulation from teenage girls affect you?' he replied, 'When I feel my head start to swell, I look at Ringo and know perfectly well we're not supermen.'

This is a curious remark, but not untypical at the time. Ringo was still regarded as a newcomer with the Beatles, as if he was still on probation.

Paul was also to say, 'We're never serious,' then he looked at Ringo and continued, 'Just look at him. How could we be serious?'

Another comment made by John was: 'Ringo doesn't know the meaning of fear, or any other word of more than three letters,' which in some ways can be taken as an insult.

However, to everyone's surprise, Ringo proved to be the most popular Beatle with American fans and most of the tribute records were about him, such as 'Ringo For President'. This must have at last boosted his confidence.

Brian Epstein noted this and stated, 'America discovered Ringo.'

The group were booked into the Plaza Hotel, but George was ill with a bad throat. His sister Louise arrived to look after him and the hotel doctor, a Dr Gordon, was called. He told George, 'I'll have to get you fit, otherwise my young relatives will blunt my needles.'

Fortunately, George recovered enough to be able to appear on the *Ed Sullivan Show* on 9 February, during which they performed 'All My Loving', 'Till There Was You', 'She Loves You', 'I Saw Her Standing There' and 'I Want To Hold Your Hand'.

The show had the largest audience in the history of television, with 73,700,000 people watching. On 11 February they travelled to Washington to appear in their first-ever American concert at the Washington Coliseum and the next night became the first pop group ever to appear at Carnegie Hall in New York. They appeared on another *Ed Sullivan Show*, this time filmed from the Deauville Hotel in Miami, and returned to Britain on 23 February.

On his return to England, Ringo was given another boost by being elected Vice President of the Leeds University Law Society.

Recording history was made on 11 March 1964 when the Beatles were placed in the top five positions in the American chart. They were: No. 1, 'Twist And Shout'; No. 2, 'Can't Buy Me Love'; No. 3, 'She Loves You'; No. 4, 'I Want To Hold Your Hand'; No. 5, 'Please Please Me'.

Their British hit singles during the year were: 'Can't Buy Me Love' (which reached No. 1), a re-entry of 'She Loves You' (No. 42), a re-entry of 'I Want To Hold Your Hand' (No. 48), 'Ain't She Sweet' (No. 29), another re-entry of 'Can't Buy Me Love' (No. 47), 'A Hard Day's Night' (No. 1) and 'I Feel Fine' (No. 1). Their EPs were 'All My Loving' (No. 1), a re-entry of 'The Beatles Hits' (No. 17), 'Long Tall Sally' (No. 1), another re-entry of 'The Beatles Hits' (No. 16), a re-entry of 'The Beatles No. 1' (No. 17), another re-entry of 'The Beatles Hits' (No. 15), a fourth re-entry of 'The Beatles Hits' (No. 19), a re-entry of 'Twist And Shout' (No. 17), a fifth re-entry of 'The Beatles Hits' (No. 13), a sixth re-entry of 'The Beatles Hits' (No. 13), a second re-entry of 'Twist And Shout' (No. 17) and 'A Hard Day's Night' (No. 1). Their album hits were *A Hard Day's Night* (No.1), a re-entry of *Please Please Me* (No. 13), a second re-entry of *Please Please Me* (No. 19), a third re-entry of *Please Please Me* (No. 17), a re-entry of *With The Beatles* (No. 19) and *Beatles For Sale* (No. 1).

In America there was an array of singles releases. This was due to the fact that Capitol, by initially refusing to accept Beatles releases because they did not think them suitable for the American market, left EMI to make deals with companies such as Swan and Vee-Jay during 1963. This left a number of companies able to issue Beatles product now that they were the biggest name on the record scene – including MGM and Atco, who were releasing the old Hamburg Polydor recordings such as 'Ain't She Sweet'.

The singles hits during 1964 were: 'I Want To Hold Your Hand', 'I Saw Her Standing There', 'She Loves You', 'Please Please Me', 'My Bonnie', 'Twist And Shout', 'Can't Buy Me Love', 'Do You Want To Know A Secret', 'Thank You Girl', 'Love Me Do', 'P.S. I Love You', 'A

Hard Day's Night', 'Ain't She Sweet', 'And I Love Her', 'I'll Cry Instead', 'Matchbox', 'Slow Down', 'I Feel Fine' and 'She's A Woman'.

Filming also began on *A Hard Day's Night*. This was a result of Noel Rodgers, a British representative for United Artists Records, witnessing Beatlemania first hand. This was in 1963 when Capitol were still refusing to issue Beatles product in the States. Rodgers was convinced that they would eventually make a breakthrough in America and he approached Bud Ornstein, the British head of production for United Artists, to suggest they make a three-picture deal with the Beatles. The aim, primarily, was to obtain soundtracks of their recordings.

Ornstein agreed and contacted Walter Shenson, an American producer who had been making films in Britain such as *Mouse On The Moon*. He contacted director Dick Lester and Brian Epstein was approached. Ornstein and Shenson had agreed that they would be prepared to give the Beatles 25% of the film deal, but when they had the meeting with Epstein, before they could even discuss a deal he said, 'I wouldn't consider anything under 7.5%.' Fortunately, lawyer David Jacobs renegotiated the deal and did obtain the 25%, although he only asked for a percentage of the net as opposed to gross. This was typical of the amateurish approach to deals that Epstein made on behalf of the Beatles that lost them a fortune, probably in excess of $100m.

The record deal they had obtained from Parlophone was bad enough. As George Martin admitted, 'The deal I offered them was pretty awful.' He offered them one penny on royalties per single, with no advance payments – and on overseas sales they would only get half of that. A 12-track album would only be regarded as six cuts and there were three-year options with an increase of a quarter of a penny at the end of the first year and an increase of a halfpenny at the end of the second year. This was to make an absolute fortune for EMI, but was a shoddy deal for the Beatles and, apparently, there were no details of Epstein trying to negotiate anything stronger, or even taking legal advice on such an inequitable contract.

Epstein had tried to cultivate the image that he was an astute businessman, but even his deal with Dick James was unfair to the group and lost them the rights to their songs for good. It was rumoured that James's music publishing business was in trouble and short of money, yet Epstein signed the deal that gave James and his partner the majority share in all future Beatles music. James and his partner Charles Silver owned 50% of the company while John and Paul only had 15% each. James was able to turn it into a public company, against the wishes of John and Paul, which resulted in them losing the rights to the ownership of everything they wrote.

The absolute incompetence of the deal he made regarding the Beatles merchandising rights is staggering. He asked lawyer David Jacobs to deal with it and Jacobs, a homosexual, met a young man, Nicky Byrne, at a cocktail party and offered him the merchandising rights, although he had no experience in such matters. Byrne demanded 90% of the rights, leaving 10% to be shared by the Beatles, Brian Epstein and NEMS Enterprises. Epstein immediately agreed. Byrne became a millionaire straight away after flying to New York to set up the deals. Capitol Records promptly offered to buy him out for $500,000. He turned them down. Epstein had Jacobs renegotiate the deal to increase the Beatles, NEMS and his own royalty to a total of 46%. Despite making the deal with Byrne, Epstein began to negotiate deals direct through NEMS and Byrne sued. Because of the legal problems a large number of major firms, including Woolworth's, pulled out of Beatles merchandising deals, losing, it is said, over $100m of potential merchandising contracts. NEMS lost the case and had to pay Byrne substantial compensation.

These are just a few of the horrifically incompetent business messes Brian Epstein made, which, by the end of the decade, left the Beatles with just a fraction of the money they had generated. There may well have been talk of Brian being scrupulously honest in his dealings, but a closer look at the facts don't bear this out. When his contract with the Beatles was running out, without informing them he signed another deal with EMI to increase the percentage of his own contract from 15% to 25%, which ran for years after his contract with the group would have expired.

In 1964 the Beatles were in too much of a rush to even think about such things. On the first day of filming *A Hard Day's Night* George met Patti Boyd and their love affair began. The film became an international success and was dubbed 'the *Citizen Kane* of Jukebox movies'.

Director Dick Lester said he did not regard Ringo as 'the greatest intellect in the world', but also said that he saw him as 'a superb actor, an absolute natural. He can take directions from a director, which is a very difficult thing to do – you might even call it an art.'

Ringo was actually credited with thinking up the title for the film in April 1964. There had been several titles suggested ranging from 'Beatlemania' to 'It's A Daft, Daft, Daft, Daft World'. After they'd been working throughout the day on the film someone began to mutter, 'We've had a hard –'

Ringo interrupted, 'A hard day? Look at that clock. You mean a hard day's night, don't you?' And that became the title.

Incidentally, a month before, in March 1964, John Lennon's first book *In His Own Write* had been published. In it there is a story called 'Sad Michael' in which John wrote: 'He'd had a hard day's night that day, for Michael was a Cocky Watchtower.'

The year 1964 didn't just consolidate their success in Britain and America – the Beatles became a worldwide phenomenon. Their tours that year began with a world tour that started in Copenhagen, Denmark, on 4 June and took them to Hong Kong, Australia and New Zealand, ending in Brisbane, Australia, on 30 June. Ringo was unable to begin the tour with the group after collapsing at a photo session and a temporary drummer was hired in the person of Jimmy Nicol (how interesting it might have been if, with some imagination, they had hired Pete Best!).

On the morning of 3 June Ringo had collapsed during the photo session the Beatles were having in Barnes for the *Saturday Evening Post*. He was rushed to University College Hospital where it was diagnosed that he had tonsillitis and pharyngitis.

The idea of having a substitute drummer was anathema to George Harrison who said, 'If Ringo's not going then neither am I, you can find two replacements.' However, he was talked into continuing and after the first show said, 'Playing without Ringo is like driving a car on three wheels, but Jimmy has grasped our rhythm very quickly.'

Ringo was discharged from hospital on 11 June and was able to join them in Australia at the tail end of the tour. Brian Epstein accompanied Ringo from London to Australia and described it in his diary:

The Pan-Am Boeing was to take Ringo and I on the first lap of our long journey halfway across the world.

The long and tiring flight had grown arduous and we were only half awake. As far as Los Angeles we had chatted and played cards with film star Horst Buchholz and the very beautiful Vivien Leigh, whom I had admired for so long and was pleased to meet.

Throughout the journey my admiration for Ringo increased. Tired as we both were, and he only 24 hours out of hospital, never once did he hesitate to comply with requests to meet fans and press, wherever our plane refuelled.

In San Francisco, Honolulu and Fiji, this fine drummer from Liverpool delighted everyone he met with his well-known and unaffected charm.

When the plane came to a standstill at Sydney airport at the specially appointed position for our disembarkation, the door opened and our ears were full with the screams and wails of our first sample of a big Australian welcome. Ringo appeared at the door of the plane, and the noise increased and seemed to reach an ever higher peak as we made for the car at the foot of the steps.

As the car toured through the airport's spectators, Ringo bowed and smiled to the fans and notices stating, 'We love you, Ringo' and 'Welcome, Ringo' and others.

Then we boarded our Viscount for Melbourne and there, too, we received a robust welcome.

As we motored, with a police escort, to our hotel in the city, the police lined our route, and on our arrival there Ringo was pushed to the ground as the police failed to make way for us through the crowd of a thousand to the entrance of the Southern Cross Hotel.

The hotel itself seemed to accommodate every pressman,

photographer and deejay in the country. As I settled in my room to unpack clothes, all at once they knocked at the doors, called on the telephone and generally persisted against the increasingly deafening noise from the growing crowd at the front of the hotel – the expectant public gathering for the arrival of John, Paul and George, with Jimmy Nicol.

At 3.30, I joined Ringo in the Beatles' suite to watch and hear the crowd who would greet the boys at 4 p.m. Ringo couldn't watch from the window, because he would be spotted, so he listened to radio and saw TV, both of which had all channels covering the occasion. When the boys actually arrived, no one knew, as it was necessary (and how!) for them to be smuggled in at the rear of the building.

We were asked to make an appearance on the balcony of the hotel. All five boys walked around to the specially erected balustrade at the centre of the hotel's third floor flat roof – John, Paul, George, Ringo, Jimmy, followed by myself.

The sight and sound of that tumultuous welcome I shall never forget, and neither will the Beatles.

The Australian leg of the tour was a phenomenon, with tens of thousands of youngsters taking to the streets to greet them. Prior to that they appeared in Hong Kong and George was to say, 'The best flight I remember was the one to Hong Kong. It took several hours and I remember them saying, "Return to your seats because we're approaching Hong Kong," and I thought, "We can't be there already." We'd been sitting on the floor drinking and taking Preludins for about twenty hours and so it seemed like a ten-minute flight. On all those flights we were still on uppers and that's what helped us get through because we'd drink a whisky and coke with anyone, even if he was the devil, and charm the pants off him.'

In Australia, the old problem of Jelly Babies came up again. These soft jelly sweets had caused the Beatles some problems during their concert performances when touring with Roy Orbison, because fans had heard that George liked them.

George said, 'They hurt. Some newspaper had dug out the old joke, which we'd forgotten about, when John once said I'd eaten his Jelly Babies. Everywhere we went I got them thrown at me. They don't have soft Jelly Babies in America but hard jelly beans like bullets!'

A publicity handout in Australia had mentioned the British fans' habit of throwing Jelly Babies and they had problems with them in Sydney. George said, 'Wherever we've been since then – America, Europe and now Australia, that stupid story has gone ahead with the result that we get Jelly Babies chucked at us till we're really fed up.'

During a performance at Sydney Stadium Paul had to stop the show on two occasions because of the hail of Jelly Babies tossed at them on stage. When he asked the audience to stop throwing them, another hail came through the air. 'Well, I asked you anyway,' he told them. Speaking to the press after the show he said, 'I keep asking them not to chuck those damned things, but they don't seem to have the sense to realise we hate being the target for sweets coming like bullets from all directions. How can we concentrate on our jobs on the stage when we are having all the time to keep ducking to avoid sweets, streamers and other stuff they keep throwing at us?'

John commented, 'It's ridiculous. They even throw miniature koala bears and gift-wrapped packages while we are going round on the revolving stage. We haven't a chance to get out of the way.'

Ringo added, 'It's all right for you lot. You can jump aside and dodge them, but I'm stuck at the drums and can't move, so they all seem to hit me.'

On their return to Britain they were to attend the premiere of *A Hard Day's Night* at the London Pavilion, which was attended by Princess Margaret and Lord Snowdon.

The northern premiere took place at the Odeon, London Road, Liverpool, following a civic reception for the group at the town hall. Over 200,000 people lined the streets from Speke Airport to the town hall itself, and their entourage of cars, led by a police motorcycle escort, was stopped four times because of the massive crowds.

It was noticed that the loudest cries were for Ringo!

Despite the critical success of *A Hard Day's Night*, John didn't like it. He said, '*A Hard Day's Night* was sort of interesting since it was the first time. We loathed the script because it was somebody trying to write like we were in real life. In retrospect Alan Owen didn't do a bad job, but at the time we were self-conscious about the dialogue. It felt unreal.'

Alan Owen had an 'ear for dialogue' and his script was well suited to the Beatles and their sense of humour. As a Liverpool/Welshman who wrote television plays with Liverpool settings, he used to visit Liverpool regularly to pick up the natural dialogue of Scousers. When commissioned to pen the script for the film, he met George in the Blue Angel club.

Having received international acclaim and an Oscar nomination for his script, he was surprised when Epstein told him that they'd recruited a different scriptwriter for their second film. Upset, Owen said to Epstein, 'I didn't get on very well with John, Ringo is fine, but not the greatest intellectual in the world. We had trouble with one scene with Paul . . . mind you, I like George very much.'

Epstein retorted, 'What would you say if I told you that the one person who doesn't want you to work on this film is George Harrison?' Alan's wife was furious and called Epstein a liar.

In July John and Cynthia moved into a new house, 'Kenwood', in the stockbroker belt of Weybridge in Surrey and the group appeared on

'The Night Of A Hundred Stars' at the London Palladium with luminaries such as Sir Laurence Olivier and Judy Garland.

Just before their US tour *A Hard Day's Night* opened in America to rave reviews. Critics even compared the Beatles to the Marx Brothers.

Their first American tour opened on 19 August 1964 at the Cow Palace, San Francisco, and ended on 20 September at the Paramount Theater, New York. The reaction at the majority of the large stadiums was the same, vast crowds of youngsters screaming throughout the sets. The *San Francisco Reporter* was to write, 'Although it was publicised as music, all that was heard and seen of the Mersey Sound was something like a jet engine shrieking through a summer lightning storm because of the yelling fans. It had no mercy, and afterwards everyone still capable of speech took note of a ringing in the ears which lasted for as long as the Beatles played.'

It was also during this trip that Bob Dylan visited them at the Delmonico Hotel in New York and introduced them to marijuana. They'd never smoked marijuana before and told him so. He was surprised and pointed out that in their song 'I Want To Hold Your Hand' they'd sung, 'I get high'. John had to explain that the words were actually 'I can't hide'!

On their return home they began an autumn tour of Britain at the Gaumont, Bradford, on 9 October, which ended at the Colston Hall, Bristol, on 10 November, and ended the year with another Beatles Christmas Show at the Odeon, Hammersmith. This was where George first made the acquaintance of the person who was to become his life-long friend, Eric Clapton, who was on the bill as a member of the Yardbirds.

Shortly before their Christmas show, Ringo was taken into University College Hospital to have his tonsils out. At the time the newspapers had been reporting that Ringo had been dating London model Vickie Hodge. His Liverpool girlfriend Maureen Cox travelled down to visit him and then spent Christmas with him. By mid-January she was pregnant and the couple were married at Caxton Hall, London, on 11 February 1965. They spent a short honeymoon at the home of their lawyer David Jacobs, the man who had helped to make such a mess of their merchandising deals. (Jacobs was later found dead, hanging in the garage of the house in December 1968.)

The Beatles had three hit singles in Britain during 1965, all of which topped the charts. They were 'Ticket To Ride', 'Help!' and 'Day Tripper'/'We Can Work It Out'.

Their EPs kept bouncing in and out of the charts. 'A Hard Day's Night Vol 2' reached No. 8, 'Beatles For Sale' reached No.1, 'A Hard Day's Night Vol 2' re-entered at No.15, 'Long Tall Sally' re-entered at No. 16, 'A Hard Day's Night Vol 2' re-entered at No. 17, 'Beatles For Sale No. 2' reached No. 5, 'A Hard Day's Night Vol 2' re-entered at No. 6, 'Beatles For Sale' re-entered at No. 17, 'Beatles For Sale' re-entered again at No. 10 and then again at No. 14, 'Beatles Million Sellers' reached No. 1 and 'Beatles For Sale' re-entered yet again at No. 18.

On the album front their album *A Hard Day's Night* re-entered at No. 18, then had a second re-entry, also at No. 18. *Help!* reached No. 1, as did *Rubber Soul*.

Their singles in the American charts included 'Eight Days A Week', 'I Don't Want To Spoil The Party', 'Ticket To Ride', 'Help!', 'Yesterday', 'We Can Work It Out' and 'Day Tripper'.

There was an EP '4 By The Beatles' and the album releases were *The Early Beatles*, *Beatles VI*, *Help!* and *Rubber Soul*.

Filming on their second movie *Help!* began in February. Despite the fact that the budget had been doubled and it was to be filmed in colour, it was not in the same league as *A Hard Day's Night*. It was based on an old movie idea about a person who was terminally ill paying someone to kill him. According to Joe McGrath, who had written an original treatment with Dick Lester, a doctor tells Ringo that he is terminally ill. Depressed, Ringo pays £500 to a contract killer to kill him. The killer has to be a master of disguise, as Ringo doesn't want to face death directly. Ringo has asked the killer to murder him when he least expects it. The next day the doctor informs him that there has been a mistake, the X-rays he'd consulted had belonged to someone else, and therefore Ringo isn't terminally ill. Unable to contact the contract killer, he panics and tells the other Beatles to track down the killer before he can carry out his assignment.

Dick Lester then discovered that another film was currently being made in Hong Kong with an almost identical plot. Changes were hastily made and the film now revolved around an Eastern cult who wished to make a human sacrifice to the Goddess Kaili. The person to be sacrificed had to wear a special ring – and it was a ring that ended up on Ringo's finger. This resulted in the cult pursuing him and the Beatles trying to elude them.

John Lennon called the film 'Crap!' and the Beatles were reluctant to make another movie afterwards. Producer Walter Shenson commented, 'I think if we'd had a sensational script or a great idea, we might have made a third film. But it just wasn't in the cards.' Perhaps they should have commissioned Alan Owen to write the follow-up after all!

The experience wasn't all that bad as far as George was concerned because of an event that occurred during filming, while they were sitting in the Rajahama restaurant in Twickenham on 8 April. George said, 'We were waiting to shoot the scene in the restaurant when the guy gets thrown in the soup and there were a few Indian musicians playing in the background. I remember picking up the sitar and trying to hold it and thinking, "This is a funny sound." It was an incidental thing, but somewhere down the line I began to hear Ravi Shankar's name. The third time I heard it, I thought, "This is an odd coinci-

dence." And then I talked with David Crosby of the Byrds and he
mentioned the name. I went and bought a Ravi record: I put it on and
it hit a certain spot in my head that I can't explain, but it seemed very
familiar to me. The only way I could describe it was: my intellect didn't
know what was going on and yet this other part of me identified with
it. It just called on me ... a few months elapsed and then I met this guy
from the Asian Music Circle organisation who said, "Oh, Ravi
Shankar's going to come to my house for dinner. Do you want to come
too?"'

On 11 June it was announced that the Beatles would be honoured by
receiving MBEs. Although the MBE (Member of the Order of the
British Empire) is the lowest form of civil award, it was quite unprecedented at the time for a pop group to receive such an honour and
furious former recipients began protesting and sending their MBEs
back. The protests, particularly from military men, annoyed John who
then said that while army officers got their awards for killing people,
'we got ours for entertaining. On balance, I'd say we deserve ours
more.'

In 1964 King Features, a major American agency for animated
shorts on television, had gained the rights to make a series of cartoons
based on the Beatles. The 67-episode series was first screened in
America on ABC Television on 25 September 1965.

British actor Lance Percival provided the voice of Ringo in the
cartoons.

The animators were given details of how to approach the drawing of
each member of the Beatles and the instructions for Ringo read: 'Ringo
is the nice, gentle Beatle, although he looks rather sad. Ringo looks a
bit disjointed whether walking or standing. Ringo walks in a Groucho
Marx pose. Keep upper lip protruding. Keep Ringo's neck thin to help
the disjointed look. Keep hair at back shaggy. Keep mouth in wavy line.
When Ringo laughs, having made a funny remark, he squints. His
clothes tend to look as though they are a bit too big. Normally, Ringo
is always deadpan but should expression be required the main move-
ment is arching the eyebrows.'

During 1965 the Beatles began a European tour, which opened in
Paris on 20 June and ended in Madrid on 3 July, taking in France, Italy
and Spain. Their next American tour opened at Shea Stadium on 15
August and ended at the Cow Palace, San Francisco, on 31 August. A
short British tour began at the Odeon, Glasgow, on 3 December and
ended at the Capitol, Cardiff, on 12 December.

The Shea Stadium appearance was another triumph. It was Sid
Bernstein's idea, the man who'd had the foresight to book the Beatles
before they'd actually made their American breakthrough. Not only
did he organise another first – an actual rock concert at Carnegie Hall
– but this vast arena was also to see its first-ever rock concert when the
Beatles opened their tour there.

The 55,600-seater was fully booked, which made it the world's largest audience for a live rock concert up to that time. It also brought in the world's biggest ever box-office receipts: $304,000, of which the Beatles received $100,000. Disc jockey Murray the K came on to announce it as 'the biggest concert ever in history' and Ed Sullivan also talked to the crowd from the stage, saying: 'Now, ladies and gentlemen, honoured by their country, decorated by their Queen, and loved here in America, HERE ARE THE BEATLES!'

A highlight of their American trip was their 26 August meeting with Elvis Presley. This took place at Elvis's home on Perugia Way, Bel Air, and had been arranged by *New Musical Express* journalist Chris Hutchins. The Beatles and Elvis were together for three hours. The outspoken John Lennon asked Presley, 'Why do you do all these soft-centred ballads nowadays? What happened to the good old rock'n'roll?' Elvis told him, 'It's my movie schedule. It's so tight. I might just do one soon, though.'

When they left, John said, 'It was just like meeting Engelbert Humperdinck.'

A few months after the meeting, Elvis issued a statement: 'People have said my absence from personal appearances has given the Beatles their big opportunities. I know nothing about that. As for the Beatles, all I can say is – more power to them. I have watched all their television appearances over here. I don't think I should say what I feel about them. It wouldn't be fair to fellow entertainers.

'I'll say the Beatles have got what it takes and in great abundance and that they've been given a heck of a vote of confidence. I'm sorry, but I have to be diplomatic and I'm honest about it. There are entertainers like myself and I guess they're as dedicated as the rest of us. Which, in the long run, is all that matters. I wish them luck.'

When John read the statement he said, 'I'm not sure who's the biggest bullshitter – him, or me!'

However, Ringo was to meet up with Elvis again in Las Vegas and at one time there was talk of Elvis and Ringo appearing together in a television special, although nothing came of it.

On 13 September 1965 Ringo and Maureen became the proud parents of a baby boy, Zak Starkey.

26 October was the day the Beatles received their MBEs, with 4,000 fans gathered outside Buckingham Palace. As their names were called out, they each stepped forward and bowed. The Queen shook hands with each of them, spoke to them and pinned a medal on them, and then they stepped back and bowed again.

The Queen asked Paul, 'How long have you been together?' He answered, 'Oh, for many years.' Ringo said, 'Forty years.' The Queen turned to him and said, 'Are you the one that started it all?' Ringo said, 'No, I was the last to join. I'm the little one.' The Queen asked John, 'Have you been working hard lately?' He replied, 'No, we've been on holiday.'

Another Beatles myth was to arise following the ceremony. When interviewed by the French magazine *L'Express*, John said that they smoked marijuana in the Palace cloakrooms. This was an example of John's bizarre sense of humour and wasn't true, but many books and magazines still accept this bogus story as fact.

John never wanted to accept an MBE as he considered it was selling out to the Establishment. In the 1960s working-class people were more conscious of the rift between themselves and the upper classes and the fact that the Establishment (Royalty, the judiciary, etc.) controlled and manipulated them. Brian Epstein talked John into accepting because he said that it would harm the Beatles if he refused. John was later to return his MBE to Buckingham Palace. However, once an MBE is accepted it can never be revoked.

1966 began with the marriage of George Harrison and Patti Boyd in January.

John and Ringo had a meeting to discuss the possibility of a third Beatles film, but nothing came of it. Over the next couple of years there were several film projects mooted, but all failed to materialise – including a Western called *A Talent For Loving*, a version of *The Three Musketeers* with Brigitte Bardot, *Lord Of The Rings* and an anarchic screenplay by playwright Joe Orton called *Up Against It*.

Their British hit singles in 1966 were 'Paperback Writer' and 'Yellow Submarine', both of which reached No 1. They had two EP hits: 'Yesterday', which topped the charts and 'Nowhere Man', which reached No. 4. They were their last EPs to chart as EMI and other record companies decided to dispense with the EP (Extended Play) format. They had two album releases, *Revolver*, which topped the charts, and a compilation album *A Collection Of Beatles Oldies*, which reached No. 7.

Their American chart singles were 'Nowhere Man', 'Paperback Writer', 'Rain', 'Yellow Submarine' and 'Eleanor Rigby'. Their American albums were *Yesterday And Today*, and *Revolver*.

1966 was their last year of touring and there were only two tours, both of which were problematic. The first was the tour of Germany and the Far East, which began on 24 June at the Circus Krone in Munich and ended at the Araneta Coliseum, Manila, in the Philippines.

Their American tour opened at the International Amphitheatre, Chicago, on 12 August and ended at Candlestick Park, San Francisco, on 30 August.

One problem arose from an interview John did with Maureen Cleave of London's *Evening Standard* newspaper on 4 March, which was to lead to a controversy on the eve of their American tour (see below). The second controversial item arose from a photographic session they did with Bob Whitaker on 25 March. This became known as 'the butcher cover'. It was originally taken to adorn the cover of their American album release *Yesterday And Today* and featured the Beatles in white coats with pieces of meat and broken dolls as props. John had said, 'Bob was into Dali and making surreal pictures. It was inspired by our boredom and resentment at having to do another photo session and another Beatles thing. We were sick to death of it. That combination produced the cover.'

In America the image was likened to the Beatles being in butchers' smocks and in an abattoir and was greeted with horror. Capitol Records apologised for the cover and immediately engaged their staff to work on replacing 750,000 covers with another photograph, a rather bland image of the group gathered around a travelling trunk. Promotional material had to be destroyed at a cost of $200,000. While some staff threw away the original sleeve, some merely pasted the new cover over it, immediately creating a collector's item.

On 11 April they recorded George's 'Love You To'. He was to comment, '"Love You To" was one of the first tunes I wrote for sitar. This was the first song where I consciously tried to use sitar and tabla on the basic track. I overdubbed the guitars and vocal later.'

When the Beatles appeared at the Nippon Budokan Hall, Tokyo, on 30 June there were a number of death threats made to the Beatles by right-wing groups who regarded the hall as a sacred place because of the traditional martial-arts exhibitions held there. A total of 3,000 police mixed with the capacity audiences at each of the concerts.

Worse was to happen when their plane reached Manila and military police boarded the plane and dragged the Beatles out by force. George recalled, 'These gorillas, huge guys, no shirts, short sleeves, took us right off the plane. They confiscated our "diplomatic bags". They took all four of us, John, Paul, Ringo and me, without Brian or Neil or Mal. Then they removed us in a boat to Manila Bay surrounded by a ring of cops, guns everywhere. Straight away we thought we were all busted because we thought they would find all the dope in our bags.'

It wasn't a raid to search for drugs, it was a case of 'protective custody' and they were initially taken to the Philippine Navy Headquarters before actually being transferred to a yacht where a wealthy Filipino showed them off to his rich friends.

They were told they were to stay on the yacht during their visit, but they insisted on being booked in a hotel and were taken to the Manila Hotel.

The Beatles appeared at their concerts, but were unaware that Imelda Marcos had invited them as guests of honour at a special event at the Malacanana Palace. When they didn't turn up there were hostile reports on the television station and the local populace was being stirred up against them. The local promoter refused to pay them for their appearances and the tax office insisted they had to pay tax for their concerts, even though they hadn't been paid. Brian Epstein arranged for the money to be paid to the tax commissionaire. There were telephone death threats and the group were harassed on their way to the airport. Brian Epstein was punched in the face and kicked to the ground, Mal Evans was kicked several times and knocked to the floor, and their chauffeur Alf Bicknell received injuries which resulted in a damaged spine and fractured rib. They were eventually allowed to leave after being intimidated by a 200-strong mob and they flew to Delhi, where Brian Epstein was violently sick and was attended by a doctor for four days.

Incidentally, George had used a cheap sitar on 'Norwegian Wood' and when they stopped off in Delhi after the Manila fiasco, he bought a proper one.

The Beatles decided that following the American tour, which had already been arranged, they would cease touring altogether.

On 29 July the American magazine *Datebook* published the interview Maureen Cleave had conducted with John. Great emphasis was given to his quotes regarding the current state of Christianity: 'Christianity will go. It will vanish and shrink. I needn't argue about that; I'm right and will be proved right. We're more popular than Jesus now; I don't know which will go first – rock'n'roll or Christianity. Jesus was right but his disciples were thick and ordinary. It's them twisting it that ruins it for me.'

While these same words had attracted no attention in Britain, they created a furore in America, particularly in the Bible Belt. There were public burnings of Beatles records, radio stations refused to play their music and Brian Epstein considered cancelling the tour and under-writing the costs himself. Despite having laryngitis he flew to New York to see if he could placate the media. Prior to the tour he talked John into making a humiliating apology, even though John didn't want to do so. He said, 'Look, I wasn't saying the Beatles are better than God or Jesus. I said "Beatles" because it's easy for me to talk about Beatles. I could have said "TV" or "the cinema"; "motorcars" or anything popular and I would have got away with it.'

The comments didn't only cause controversy in the United States – there was an immediate ban on Beatles records in South Africa and Spain and there were moves in Holland to ban any future appearances by the Beatles there.

Commenting on the burning of the records, George said, 'They've got to buy them before they can burn them.'

During the tour Christian demonstrators picketed their coach, screaming abuse, people threw rubbish on stage, and the Ku Klux Klan demonstrated outside the Mid South Coliseum in Memphis.

Their final concert took place at Candlestick Park, San Francisco, on 29 August. After it was all over George, who hated touring, said, 'I'm not a Beatle any more.'

On their return John began filming an appearance in *How I Won The War* and George and Patti flew to Bombay where George was to take sitar lessons.

1967 saw the beginning of what were their 'recording years'. Of course, they had been recording all along and developing their music in excellent albums such as *Revolver* and *Rubber Soul*, but now, without the distraction of touring, they were to devote far more time on their recorded product.

Their first record of the year was a double A side 'Penny Lane'/'Strawberry Fields Forever', which was their first single since 1963 not to go straight to the top of the charts, being held at the No. 2 position by Engelbert Humperdinck's 'Release Me'. George Martin was to admit to some of the blame for choosing to release a double A side, which actually split the sales of the single.

The two sides were originally scheduled to be part of an album about Liverpool, but Martin needed to release a single quickly and decided to issue the two numbers, the 'Penny Lane' number written by Paul and 'Strawberry Fields Forever' by John. As a result the Liverpool concept was dropped and the seeds of *Sgt Pepper's Lonely Hearts Club Band* were sown. Their next two singles 'All You Need Is Love' and 'Hello Goodbye' topped the charts and their final release was the double EP 'Magical Mystery Tour', which reached No. 2.

Their sole album release that year was *Sgt Pepper's Lonely Hearts Club Band*, which, naturally, topped the charts.

Their American singles were 'Penny Lane', 'Strawberry Fields Forever', 'All You Need Is Love', 'Baby You're A Rich Man' and 'Hello Goodbye'.

In America there were two album releases, *Sgt Pepper's Lonely Hearts Club Band* and *Magical Mystery Tour*, the latter being issued as an album rather than a double EP set as in Britain.

Paul flew to America in April to celebrate Jane Asher's birthday with her. She was currently touring with the Bristol Old Vic. It was during his flight home that he conceived the idea of *Magical Mystery Tour*, possibly inspired by Ken Keysey and his Merry Pranksters, who were travelling around America in a bus painted in a psychedelic design. The following month, on 15 May, he was introduced to Linda Eastman at the Bag O' Nails club.

The *Sgt Pepper* album was released on 1 June and was one of the most anticipated record releases of all time. It also featured a ground-breaking and much imitated album sleeve, one of the most identifiable images of the twentieth century, designed by artist Peter Blake. There were over seventy figures on the album cover, which were supposed to be the individual Beatles' choices of their heroes. In fact, the majority of icons were probably chosen by gallery owner Robert Fraser (who included a lot of his own clients such as Richard Lindner on the sleeve, which is why there are so many contemporary artists). George chose four Indian holy men and Ringo didn't choose anyone. A number of selections by Paul and John weren't included. A major icon for Paul was Brigitte Bardot and he included her on a sketch he made, six times larger than anyone else – but Blake put Diana Dors there instead, simply because he'd borrowed a waxwork of her. John's selections, ranging from Gandhi to Adolf Hitler (not exactly a hero, but you have to take John's bizarre sense of humour into consideration), were vetoed.

Shirley Temple, a child actress of the 1930s and 40s, is actually represented three times. Who chose her is not known, but it wasn't a Beatle. George hated her. When she came backstage at the Cow Palace, San Francisco in August 1964 to see them, George refused point blank to meet her.

George Martin turned down George's 'Only A Northern Song', but accepted his single contribution to the album, 'Within You, Without You'.

Another unique Beatles 'first' was their appearance on the *Our World* live TV link-up on 25 June, a six-hour spectacular which was transmitted throughout the world by satellite to the largest television audience of all time up to that point – 400 million people. Britain's contribution was to present the Beatles performing a new number live – 'All You Need Is Love'.

Via Patti Harrison, the Beatles were to come under the influence of the Maharishi Mahesh Yogi, and they all attended a lecture by the guru at the Hilton Hotel, London on 24 August, after which they accepted an invitation to join him at his seminar that weekend at Bangor University, Wales. It was while they were in Bangor, on 27 August, that they received the news that their manager Brian Epstein had been found dead.

In an effort to keep the Beatles together, Paul suggested that they make a film of *Magical Mystery Tour*. Painted in psychedelic style, the coach set off with the Beatles and a total of 43 passengers, including fan-club secretaries, actors and actresses, comedians and a bunch of dwarfs.

October saw John visiting the Lisson Gallery in London on 11 October, where he met Yoko Ono. The same month *How I Won The War*, in which John was featured, was premiered in Britain.

On 22 November George began work on his *Wonderwall* sound-track and the following month Ringo was filming *Candy* in Italy.

Ringo had been such a success in *A Hard Day's Night* and *Help!* that there had been several film parts offered. Beatles PR man Tony Barrow was to comment: 'Ringo emerged as the most promising in terms of screen potential. He found it easy to pull faces. There were elements of likeable lunacy in his personality which lent themselves to movie photography.'

Brian Epstein helped Ringo to sort out the scripts and Ringo said, 'We decided that *Candy* was good for me as a trial because it was only two weeks' work.'

A major step in 1967 was the creation of Apple, a business venture they started on the advice of Brian's brother Clive Epstein, who said they needed to start some kind of business to offset income tax.

In some ways it was an annus horribilis, with the shock of Manila, the reaction to John's 'more popular than Jesus' quote, the death of Epstein and the year ending with a critical mauling for their *Magical Mystery Tour* film. On the other hand, it was the year of *Sgt Pepper* and the launch of Apple.

Magical Mystery Tour was given its world premiere on BBC Television on 26 December, but the colour film was screened in black-and-white. For the first time the Beatles were crucified by the British press, something that had never happened before. The film was savaged.

Paul had to appear on television and radio shows in an attempt to repair the damage. He said, 'Was the film really so bad compared to the rest of Christmas TV? You could hardly call the Queen's speech a gasser. Our problem is that we are prisoners of our own fame.'

It was screened in colour on BBC2 on 5 January 1968, but the damage had been done. American networks CBS, NBC and ABC had been negotiating to buy the film for screening in the US for $1m, but the bad reviews in the British press put paid to that and the American networks all withdrew.

It's hard to see why the critics were so vicious. The film was funny, surreal, entertaining and stands the test of time. It was certainly more innovative than their feature film *Help!* Due to the hysterical criticism, a direction which British television could have taken as an inventive way of presenting music was dropped. The Rolling Stones, who were making *The Rolling Stones Rock'n'Roll Circus*, got cold feet and decided not to show their special on television in case they received a similar mauling. Another example of how critics can kill something that does entertain and have value.

Their British hit singles in 1968 were 'Lady Madonna' and 'Hey Jude', both of which topped the charts. An import of the American *Magical Mystery Tour* album reached No. 31 in the British charts and their *The Beatles* double album also topped the charts.

Their American singles were 'Lady Madonna', 'Hey Jude' and 'Revolution' and their chart-topping double album *The Beatles* had advance orders of 1.9 million.

1968 is the year in which the Beatles are remembered for attending the Maharishi Mahesh Yogi's ashram in Rishikesh, India, and for the expansion of their Apple concept – and also for the romance between John and Yoko.

Paul and John were the two most enthusiastic supporters of the new Apple business venture with Paul saying, 'Instead of trying to amass money for the sake of it, we're setting up a business concern at Apple – rather like Western Communism – we've got all the money we need. I've got the house and the cars and all the things that money can buy.'

George and Patti, together with John and Cynthia, began their journey to Rishikesh on 16 February. Paul and Jane Asher and Ringo and Maureen followed a few days later. The course was due to last three months but Ringo and his wife weren't enamoured of the ashram and left after ten days, with Ringo declaring it was like a Butlin's holiday camp. Ringo couldn't stand the food as lunch and dinner consisted of soup followed by a vegetarian main dish. George and John were already vegetarians but Ringo had to arrange for Mal Evans to provide him with lots of eggs, which he had poached, boiled, fried and scrambled.

Despite not liking the ashram, Ringo was to praise the Maharishi, saying, 'The four of us have had the most hectic lives. We have got almost anything money can buy. But when you can do that, the things you buy mean nothing after a time. You look for something else, for a new experience. It's like your dad going to the boozer and you want to find out what the taste of drink is like. We have found something now which fills the gap. Since meeting His Holiness, Maharishi Mahesh Yogi, I feel great.'

Paul and Jane also left after ten weeks, earlier than anticipated, leaving George and John, who had been joined by 'Magic Alex' Mardas, Apple's 'electronics wizard'.

The official name of the ashram was the Academy of Transcendental Meditation and it stood 150 feet above the Ganges River. Outside was a banner with the word 'WELCOME' and a Hindu guard stood in front of a wooden gate in a barbed-wire fence. Behind a fenced compound there were six *puri*, single-storey concrete barrack-style structures, each with ten simple rooms. A grand path connected the buildings, and there was a kitchen and dining area.

The fifty or so people gathered were of all ages and nationalities. They included Tim Simcox, a television actor; Walter Koch, a physicist from Santa Barbara; Anneliese Braun, who was said to be able to heal people by laying on hands; lawyer Fred Smithline and his wife Susie; Nancy Jackson; Larry Kurland, a Lufthansa pilot; a blackjack dealer from a Los Angeles casino, and so on. The specific course they were on cost $500 and meant three months in the ashram to study to become initiators in their native country. They would then proceed by chartered jet to Kashmir where the Maharishi maintained a second establishment aboard a string of houseboats where they would take written and oral examinations.

There were several other celebrities present apart from the Beatles: Donovan, Mike Love of the Beach Boys and actress Mia Farrow with her sister Prudence.

The ashram sojourn proved inspirational to George, John and Paul, who wrote a large number of compositions while they were there – even Ringo was to compose a number, 'Don't Pass Me By', which was included on the next Beatles album! One interesting song was inspired by Mia Farrow's younger sister Prudence, who remained in her room meditating for so long that John was asked to be the person to persuade her to come out of her solitude – he was to write the song 'Dear Prudence'.

Mia was also the subject of another myth: that George and John left the ashram because the Maharishi had molested her. This was due to John's later statement: 'There was this big hullabaloo about his trying to rape Mia Farrow or somebody and trying to get off with a few other women and things like that.'

This situation arose because of Alexis Mardas, who was alarmed at what he saw at Rishikesh: 'An ashram with four-poster beds? Masseurs, and servants bringing water, houses with facilities, an accountant – I never saw a holy man with a book-keeper.'

When he heard that the Maharishi expected the Beatles to donate 10–15% of their annual income to a Swiss account in the Maharishi's name he confronted the Maharishi, accusing him of exploiting the Beatles. He said that he was then offered a bribe to build a radio station in the grounds of the ashram.

Alexis began to sneak wine in for some of the women and question them about the Maharishi. A nurse told him that the Maharishi had invited her for a chicken dinner and then made sexual advances to her. He told George and John, but George was unconvinced and John wasn't sure. Alexis then approached some other women and told George and John about it, resulting in their confrontation with the Maharishi and their decision to leave Rishikesh.

It had nothing to do with Mia Farrow who, on discovering the Beatles were at the ashram, thought there would be hordes of press descending on them, so she left and set out on a three-week journey across India. Discussing her brief stay at Rishikesh she was to say, 'Everyone made the mistake of trying to make a Christ figure out of him. He's a man. No religious man should try and become another Pope-like figure.' She did add, 'The Maharishi did do one thing right. He put meditation in terms that the Western world could understand. That was important.'

At the beginning of the year the Beatles had changed their company from Beatles Limited to Apple Corps Limited and soon began to employ their staff and set up various business arms – Apple Records, Apple Electronics, Apple Retail, Apple Television, Apple Music Publishing and Apple Wholesale.

The music publishing company was run by Terry Doran, an old friend from Liverpool days who was once a business partner of Brian Epstein in Brydor Cars. He later worked for George at Dark Horse Records and became George's personal assistant and manager of Friar Park for some years. George sacked him when Dhani was born, allegedly because Terry was gay and George didn't want the presence of a homosexual around his son.

Other Liverpool friends at Apple included Neil Aspinall, their former road manager, as managing director of Apple Corps Ltd, Mal Evans as a personal assistant to the Beatles, Derek Taylor heading the

Apple press office, Tony Bramwell as record plugger, Peter Brown as
co-ordinator to the Beatles (a sort of manager to the group) and Brian
Lewis as business consultant.

Apple Electronics was run by Alexis Mardas, known as 'Magic
Alex', who dazzled the Beatles – particularly the gullible John Lennon
– with gadgets. He promised to build a 72-track recording studio at
Apple, which turned out to be a disaster.

Joan Collins's husband Ron Kass was appointed head of Apple
Records, with Peter Asher as A&R man.

John was to say, 'The aim of the company isn't a stack of gold teeth
in the bank. We've done that bit. It's more of a trick to see if we can get
artistic freedom within a business structure; to see if we can create
things and sell them without charging three times our cost.'

John and Paul also went to America to promote the company on
television and Paul busied himself working on design ideas and advertisements. George and Ringo didn't participate as much on the business
side, although George became mostly concerned with Apple Records,
signing and recording artists he liked, enjoying his stint producing
records and contributing to the productions by playing guitar or
providing compositions.

George asked Apple to help promote a single by Steven Friedland, a
twenty-year-old New Yorker who'd recorded a number 'King Of Fuh'.
It didn't receive any airplay, Apple didn't sign him and the record was
eventually released in America under Brute Force Records. George also
wanted Apple to release an album by Delaney and Bonnie, who he
joined on a British tour, but business problems prevented it and they
were signed to the Electra label.

Jackie Lomax was another friend from Liverpool, former lead singer
with the Undertakers. Jackie was initially signed as a songwriter, but
George offered to produce some tracks by Jackie as a solo singer. He
wrote a number for him, 'Sour Milk Sea', which had a superstar line-
up of musicians – George and Jackie on rhythm guitars, Paul on bass,
Ringo on drums, Nicky Hopkins on piano and Eric Clapton on guitar.
The single was among the first four Apple releases, but didn't succeed.
Undeterred, George tried again, this time producing a complete album
Is This What You Want? which was partly recorded in Los Angeles.
Even Paul was to take a hand in promoting Jackie and on the eve of his
marriage to Linda, he recorded the old Coasters hit 'Thumbing A Ride'
with Jackie – with George and Billy Preston playing on the track.

None of Jackie's recordings had any success and when Allen Klein
took over at Apple he was dropped, leaving an unreleased track,
'Going Back To Liverpool'.

George was quite happy to sign up his old friend Ravi Shankar, was
able to have a couple of hits with the Radha Krishna Temple and also
worked with Billy Preston, Doris Troy, Ronnie Spector and Lon and
Derrek Van Eaton.

During 1968 they recorded their double album *The Beatles*, which was originally to have been called 'A Doll's House'. It was designer Richard Hamilton who asked if they had ever had an album released simply using the group name; he also designed a plain white cover in contrast to the elaborate *Sgt Pepper* sleeve. As a result *The Beatles* has often been called the 'White Album'. It was the first Beatles album on Apple and took five months to record.

Designer Richard Hamilton commented, 'I began to feel guilty at putting their double album under plain wrappers; I suggested it could be jazzed up with a large-edition print, an insert that would be even more glamorous than a normal sleeve.

'That's why the album ended up the way it did. Most people, among them Yoko, think it was Yoko's idea. I've no doubt that she would have been very supportive ... but my contact with the project was only through Paul – even EMI was held off.'

There were thirty tracks on the double album, most of which had been written during the spell at Rishikesh. George Martin was unhappy at dealing with so many tracks and wanted them to pare down the number of songs and just release a single two-sided album. He was overruled. George commented, 'I think in a way it was a mistake doing four sides, because it's just too big for most people to really get into. I listen mainly to side one, which I really like.' After having said this, George was to make his solo debut with a triple album!

The large amount of songs leading to the double album was the result, once again, of Paul and John trying to get as many of their compositions onto the album as possible. George, who had also written a large amount of songs at Rishikesh, was left with a paltry four tracks on the double LP.

This is probably why George began planning his first solo album while he was still a member of the Beatles, obviously frustrated that he had so much difficulty in getting his own numbers accepted as Beatles tracks due to the fact that priority was given to the Lennon and McCartney material.

In October 1969 he was to discuss his solo album. 'It's mainly just to get rid of all the songs I've got stacked up. I've got such a backlog, and at the rate or two or three an album with the group, I'm not even going to get the ones I've already done out for three or four years. I suppose I'm waiting till I've got myself a proper studio at home. And then I can just knock 'em off when I feel like it.

'In future, though, the Beatles are going to get an equal rights thing, so we'll all have as much on the album.'

1968 was the year John became besotted with Yoko. In May John's wife Cynthia had gone to Greece on holiday with some friends. When Cynthia arrived back she found John and Yoko together in the house and it was quite obvious that they had slept together, yet Cynthia asked

John if he would like to go out for dinner. He said, 'No thanks,' and Cynthia remembers that Yoko then gave her 'a very positive, confident look'.

Cynthia capitulated, didn't fight to keep her husband, and the couple were eventually to divorce.

In the meantime, Yoko stuck to John like a limpet and broke a long-standing agreement that wives and girlfriends wouldn't hang around at recording sessions.

When she was involved in a minor road accident she had Harrods deliver a double bed to Olympic Studios where the Beatles were currently recording and lay there for days on end with a microphone near to her mouth enabling her to make comments while the Beatles were recording.

George Martin became annoyed at her presence and was to say, 'It was a bit difficult to deal with. Suddenly she would appear in the control room. Nobody would say anything to me. I wasn't even introduced to her; she would just sit there. And her influence would be felt. To begin with, everyone was irritated by her.'

One observer said that she clung to John 'as if she had been surgically attached'.

George detested her and even Ringo was to comment, 'Listen, John, does Yoko have to be there all the time?'

On 17 July 1968 the world premiere of *Yellow Submarine* took place and the Beatles all attended a celebration party at a disco at the Royal Lancaster Hotel, which had been renamed Yellow Submarine.

The Beatles had originally not really been interested in the animated film, but had agreed to it being made as they were under the impression that that would fulfil their obligation to United Artists under a three-film deal. It didn't.

Once the film was made they were impressed and made a brief appearance at the end of it, inviting the audience to join them in a song.

Paul's affair with Jane Asher had ended when the actress discovered that in her absence Paul had been sharing her home – and their bed – with a girl called Francie Schwartz.

The Apple Retail side of the business hadn't been doing too well and the Baker Street Boutique was closed down.

During *The Beatles* album sessions, tension was growing between the group and, surprisingly, on 20 August it was Ringo Starr who walked out on the group.

This occurred because Paul made a comment to him that he'd fluffed while playing a tom-tom. He walked out threatening to quit and spent the following fortnight on Peter Sellers' yacht in the Mediterranean, during which he was inspired to write a song, 'Octopus's Garden'.

When he returned to Abbey Road Studios on 3 September there were flowers and a 'Welcome home' banner on his drum kit. He was to point out, 'Paul is the greatest bass player in the world. But he is also very determined; he goes on and on to see if he can get his own way. While that may be a virtue, it did mean that musical disagreements invariably arose from time to time.'

In November George's *Wonderwall* album was issued and he spent seven weeks in Los Angeles recording the Jackie Lomax album. The same month John and Yoko released their *Unfinished Music No. 1 – Two Virgins* album, which featured them both in the nude on the cover. John commented, 'We were both a bit embarrassed when we peeled off for the picture – so I took it myself with a delayed action shutter.' Despite what John said, a photograph exists of John, Yoko and another male, completely nude, and this 'third virgin' is the one who took the photograph of them.

EMI refused to release it and it was issued by a label called Tetragrammaton, but issued with a brown-paper sleeve covering the offending parts with a cutout allowing their two heads to peek through. The authorities confiscated copies of the record when they reached New York. During the same month Yoko suffered a miscarriage and *The Beatles* white album was released.

The year ended with a party at Apple on 23 December. George had sent a memo informing everyone: 'Hell's Angels will be in London within the week, on the way to straighten out Czechoslovakia. There will be twelve in number complete with black leather jackets and motorcycles. They will undoubtedly arrive at Apple and I have heard they may try to make full use of Apple's facilities. They may look as though they are going to do you in but are very straight and do good things, so don't fear them or uptight them. Try to assist them without neglecting your Apple business and without letting them take control of Savile Row.' John and Yoko attended the party dressed as Mother and Father Christmas.

Their British hit singles in 1969 were 'Get Back', 'Ballad Of John And Yoko', which both topped the charts and 'Something', which reached No. 4. Their album-chart placings were *Yellow Submarine* at No. 3, a re-entry for *Yellow Submarine* at No. 14, a re-entry for *The Beatles* at No. 13, a second re-entry for *The Beatles* at No. 31, a re-entry for *Sgt Pepper's Lonely Hearts Club Band* at No. 38, a third re-entry for *The Beatles* at No. 14, another re-entry for *Yellow Submarine* at No. 4 and *Abbey Road* at No. 1.

Their American singles were 'Get Back', 'Don't Let Me Down', 'The Ballad Of John And Yoko', 'Come Together' and 'Something'. In America 'Something' topped the charts, as did the *Abbey Road* album.

At the beginning of 1969 the Beatles had begun filming their 'Get Back' project at Twickenham Studios. The situation between the members was now getting tense. On 10 January George and John had a big argument because John had been putting down George's songwriting. With John continuing to criticise him, saying that he was contributing nothing to the sessions, and with the feeling that Paul was treating him as an inferior, together with the fact that he was irritated by Yoko's continual presence, George walked out on the group, saying he'd quit and would see them around the clubs.

George returned on 15 January, during which there was a five-hour talk. As a result George agreed to continue with the filming but said he would leave the group if a proposed live appearance went ahead. That idea was dropped and eventually ended up as a Savile Row rooftop session.

A few days later John put the cat among the pigeons when he told journalist Ray Coleman that Apple was going bust. It was an exaggeration, because they still had quite a large amount of money available. However, this was the interview that set Allen Klein on a mission to become their manager.

He contacted John and arranged to meet John and Yoko at the Dorchester Hotel. He'd researched Yoko's background as well as John's and included her throughout the conversation, promising to set up an exhibition for her in America. John recalled, 'We had him because Klein was the only one Yoko liked.'

The Beatles, acting on the advice of Linda's brother John Eastman, were about to purchase NEMS for £1million, which EMI had agreed to advance them against future royalties. This was a very good deal as NEMS was entitled to take 25% of their royalties for a further nine years in a deal Brian Epstein had made, without informing them. Allen Klein met all four Beatles and advised them not to buy NEMS. Paul walked out of the meeting. He was right to be upset; buying NEMS would have been in the interests of the group.

The Beatles then tried to buy Northern Songs. The balance of power lay with a consortium of city investors who agreed to support the Beatles in gaining control of the company. However, John made a statement saying, 'I'm sick of being fucked about by men in suits sitting on their fat arses in the City.' The consortium was furious, sold their shares to Lew Grade, and the Beatles lost control of their songs forever.

Klein then took over the reins of Apple and made wholesale sackings, leaving the company as just a virtual collecting agency for Beatles royalties.

The famous rooftop appearance took place on 30 January 1969 and it was the last-ever live appearance by the Beatles. They performed 'Get Back', 'Don't Let Me Down', 'I've Got A Feeling', 'One After 909' and 'Dig A Pony'. After they'd finished, John said, 'I'd like to say "thank you" on behalf of the group and ourselves and I hope we passed the audition.'

A schism now appeared between John, George and Ringo on the one hand and Paul on the other. Paul refused to sign up with Klein as he didn't trust him – and Mick Jagger, who'd once been under Klein's control when he'd managed the Rolling Stones, sent a note to Paul warning him off Klein. Paul wanted Linda's father's firm Eastman & Eastman to look after the Beatles' affairs.

On 12 March 1969 Paul and Linda were married. Due to the unhappy dispute between them, no other members of the Beatles were present at the ceremony, although George and Patti attended the reception later on.

As if to counter the marriage of Paul and Linda, John and Yoko flew to Paris on 15 March intending to get married, but were unable to do so because of rules regarding the length of residency. Peter Brown arranged for them to be married in Gibraltar and they were married on 20 March and then went on to Amsterdam on the first of their bed-ins. In April John changed his name to John Ono Lennon and rumours began in America that Paul had been killed in an accident – the 'Paul Is Dead' rumours continued for years and in typical 'conspiracy theory' fashion, spun a web of intricate details surrounding the alleged accident and a Beatles cover-up to maintain he was still alive!

John and Yoko issued another avant-garde album *Unfinished Music No. 2 – Life With The Lions* on 26 May. A new Beatles single 'The Ballad Of John And Yoko' was issued a few days later and the pair held another bed-in at the Queen Elizabeth Hotel, Toronto, Canada.

Due to all the tensions and disputes, the 'Get Back' recordings had become something of a mess and Paul had talked the others into making another album instead, *Abbey Road*. Paul had an idea for the cover and drew a sketch for photographer Iain Macmillan – and the Beatles were photographed crossing the Abbey Road zebra crossing, another major twentieth-century image!

Their twelfth album went straight to No. 1 in the charts and featured two numbers by George, 'Something' and 'Here Comes The Sun', which were among the best tracks on the album, better than some of the tracks by John and Paul. So much for John's criticisms of George's songwriting – and he admitted it by saying that George's numbers were the best on the album. Allen Klein agreed and released 'Something' as a single, George's first and only A side of a Beatles record.

In September, John hastily assembled a group to back him at the Toronto Rock'n'Roll Revival Concert and called them the Plastic Ono Band. John recalled, 'I said to Paul, "I'm leaving." I knew on the flight over to Toronto or before we went to Toronto: I told Allen I was leaving. I told Eric Clapton and Klaus that I was leaving then, but that I would probably like to use them as a group. I hadn't decided how to do it – to have a permanent new group or what – then later on, I thought fuck, I'm not going to get stuck with another set of people, whoever they are.'

Allen Klein talked John out of announcing that he was leaving the Beatles in case it affected their current business negotiations.

So John was, in fact, the third Beatle to announce he was leaving the fold.

Abbey Road was released on 26 September.

It was obvious by now that the relationship between John and Yoko was taking precedence with John over the Beatles. Another album, *The*

Wedding Album, was released on 20 October, they appeared in a BBC documentary *The World Of John And Yoko, The Plastic Ono Band – Live Peace In Toronto* was released in December and the same month they appeared at the Lyceum Ballroom, London, in a UNICEF concert as John And Yoko's Plastic Ono Supergroup – with George Harrison and Eric Clapton among the members.

On 24 October the second Plastic Ono Band single 'Cold Turkey' was issued. John had originally wanted to record it with the Beatles, but Paul thought such an overt drugs song was not suitable for the Beatles. In the past they'd had records banned because of the suspicion of a drugs reference. As a result, John broke the pact they had that every song written, even if it was just a solo effort of either of them, would go out under the Lennon and McCartney banner.

This had benefited John in the past because Paul had written songs recorded by Chris Barber, Billy J. Kramer (two numbers), Badfinger, Peter and Gordon (four numbers), Cilla Black (three numbers), the Applejacks, Mary Hopkin, Tommy Quickly, the Black Dyke Mills Band, Jackie Lomax, and Mike Shannon and the Strangers, while John had only given two numbers to the Fourmost and one to Billy J. Kramer.

In 1970 the Beatles' British singles hits were 'Something' and 'Let It Be'. The album *Let It Be,* their thirteenth and last album before they split (unlucky number?), went straight to No. 1 in the charts.

Their two American singles in 1970 were 'Let It Be' and 'The Long And Winding Road' and their two albums released were *Hey Jude* and *Let It Be.*

On 11 February 1970, John issued 'Instant Karma' by the Plastic Ono Band and on 12 March George and Patti moved into Friar Park. He was later to say, 'When I first came to this house, it was occupied by nuns. I brought in this poster of Vishnu. You just see his head and shoulders and his four arms holding a conch shell and various other symbols, and it has a big *oa,* this transcendental syllable, which represents Krishna and has been chanted by many persons throughout history for spiritual perfection, written above it. He has a nice aura around him. I left it by the fireplace and went out into the garden. When we came back in the house, they all pounced on me, saying, "Who is that? What is it?" as if it were some pagan god. So I said, "Well, if God is unlimited, then he can appear in any form, whichever way he likes to appear. That's one way. He's called Vishnu."'

The Beatles were all busy with various projects, Ringo recording his solo *Sentimental Journey* album, John with his various Yoko projects, Paul recording his solo album and George producing his Radha Krishna Temple records.

In the meantime, Phil Spector was called in to see if he could make the 'Get Back' tapes into a serviceable album. Paul was to say, 'The album was finished a year ago, but a few months ago American record producer Phil Spector was called in by John Lennon to tidy up some of the tracks. But a few weeks ago I was sent a remixed version of my song "The Long And Winding Road" with harps, horns, an orchestra and women's choir added. No one had asked me what I thought. I couldn't believe it. I would never have female voices on a Beatles record. The record came with a note from Allen Klein saying he thought the changes were necessary. I don't blame Phil Spector for doing it but it just goes to show that it's no good me sitting here thinking I'm in control because obviously I'm not. Anyway I've sent Klein a letter asking for some of the things to be altered but I haven't received an answer yet.'

George Martin said, 'It was a very good McCartney song, but when it came back from being handled by Phil Spector, it was laden down with treacle and choirs and scoring and so on.'

Klein never answered Paul's letter and took no notice of his request to have Spector's changes and his 'wall of sound' removed. 'The Long And Winding Road' was released as a single in May.

In fact, the whole concept of the final album was for it to have a simple feel to fall in line with the film documentary.

George Martin was to say, 'It was always understood that the album would be like nothing the Beatles had done before. It would be honest, no overdubbing, no editing, truly live, almost amateurish. When John brought in Phil Spector he contradicted everything he had said before. When I heard the final sounds I was shaken. They were so uncharacteristic of the clean sounds the Beatles had always used. At the time Spector was John's buddy, mate and pal, still is. I don't know. I was astonished because I knew Paul would never have agreed to it. In fact I contacted him and he said nobody was more surprised than he was.'

Seemingly with no control over his own work, where other people could alter his music without his permission and get away with it, Paul needed to seek advice. He was told that under his contract he had to let Klein manage him. When he was told he could sue Klein he said, 'Great, I'll sue him,' but he was told he would also have to sue Apple.

Paul was reluctant to do this and it took him two months to make a decision, but he then decided to go ahead as the current position was untenable.

As John Lennon had gone ahead and recorded his solo albums, Paul McCartney began to work on his solo debut album, *McCartney*. He approached Allen Klein to inform him that he wanted it released on 17 April 1970. Klein told him that was impossible as Apple had already decided to release the *Let It Be* soundtrack around that time to coincide with the United Artists release of the *Let it Be* film. They had also already scheduled the release of Ringo's first solo album *Sentimental Journey* near to that time and stated that it was obvious that if all the albums were issued at same time, they would be competing with each other unnecessarily.

Since Ringo had been the most neutral member in the conflict between them all during the break-up fiasco, George and John elected him to visit Paul at his home in Cavendish Avenue, St John's Wood, to see if he could persuade him to change the date of the solo album release.

Ringo went along and rang the bell. Paul made him remain outside while he demanded to know what he wanted. He was then allowed into the house and had to explain his mission to Paul. Paul went into an uproar.

Ringo recalled, 'He shouted at me, prodding his fingers towards my face, and said, "I'll finish you now!" and "You'll pay!" He told me to put on my coat and get out.'

Ringo suggested to the other members that since releasing his solo album meant a lot to Paul he felt they should let him go ahead and should show their friendship by pushing back the release dates of the other two albums.

The final arrangment was that *Sentimental Journey* was issued on 27 March, *McCartney* on 17 April and *Let It Be* on 8 May.

With the release of his solo album *McCartney* Paul issued a question-and-answer sheet, which made it clear that he was leaving the Beatles. Among the Q&A was:

Q: Is this album a rest away from Beatles or start of a solo career?

A: Time will tell. Being a solo album means 'the start of a solo career' . . . and not being done with the Beatles means it's a rest. So it's both.

Q: Is your break with the Beatles temporary or permanent, due to personal differences or musical ones?

A: Personal differences, business differences, but most of all because I have a better time with my family. Temporary or permanent? I don't know.

Q: Do you foresee a time when Lennon/McCartney becomes an active songwriting partnership again?

A: No.

Paul went ahead with his legal steps to dissolve the partnership and the greatest group in the history of pop music had come to an end.

Strangely, Paul had been the last of the members to announce he was leaving. He was the one who, all along, had striven to keep the group together, particularly after the death of Brian Epstein. He was the one who kept them going with *Magical Mystery Tour*, and who had suggested the *Abbey Road* album when the 'Get Back' project was dragging behind. He had wanted to stage a major concert, but George wouldn't hear of it. His decision had more to do with Klein's interference than anything else.

He was to be proved right. The Eastmans would probably have done well for the Beatles. It was their advice encouraging Paul to build up a music publishing empire that made him the richest Beatle of the four.

Paul's action to dissolve the Beatles went to the High Court and Ringo's affidavit was read out in court on 23 February 1971. It stated: 'The Beatles might yet stay together as a group. Paul is the greatest bass player in the world. He is also determined. He goes on and on to see if he can get his own way. While that may be a virtue, it did mean that musical disagreements inevitably rose from time to time. But such disagreements contributed to really great projects.'

He also contended, 'I was shocked and dismayed after Mr McCartney's promises about a meeting of all four Beatles in London in January, that a writ should have been issued on December 31. I trust Paul and I know he would not lightly disregard his promise. Something serious, about which I have no knowledge, must have happened between Paul's meeting with George in New York at the end of December.' He ended, 'My own view is that all four of us together could even yet work out everything satisfactorily.'

Eventually, Ringo, John and George also found Klein was not to their liking and they too sued him, although it cost them a great deal of money. They dispensed with his services and John was to say, 'There are many reasons why we finally gave him the push, although I don't want to go into the details of it. Let's say possibly Paul's suspicions were right – and the time was right.'

In June 1973 Klein sued Apple, and for John, George, Paul and Ringo to finally rid themselves of him, they had to pay a settlement of $4 million. Paul's suspicions about him were further proved when Klein was jailed for two months in May 1979 for tax evasion relating to the income he'd derived from illegal sales of the *Concert For Bangla Desh* album. When George was being sued by Bright Tunes over the 'My Sweet Lord' plagiarism accusation, Klein bought the company hoping to get a big pay-off from George.

Apart from the initial euphoria when the unknown group from Liverpool began to attract audiences in Hamburg, Liverpool and then internationally, George was always unhappy as a Beatle. He didn't like touring, he didn't like the media, and he spent a great deal of his solo career complaining of people's obsession with the Beatles and their desire for the group to re-form.

Discussing the Beatles in 1992, he said, 'It all shrivelled up. The spotlight caused a lot of damage really. It wasn't all negative – it was a success, a wonderful thing – but there were hidden pitfalls; you've got to watch you don't go off the rails and get carried away. Plus, as a musician, if you find yourself playing the same ten tunes day in, day out, the skills of being a musician start disappearing.'

He said, 'At the height of Beatlemania, all we did was stand on a stage, sing a few tunes very quickly, shake our heads and go "Oooooh!" For years the Beatles whipped up this frenzy. That was what mania was – even the police would go: "The Beatles are coming," and they'd all go hop on their motor bikes and go crashing into each other. I just didn't want to know about that side of things. I think that's the reason why Eric (Clapton) went in and out of bands – every time they started getting too famous, he left.'

Ringo's first solo album *Sentimental Journey* appeared in March 1970.

With the impending break-up of the group, Ringo felt lost and wondered what he would do. He then thought of the songs he was brought up on that his uncles and aunts used to sing. He called George Martin and said 'Why don't we make a sentimental album?'

He recalled, 'The great thing was that it got my solo career moving. Not very fast, but just moving. It was like the first shovel of coal in the furnace that makes the train inch forward.' It also motivated him into writing a No. 1 hit with 'It Don't Come Easy' and a million-seller with 'Back Off Boogaloo'.

In his solo recording career, Ringo found the encouragement and support that he had never enjoyed with his recordings as a member of the Beatles. John, Paul and George all wrote numbers especially for him, helped to produce his records and also gave him advice and whatever help he needed in his solo years.

John Lennon, for instance, used to record demos of guide vocals for Ringo, or ones he found for him to record, like 'I'm The Greatest', 'Goodnight Vienna' and 'Only You'.

Ringo recalled, 'We always used to do that. It was great! It's easier for me when I'm playing if someone's singing the song, because you can feel where it needs bringing up or bringing down. John was always great fun to have in the studio and great energy. And when it came to those Seventies sessions, I knew him so well that it was always relaxing. Then I'd have to go and do the vocals after him, of course. And he'd be in the booth with me, just willing me on. You know, "Come on, let's go!" It was just great energy and great support.'

The former Beatles were also keen to praise their former drummer. John Lennon said, 'Ringo was a star in his own right before we even met. His talents would have come out one way or another. Whatever that spark is in Ringo, we all know it but we can't put our finger on it. There's something in him that's projectable and he would have surfaced as an individual.' Paul McCartney said, 'When Ringo joined us we got a bit more kick, a few more imaginative breaks.'

John was also to say, 'Ringo is Ringo, that's all there is to it. And he's every bloody bit as warm, unassuming, funny and kind as he seems – he was quite simply the heart of the Beatles.'

In an interview with *Entertainment Tonight* in November 1981 Ringo had been asked if being a former Beatle was a burden. He answered, 'It's never really a burden. That's the wrong word. It used to get in the way sometimes, and still every interview you do people like you ask about them. There's no madness out there like it used to be. I was a Beatle, I'm still Ringo Starr and I'm doing my own records now. It's more exciting for me to talk about my records than Beatles records, because we've been talking about them for twenty years.'

However, despite the fact that the group had disbanded, there were other Beatles projects to emerge over the coming decades, most notably the Beatles *Anthology* project of a series of CDs and a set of video/DVDs, followed by the singles 'Free As A Bird' and 'Real Love' and the release of the album *The Beatles 1*, a phenomenal seller.

The first major Beatles event following their break-up occurred in November 1995 when a double-CD package called *The Beatles Anthology, Volume 1*, containing outtakes, home demos and live recordings was released simultaneously around the world. This was followed by *The Beatles Anthology, Volume 2* and *The Beatles Anthology Volume 3*.

A quarter of a century after they'd disbanded, the Beatles had once again created a musical innovation – ever since, every major artist has copied the package and come out with their own 'anthology'.

The first release also coincided with a five-part six-hour television history of the Beatles' career, *Anthology, The TV Series*. The release mentioned that: 'The unprecedented musical will feature John, Paul, George and Ringo, with the latter three bringing additional instrumentation, voices and arrangements to two John Lennon songs on which he sings and plays.'

The idea of a television series of the Beatles' lives and careers had originally begun with the Beatles' close associate Neil Aspinall conceiving a project called 'The Long And Winding Road' at the close of the 1960s. The idea was never abandoned, but when it finally came time to put it into practice, George Harrison didn't want the Beatles' history to fall under the name of a Paul McCartney composition, so the term 'Anthology' was chosen for the project instead.

This television series was followed in September 1996 by *The Beatles Anthology*, an 8-volume video set with a running time of 9 hours and 51 minutes.

The final part of the project was published some years later in 2000 as a lavish book *The Beatles Anthology*, the delay probably caused by the death of Derek Taylor, a close friend of the Beatles who was originally commissioned to co-ordinate the book project.

Commenting on the 'Anthology' project, Ringo said, 'I thought it was great therapy for the three of us. We went over things that we thought were really big at the time, and they aren't that big at all. Those little arguments that form up in your mind.

Discussing the two singles, 'Free As A Bird' and 'Real Love', he said: 'Originally, we took the easy route, which was to do some incidental music, because what else can we do? There were four Beatles and there are only three of us left. We were just going to do some incidental music and just get there and play the instruments and see what happened.

Then we thought, well, why don't we do some new music? And then
we always hit the wall and, OK, Paul had a song, or George had a song
or I had a song, well, that's the three of us, why don't the three of us go
in and do this. And we kept hitting the wall, because this is the Beatles;
it's not Paul, George or Ringo.'

Following the 'Anthology' came yet another innovation, an album
The Beatles 1, released on 14 November 2000 and containing 27
tracks of Beatles singles that had reached the No. 1 spot in Britain or
America. Released thirty years after the Beatles had disbanded, it
became the biggest-selling album of the year. Record companies have
been quick to spot a Beatles groundbreaker once again and have been
releasing CDs of No.1 tracks by other major artists ranging from Elvis
Presley to Michael Jackson.

The tracks were: 'Love Me Do', 'From Me To You', 'She Loves You',
'I Want To Hold Your Hand', 'Can't Buy Me Love', 'A Hard Day's
Night', 'I Feel Fine', 'Eight Days A Week', 'Ticket To Ride', 'Help!',
'Yesterday', 'Day Tripper', 'We Can Work It Out', 'Paperback Writer',
'Yellow Submarine', 'Eleanor Rigby', 'Penny Lane', 'All You Need Is
Love', 'Hello Goodbye', 'Lady Madonna', 'Hey Jude', 'Get Back', 'The
Ballad Of John And Yoko', 'Something', 'Come Together', 'Let It Be'
and 'The Long And Winding Road'.

It's interesting to note who composed the chart-toppers. George
wrote one, John and Paul composed three as a team, John composed
eight and Paul composed fifteen.

The Beatles story on record didn't end there. On 18 November 2003
Let It Be ... Naked was released. This was the much anticipated
version of the *Let It Be* album as it was originally envisaged by the
Beatles themselves, stripped of the choirs, harps, orchestras and 'wall
of sound' of Phil Spector's version.

In 1989, at the press reception for the first All-Starr tour, Ringo said:
'I'm better off now not thinking about what I did a hundred years ago.
I can't get away from the Beatles. I am one of them. But it gets busy
sometimes, you know. I am a human being, and I do different things
today. Back then we all had one common aim, and that was the band.
We were all different forces there, but we were focused on one aim.
Now those forces are sparkling all over.'

In 2003, when asked to comment on the fact that Paul had changed
the songwriting credits of Beatles songs he had written from Lennon
and McCartney to McCartney and Lennon, Ringo said, 'I think the
way he did it was underhanded. He's wanted to do it for years. I'm not
going to tell you all his reasons. He'll tell you them. I thought he should
have done it officially with Yoko. But he didn't. It was the wrong way
to go about it.'

As if to comment further, Ringo had the following credits on the
back cover of his *Ringo Rama* album: 'Produced by Mark Hudson and
Ringo Starr. Produced by Ringo Starr and Mark Hudson.'

Beaucoups Of Blues (album)

Ringo's second solo album, which he began recording in Nashville, Tennessee, on 30 June and completed on 1 July 1970 using 21 of Nashville's leading musicians. Pete Drake produced the album and Scotty Moore, Elvis Presley's former guitarist, was the engineer.

Ringo said, 'I was trying to get it together over here in Britain, which is really silly. I was trying to fly in twelve guys from Nashville and all that rubbish and suddenly I was playing on George's album and Pete Drake was there and I was talking to him about it and he said, "Look here, son, why don't you come over to Nashville? I'll get it together in a week," and I said, "Come on, you can't get an album together in a week, it's impossible." He said, "But Dylan's only took two days." I said, "OK, you go back and fix it up and I'll fly out a few days later." We did the album in two nights. I did a few other tracks that we didn't put out. I was only there three days recording. I'd learn five songs in the morning and I'd go and record five songs that night. It was really good.'

The musicians included: Buddy Harman, bass; Charlie Daniels, guitar; Dave Kirby, guitar; Chuck Howard, guitar; the Jordanaires, backing vocals; Charlie McCoy, harmonica; Sorrels Pickard, guitar; Jerry Kennedy, guitar; Jerry Shook, guitar; George Richey, fiddle; Grover Lavender, fiddle; Jim Buchanan, fiddle; Roy Huskey Jr, bass; Pete Drake, pedal steel guitar; Ringo Starr, acoustic guitar and drums; D.J. Fontana, drums; Ben Keith, steel guitar; Jerry Reed, guitar and Jeannie Kendall.

The tracks were: 'Beaucoups Of Blues', 'Love Don't Last Long', 'Fastest Growing Headache In The West', 'Without Her', 'Woman Of The Night', 'I'd Be Talking All The Night', '$15 Draw', 'Wine, Women And Loud Happy Songs', 'I Wouldn't Have You Any Other Way', 'Loser's Lounge', 'Waiting' and 'Silent Homecoming'. He also recorded 'Early 1970' and 'Coochy-Coochy'. The latter was issued as the flipside of the American 'Beaucoups Of Blues' single.

The photographs for the sleeve were taken in Nashville by Marshall Fallwell Jr, with the back-sleeve image featuring most of the musicians contributing to the album. John Kosh designed the gatefold sleeve.

Beaucoups Of Blues (single)

The title track of Ringo's second solo album, 2 minutes and 30 seconds in length. Buzz Rabin penned the number.

It was released in America only on Apple 2969 on 5 October 1970 with 'Coochy Coochy' on the flip. It peaked at the No. 87 position in the *Billboard* charts.

Beautiful Night

A track from Paul McCartney's 1997 album *Flaming Pie* in which Ringo's vocals are to the fore. Paul said, 'I'd written it a few years ago and I'd always liked the song, and I'd done a version in New York, but I didn't feel we'd quite pulled it off.

'So I got this song for when Ringo was coming, changed a few of the lyrics, and it was like the old days. I realised we hadn't done this for so long, but it was really comfortable and it was still there. So we did "Beautiful Night" and we tagged on a fast bit at the end which wasn't there before.'

Bernstein, Sid

Bernstein was the first American promoter to see the potential of the Beatles in the United States and he promoted them at the Carnegie Hall and Shea Stadium concerts in 1964 and 1966.

On Friday 17 September 1976 he took out a full-page advertisement in the *New York Herald Tribune* asking that the Beatles unite for a charity concert. As Ringo was currently involved in interviews to promote his new album *Ringo's Rotogravure*, journalists were eager to hear his comments.

When asked if he'd seen the advert, he said, 'I haven't read it properly. But if it is another one of those things that offers us the moon to do one concert – as of now, it is out! Look, people have been asking us to do this thing for so long and offering us God knows how much, but they don't seem to realise – we didn't start doing it for money, and we aren't going to end it that way. The Beatles were formed because four guys wanted to get together and play. Now those four guys are going their separate ways. I can't speak about what might happen in five years time, but as of now – no Beatles! We just don't need it!'

While conducting interviews in Paris on 20 September he was asked to comment on the advertisement by Tony Prince, a disc jockey with Capitol Radio. He said, 'I think Sid Bernstein is trying to get his name in the papers. When I got up someone said, "Have you seen this?" But I hadn't, it was too long to read. I realised the whole gist of the situation is that he wants to give us $230 million. I don't know how long he wants us to play, it's good for five minutes, but I don't know why all this pressure is on us. We're busy all the time. I'm here promoting this album and he's put that out and all I'm going to get from you and everyone else is "Sid Bernstein said this". I don't care about Sid Bernstein; I'm promoting my record. I don't know what the others are going to say about it, but it won't be now.

'Next week someone's going to come in with $500 million. It annoys me because I have to spend all this energy all the time talking about it when we should be talking about something else. That's when it annoys me. If that hadn't been in the papers we would have passed right over it. We've just spent ten minutes talking about this guy who writes to a newspaper.'

Best Of Ringo Starr & His All-Starr Band: So Far, The

A 93-minute video and DVD set issued in America by Image Entertainment on 23 October 2001. The video was on ID0827RD and the DVD on IDO828RODVD.

Paul McCartney provides a voice-over introduction that he ends with the words, '... from the greatest band of all time, what's his name? It's Ringo STAAAAARR!'

The live performances were taken from concerts at several different venues. The tracks were:

'Honey Don't' and 'Photograph' by Ringo, 'Iko Iko' by Dr John, and 'The Weight' by Levon Helm, all recorded at the Greek Theater, Los Angeles, in 1989.

'Don't Go Where The Road Don't Go', 'You're Sixteen', 'Yellow Submarine' and 'I Wanna Be Your Man' by Ringo, 'Rocky Mountain Way' by Joe Walsh, 'Bang The Drum' by Todd Rundgren, recorded at the Montreux Jazz Festival in 1992.

'No No Song' by Ringo, recorded at the Empire Theatre, Liverpool, in 1992.

'Groovin'' by Felix Cavaliere, 'You Ain't Seen Nothing Yet' by Randy Bachman and 'Boys' by Ringo, recorded in Japan in 1995.

'Sunshine Of Your life' by Jack Bruce, 'Norwegian Wood' by Peter Frampton, 'A Whiter Shade Of Pale' by Gary Brooker and 'It Don't Come Easy', 'Act Naturally' and 'With A Little Help From My Friends' by Ringo, recorded at Pine Knob, Detroit, in 1997.

Best, Pete

The Beatles' drummer from August 1960 to August 1962, born in Madras, India, on 24 November 1941. There had been a couple of previous drummers with the group such as Norman Chapman and Tommy Moore, but they had only been with the group for a short time.

When the Beatles had a booking cancelled at the Grosvenor Ballroom, Wallasey, on 6 August 1960, they visited the Casbah club where Pete was playing with his band the Blackjacks. They particularly admired his new drum kit and Paul McCartney phoned him the next day to ask if he'd join the Beatles. As the Blackjacks were on the verge of disbanding, Pete agreed and auditioned with them at the Wyvern club. He was accepted and travelled to Hamburg with them, initially playing at the Indra club and then the Kaiserkeller. When Allan Williams wanted to record the Hurricanes' lead singer with the Beatles at the Akustic Studios, Pete was in Hamburg city centre buying new drumsticks and Ringo sat in with them.

During their stint in Hamburg, the Beatles underwent a transformation, both musically, personally and visually. Pete also developed a new style called the 'Atom Beat', which helped drive their music in a powerful way, a style other Liverpool bands began to copy.

When the Beatles received their recording audition at Abbey Road Studios, George Martin suggested that for their next recording he would prefer to have a session drummer. This was standard practice with A&R men at the time – although Martin was comfortable with the vocals and guitar work of artists in a studio, he felt that session drummers were more aware of what was required in a studio.

This was used as an excuse to sack Pete, a decision pushed forward mainly by George Harrison and Paul McCartney. John Lennon wasn't happy with it and neither was Brian Epstein, but George Martin's action did have an influence.

Pete was called in to see Epstein, who told him that he was sacked and that the group had already hired Ringo Starr of Rory Storm and the Hurricanes. Epstein wanted Pete to join the Merseybeats, but he refused.

When Ringo appeared at the Cavern for the first time as a member of the Beatles, there was something of a melee due to fans angered at Best's removal, and George Harrison received a black eye from a Best fan called Bruno.

The EMI recording session took place, but apparently George Martin, Ron Richards and Paul McCartney were not happy with Ringo's drumming and rearranged the date with session drummer Andy White. Despite this, the version of 'Love Me Do' that Ringo played on was the version used on the single, yet Ringo believed otherwise for the rest of his career, even recording another version of 'Love Me Do' with the Roundheads decades later.

Best immediately joined Lee Curtis and the All Stars who, as a result, were voted No. 2 to the Beatles in the *Mersey Beat* poll. Lee Curtis signed with Decca, who wanted him to record as a solo artist, and Decca wanted to push Pete's name, so the group was now called the Pete Best Four. Their single 'I'm Gonna Knock On Your Door' was unsuccessful and Decca dropped them.

In February 1963, in a Beatles interview in the American *Playboy* magazine, John Lennon intimated that Pete was always off sick, which was the real reason he was fired. This was untrue as Pete was only off ill for four gigs in the entire two years. However, Ringo commented on John's accusation by saying, 'He took little pills to make him ill.'

Pete sued and received an out-of-court settlement.

He married his girlfriend Kathy in August 1963 (August seemed to be a momentous month for him). With the phenomenal success of the Beatles, Pete became terribly depressed. He had contributed to the Beatles' fame when he was with them and had been sacked without any compensation. He attempted suicide.

He flew to the States with a quintet, the Pete Best Combo and made a number of albums, including *Best Of The Beatles* and *The Beatle That Time Forgot*, which were unsuccessful.

Pete then got the offer of an audition to become one of the Monkees. He was about to fly to Hollywood when he found that his work permit had run out and that he'd have to fly back to England and apply for another one. The alternative was to become an American citizen, but that would have meant he would have been eligible to be drafted for the Vietnam War. He returned to Liverpool and became a civil servant.

He was to take early retirement and return to music leading a band in 1994. The following year the tracks he'd recorded with the Beatles for Decca Records were included on the *Beatles Anthology*, which at last brought him a substantial sum for his time in the early Beatles.

In recent years Pete has been touring the world with his band, achieving a success previously denied him, and his story has been the subject of three books.

Black, Cilla

Liverpool singer, born Priscilla White on 27 May 1943. She began singing with local bands, one of which was Rory Storm and the Hurricanes, and she duetted on the song 'Boys' with Ringo. A mistake by Bill Harry in the *Mersey Beat* newspaper dubbed her 'Cilla Black' and she decided to keep the name.

Ringo appeared as a guest on her television show *Cilla* on 6 February 1968, singing a duet with Cilla, 'Do You Like Me', and the music-hall song 'Nellie Dean'.

He appeared on the show again on 1 October 1970 when he and Cilla duetted on 'Act Naturally'.

George Harrison wrote and produced two songs for her at Apple Studios in 1972 with 'You've Got To Stay With Me' and 'I'll Still Love You'. The line-up on these tracks comprised Ringo on drums, Eric Clapton and George on guitar and Klaus Voormann on bass.

The numbers weren't released and Ringo eventually re-recorded 'I'll Still Love You' for his *Rotogravure* album.

At one time Ringo offered Cilla the number 'Back Off Boogaloo', but she rejected it, saying she wanted 'Photograph' instead. However, Ringo decided to record it himself and it became a chart-topper.

Blades, Jack

A guitarist, born 24 April 1954 in Palm Springs, California. He began to take an interest in music at the age of eight, inspired by the Beatles. His first group was called Rubican, formed in 1976. They disbanded in 1979 and his other groups have included Stereo, Ted Nugent's Night Ranger and Damn Yankees.

He became a member of Ringo and the Roundheads.

Blast From Your Past

A compilation of hits with eight American chart singles, five of which were also British hits, together with one B side and an album track.

This was the last album to appear on the Apple label and Roy Kohara designed the sleeve.

It was issued in Britain on Apple PCS 7170 on 12 December 1975. Incidentally, the sleeve contains a quote from 'a local Gynecologist: "You don't have to be first, but make sure you're not last!"'

The compilation was issued in America on Apple SW 3422 on 20 November 1975 where it reached No. 30 in the charts, although it had no chart placing in Britain.

The tracks were: Side One: 'You're Sixteen', 'No No Song', 'It Don't Come Easy', 'Photograph', 'Back Off Boogaloo'. Side Two: 'Only You (And You Alone)', 'Beaucoups Of Blues', 'Oh My My', 'Early 1970', 'I'm The Greatest'.

It was reissued as a budget album in Britain on Music For Pleasure MFP 50524 on 25 November 1981 and in America on Capitol SN-16236 in September 1981.

Blindman (film)

Produced by Saul Swimmer, who went on to produce *The Concert For Bangla Desh* film, and directed by Ferdinando Baldi in Almeria, Spain, in 1971. The Italian western had been written by Tony Anthony, who also played the lead. Ringo's appearance was arranged by Allen Klein (who also appeared in the movie, along with Mal Evans).

The film was in colour, ran for 105 minutes and received an X Certificate in the UK.

Apart from Anthony as the title character, Ringo was cast as a baddie called Candy, Agneta Eckmyr was Pilar, Lloyd Batista was Domingo and Magda Konopka was Sweet Mama.

As usual with spaghetti westerns, the location was Spain and the filming took place between June and August 1971.

Although Ringo wrote some music for the film, his soundtrack was never used. The song 'Blindman', which he'd intended to be the main tune, ended up as the B side to 'Back Off Boogaloo'.

The film did not receive the international distribution of his previous movies. It opened in Rome on 15 November 1971 and in America received its premiere in Chicago on 12 January 1972. Later that year it received a limited showing in Britain. The film's plot concerns a blind gunslinger who is hired to escort fifty beautiful women to an equal number of miners from Texas who have marriage in mind. On his way to collect his charges he discovers a ruthless Mexican bandit called Domingo has hijacked them. He sets off for the border, riding a horse that seems to know the way. He comes across an old man whose daughter Pilar has been ravished and kidnapped by Domingo's brother, Candy. The old man leads him to the bandit's camp. Domingo and his sadistic sister Sweet Mama have sold the girls to a group of Mexican soldiers; they then massacre the men before imprisoning their general.

Blindman captures Candy and offers to exchange him for the girls. He is tricked and ends up with 49 aged Mexicans and Sweet Mama, who captures him and puts him in a cell with Pilar and the general.

Blindman escapes from jail with the general and later kills Candy. Domingo then arranges a bizarre funeral-marriage between Candy and Pilar. The general arrives with his troops and routs the bandits while Blindman kills Domingo. He discovers that the general has taken all the girls and sets off, once more, in pursuit.

The *Monthly Film Bulletin* commented: 'There are some nice ideas here and there, notably the spectacle of the fifty girls twittering through the desert in their nighties and being rounded up like a herd of cattle, and of Ringo Starr tethered to a locomotive and hung with cowbells lest he move without alerting the Blindman.'

Blindman (song)

A number Ringo wrote for his 1971 film *Blindman*. Ringo and Klaus Voormann produced it on 18 and 19 August 1971 and it was issued as the flipside of 'Back Off Boogaloo'. Pete Ham also plays on the track. It was rumoured that Ringo was to compose the film's soundtrack but when the producers heard this number, they cancelled it. The number is 2 minutes and 40 seconds in length.

Blue Christmas

One of the numbers featured on Ringo's 1999 album *I Wanna Be Santa Claus*. It was written by Jay W. Johnson and Billy Hayes. Ringo is on lead vocals, drums and percussion, Mark Hudson on bass and backing vocals, Steve Dudas on electric guitar, Jaydee Maness on pedal steel guitar and Gary Burr on backing vocals. It is 2 minutes and 58 seconds in length.

Blue Moon Of Kentucky

A number penned by Bill Monroe that became a classic Elvis Presley track. When Ringo, George and Paul were jamming at George's Friar Park recording studios, working on the *Anthology* project, they began playing the number following a conversation about Elvis Presley. They were filmed performing the number, and a clip of it, lasting a minute and a half, was shown on ABC TV's *Good Morning* show in America in December 1995.

Blue Turning Grey Over You

This track on *Sentimental Journey* was written by Andy Razaf and Thomas 'Fats' Waller and was a hit for Louis Armstrong in 1930. Oliver Nelson arranged this version. Ringo recorded the basic track on 4 December 1969 and completed it on 24 February 1970. This was the final track Ringo recorded before he went on a trip to America. It is 3 minutes and 18 seconds in length.

Boardwalk Records

The record company that signed a multi-album contract with Ringo early in 1981. They parted company after one album release, *Stop And*

Smell The Roses. This was arguably due to the death that year of one of the label's founders, Neil Bogart, who was a personal friend of Ringo.

Their Los Angeles office then turned down his new album *Old Wave* and even RCA in Britain, who Ringo signed with in 1981, were reluctant to release that album.

Instead, Boardwalk released it in Germany on 16 August 1983 on Boardwalk 266.16.029, together with a single from the album, 'In My Car', which Ringo had co-written.

Bogie, Colonel Doug

Ringo once said that one of his favourite performers was a British entertainer called Colonel Doug Bogie. He signed him up to Ring O' Records and the artist had one single released in Britain, the old Jimmy Kennedy dance number 'Cockey Cockey' and the traditional carol 'Away In A Manger'. The single was issued in Britain on Ring O' 2017 104 on 21 November 1975. Ring O' Records didn't want to issue it in America, but ABC picked it up as a Christmas disc and issued it on 8 December 1975 on ABC 12148.

There were rumours that Ringo played drums and Eric Clapton played guitar on the single, although no musicians' credits were given.

Bolan, Marc

A British singer/songwriter/guitarist/poet, born Marc Feld in London on 30 September 1947.

He initially appeared as Toby Tyler, then Marc Bowland and finally Marc Bolan, and made his recording debut with 'The Wizard' in 1966. He joined John's Children in 1967, then teamed up with Steve Peregrine Took in Tyrannosaurus Rex later the same year.

Took suffered from drugs problems and was replaced by Mickey Finn in 1968. The group truncated their name to T. Rex and became a quartet, issuing a string of major hits including 'Ride A White Swan', 'Hot Love', 'Telegram Sam', 'Children Of The Revolution' and 'The Groover'.

In 1970 Marc married his girlfriend June Child, but they were to split three years later when he fell in love with Gloria Jones, an American singer, with whom he had a child, Rolan.

Bolan was one of the acts associated with glam rock and Ringo said, 'Bowie is a step beyond what Marc is doing and you've got Alice (Cooper) somewhere in between.'

Ringo and Marc became good friends and Ringo was intrigued about the T. Rexmania that was occurring. He became something of a father figure to Bolan, who presented Ringo with a Les Paul electric guitar.

Ringo decided to make a film of a T. Rex concert and filmed them at their Empire Pool, Wembley, concert on 18 March 1972. When editing the film at Twickenham Studios he commented, 'Everyone in the audience was getting something different. That's why we used all those close-ups. There's one guy and his chick and they're just sitting very still, watching it. Then there are the chicks who are going completely insane.'

While editing it he came to another decision: 'I wanted to do some more. You see, my theory about filming concerts is that you can't create the atmosphere that's in the hall. We got him to write a few things and set up a couple more days' shooting.'

The film was called *Born To Boogie*.

It was also a phrase Marc had come out with that inspired Ringo to write the number 'Back Off Boogaloo'.

Tragedy occurred on 17 September 1977. Bolan, who had never learned to drive because he hated cars, was on his way home, with Gloria at the wheel. The car swerved off the road and crashed into a tree on Barnes Common in London. He was killed instantly. It was two weeks before his thirtieth birthday and, bizarrely, he had always believed he would not reach the age of thirty.

Bonnet, Graham

A singer who Ringo signed to his Ring O' Records label in 1977. He had two singles issued on the label, the Bob Dylan composition 'It's All Over Now, Baby Blue' c/w 'Heroes On My Picture Wall', issued in Britain on Ringo O' 2017-105 on 3 June 1977 and 'Danny' c/w 'Rock Island Line', issued in Britain on Ring O' 2017-106 on 12 August 1977.

An album was issued in September 1977.

Born To Boogie

Ringo made his directorial debut with *Born To Boogie,* filmed between March and April 1972. An Apple Films production, the 90-minute colour film was made entirely on location in London, mainly at a concert at the Empire Pool, Wembley.

Filming began on Saturday 18 March 1972 at the Marc Bolan/T. Rex concert at the Empire Pool, Wembley. Ringo filmed both evening concerts from his position in the photographer's pit below the stage. On 21 March Marc Bolan and T. Rex were with Ringo at Tittenhurst Park filming further scenes for the film. They settled in John's Ascot Sound Studio (ASS) and a jam session took place with T. Rex, Elton John and Ringo, which was filmed. The numbers were 'Tutti Frutti', 'Children Of The Revolution' and 'The Slider', although only the first two numbers appeared in the film. Then, on 22 March, still at Tittenhurst Park, they filmed the Mad Hatter's Tea Party sequence for the film.

In 1972 pop superstar Marc Bolan was a friend of the then 32-year-old Ringo. The former Beatle had been impressed by scenes of T.

Rextasy that had accompanied Bolan's concerts and decided to record the atmosphere on film. Ringo also acted as a cameraman, along with Nick Knowland, Mike Dodds, Mike Davis, Jeremy Stavenhagen and Richard Stanley. Marc Bolan summarised the movie, saying, 'The film was made purely as a piece of rock'n'roll entertainment.

'I feel it documents the phenomenon that has been T. Rex through the past year – and that was the purpose of the film initially. But as Ringo and I became more involved in the making of *Born To Boogie*, we decided to add several more scenes – bringing in 'accident' humour and also to shoot from recorded music – actually 'live' without dubbing.

'By doing so we were endeavouring to get a spontaneity which does not come naturally from some films. In some of the scenes outside of the concert we let our imaginations take their course and, with the aid of props and a dwarf, let whichever happened, happen.

'We made the film strictly for a teenage audience who demand youthful excitement in the cinema – as well as on television and in the theatre. I think the film does that – no more, no less.'

Elton John, Keith Moon and Ringo himself made cameo appearances and the numbers performed on stage by T. Rex included 'Jeepster', 'Hot Love', 'Get It On', 'The Slider', 'Union Hall Poem' and 'Chariot Choogle'.

At the press screening of the film on Wednesday 13 December 1972 at the Oscar One cinema, London, Ringo held a brief press conference.

Q: How did you come to be filming Marc Bolan?

Ringo: I telephoned him one day and said, 'Come and see me. I've got this idea. See what you think. Yes or no.' And on that particular thing it was 'no'. But through that meeting we got to know each other and became friendly. Then I heard he was going to be filmed at his Wembley show. Well, Apple has a film company so I said, 'Why don't you let me do it? I'm your pal.' And he said, 'OK. We'll do it together.' After the show we looked at the footage we had got and decided to add to it. You see, my theory about filming concerts is that you cannot create the atmosphere that was in the hall. So I needed to do more. We got him to write a few things and set up a couple more days shooting.

Q: What about the 'Some people like to rock – some people like to roll' sequence?

Ringo: Oh, yes! It was so messy that it had to be included!

Q: Was the Wembley show in any way a nostalgic experience for you?

Ringo: Very much so. They were screaming and shouting and I love that.

Q: So you enjoy the screams, then?

Ringo. Oh, yeah. If they had been quiet when I played I would have died. I wouldn't have known what to do.

George Melly, writing in the *Observer* newspaper, commented, 'The film is directed and in part filmed by Ringo Starr. The incidental humour is drawn from the nursery surrealist world of *The Magical Mystery Tour*, but lacks that famous disaster's pretensions. Nuns, one bearded, take tea, a dwarf gnaws ravenously at a car's offside mirror. Simple oral-fixation, but the music goes like the clappers.'

The *Morning Star* newspaper reviewer wrote, 'Made by Apple films and directed by Ringo, this is the best teeny-bopper entertainment since the Beatles succumbed to insecticide.'

Fergus Cashin noted in the *Sun*, '*Born To Boogie* will open at boxer Billy Walker's cinema, Oscar, with a U. It's the nearest it will ever get to an Oscar.

Bottom Line Cabaret Theater, The

The first live appearance of Ringo and the Roundheads took place at this Greenwich Village, New York, venue on Tuesday 12 May 1998. Ringo hadn't played in a nightclub for 35 years. Apart from Ringo, the group comprised Joe Walsh, Mark Hudson and Steve Dudas on guitars, Jack Blades on bass, Jim Cox on keyboards, Gary Burr on guitar, Simon Kirke on drums and Scott Gordon on harmonica.

The 45-minute set took place during the evening before an audience of 300, which included Diana Ross, Patti Smith, Vini Poncia, Barbara Starkey and Will Lee, the bassist from *The Late Show With David Letterman*.

The group performed 'With A Little Help From My Friends', 'It Don't Come Easy', 'I Was Walkin'', 'Don't Pass Me By', 'Back Off Boogaloo', 'King Of Broken Hearts', 'Octopus's Garden', 'Photograph', 'La De Da', 'What In The . . . World' and a medley of 'Love Me Do'/'With A Little Help From My Friends'.

Later Ringo and the band attended an after-show party at the home of Mercury Records executive Danny Goldberg.

The show was a rehearsal for the taping of the VH-1 *Storytellers* programme to be performed the following evening.

Ringo Starr and the Roundheads appeared at the venue again for a promotional appearance on 22 March 2003. They played a 35-minute 8-song set from 11 a.m. for the media. Ringo's fellow musicians were Mark Hudson, Gary Burr and Steve Dudas on guitar, Mark Hart on keyboards, Matt Bisonette on Hofner bass and Greg Bisonette on drums. Two of the numbers were from his new *Ringo Rama* album, 'Memphis In Your Mind' and 'Never Without You'. The other songs were 'It Don't Come Easy', 'I Wanna Be Your Man', 'Boys', 'Photograph', 'Yellow Submarine' and 'With A Little Help From My Friends'. During their 'With A Little Help From My Friends' encore they were joined by Grammy award winner Norah Jones, who is Ravi Shankar's daughter.

Boys
A song that Ringo has probably performed for a longer time than almost any other, a Luthor Dixon/Wes Farrell composition that the Shirelles included on the flipside of their 1960 hit 'Will You Love Me Tomorrow'. Liverpool groups generally played B sides of records seeking new numbers for their repertoire. The Beatles included it in their set, with Pete Best on vocals. When Ringo replaced Best he took over the song.

Ringo was familiar with 'Boys', as he performed the song in his 'Ringo Starrtime' spot in Rory Storm and the Hurricanes. When Cilla Black got up to sing 'Boys' with the group at one time, Ringo was slightly irked as he had to share the single microphone with her.

The Beatles recorded the number in one take at Abbey Road Studios on 11 February 1963, and it provided Ringo with his first lead vocal on a Beatles track.

He performed it on stage during the group's 1964 tour of North America and it is also on the albums *Introducing The Beatles*, *The Early Beatles*, *Rock And Roll Music* and *The Beatles At The Hollywood Bowl*.

Ringo decided to revive the number with his All-Starr Band.

At the press conference for his 1989 tour he said he would be playing 'Boys' because 'it would be interesting to do because it was the first song I recorded, so I have a lot of love for that song. And I sound great!'

Bramlett, Delaney
Delaney and Bonnie were a husband-and-wife team, Delaney and Bonnie Bramlett, who toured Britain and Europe as Delaney and Bonnie and Friends, with George Harrison one of the backing musicians.

Bonnie was born Bonnie Lynn O'Farrell on 1 July 1939 in Pontotoc, Mississippi and was once a member of Ike and Tina Turner's Ilettes.

The couple broke up in 1972 and Delaney began recording as a solo artist. When her album *Delaney And Friends – Class Reunion* was issued in 1978, she claimed that Ringo had played drums on the tracks 'For Old Time Sake', 'I Think I Got It', 'I Wish It Would Rain', 'Locked Up In Alabama', and 'You Were The Light', although he is uncredited.

Bonnie became a member of the Bandaloo Doctors, who Ringo asked to be the opening act of his 1992 All-Starr tour.

Brooker, Gary
A British musician, born in Essex on 29 May 1945. He was keyboards player with the Paramounts and then became a founder member of

Procol Harum, whose 'A Whiter Shade Of Pale' was a major hit. The only other hit of note was 'Conquistador'.

Brooker became a friend of the Beatles, in particular George and Ringo, and he played on George's albums *All Things Must Pass*, *Somewhere In England* and *Gone Troppo*. He also played on Ringo's *Old Wave* album and joined the Fourth All-Starr Band in 1997, performing 'The Devil Came From Kansas', 'Conquistador' and 'A Whiter Shade Of Pale'.

Brookfield House

The property that Ringo bought from Peter Sellers. While they were filming *The Magic Christian*, Ringo heard that Sellers was going to put his house on the market. It was a fifteenth-century oak-beamed mansion in Elsted, Surrey, set in several acres of grounds with its own lake, paddocks, walled gardens and barns. Sellers had spent an additional £50,000 on renovations and had a gymnasium, changing rooms, sauna and private cinema built into the barns.

Ringo offered Sellers £70,000 for the property and Sellers accepted. Then John Lennon, who also liked the house, put in an offer of £150,000, but Sellers decided to keep his word to Ringo and sold it to him.

Ringo and family moved into the mansion in mid-November 1968, but only lived there until 5 December 1969, when he decided to buy Lennon's Tittenhurst Park.

Ringo later sold the house to American singer Stephen Stills.

The property was sold in 1988 for £1.7 million.

Bruce Willis – The Return Of Bruno

A spoof rock video by Bruce Willis lasting 52 minutes that was screened in Britain on BBC2 on 31 August 1987 and issued on home video on 14 September. Ringo made a cameo appearance in the film.

Bruce, Jack

A British musician, born in Glasgow, Scotland, on 14 May 1943. He won a scholarship to the Royal Scottish Academy of Music and later moved to London where he became a member of Alexis Korner's Blues Inc. His other bands included the Graham Bond Organisation, Manfred Mann and John Mayall's Bluesbreakers. His most famous band was with Eric Clapton and Ginger Baker in the trio Cream. When the group broke up in 1968 he recorded the solo album *Songs For A Tailor*. During the 1970s he appeared in West, Bruce and Laing, in the 1980s in BLT with Robin Trower and Bill Lordan and in the 1990s with Gary Moore. He was a member of the All-Starr Band in 1997 and 1998 and performed the numbers 'I Feel Free' and 'White Room'.

He recalls the All-Starr's tours as being great fun. 'The most enjoyment I had on the tour was playing other people's songs; it's not often one gets a chance to play such classic songs. It was very satisfying to get on stage to rock out with such high-calibre musicians like those on the All-Starr Band and make the audience climb the walls. It was also nice to see Ringo playing so well. To turn around on stage and see Ringo smiling when we were all playing together was a great feeling. The whole experience was tremendous fun.'

Bye Bye Blackbird

A track on Ringo's *Sentimental Journey* album. Mort Dickson and Ray Henderson originally wrote the number especially for a Vaudeville performer, George Price, in 1927 and Maurice Gibb arranged this version for Ringo.

It was recorded at Morgan Studios in London on 5 March 1969 and is 2 minutes and 10 seconds in length.

Cable Music

A company Ringo formed with Richard Branson in 1987. The original aim was to present a 24-hour music channel, a British version of MTV.

Caldwell, Iris

The sister of Rory Storm, leader of Rory Storm and the Hurricanes, who Ringo played drums with prior to joining the Beatles. Iris was also a girl-friend of George Harrison and Paul McCartney and was to marry Shane Fenton (who became a chart artist with a name change to Alvin Stardust).

Iris recalled the time Ringo was a member of Rory Storm's group at Butlin's in Pwllheli. 'The group decided they would look more professional in make-up, but Ringo refused point blank and said he wouldn't "put that muck on my face". He gave in in the end, only smearing a thin layer over his face.

'I remember that he was very popular with the girls staying at the camp. They all loved the grey streaks in his hair, even though Ringo hated them.

'Rory thought a lot of Ringo and gave him his own spot in the act called "Ringo Starrtime". Ringo sang "Matchbox" and "Boys".

'He did not grow his beard until their second season at the camp in Pwllheli. I think it was to try and draw attention away from the streaks in his hair.'

Caldwell, Vi

The mother of Alan Caldwell, known as Rory Storm, who led the Hurricanes, the group in which Ringo was the drummer. Ringo spent many hours at the Caldwell house and got to know the family well. The Beatles used to write to her when they were in Germany.

When she was asked to recall the days when Ringo was a member of the Hurricanes, she remembered his first swimming lesson.

'Rory found out that Ringo could not swim a stroke so he decided to try and teach him. It was fine at first, but then they became more ambitious and decided to go underwater swimming, which almost caused a tragedy. Rory told me that suddenly a pair of hands appeared beneath the waves, desperately searching for something to grab on to. Ringo's swimming obviously wasn't good enough for underwater yet. Luckily Rory saw what was happening and pulled him out.

'In 1961 Ringo was going out with a girl called Gerry. They were seen everywhere together and I believe the only reason that they broke it off was because Ringo refused to give up show business.

'He was a constant visitor to our house and usually came home with Rory after they had finished playing. They used to sit there chatting for hours. But I seem to remember that it was Rory who did most of the talking while Ringo did most of the listening. Often they would sit there until the early hours of the morning, and occasionally even until dawn broke.

'I remember that Ringo's moods used to vary a lot. Sometimes he'd be very happy and animated and other times miserable and depressed. But he had a very strong effect on all the others present and if he was feeling happy they all ended up feeling happy too. If he was sad then everyone seemed to be miserable.

'He always seemed to be getting into scrapes. I remember the time he went to Hamburg for the first time. He travelled alone on the train and had to change in Paris. During the usual scramble he lost track of his drum kit. He told me that he stood on the platform unable to speak a word of French and did his best to describe what had happened in sign language. The French people thought he was mad and called the gendarmes. Fortunately, one of them did understand English, and realised what had happened. He still had to stay in Paris overnight, but his drums were found by next morning.

'I know that from the very first time that he met them, Ringo admired John, Paul and George very much, and I think it was the biggest moment of his life when he was given the opportunity of playing with them on their first recording session.

'It certainly changed his whole life and looking back on all the troubles that Ringo went through as a child I'm very glad that he has become so successful and famous.'

Sadly, both Vi and Rory were found dead at their home in Liverpool on 28 September 1972. Rory had been in Amsterdam working as a disc jockey when he received news that his father had died. He rushed home to console his mother. Rory had a chest condition and couldn't breathe properly. He found it difficult to sleep and took a number of pills, along with some whisky, which may have resulted in his death. It's thought that Vi found his body, and was so distraught that she took her own life.

California Calling

A track on the album *The Beach Boys,* on which Ringo plays drums. The album was issued on CD by CBS on 27 September 1985 on CBS CD 26378.

Call Me

A track from the *Goodnight Vienna* album, penned by Ringo, which was issued as the flipside of the 'Only You (And You Alone)' single. It is 4 minutes and 2 seconds in length.

Candy

Ringo was offered his first film role in a non-Beatles film in 1968. *Candy* was an updating of Voltaire's *Candide.* The movie was scripted by Buck Henry from the rather risqué comic novel by Terry Southern and Mason Hoffenberg that had originally been printed in Paris by the Olympia Press. When it was eventually published in the United States it became a bestseller.

The film was an Italian/French co-production, filmed in Italy by producer Richard Haggiag and director Christian Marquand. The colour movie, with a running time of 128 minutes, was given an X certificate. Other stars who appeared in the film included Marlon Brando, Richard Burton and James Coburn.

Ringo played the part of Emmanuel, a Mexican gardener who attempts to seduce Candy Christian.

The comparatively unknown Swedish actress Ewa Aulin starred in the title role. Richard Burton portrayed Professor McPhisto, a college lecturer, the first in a line of would-be seducers. Italian actress Elsa Martinelli appeared as Candy's Aunt Livia. Marlon Brando played a randy Eastern guru.

McPhisto attempts to seduce Candy after she has attended his lecture and tries again while driving her home. When she arrives she finds that he has spilled whisky on her dress so she takes it off and begins to sponge it. Emmanuel the gardener enters the room and grabs her, attempting to make love to her on a pool table.

Her father (played by John Astin) arrives and the gardener is thrown out. His pride hurt, Emmanuel complains to his relatives and this ill-assorted group of Mexicans pursue Candy and her father to the airport on motorbikes. One of Emmanuel's kinfolk hurls a bolas, which splits open the head of Candy's father.

Apart from a brief appearance at the end of the movie, Ringo takes no further part in the film. Though much publicised, his part was little more than a cameo role with only a few lines of dialogue of the 'Dis no good' variety – wearing a suitably lustful leer on his moustachioed face as he tries to seduce Candy.

Candy flies off and is involved in an incident with the pilot when she shows him her breasts. Having been isolated in his cabin for years, he is so shocked he parachutes out of the plane. Miraculously the aircraft lands in New York, where Candy's father undergoes an operation during which his blonde daughter has to fight off the attentions of the doctors. Her other encounters include a film director, a hunchback and a holy man. She escapes the attentions of the latter to find herself in a temple, where she discovers the bound body of her father.

Terry Southern was also the author of *The Magic Christian,* on which Ringo's second solo movie was based.

Cappello, Tim

An American musician who played sax and percussion in the second and fifth All-Starr Bands in 1992 and 1999 respectively.

Career after the Beatles

Initially, it seemed as if Ringo's solo career had got off to a rocky start following the modest success of his debut album *Sentimental Journey,* which reached the British Top 20 and hit the No. 22 spot in America, and the lack of chart success of his second album *Beaucoups Of Blues.*

Then success struck home with his first solo single, 'It Don't Come Easy' becoming a massive hit, followed by a second hit with 'Back Off Boogaloo' and a third successful single with 'Photograph'. His third album *Ringo* was a triumph, followed by another million-selling single 'You're Sixteen'. 'Only You (And You Alone)' had modest chart success, followed by the *Goodnight Vienna* album, which also charted. His sixth single 'Snookeroo' failed to make the charts and a compilation album, *Blast From Your Past,* failed to make a stir.

In succeeding years there were many albums and singles, but none were ever to make the impact of his initial releases. Major record companies showed a lack of interest and Ringo moved from EMI/Capitol to Atlantic, then to Portrait, followed by Boardwalk – when he moved to The Right Stuff with his *Old Wave* album, a release couldn't be found for it in America or Britain. Rhino, Rykodisc, Private Music, Music Masters, Mercury, King Biscuit and Koch were other labels that took a chance on him – and he finally found a niche with his 'All-Starr Band' albums, live recordings of his tours with the All-Starr Band, which did find a ready market. 2003 saw him return to a studio album with *Ringo Rama,* which received reviewer acclaim and steady sales.

During this time his film career floundered and he decided to close the book on acting and concentrate on his music. In 2003, when asked if he had any further films or TV parts planned, he said, 'No. I've decided I'm just going to do music from now on. That's what I love. I'm a musician and that's all I want to be. I'm turning down everything else.'

His personal life was also to have its ups and downs over the years. Following his marriage to Maureen (they were married under her real name Mary Cox) in 1965, the couple moved into an apartment in Montague Square in London's West End, but when their son Zak was born in September that year, they moved into a house, Sunny Heights, in Weybridge. Their second son Jason was born in August 1967 and their daughter Lee in November 1970.

The marriage seemed a strong one until a bizarre situation occurred when Ringo and Maureen invited George Harrison and his wife Patti to dinner at their Tittenhurst Park estate in Ascot.

The events of that night have been reported in various books and have never been denied by any of the concerned parties.

For example, it was reported in the 1983 book *The Love You Make*, written by Peter Brown, a Beatles 'insider' and former executive of Apple. He claimed that when the meal was finished, George blurted out that he was in love with Maureen. Maureen became terribly embarrassed, Ringo stormed off and Patti burst into tears and locked herself in the bathroom. After a while, George and Patti left.

That part of the story appears to be accurate, as even Maureen was to recall that she began clearing the dining table after the meal and George approached Ringo and said, 'I have to talk to you. I'm deeply in love with Maureen and I have been for three years.'

There is no confirmation of what Brown alleges happened next. He wrote that a few weeks after the abortive dinner incident, Patti returned home from a shopping spree in London and found George in the bedroom of their Friar Park home with Maureen.

Maureen and Patti were to neither confirm nor deny the incident, but when George was asked why he'd slept with his friend's wife, he shrugged his shoulders and said, 'Incest.'

Other events seem to indicate that there may be some truth in the stories. Eric Clapton, George's best friend, ended up with George's wife. Rolling Stone member Ronnie Wood and his wife Chrissie were guests at Friar Park for a month in October 1973. Wood then issued a statement to the press that he had a liaison with Patti. A decade later, in January 1984, Chrissie Wood related to the *News of the World* newspaper that it had been a case of wife swapping, that she went on a holiday to Portugal with George while Ronnie and Patti went on holiday together to the Bahamas.

After the alleged incident with Maureen and George, Ringo and his wife began to live virtually separate lives and eventually divorced in 1975, having been married exactly ten years.

Despite this, George and Ringo remained friends and George was always ready to aid Ringo on his recordings, whether to contribute a guitar solo, write a song or produce a track.

Ringo became heavily dependent on drink and drugs and began to move between London, Monte Carlo and Los Angeles. He was regularly in the company of two of his closest friends, both heavy drinkers – Keith Moon and Harry Nilsson. This trio, together with John

Lennon, found themselves sharing a house together during John's 15-month 'lost weekend' in Los Angeles during which John was to involve them all in his recording sessions for his rock'n'roll album and in the album he was producing for Nilsson called *Pussy Cats*.

Ringo was also to form his own record label, Ring O' Records, but with no record success in 1977/78, the label was closed down.

No longer a settled family man, Ringo was something of an international playboy and was rarely seen without an attractive woman on his arm. He was to say, 'Well, I'm a jet-setter. Whatever anyone may think and whoever puts it down, I am on planes half the year going different places. And in people's eyes, Monte Carlo is a jet-set scene. Los Angeles is a jet-set scene. London, swinging London, not that it swings any more. Amsterdam, you know. It's a crazy kind of world. Wherever I go it's a swinging place, man.'

His taste for the high life became well known and one journalist, noting Ringo's penchant for attending party after party, wrote, 'He'd go to the opening of an envelope.'

He became a tax exile, spending several months of the year at his home in Monte Carlo (he also had homes in Los Angeles and London), but still suffered from poor health. He became seriously ill with peritonitis again, an ailment of his childhood, and was taken to the Princess Grace Hospital in Monte Carlo on Saturday 28 April 1979. He almost died and during an operation several feet of intestines had to be removed.

Another blow came later that year when a devastated Ringo watched helplessly as his home in the Hollywood Hills was completely destroyed by fire, taking with it his priceless and irreplaceable collection of memorabilia and causing £67,000 worth of damage.

At the end of the following year came the tragic news that John Lennon had been murdered.

Ringo and his close companion Barbara Bach were on holiday in the Bahamas at the time. Barbara's daughter phoned them from England, but it wasn't clear to them whether the shots had been fatal.

Ringo phoned Maureen, his ex-wife – and John's former wife Cynthia happened to be with her at the time.

Ringo and Barbara immediately ordered a chartered plane to take them to New York and entered the Dakota building by a back door to evade the gathering crowds. Ringo had contacted Yoko by a payphone to let her know that his arrival was imminent. Yoko requested that Ringo come alone, but he told her, 'Where I go, Barbara goes too.'

As Ringo and Barbara left, fans began trying to touch him. He was to say, 'I was disgusted, not with the idea that they were there, but with the fact that you had a lot of dummies in the crowd all shouting at Yoko and saying, "Come to the window." She didn't want to deal with it at the time you know, the very next day after John's death. I also didn't want to hear people saying how much they loved the Beatles. I was there for a friend, not because he was a member of a pop group.'

It illustrates Ringo's personality that when he heard of the death he immediately rushed to Yoko's side to offer his condolences in person. Paul was also shocked, of course, and told reporters, 'It's a drag.' He did phone Yoko, but didn't fly to New York. Neither did George.

Ringo had met Barbara during the filming of *Caveman* in Mexico in 1980. Ringo then shed his longtime girlfriend Nancy Andrews and the two became inseparable. They were married on 27 April 1981 at Marylebone Register Office in London.

During 1984 Ringo became the narrator of the *Thomas The Tank Engine* series and the following year he became the first ex-Beatle to become a grandfather when his son Zak and wife Sarah had a baby daughter, Tatia Jane.

Unfortunately, Ringo hadn't got out of the habit of hard drinking and since Barbara was his constant companion, the drinking affected her. The two suffered from the effects of alcohol, resulting in constant arguments. They entered one of the down periods of their married life. Both Ringo and Barbara had been drinking far more alcohol than was good for them for some time. Their addiction became public knowledge, and during an interview on the American programme *Entertainment Tonight* Ringo intimated that both he and Barbara were taking the pledge. He mentioned that Barbara would 'try to straighten us out every couple of months, but then we'd fall back into the trap. I knew I should be doing something to get help but I just never got around to it.'

In October 1988 he and Barbara checked into an exclusive rehabilitation centre. The idea was to keep everything secret, which is why they decided on the Sierra Tucson Clinic in the desert, twenty miles away from the nearest town. They didn't want the press to get wind of their decision because they anticipated they would report it.

Unfortunately, Ringo blew his own cover at Tucson airport. He said, 'I landed as drunk as a skunk. I drank all the way and got off the plane totally demented. I thought I was going to a lunatic asylum.'

As they'd suspected, the press had a field day, with headlines in the papers and gossip sheets such as: 'Ringo and Wife In Booze Hell!', 'Shame Of Crazed Beatle' and 'Starr's Vicious Secret'.

They were on the course for five weeks, during which time they had to sleep apart and were awakened at the crack of dawn each day.

The vice president of the clinic, Judy Schieb, described the course the couple was taking as 'The Minnesota Method'. She expressed her opinion about alcoholism, 'It's a disease of the mind, body and spirit. We assist people in dealing with their feelings and they start seeing some of the reasons why they are not willing to face life on life's terms. We ask that they take a look at their family of origin and how that might have transferred into their adult life.'

Ringo recalled, 'Eight days in, I decided I am here to get help because I know I'm sick – and I just did whatever they asked.' He also said, 'You get so safe in the clinic. I didn't want to leave.'

As well as counselling, much of it by recovered sufferers, the treatment included compulsory exercise, group therapy and detoxification. They were confined to the premises and sex was taboo.

On their 'release' from the course, Ringo was to say, 'We've been given our lives back,' and gave out this message: 'Now, if any of my friends can't deal with me being sober, then I just don't bother with them because, for me, to live is more important than a friend getting uptight just because I won't have a drink.'

He also said, 'I feel physically and mentally strong and spiritually strong. And I'm ready. I was in a mess and I sought help and I got it and I feel a lot better by it. I'm just sorry I waited so long, really.'

After the dark days of the 1980s, in which the sparkling light had been his marriage to Barbara, things began to improve tremendously for Ringo, and the 1990s became the decade of his revived fortunes.

February 1989 saw Rhino Records release *Starr Struck: Best Of Ringo Starr. Volume 2* and the *Thomas The Tank Engine* series was transformed in America into a children's series, *Shining Time Station*, in which Ringo became a hero to a new generation of fans (admittedly in the three to four-years-old category) as 'Mr Conductor'. The series ran on American television from January to June.

Since leaving the Beatles, Ringo had made few stage appearances. Apart from one or two one-off performances, he had appeared with the Band, Bob Dylan's Rolling Thunder Revue, the New Barbarians, Todd Rundgren and the Beach Boys.

He was then approached by promoter David Fishof with a brilliant idea – he should tour again, forming a band of musicians who had all had major hits in their own right. They would be called Ringo Starr and the All-Starr Band.

It was a hugely successful concept and was to take Ringo through the entire decade of the 1990s and into the 21st century with regular tours, almost annually, and a string of popular live-album releases. It also brought his confidence back and his love of actual stage performing.

Carmen, Eric

An American singer/songwriter, born on 11 August 1949 in Cleveland, Ohio. Eric began playing the violin at the age of six and by the age of eleven was playing piano and composing songs. The Beatles became a big influence on his life and when he was at John Carroll University he joined the rock group Cyrus Erie that, with some personnel changes, developed into the Raspberries who had several hits, including 'I Wanna Be With You' and 'Overnight Sensation'. When they disbanded in 1974 he went solo and over the years was to have several hits in his own right, including 'All By Myself' and 'Never Gonna Fall In Love

Again'. The film *Dirty Dancing* sparked off his career once again when it featured one of his numbers, 'Hungry Eyes', which led to further hits.

He became a member of the sixth All-Starr Band in 2000 after an approach by his manager David Spero, who also managed Joe Walsh, and he performed 'Go All The Way'.

Carrack, Paul

A keyboardist and vocalist who appeared with Ringo Starr's All-Starr Band in 2003. Sheffield-born Carrack initially performed with a group called Warm Dust, followed by Ace, who had an international hit with his song 'How Long', which reached No. 3 in the American charts. The group disbanded at the end of the 70s and with the advent of punk Paul became a session man, recording and appearing with artists such as Frankie Miller and Roxy Music, and on albums by the Undertones, the Smiths and the Pretenders.

He joined Squeeze but left the group for a solo career before teaming up with Nick Lowe. In 1985 he joined Mike Rutherford in Mike and the Mechanics.

Carrack continued to release solo albums and also penned numbers with Squeeze lyricist Chris Difford while launching his own record label, Carrack-UK.

Ringo invited him to join the All-Starr Band tour in 2003 and in April Paul was to comment; 'He does a tour every year as Ringo's All-Starrs. He basically puts together a band made up of people who have had a hit or two somewhere along the line and can do a turn. He does 'With A Little Help From My Friends', 'Yellow Submarine', 'Photograph' and all those great songs, so everyone's turn comes round a few times. I've been up for doing it for a couple of years, but for one reason or another it didn't happen, and fortunately he asked me again this year. And when a Beatle calls you have to say yes.'

Casino Rama

A venue in Rama, Ontario, Canada where Ringo launched his All-Starr Band tour in 2001.

On Tuesday 24 July 2001 he held a press conference there to announce details of his All-Starr tour, which was to begin at the Casino on 26 July. At the time the band were rehearsing in the Chippewa Community Hall, across the street from the casino.

David Fishof introduced them and they played a medley of songs from their tour set list. Ringo and some of his band – Sheila E, Roger Hodgson, Ian Hunter, Howard Jones, Greg Lake and Mark Rivera – then answered questions from the press, and also from fans. The conference was presented live online by yahoo.com. Ringo discussed the lack of airplay of his recent albums.

Ringo also held a musical press conference there on 23 July 2003 to launch his eighth All-Starr tour.

Cavaliere, Felix

An American musician, born in Pelham, New York, on 19 November 1944. After studying classical piano, he was part of doo-wop group the Stereos while still at high school, and when at Syracuse University he formed Felix and the Escorts. For a time he was a member of Joey Dee and the Starliters, but after being influenced by the Beatles he formed a new band, the Rascals. Sid Bernstein, who had promoted the Beatles appearances at Carnegie Hall, became their manager. He then promoted the Beatles at Shea Stadium on 15 August 1965 and placed the slogan 'The Rascals Are Coming' on the stadium scoreboard. A furious Brian Epstein, the Beatles' manager, made him take it off.

The group's second single 'Good Lovin'' topped the American charts. They had further hits but disbanded in 1972.

Ringo invited Felix to join the All-Starrs for their official 1995 world tour, on keyboards. He performed his hits such as 'Groovin'' and 'Good Lovin'', in addition to numbers by other artists. He was to comment, 'I'm very fortunate that I'm still able to be involved in music. I've been very lucky over the years and I had a dream come true working with Ringo.'

Caveman

Ringo's largest film role was a starring one in this 'prehistoric comedy'.

Producer Lawrence Turman first thought of the idea for the film in 1977. He and his partner David Foster approached United Artists, who gave the project the thumbs up. Screenwriter Carl Gottlieb collaborated on the script with Rudy De Luca and was then appointed director.

An international cast was assembled starring Ringo and Barbara Bach. Ringo commented, 'It's right that people forget that since the break-up ten years ago I have had a very good career on my own, and not only as a recording artist. As an actor, people only really think about *Help!* and *A Hard Day's Night*. I've never really starred in a movie before. I've just done parts ... and as for lessons in acting, I think I have had the best lessons by working with the best craftsmen, like Peter Sellers and Richard Burton – people like that. Practical experience is a thousand times better than any class. They all taught me a hell of a lot.'

Filming began in February 1980 and the film was released in 1981.

The basic story concerns Atouk (Ringo) who, because of his lust for the tribal chief's woman Lana (Barbara Bach), goes out into the world, learns to stand upright, tames dinosaurs, becomes leader of his own tribe, discovers fire, returns to fight and defeat the gigantic tribal chief Tonda (John Matuszak) and finally wins his heart's desire. What does he do next? Holding the tanned body of his potential mate, her skin covered only by the briefest of animal skins, he suddenly tosses her over a boulder into a gigantic heap of dinosaur dung!

Caveman is played for laughs, tosses any attempt at historical accuracy out of the window, pokes gentle fun at *One Million Years BC* and *2001: A Space Odyssey* and is set one zillion years ago!

As Lana, Barbara Bach looks rather like Raquel Welch in *One Million Years BC*. Ringo, however, is nothing like John Richardson's macho Tumak of that film. Initially, we see him scrabbling for berries and being tossed out of the way each time he spots any by the other burly tribesmen. Since the cave people are shown walking with a stoop, Ringo at times reminds the viewer of Groucho Marx. Fortunately – in a spoof on *2001: A Space Odyssey* – Ringo and his best friend Lar (Dennis Quaid) discover how to straighten each other's backs. Now, with the confidence befitting *Homo erectus*, they spend time conveying the information to everyone else. Eventually, with much snapping and cracking of bones, the cast are able to walk upright.

There is little dialogue, apart from that of a Chinese caveman who creates English words. A special fifteen-word language was created for the film – and the following words are repeated throughout, with many gestures and some help from the soundtrack. The characters seem to relish the opportunity of indulging in belches, grunts and groans and other, rather more indiscreet anatomical noises!

The language consists of:

Aieee: Help, save me
Aloonda: Love, to love, affection, desire, goodness
Bo-bo: Man, friend, human, one-of-us
Ca-ca: Excrement, dung
Fech: Bad, no good, ugly
Gwee: To go, go on, go.
Haraka: Fire, burning thing
Kuda: Come here, where we are now, to come, this way, right here
Ma: Me, I, myself
Macha: Wild animal, beast, nonhuman creature
Nya: No, none, not happening, negative
Ool: Food, edible stuff
Pooka: Hurt, injured, messed up, no good
Whup: Stop, whoa, hold it
Zug-zug: Sexual intercourse, doing it, lustful expression

The role proved ideal for Ringo, who commented, 'I'm a very visual person, so for me, *Caveman* is a great piece. It's more than dialogue, and it's far more creative to me to transmit all those feelings.' And transmit them he does; with rolling eyes and a cheeky grin, Ringo gives full rein to the Chaplinesque qualities many observers spotted in his performance in *A Hard Day's Night*.

Caveman was filmed in Mexico and its locations are spectacular: huge, exotically shaped boulders and 'prehistoric-looking' mountains.

The dinosaurs are the cutest you've ever seen, with a tyrannosaurus rex looking so comical, even when pursuing humans in search of his dinner. The most fearsome-looking creature is an abominable snowman who attacks the tribe when they stray into a nearby ice age, but even he is reduced to tears by the frustration of trying to get the better of Ringo.

The secret of the film, of course, is that the underdog triumphs. From the moment we see our pale and weedy hero being pushed around by brawny musclemen, the audience is on his side, and he continues to overcome every obstacle, more by luck than judgement.

The film's one false note is Ringo's inexplicable obsession with the stunning Lana, at the expense of the little blonde in the cave next door, Tala (Shelley Long), who stands by our intrepid caveman through thick and thin. Lana is just concerned with backing whoever is chief in order to get first pick of the dinosaur meat!

Century 21

The company that sponsored Ringo's 2000 All-Starr tour. Ringo filmed a TV spot for the firm which was premiered on NBC's *Today* show on 15 May. The company also set up a press conference at the Plaza Hotel, New York on 1 May to promote the tour and their own website.

Century 21 gave Ringo a laptop computer and he was asked if he used the Internet and email. He said, 'I've sent three emails in my life. And my wife Barbara typed two of them. Not being that type, I'm waiting for the real talky box because I can really talk but I can't type.'

When asked about musicians going on the road in their fifties and sixties, Ringo said, 'Well, we're pleased we're still alive. And we're blessed that people would like to come and see us. And it's a privilege to be able to get to know each other again and we have to rehearse. They're long days, we do seven or eight hours of rehearsal. But it takes that, in my case, so that I'm really comfortable when we do the show. 'Cause I don't think people should pay money to come and see us rehearse.'

On the forthcoming *Beatles Anthology* book he commented, 'It's very big. Big book. I can tell you that it's really a very nice piece, I've seen the mock-ups, I've read my part in it, and I spoke to people who've actually been involved in reading it all and other people now getting involved who have to read it, and it just seems really interesting. They're excited. There's a lot of stuff in there that they didn't know. So I think it's going to be a worthwhile piece of stuff, because it's mainly from our lips, not other people's.

Christmas Dance, The

An original Christmas number penned especially for Ringo's 1999 Christmas album *I Wanna Be Santa Claus*. It was composed by Starkey/Hudson/Jim Cox/Steve Dudas. Ringo provides lead vocals, drums and percussion, with Jim Cox on bass, string and horn arrangements, Mark Hudson on acoustic guitar, electric guitar and backing vocals, Steve Dudas on acoustic guitar and electric guitar, Dan Higgins on saxophone and Gary Burr on backing vocals. It tells of a very shy guy who eventually plucks up the courage to ask a girl for a dance, and is 4 minutes and 13 seconds in length.

Christmas Eve
An original Christmas number penned especially for Ringo's 1999 Christmas album *I Wanna Be Santa Claus*. It was composed by Starkey and Hudson. Ringo is on lead vocals, drums and percussion, Armand Sabal-Lecco on bass, Mark Hudson on acoustic guitar, electric guitar and backing vocals, Jim Cox on piano and string arrangement and Gary Burr on backing vocals. It is 4 minutes and 26 seconds in length, and is the story of a man whose girlfriend has walked out on him the day before Christmas.

Christmas Time Is Here Again
This was originally a number that the Beatles included on their 1967 Christmas message record to fans. Ringo and his band added their own voices and instruments to the number, bringing it to a length of just over four minutes on Ringo's 1999 album *I Wanna Be Santa Claus*. It was written by Lennon/McCartney/Harrison/Starr.

Ringo is on lead vocals, drums, percussion and bellows, with Mark Hudson on acoustic guitar, percussion and backing vocals, Steve Dudas on acoustic guitar and electric guitar, Jim Cox on accordion and keyboards, Matt Hurwitz on acoustic guitar, Bob Murphy, Ian Holliday, Roger Houth and Willie Cochrane on bagpipes; Joe Perry provides the guitar solo and John Tila, Gary Burr, Sarah Hudson, Bill Hudson, Steffan Fantini, Marc Fantini, Kiley Oliver, Tess Whitehart and Dick Monda provide backing vocals. It is 4 minutes and 6 seconds in length.

Chronology

1940
7 July. Richard Starkey born at 9 Madryn Street, Liverpool 8.

1960
11 March. The Beatles and Rory Storm and the Hurricanes, Ringo's band, appear together on the bill of 'An All Night Rock And Roll Ball' at Aintree Institute, Liverpool.
16 October. A recording takes place at the Akustic Studio in Hamburg when Ringo joins John, George and Paul to record together for the first time, backing singer Lu Walters from Rory Storm and the Hurricanes.

1961

18 August. Ringo plays on stage with the Beatles for the first time at the Cavern. He recalled, 'One day Pete Best went sick. A car came for me and the driver asked if I would play drums for the Beatles at a lunchtime session down at the Cavern. What a laugh it turned out to be. We knew all the same numbers, but we did them differently. I didn't fit in at all well at first.'

1962

5 February. When Beatles drummer Pete Best is ill again, Ringo deputises for him at the Cavern and the Kingsway Club, Southport.

18 August. Ringo makes his debut as a Beatle at the Horticultural Society Dance at Hulme Hall, Port Sunlight, following a two-hour rehearsal together prior to the gig.

19 August. Ringo makes his debut as a member of the Beatles at the Cavern and Pete Best fan Bruno gives George Harrison a black eye.

11 September. At the EMI recording session Ringo is asked to play tambourine and maracas while session drummer Andy White works with the Beatles. He thinks, 'Are they doing a Pete Best on me?'

1963

16 September. Ringo and Maureen leave for a holiday in Greece with Paul and Jane Asher. He says, 'I did a lot of swimming during the day while Paul had a bash at water-skiing. During the evenings we used to join in with the local Greek group called the Trio Athena because they didn't play pop stuff – not until we turned up at any rate. Now they'll have a go at the top ten!'

2 October. Ringo and Maureen and Paul and Jane return to London.

3 October. Ringo drives to Southend, Essex, to see the Everly Brothers, Bo Diddley and the Rolling Stones at the local Odeon cinema.

23 October. The Beatles record Ringo's track 'I Wanna Be Your Man'.

28 November. Ringo has to interrupt rehearsals at the ABC Cinema, Lincoln, due to earache.

1964

3 June. Ringo is rushed to hospital just prior to the Beatles tour.

4 June. Jimmy Nicol is brought in as a substitute for Ringo.

13 June. Ringo and Brian Epstein leave London for Australia.

15 June. Jimmy Nicol leaves for London as Ringo rejoins the Beatles at Melbourne Festival Hall.

25 July. Ringo records his appearance on *Juke Box Jury* for screening the following week.

31 July. 'Ringo's Theme (This Boy)' c/w 'And I Love Her' by the George Martin Orchestra, is issued in the US by United Artists on UA743.

1 August. Ringo appears on *Juke Box Jury*.

7 August. George Martin's single 'Ringo's Theme' is issued in Britain on Parlophone R 5166.

27 September. Ringo is one of the judges of the Oxfam Beat Contest at the Prince of Wales Theatre, London, along with Cilla Black, Brian Epstein, Alan Freeman, journalist Betty Hale and Billy Hatton of the Fourmost.

30 November. The novelty disc 'Ringo's Dog' by Jack Dorsey is issued in Britain on Pye N 15730.

1 December. Ringo is admitted to University College Hospital where his tonsils are removed.

9 December. Paul McCartney visits Ringo in hospital.

10 December. Ringo leaves University College Hospital.

1965

3 February. Ringo and Maureen have lunch with Paul Getty in London.

11 February. Ringo and Maureen are married. John and George attend, but Paul is away on holiday in Africa.

7 April. Ringo and Maureen announce that they are expecting their first child.

2 June. Ringo, John and George attend the premiere of Dick Lester's film *The Knack* at the London Pavilion.

13 September. Ringo and Maureen's first child, a son named Zak (the name Lee had already been chosen if the baby had been a girl), is born at Queen Charlotte's Hospital, London. As news had been announced that John Lennon was going to send his son Julian to a private school, Ringo says, 'A state school was good enough for me, so it'll be good enough for Zak.'

7 October. Pete Best instigates a lawsuit against Ringo for alleged libellous remarks that Ringo had made in a *Playboy* magazine interview.

1966

12 January. Ringo and Maureen and John and Cynthia fly to Trinidad for a ten-day Caribbean holiday.

23 January. Ringo and Maureen and John and Cynthia return from their holiday.

4 October. Ringo and Maureen travel to Spain to visit John, who is filming *How I Won The War*.

31 October. Rumours appear in the media that Ringo is to be offered a part in the next James Bond film.

7 November. Ringo and Brian Epstein greet the Four Tops at Heathrow Airport.

8 November. Ringo denies rumours that the Beatles have broken up.

20 November. Ringo visits his relatives in Liverpool.

22 December. Ringo and George are interviewed for the *New Musical Express* by Andy Gray.

24 December. Ringo arrives in Liverpool for a family Christmas.

1967

19 February. Ringo and John attend the Chuck Berry show at the Savile Theatre.

19 April. Ringo, John, Paul and George sign an agreement as 'The Beatles & co.'

23 April. It is announced that Ringo and Maureen are expecting a baby in August.

19 August. Ringo and Maureen's second son, Jason, is born at Queen Charlotte's Hospital in London.

3 December. Ringo leaves London for Italy to appear in the film *Candy*.

17 December. Ringo returns to London after completing his role in *Candy* in Rome.

1968

8 February. Ringo appears live on the television show *Cilla* with Brian Epstein stablemate Cilla Black, with whom he sings and performs some comedy sketches.

19 February. Ringo and Maureen and Paul McCartney and Jane Asher leave to join the Maharishi Mahesh Yogi's ashram in India.

1 March. Ringo and Maureen leave Rishikesh in India.

13 March. Ringo is interviewed by the *New Musical Express*.

17 March. Ringo visits members of his family in Liverpool.

22 March. The interview with Ringo is published in the *New Musical Express*.

1 April. Ringo and Maureen attend a business meeting at Apple.

18 April. Ringo and John Lennon are at the Revolution Club in Bruton Place, London, to attend a launch for the UK branch of Bell Records.

28 April. Ringo and John attend the West End musical *Charlie Girl*, in which Gerry Marsden, former leader of Gerry and the Pacemakers, appears.

9 May. Ringo has a meeting at the Apple offices with John to discuss the projected Apple School.

17 May. Ringo and Maureen and George and Patti attend the premiere of the film *Wonderwall*.

7 June. Ringo and Maureen and George and Patti fly to California.

8 June. Ringo and George visit Joan Baez in Carmel, California.

9 June. Ringo and George play golf in Monterey.

12 June. Ringo and George arrive in Los Angeles.

13 June. Ringo and George jam with Peter Tork of the Monkees, David Crosby of the Byrds and Peter Asher in Los Angeles.

16 June. Ringo and George arrive in New York. In the evening Ringo and Maureen attend a Jimi Hendrix club show.

22 August. During a recording session at Abbey Road, Ringo announces that he is quitting the Beatles. He returns on 5 September.

19 November. Ringo and family move home from Weybridge to Elstead.

3 December. Ringo and Maureen, along with Geoffrey Ellis, managing director of NEMS, and Mal Evans fly to Italy for the premiere of *Candy*. In the evening they visit the Titan and Piper clubs in Rome.

17 December. *Candy* is released in America, where the critics pan it.

1969

20 February. *Candy* is released in Britain.

28 February. The case against Ringo by Brymon Estates is settled out of court and Ringo sells his Montague Square leasehold.

23 March. Ringo flies to New York for location filming for *The Magic Christian*.

27 March. Ringo tells the media that the Beatles will never perform live in public again.

2 May. Ringo finishes filming *The Magic Christian*.

29 May. Ringo returns from America.

4 July. Ringo and Maureen deputise for John and Yoko, who have been involved in a motoring accident during a trip to Scotland, at the press reception for the Plastic Ono Band's 'Give Peace A Chance' at Chelsea Town Hall.

7 July. Ringo, George and Paul record 'Here Comes The Sun' at Abbey Road on Ringo's 29th birthday.

3 August. Ringo and Maureen and Mal and Lil Evans attend the Hank Snow concert at the London Palladium.

1 September. Ringo and John Lennon return from Dylan's Isle of Wight concert

8 September. Ringo is admitted to the Middlesex Hospital with a stomach complaint.

5 October. Yorkshire Television invites Ringo, the Hollies and Peter Sellers to appear in a George Martin television special at Christmas.

18 October. Ringo and Maureen, together with Paul and Linda, attend the opening night of Mary Hopkin's cabaret season at the Savoy Hotel, London.

27 October. Ringo begins recording his first solo album at Abbey Road.

2 November. There are reports in the press that Ringo is making a second album and may also be appearing in Elvis Presley's next television special.

8 December. Ringo re-records 'With A Little Help From My Friends' for a George Martin television special.

10 December. Ringo appears on the BBC2 programme *Late Night Line-up*.

11 December. *The Magic Christian* receives its British premiere.

14 December. Ringo records his appearance for the George Martin special at Yorkshire television studios.

24 December. Ringo's appearance as a guest on the George Martin television special 'With A Little Help From My Friends' is screened. He performs 'Octopus's Garden' backed by the George Martin Orchestra.

1970

11 January. An announcement is made that Ringo will be appearing on NBC TV's *Rowan And Martin's Laugh-In*.

29 January. Ringo and Maureen attend the American premiere of *The Magic Christian*.

23 February. Ringo's appearance on *Rowan And Martin's Laugh-In* is broadcast.

5 March. The *New Musical Express* interviews Ringo and George.

8 March. The recording of 'It Don't Come Easy' is completed at Trident Studios in London.

27 March. Ringo's *Sentimental Journey* album is released in Britain.

29 March. Ringo appears on the *The David Frost Show* and performs 'Sentimental Journey', backed by the George Martin Orchestra.

1 April. Ringo overdubs his drum parts of 'Across The Universe'/'The Long And Winding Road'/'I Me Mine', becoming the last Beatle to play at a Beatles recording session at Abbey Road.

5 April. Ringo appears on Radio One's *Scene And Heard*.

10 April. The front-page story in the *Daily Mirror* reads 'Paul Is Quitting The Beatles'. Ringo says, 'This is all news to me.'

24 April. Ringo's *Sentimental Journey* album is released in America.

9 May. Ringo and Maureen are guests of honour at the screening of *Woodstock* at the Cannes Film Festival.

17 May. Ringo's promo of 'Sentimental Journey' is shown on *The Ed Sullivan Show* in America.

22 May. Clips of Ringo and Maureen at the Cannes Film Festival are show on London Weekend Television's *Aquarius* programme.

21 June. There is an announcement that Ringo will star in his own American TV series.

29 June. Ringo leaves for Nashville to record a new album.

30 June. Ringo begins recording at Music City Records studio in Nashville.

1 July. Ringo completes his two-day recording session in Nashville for *Beaucoups Of Blues*.

7 July. Sadly, on Ringo's birthday, George Harrison's mother dies.

17 September. Ringo attends a Mike Nesmith concert at the Nashville Rooms in London.

25 September. Ringo's album *Beaucoups Of Blues* is released in Britain.

28 September. Ringo's album *Beaucoups Of Blues* is released in America.

1 October. Ringo records an appearance on the BBC1 show *Cilla*, duetting with Cilla Black and also singing 'Act Naturally'. (The show is not transmitted until 13 February 1971.)

5 October. The single 'Beaucoups Of Blues' c/w 'Coochy-Coochy' is released in America on Apple 2969.

18 October. Apple announces that they will be issuing a second album of Ringo's Nashville recordings.

1 November. Ringo films more clips for Cilla Black's TV show.

11 November. Ringo and Maureen's daughter Lee Parkin is born at Queen Charlotte's Hospital, Hammersmith, London.

31 December. Ringo holds a New Year's Eve party at Ronnie Scott's club in London. There is a jam session with Ringo and Charlie Watts sharing drums, Klaus Voormann and Maurice Gibb sharing bass, Eric Clapton on guitar, Bobby Keys on sax and Georgie Fame on organ.

1971

25 January. Ringo begins five days of rehearsals for his appearance as Larry the Dwarf in Frank Zappa's *200 Motels* at Pinewood Studios in Iver, Buckinghamshire.

1 February. Ringo begins filming *200 Motels* at Pinewood Studios; the film is described as 'an account of what it is like to be a pop musician on the road in 1971'.

8 February. Ringo and Maureen holiday in Switzerland.

13 February. Ringo's guest appearance on the show *Cilla* is screened.

19 February. A two-minute clip of Ringo's appearance on *Cilla* is screened on BBC1's *Ask Aspel*.

23 February. Ringo's affidavit regarding Paul's case to end the Beatles' partnership is read out in court.

15 March. Ringo and George meet to discuss the legal battle with Paul.

9 April. 'It Don't Come Easy', produced by George Harrison c/w 'Early 1970' is released in Britain. George also played guitar on the A side.

16 April. Ringo's single 'It Don't Come Easy' c/w 'Early 1970' is issued in America.

22 April. The Apple promotional film of 'It Don't Come Easy' is shown on *Top Of The Pops*.

27 April. Ringo is in Norway making a second promotional clip for 'It Don't Come Easy'. Produced by Michael Hurll, it shows Ringo singing at a piano in the snow and clips of him skiing and riding a skimobile.

29 April. Ringo's Norway promo is shown on *Top Of The Pops*.

5 May. A kinetic sculpture designed by Ringo and Robin Cruikshank goes on sale in Zatach in Sloane Square, London. It is a mercury-filled object with zigzagging discs powered by a small motor that sits in the opaque light box underneath, all housed in a transparent Perspex case. It retails for £60.

12 May. Ringo and Maureen and Paul and Linda charter a plane to St Tropez in the south of France to attend the wedding of Mick Jagger to Bianca.

13 May. Ringo and Maureen are joined by George and Patti and Cilla Black on the yacht *Marala* in the south of France.

27 May. It is announced that Ringo will be starring in a spaghetti western called *Blindman*. He comments, 'I want to be, like, in this film, a crazy cowboy or whatever part I get. We're talking about me being an actor now, not being used for the name like I have been. In this film I really feel as if I'm acting.'

8 June. Ringo is in London recording with guitar legend B.B. King.

17 June. Ringo begins filming *Blindman*.

24 June. Ringo is in Scandinavia filming his third television appearance with Cilla Black for the special 'Cilla In Scandinavia'.

11 July. Ringo gives a lengthy three-part interview to *Melody Maker* during a break in the filming of *Blindman*. (The interview is published on 31 July, 7 and 14 August.)

3 September. Ringo and Robin Cruikshank officially launch their design company Ringo Or Robin Limited.

14 September. A two-week exhibition of Ringo and Robin Cruikshank's furniture opens at Liberty's store in London.

8 October. Ringo contributes an avant-garde work in a plastic bag to be exhibited at Yoko Ono's 'This Is Not Here' exhibition at the Everson Museum of Art in Syracuse, New York.

9 October. Ringo is a guest at John Lennon's 31st birthday party at the Hotel Syracuse in Syracuse, New York.

10 November. The film *200 Motels* opens in New York.

27 November. BBC screens the TV special 'Cilla In Scandinavia' in which Ringo is a guest.

16 December. The film *200 Motels* opens at the Classic Cinema, Piccadilly Circus, London.

1972

28 January. Ringo films a one-minute sketch with Lulu and Michael Palin for *Monty Python's Flying Circus*. It's a nonspeaking role in an episode that is first screened in October by BBC2.

27 February. Ringo and Maureen attend the two-day 40th birthday party for Elizabeth Taylor at the Intercontinental Hotel in Budapest. Other guests include Princess Grace of Monaco and Frankie Howerd.

17 March. Ringo's single 'Back Off Boogaloo', produced by George Harrison, is released in Britain.

18 March. Ringo films the two Marc Bolan concerts at the Empire Pool, Wembley, for his projected film *Born To Boogie*.

20 March. While at John Lennon's Tittenhurst Park mansion Ringo films a promo for 'Back Off Boogaloo'. It is filmed by Caravel Films and features Ringo wandering around the grounds looking for the Frankenstein monster he's created. 'Back Off Boogaloo' is released in America.

21 March. Ringo films additional material for *Born To Boogie*.

22 March. Ringo films the Mad Hatter's tea-party sequence at Tittenhurst Park for the *Born To Boogie* movie.

22 April. Ringo and Maureen attend Jerry Lee Lewis's concert at the London Palladium.

15 August. A concert is filmed at Surrey Docks for Ringo's film *Count Downe*. The musicians are Ringo, Harry Nilsson, Keith

Moon, Peter Frampton, Klaus Voorman, Rikki Farr, Bobby Keyes and Jim Price – an outfit called the Count Downes. John Bonham replaced Moon on the second day as Keith had rejoined the Who on their European tour.

16 August. The second and final day of the filming of the Surrey Docks concert.

3 September. Ringo appears as a guest on the 'Jerry Lewis Muscular Dystrophy Telethon'.

9 September. An interview with Ringo conducted by Ray Connolly appears in the *Evening Standard*.

12 September. The *Daily Mirror* publishes a report on the filming of Ringo's film *Count Downe*.

30 September. Rory Storm, leader of Ringo's former group Rory Storm and the Hurricanes, is found dead at his home in Liverpool. Later, when asked why he didn't attend Rory's funeral, Ringo said, 'I wasn't at his birth, either.'

23 October. Ringo is at Butlin's holiday camp on the Isle of Wight to begin filming the seven-week shoot of *That'll Be The Day*. The film is completed on 4 December.

26 October. The *Monty Python Flying Circus* episode, which features a brief sketch with Ringo and Lulu, is screened by BBC2.

24 November. The album *Tommy*, featuring two tracks by Ringo, is released in Britain.

25 November. An interview with Ringo from the set of *That'll Be The Day* is featured in the magazine *Cinema & TV Today*.

27 November. The *Tommy* album, with Ringo's contribution as Uncle Ernie, is issued in America.

2 December. Ringo and Maureen attend the premiere of *Alice In Wonderland* at the Odeon, Marble Arch. Her Majesty the Queen is also in attendance. Ringo and Maureen go to the post-premiere party at the Inn On The Park.

12 December. Ringo promotes his *Born To Boogie* film live on the children's TV show *Magpie*.

13 December. The press screening of *Born To Boogie* takes place at the Oscar One Cinema in London.

14 December. The premiere of *Born To Boogie* takes place at the Oscar One Cinema in Brewer Street, London, with Ringo and Maureen, Marc Bolan, Mickey Finn and Elton John in attendance.

25 December. Dressed as Father Christmas and arriving in a sleigh pulled by reindeers, Keith Moon arrives at Tittenhurst Park to surprise Ringo and Maureen.

1973

1 January. The *Liverpool Echo* publishes an interview with Ringo conducted by Rex Reed in which Ringo discusses his *Son Of Dracula* film.

3 January. *Daily Express* reporter David Wigg interviews Ringo for the Radio One programme *Scene And Heard*. The interview is broadcast on 6 January.

6 January. The David Wigg interview with Ringo is transmitted on *Scene And Heard* and is later included on the 1976 Polydor album *The Beatles Tapes*.

13 January. Ringo and George Harrison attend the Eric Clapton concert at the Rainbow Theatre, London.

5 March. Ringo begins recording his *Ringo* album at Sunset Sound Recorders Studio in Los Angeles.

10 March. George Harrison turns up at the Sunset Sound Recorders Studio to see Ringo and hear some of the recordings Ringo has completed. In the evening Ringo records an anti-drug commercial, which is to be issued to US radio stations by the National Association of Progressive Radio Announcers.

12 March. George returns to Sunset Sound Recorders Studio to provide some backing vocals for Ringo.

13 March. In addition to George, John and Yoko turn up at Sunset Sound Recorders Studio and Ringo, John and George perform together on John Lennon's number 'I'm The Greatest'.

17 March. Due to the recording session on 13 March, rumours circulate in the papers about a Beatles reunion. *Melody Maker* reports: 'Rumours flashed through Los Angeles this week that three of the Beatles have teamed up for recording purposes. John Lennon, George Harrison and Ringo Starr are all in Los Angeles with Klaus Voormann, the bassist rumoured to replace Paul McCartney after his departure from the group.'

28 March. Ringo and his record producer Richard Perry fly in to London to continue work on the *Ringo* album.

29 March. Ringo videotapes his appearance for London Weekend Television's *The Russell Harty Show*, to be broadcast on 31 March.

12 April. *That'll Be The Day* receives its world premiere at the ABC2 cinema in London. Ringo and Paul McCartney are in attendance.

15 April. *Born To Boogie* goes on general release in Britain.

16 April. Paul and Linda join Ringo at Abbey Road Studios to record the track 'Six O'Clock' for the *Ringo* album.

13 May. *That'll Be The Day* goes on general release in Britain.

3 July. Ringo attends the last performance of David Bowie's *Ziggy Stardust And The Spiders From Mars* at the Odeon, Hammersmith.

24 July. Ringo oversees the mixing of his *Ringo* album at Sunset Sound Recorders Studio in Los Angeles.

26 July. Ringo forms a music publishing company – Wobble Music Ltd.

18 September. Ringo buys Tittenhurst Park.

24 September. Ringo's single 'Photograph' c/w 'Down And Out' is released in America. The number was co-written with George Harrison, who also co-produced it.

19 October. 'Photograph' c/w 'Down And Out' is released in Britain.

22 October. The Press reports that Ringo has teamed up with Liverpool comedian Arthur Askey and Cilla Black in a consortium to obtain a radio licence in Liverpool.

2 November. The album *Ringo* is released in America, where it is to reach No. 2 in the charts.

8 November. Ringo's album *Ringo* is awarded Gold Disc status in America.

9 November. The album *Ringo* is released in Britain, where it is to reach No. 7 in the charts.

24 November. Ringo's single 'Photograph' tops the American charts.

3 December. Ringo's single 'You're Sixteen' c/w 'Devil Woman' is released in America.

9 December. Ringo's album *Ringo* is awarded a Gold Disc.

27 December. *Blindman*, the spaghetti western in which Ringo appears, receives its British premiere at the Astoria Cinema in Charing Cross Road, London.

28 December. Ringo's single 'Photograph' attains Gold Disc status in America.

1974

1 January. Ringo announces that he has turned down a role in *Stardust*, the sequel to *That'll Be The Day*.

26 January. Ringo's single 'You're Sixteen' tops the American charts.

6 February. Ringo records an interview with Brian Matthew for the Radio One programme *My Top Twelve*. His favourite records include 'Strange Brew' by Cream, 'You Are The Sunshine Of My Life' by Stevie Wonder, 'Heartbreak Hotel' by Elvis Presley, 'Something Else' by Eddie Cochran and 'Everything I Do Has To Be Funkin'' by Leo Dorsey.

8 February. Ringo's single 'You're Sixteen' is released in Britain.

18 February. Ringo's single 'Oh My My' c/w 'Step Lightly' is issued in America.

23 February. Ringo and Harry Nilsson are spotted together in Macon, Georgia, where they are about to cut an album.

20 March. George Harrison denies rumours that he will be touring American with Ringo.

22 March. Renting a house in Santa Monica for the recording of Harry Nilsson's *Pussy Cats* album, John Lennon is joined there over the next fortnight by Ringo and his manager Hilary Gerrard, Keith Moon, Harry Nilsson and Klaus Voormann.

28 March. Ringo plays drums on the first day of the recording of Nilsson's *Pussy Cats* album. Discussing the recording, John Lennon says, 'The main thing was we had a lot of fun. There was Keith Moon, Harry, Ringo and me all living together in the house and we had some moments.'

29 March. Further recordings of the *Pussy Cats* album take place at Burbank Studios.

31 March. While Ringo, Keith Moon and Harry Nilsson are clubbing it in Los Angeles, a jam session takes place at the beach house in Santa Monica with John Lennon on guitar and Paul McCartney on drums. The same day it is announced that the London Playboy Club has banned Ringo and Moon because they had caused damage in the club amounting to £30.

1 April. When Ringo returns to the beach house with Moon and Nilsson he notices someone has used his kit and asks, 'Who's been fiddling with my drums?' He's told that Paul McCartney has been there. In the meantime, the *Son Of Dracula* soundtrack is released in America.

2 April. Ringo, Nilsson and Moon turn up at the beach house again.

3 April. Further sessions for *Pussy Cats* take place at Burbank Studios.

7 April. Ringo's appearance on Radio One's *My Top Twelve* is broadcast.

14 April. Controversy is aroused and radio staff are sacked when Ringo appears on radio station KROQ and uses bad language.

19 April. Ringo and Keith Moon attend the premiere of *Son Of Dracula* in Atlanta, Georgia.

20 April. Ringo meets Paul, John and George at the Beverly Wilshire Hotel in Los Angeles for a meeting.

24 May. The *Son Of Dracula* soundtrack is released in Britain.

28 June. John Lennon records a demo disc of 'Goodnight Vienna' for Ringo. Ringo forms another company, Reckongrade Ltd.

19 August. *Pussy Cats*, the Nilsson album produced by John Lennon and featuring Ringo Starr and Keith Moon on drums, is issued in America.

24 August. John Lennon supervises Ringo's recordings of 'Goodnight Vienna' and 'Only You'.

30 August. *Pussy Cats* is released in Britain by RCA.

17 September. Ringo announces in Los Angeles that he will be campaigning against young people taking drugs.

5 November. Eric Clapton and Patti Harrison are among Ringo's guests when he hosts a Bonfire Night celebration at his Tittenhurst Park mansion.

11 November. 'Only You (And You Alone)' c/w 'Call Me', Ringo's latest single, is issued in America.

15 November. Ringo's album *Goodnight Vienna* and his single 'Only You (and You Alone)' c/w 'Call Me', are issued in Britain.

23 November. An interview with Ringo appears in *Melody Maker*. He is asked if the Beatles will ever get back together and states that they couldn't because George would never play with Paul again.

11 December. Ringo changes the name of one of his companies and Reckongrade Ltd becomes Pyramid Records Ltd.

19 December. The promo film for 'Only You' is premiered on *Top Of The Pops*.

31 December. Ringo hosts a New Year party at Tittenhurst Park. His guests include Eric and Patti Harrison.

1975

27 January. Ringo's single 'No No Song' c/w 'Snookeroo' is issued in America.

3 February. Ringo begins filming *Lisztomania* at Shepperton Studios in Middlesex. He appears in the role of the Pope.

7 February. Ringo and his girlfriend Nancy Andrews leave London for California.

21 February. Ringo's single 'Snookeroo' c/w 'Oo Wee' is released in Britain.

29 March. Ringo attends the premiere of the Who's rock opera *Tommy* at the Leicester Square Theatre, London. After the screening he joins the after-show party at the Inn On The Park.

4 April. Ringo forms his new record label Ring O' Records, a name suggested by John Lennon. He embarks on a series of interviews to promote it.

5 April. The 'No No Song' reaches its highest position in the American charts – at No. 3.

12 April. An interview with Ringo, conducted by Steve Lake, appears in *Melody Maker*.

21 May. The ABC TV special 'David Frost Salutes The Beatles' is screened in America and among the clips is one of Ringo appearing in *That'll Be The Day*.

2 June. Ringo's latest American single release is a medley comprising 'It's All Down To Goodnight Vienna', 'Goodnight Vienna (Reprise)' and 'Oo Wee'.

21 June. Ringo is spotted backstage at the Wembley Stadium concert featuring the Beach Boys and Elton John.

7 July. The Rolling Stones are among the guests at Ringo's 35th birthday party at the Beverly Wilshire Hotel in Los Angeles. During the day Keith Moon had hired a plane to skywrite 'Happy Birthday Ringo' in the skies above the city.

17 July. In London Maureen is granted an uncontested divorce from Ringo on the grounds of adultery.

23 August. To celebrate their signing of Dr John (Mac Rebennack), United Artists hold an event at the Cherokee club in Los Angeles. Ringo and Eric Clapton join Dr John on stage.

10 October. *Lisztomania* is premiered in New York.

13 November. *Lisztomania* is premiered in London.

16 November. *That'll Be The Day* is re-released as a support to the sequel *Stardust*, which premieres in London.

17 November. The double bill of *That'll Be The Day* and *Stardust* goes on general release in Britain.

25 November. Ringo's compilation album *Blast From Your Past* is released in America.

12 December. *Blast From Your Past* becomes the last Ringo album to appear on the Apple label.

14 December. Ringo returns from his tax haven in Monte Carlo to attend Queen's concert at the Odeon, Hammersmith, London.

18 December. Ringo and Lynsey De Paul attend the Royal European Film Premiere of *The Man Who Would Be King* at the Odeon, Leicester Square, London.

1976

9 January. Ringo's single 'Oh My My' c/w 'No No Song' is released in Britain.

25 January. At the Houston Astrodome in Texas, Ringo appears on stage with Bob Dylan and the Band to partake in 'Night Of The Hurricane's 11', a benefit concert for convicted murderer Rubin 'Hurricane' Carter.

26 January. The Beatles' contract with EMI finally ends, allowing the different members to sign with other labels and for Ringo to sign with Atlantic.

10 March. Ringo signs with Atlantic Records for his North American releases and Polydor International for Britain.

9 May. Ringo and George are in the audience for the Wings concert at Maple Leaf Gardens, Toronto, Canada.

12 June. Ringo is recording his *Ringo's Rotogravure* album at Cherokee Recording Studios in Hollywood, where he is joined by John and Yoko. They record 'A Dose Of Rock 'N' Roll', with John on piano, and John's composition 'Cookin' (In The Kitchen Of Love)'.

19 June. Taking time off from the Wings tour, Paul and Linda McCartney join Ringo at the Cherokee Recording Studios in Los Angeles to record 'Pure Gold', a number penned by Paul for Ringo.

30 July. Ringo and George have attempted to prevent the release of Polydor's *The Beatles Tapes* albums, based on interviews conducted by David Wigg for the BBC *Scene And Heard* programme. They are unsuccessful and are denied a High Court injunction.

17 September. *Ringo's Rotogravure* is released in Britain. Ringo refuses to comment on a full-page advert, taken out in the *New York Herald Tribune* this day, requesting that the Beatles unite for a charity concert.

19 September. Ringo is in Copenhagen promoting his new album.

20 September. Ringo's single 'A Dose Of Rock 'N' Roll' c/w 'Cryin'' is released in America. As he is now a UK tax exile, Ringo has to do all his promotional interviews outside the country and holds his interview sessions at the George V Hotel in Paris. Among the interviews is one by Tony Prince of Capitol Radio and another by Radio Luxembourg.

23 September. Ringo holds further interviews for his new album at a press conference in Milan, Italy.

27 September. *Ringo's Rotogravure* is released in America and is to reach No. 28 in the charts.

1 October. The Capitol Radio interview with Ringo, conducted at the George V Hotel in Paris, is aired.

2 October. The first part of a Radio Luxembourg interview recorded at the George V Hotel in Paris is aired. *Melody Maker* also publish an interview with Ringo conducted at the George V Hotel by Ray Coleman.

4 October. Ringo is interviewed by the Dutch fanzine *Beatles Unlimited*.

5 October. Ringo is in Holland promoting his latest album. He appears for fifteen minutes live on *Voor De Vuist Weg*, an Avro NED2 programme, hosted by Williem Duys.

9 October. As a surprise for John Lennon's 36th birthday, Ringo sends Cherry Vanilla to the Dakota apartments to give John her own version of *Romeo And Juliet*.

10 October. The second part of the interview with Ringo is aired on Radio Luxembourg.

15 October. Ringo's single 'A Dose Of Rock 'N' Roll' c/w 'Cryin'' is released in Britain.

19 October. Ringo records 'I Can Hear You Calling' at the studios of Atlantic Records in New York.

22 November. Ringo's single 'Hey Baby' c/w 'Lady Gaye' is released in America.

24 November. The Band hold their farewell performance at the Winterland ballroom in San Francisco and Ringo appears with them on drums to perform 'I Shall Be Released'. The concert is filmed by United Artists who release it as the movie *The Last Waltz*.

29 November. Ringo's single 'Hey Baby' c/w 'Lady Gaye' is released in Britain.

1977

12 February. Ringo's version of the Bruce Channel 1962 hit 'Hey Baby' only reaches No. 74 in the American charts.

16 August. Ringo and Keith Moon film scenes for *The Kids Are Alright* at Moon's house on Victoria Point Road on Malibu Beach in California.

25 August. Ringo's single 'Wings' c/w 'Just A Dream' is released in America.

5 September. Ringo is interviewed by disc jockey Dave Herman in Los Angeles to promote his new single.

16 September. Ringo's single 'Drowning In A Sea Of Love' c/w 'Just A Dream' is released in Britain.

20 September. Ringo's album *Ringo The 4th* is released in Britain.

26 September. *Ringo The 4th* is released in America.

18 October. Ringo's single 'Drowning In A Sea Of Love' c/w 'Just A Dream' is released in America.

9 December. The Polydor album *Scouse The Mouse* is released in Britain, with Ringo as 'Scouse the mouse' performing eight of the seventeen tracks on the LP.

1978

11 February. Ringo begins filming his television special 'Ringo' for the next ten days in Hollywood.

18 April. Ringo's single 'Lipstick Traces' c/w 'Old Time Relovin'', is released in America.

21 April. Ringo's new album *Bad Boy* is released simultaneously in Britain and America. It will only reach No. 129 in the American charts.

26 April. The television special 'Ringo' is screened in America.

6 July. Ringo's single 'Heart On My Sleeve' c/w 'Who Needs A Heart' is released in America.

15 July. Ringo attends the Bob Dylan concert at the Aerodrome in Camberley, Surrey.

21 July. Ringo's single 'Tonight' c/w 'Old Time Relovin'' is issued in Britain. He also begins work on a 30-minute special in Monte Carlo to promote his latest album, but it is never completed.

22 July. Ringo and Nancy Andrews fly to Copenhagen where he records 'She's So In Love' and 'On The Rebound' at the Sweet Silence Studios.

23 July. Still at the Sweet Silence Studios, Ringo records 'One Way Love Affair' and 'As Far As We Can Go'.

6 October. Ringo appears on the American chat show *Everyday*.

1979

28 April. In Monte Carlo Ringo becomes ill with peritonitis and is taken to the Princess Grace Hospital for surgery.

14 May. The Who documentary film *The Kids Are Alright*, featuring a cameo appearance by Ringo, is premiered at the Cannes Film Festival.

19 May. Ringo is at Eric Clapton's Hurtwood Edge home to celebrate Clapton's marriage to George Harrison's ex-wife Patti and joins in a jam session with Paul McCartney, George Harrison, Mick Jagger, Lonnie Donegan, Ginger Baker, Denny Laine and Clapton.

29 May. Ringo visits John Lennon at the Dakota Building in New York.

8 June. During an appearance with Ronnie Wood on the American TV show *Midnight Special*, Ringo plays drums on Wood's track 'Buried Alive'.

3 September. Ringo is a guest on the American fundraising television show 'The Jerry Lewis Muscular Dystrophy Telethon'. He takes pledges on the phone and joins in a jam session of 'Money', 'Twist And Shout' and 'Jumpin' Jack Flash' with Bill Wyman, Kiki Dee, Todd Rundgren and Doug Kershaw.

4 September. Ringo is once again interviewed by disc jockey Dave Herman.

18 October. The show *Beatlemania* opens in London at the Astoria Theatre with Louis Colucci and Bobby Taylor taking the role of Ringo.

5 November. Ringo visits John Lennon at the Dakota building once again and John gives him a demo of the number 'Life Begins At 40', which he wants Ringo to record.

28 November. Ringo's home in Los Angeles is destroyed by fire, incinerating his precious collection of Beatles memorabilia.

1980

22 January. Ringo is asked to comment on the jailing in Japan of Paul McCartney due to drugs being found on him when he entered the country. Ringo says, 'It's the risk you take when you're involved with drugs. He's just been unlucky.'

10 February. In America Ringo is interviewed for a radio show by disc jockey Robert W. Morgan.

17 February. Ringo is strip-searched by customs as he enters Mexico to film *Caveman*.

18 February. Ringo begins filming *Caveman* at Churubusco Studios in Mexico.

25 March. Filming ends of *Caveman*.

31 March. A photograph of Ringo in his *Caveman* outfit appears in the *Daily Mirror*.

8 May. Ringo and Barbara Bach refuse to discuss their romance with *Daily Mirror* reporters in England.

19 May. Following a party in London, Ringo and Barbara are involved in a road accident when the Mercedes car they are driving in crashes. They are taken to St Mary's Hospital, then spend the night at the Dorchester Hotel.

11 June. Ringo announces that he and Barbara are to be married.

4 July. Ringo and Barbara fly to London where he confirms with reporters that they will soon be married.

9 July. Ringo and Barbara travel to France where Ringo will be recording his new album.

27 July. Following a short holiday in France after the album sessions, Ringo and Barbara fly to Los Angeles.

28 July. Ringo and Barbara appear on the American television programme *The John Davidson Show*.

11 August. Ringo continues recording for the *Can't Fight Lightning* album (later to undergo a name change to *Stop And Smell The Roses*) at the Devonshire sound studio in Hollywood.

4 September. Ringo enters Cherokee Studios in Los Angeles to continue recording for his album.

23 September. Ronnie Wood of the Rolling Stones joins Ringo at Cherokee Studios to appear on an early version of 'Dead Giveaway'.

25 September. Ringo and Ronnie Wood record the track 'Brandy' at Cherokee Studios.

27 September. Ringo records at Cherokee Studios once again.

6 November. Accompanied by Ronnie Wood, Ringo records a demo of 'I Don't Believe You' at Cherokee Studios.

10 November. On his return to Tittenhurst Park, Ringo phones up George and asks him to appear on his next album.

19 November. Ringo joins George Harrison for a recording session at George's Friar Park Studio.

30 November. Ringo, along with Harry Nilsson and engineer Paul Jarvis, listen to the session tapes for the *Can't Fight Lightning* album at Compass Point Studios in Hollywood.

1 December. Ringo records the vocals on the 'Can't Fight Lightning' track at Compass Point Studios.

2 December. Ringo and engineer Paul Jarvis begin the mixing for his forthcoming album at Compass Point Studios.

3 December. Ringo and Jarvis continue mixing the tracks for the new album.

4 December. Ringo records his vocals for the new version of 'Back Off Boogaloo'.

5 December. Ringo completes his album sessions and flies to the Bahamas to join Barbara.

8 December. John Lennon is murdered by a disturbed fan. Ringo and Barbara, still in the Bahamas, receive the news when Barbara's daughter phones them from England. Ringo phones Yoko to say he is coming to see her immediately.

9 December. When Ringo and Barbara arrive at the Dakota, Yoko says she only wants to see Ringo, but he replies, 'Where I go, Barbara goes too.'

1981

14 January. Ringo begins another three days of recording at Cherokee Studios, once again accompanied by Ronnie Wood.

20 January. Ringo resumes his recording sessions at Cherokee Studios.

13 February. The final mixing sessions for Ringo's forthcoming album take place at Compass Point Studios and ten of the fifteen tracks are selected for the album.

15 February. Ringo and Barbara fly to the island of Montserrat to join Paul McCartney and George Martin for recording sessions.

16 February. Ringo plays drums on the track 'Take It Away' for Paul McCartney's forthcoming album.

19 February. Ringo and Barbara return to Los Angeles.

24 March. Ringo holds a press conference in Chicago to promote the film *Caveman*.

31 March. Ringo and Barbara are interviewed on the 'Barbara Walters Special' television show.

1 April. Ringo's former partner Nancy Andrews files a lawsuit against Ringo for $5 million.

9 April. *Caveman* is given a press screening at the Rivoli Theater in New York.

10 April. The world premiere of *Caveman* takes place at the Rivoli Theater, with Ringo commenting, 'I'm a very visual person, so for me, *Caveman* is a great piece. It's more than dialogue, and it's far more creative to me to transmit those feelings.' Perhaps this refers to the fact that there are only fifteen words of dialogue in the entire film.

27 April. Ringo and Barbara are married. The witnesses are Roger Shine and Hilary Gerrard. Guests include Ringo's mother Elsie Graves and his stepfather Harry Graves, Barbara's parents Marjorie and Howard Goldbach, her daughter Francesca, her sister Marjorie, her brother-in-law Phillipe and her brother Peter Goldbach and his wife Jo.

7 May. David Hartman interviews Ringo and Barbara by satellite for the ABC television show *Good Morning America*.

11 May. Ringo and Barbara appear on the American television show *PM Magazine*.

5 July. Ringo and Barbara appear on *Good Morning America*.

23 July. *Caveman* is premiered in London at the Studio Cinema, London.

24 August. Ringo and Barbara return to England.

16 September. Ringo begins filming promos for 'Stop And Smell The Roses' and 'Wrack My Brain' at Egham Aerodrome in Surrey.

17 September. Ringo continues filming his promos, both directed by Keef & Co.

18 September. Ringo films interior scenes for 'Wrack My Brain' in London.

19 September. The promo for 'Stop And Smell The Roses' is prepared for screening on television.

16 October. Ringo is in Los Angeles and poses for promotional pictures to accompany his 'Stop And Smell The Roses' promo.

26 October. Ringo embarks on a series of interviews, lasting a month, to promote his new album, beginning with the radio station KLOS in Los Angeles.

27 October. The album *Stop And Smell The Roses* is released in America, in addition to the single 'Wrack My Brain' c/w 'Drumming Is My Madness'. Ringo appears on the television breakfast show *Good Morning America*.

29 October. Ringo appears on the WBEN Buffalo radio show to promote his *Stop And Smell The Roses* album.

3 November. The *LA Times* publishes an interview with Ringo.

4 November. The *Indianapolis News* publishes an interview with Ringo.

13 November. The single 'Wrack My Brain' c/w 'Drumming Is My Madness' is released in Britain.

19 November. Ringo appears on the CBS TV show *Entertainment Tonight.*

20 November. The album *Stop And Smell The Roses* is released in Britain.

22 November. Britain's *Sunday Mirror* newspaper features an interview with Ringo.

24 November. Ringo appears live on *The Merv Griffin Show* in America and then flies to England to spend Christmas at Tittenhurst Park.

25 November. A pre-recorded interview with Ringo, conducted by Tom Synder, is featured on NBC's *Tomorrow* show.

27 November. Michael Heseltine, the Minister for the Environment, opens a series of streets in Liverpool based around the Beatles. They are Ringo Starr Close, Paul McCartney Way, John Lennon Drive and George Harrison Close.

2 December. Ringo is interviewed on Capitol Radio in London promoting *Stop And Smell The Roses.*

7 December. An interview with Ringo appears in the American magazine *People.*

8 December. Ringo's Capitol Radio interview is repeated.

12 December. Ringo and Barbara appear on the BBC TV chat show *Parkinson.* An interview with Ringo also appears in the *New Musical Express.*

1982

13 January. Ringo's single 'Private Property' c/w 'Stop And Smell The Roses' is released in America. Between today and 15 January, Ringo and Barbara and Paul and Linda McCartney film an 11-minute promo 'The Cooler' in London.

27 February. Ringo and Barbara attend the London club Legends to celebrate Elizabeth Taylor's 50th birthday.

20 March. Ringo phones the *Sunday Mirror* newspaper to tell them that rumours that his marriage was in trouble were false.

21 March. The *Sunday Mirror* publishes the piece on Ringo's marriage while the couple fly to America, with Ringo giving an interview to radio WZZP in Cleveland soon after they arrive.

3 April. Ringo and Barbara are at the Sheraton Plaza Inn, New Rochelle, New York, to attend the wedding of Barbara's brother.

5 April. The wedding takes place of Barbara's brother Dr Peter Goodbach and Dr Jo Shapiro.

6 April. Ringo and Barbara arrive home and Ringo enters his Startling Studios with former Eagles member Joe Walsh, who is producing, to begin recording for his next album.

24 April. Ringo and Barbara attend a party and meet up with Lynsey De Paul and James Coburn.

14 May. The 1978 film *Sextette*, in which Ringo appeared with Mae West, is re-released in New York.

24 May. Both Ringo and Paul attend the Cannes Film Festival where 'The Cooler' is entered in the 'Best Short Subject' category.

31 May. Ringo continues recording for his forthcoming album *Old Wave* at his Startling Studios in Tittenhurst Park.

11 June. Ringo and Barbara fly to Los Angeles.

14 June. Ringo and Barbara return to England.

18 June. Barbara and Ringo are at Elstree Film Studios where Paul is recording a promo clip for 'Take It Away'. A party for Paul's 40th birthday also takes place there.

23 June. Ringo has been recording at Elstree Studios for Paul's promo for 'Take It Away'.

15 August. After another visit to America, Ringo and Barbara return, with Ringo telling the press that he won't be appearing in the film *Yellowbeard*.

7 September. Ringo and Barbara and Paul and Linda McCartney are at the Lyceum Ballroom in London for the Buddy Holly Week event, the Rock'n'Roll Championship.

20 September. *Sextette* is released on home video in Britain.

26 September. Ringo and Barbara fly to Australia.

28 September. Ringo and Barbara are interviewed on *Parkinson In Australia*. Ringo plays drums on a medley of 'Honey Don't' and 'Blue Suede Shoes', backing singer Glenn Shorrock.

8 October. *The Parkinson In Australia* show featuring Ringo is aired.

29 October. The 1969 film *The Magic Christian* is issued in Britain on home video by Videoform Pictures.

30 October. Ringo takes part in a phone-in on the WBEN station in Buffalo, New Jersey.

21 November. Casey Kasem's *America's Top Ten* TV show features an interview with Ringo.

8 December. Ringo is criticised by a Labour member of the local council for applying for a grant of £500 for restoration work at Tittenhurst Park.

12 December. Ringo and Barbara appear on *Parkinson* and the promo for 'Wrack My Brain' is shown. The finale features Ringo on drums backing Tim Rice, Jimmy Tarbuck and Michael Parkinson performing 'Singing The Blues'.

28 December. The Christmas edition of BBC1's *Pop Quiz*, hosted by Mike Read, features 'Beatles Pop Quiz' with questions set by Ringo and Paul.

1983

2 January. Ringo's American television special 'Ringo' is finally shown in Britain when it is premiered on Channel Four.

16 February. The local council rejects Ringo's application for a grant to repair part of Tittenhurst Park.

12 March. Ringo is in hospital in London having a medical checkup.

27 April. Ringo and Barbara celebrate their second wedding anniversary at St James' club in London with their guests Paul and Linda McCartney.

11 May. The *Daily Mirror* prints photographs of Ringo and Paul during the filming of *Give My Regards To Broad Street*.

13 May. Ringo and Barbara begin filming *Princess Daisy*, the TV miniseries in which they appear as Robin and Vanessa Valerian. They received the roles above Rod and Alana Stewart and Mick and Bianca Jagger (although Mick and Bianca were no longer married).

16 May. In America Ringo and Barbara are pictured on the set of *Princess Daisy*.

4 June. The 26-part ABC radio series *Ringo's Yellow Submarine* is transmitted in America.

16 June. Ringo's album *Old Wave* receives a limited release in Germany, together with a single 'In My Car' c/w 'As Far As We Can Go'.

24 June. Ringo's album *Old Wave* is released in Canada.

8 July. *Caveman* is issued as a rental video in Britain by Warner Home Video.

25 July. Ringo meets up with George Harrison and Paul McCartney at the Gore Hotel in London.

15 September. Ringo and Barbara attend the Variety Club party to celebrate Tommy Steele's 25th anniversary in show business.

22 September. Ringo and Barbara, Paul and Linda, Eric Clapton and Micky Dolenz attend an Albert Hall concert by the Everly Brothers.

26 September. Ringo appears on the London Weekend Television programme 'Cilla – A Celebration'. During the interview he reveals that when he visited Elvis Presley at Graceland he noticed that a record by Cilla was on Elvis's jukebox.

12 October. Liverpool City Council announces that they are inviting Ringo, Paul, George and Yoko to Liverpool to receive Freedom Of the City awards.

30 October. Ringo and Barbara are interviewed by the *Dallas Morning News* to promote their appearance in *Princess Daisy*.

2 November. In an interview in *Family Circle* magazine, Barbara points out that Ringo is a good father to his children.

3 November. The American newspaper *USA Today* features an interview with Ringo and Barbara promoting *Princess Daisy*.

7 November. Ringo is interviewed on *Entertainment Today* discussing *Princess Daisy*.

11 November. Ringo is interviewed about his friendship with Marc Bolan for the Channel Four show *The Tube*.

25 November. The edition of *The Tube* featuring a brief interview with Ringo is screened, also including a clip from the *Born To Boogie* movie.

26 November. The final part of *Ringo's Yellow Submarine* is transmitted in America.

1 December. Ringo meets up with Paul, George and Yoko at the Dorchester Hotel in London to discuss Apple business. When asked if the Beatles were getting back together, Ringo replies, 'Don't be daft.'

1984

28 February. A home video of the American TV miniseries *Princess Daisy*, which features Ringo and Barbara as a married couple, is issued in Britain by Videoform Pictures (MGS 037).

8 March. The *Daily Express* reports that Ringo has agreed to accept his Freedom of the City award from Liverpool Council.

14 May. Ringo appears as a surprise guest on the Thames television show *What's My Line?*

4 July. Ringo appears as a guest drummer with the Beach Boys for two concerts, one in Washington DC, the other in Miami, Florida.

16 September. The first part of the *Princess Daisy* miniseries is screened in Britain on the ITV network, followed on 17 September by the second and final part.

9 October. Ringo appears on the *Good Morning Britain* television show to promote *Thomas The Tank Engine And Friends,* which begins its 13-week run on the ITV network that day.

22 November. Ringo and Barbara attend the premiere of the HandMade Film *A Private Function.*

28 November. *Give My Regards To Broad Street*, in which Ringo appears, is premiered in London.

3 December. On the BBC2 show *Film '84* critic Barry Norman reviews Paul McCartney's film *Give My Regards To Broad Street* and comments, 'Ringo Starr drifts in and out in a performance which suggests he should run, not walk, to the nearest acting school.'

1985

22 January. Ringo's son Zak marries Sarah Menikides in Bracknell, Berkshire, without informing either of his parents.

24 January. Ringo and Barbara organise a wedding party for Zak and Sarah at Tittenhurst Park.

15 February. Warner Home Video issues *The Last Waltz* in Britain, a film of the Band's last concert in which Ringo makes an appearance.

11 March. Ringo plays the part of a caretaker in a charity video *Willie And The Poor Boys – The Video* at Fulham Town Hall, London.

12 March. Ringo completes filming the charity video, which was organised by Bill Wyman in aid of ARMS (Action Research into Multiple Sclerosis).

24 May. Ringo and Barbara attend the premiere of *Wild Geese II.*

25 May. Polygram Music Video issues *Willie And The Poor Boys – The Video.*

13 June. The TVS television channel screens details of the making of *Willie And The Poor Boys – The Video.*

7 September. Ringo becomes a grandfather when his daughter-in-law Sarah Menikides Starkey and his son Zak become the parents of a 7lb 2oz girl, Tatia Jayne, born in a private hospital in Ascot.

25 September. Ringo and Barbara attend the launch party for photographer Terry O'Neill's exhibition 'Legends' at Hamilton's Gallery, London.

14 October. Ringo and Barbara attend the Chelsea Arts Club Ball at the Royal Albert Hall.

21 October. Ringo and George videotape their appearance on the Carl Perkins television special 'Blue Suede Shoes' at Limehouse Studios in London. Ringo is the first guest and performs 'Honey Don't' and 'Matchbox'.

22 October. Radio One's *Newsbeat* programme features an interview with Ringo and George Harrison discussing the Carl Perkins special.

26 October. Ringo and Barbara are among the audience of the London Weekend television special 'An Audience With Billy Connolly'.

5 November. Ringo, Barbara and Olivia Harrison attend 'Fashion Aid' at the Royal Albert Hall.

11 November. *Thomas The Tank Engine* audiocassettes, featuring narration by Ringo, are released in Britain.

18 November. Ringo begins recording a further series of *Thomas The Tank Engine* narrations.

9 December. The CBS special *Alice In Wonderland*, featuring Ringo as the Mock Turtle, is transmitted in America.

11 December. Ringo is a guest on the *This Is Your Life* tribute to photographer Terry O'Neill.

1986

31 January. Ringo appears on a CBS radio show in America, *Top 30 USA*.

2 February. Ringo is featured in a one-hour radio special, which is syndicated throughout the United States.

22 April. Ringo and George discuss the HandMade Film *Mona Lisa* on the BBC TV show *Film '86*.

20 June. Virgin Video issue *Carl Perkins And Friends – A Rockabilly Session* in Britain.

18 July. Ringo appears on the syndicated radio show *Ticket To Ride* in America.

27 July. Ringo and Barbara attend an England v. Mexico polo match at Windsor.

12 September. Ringo and Barbara attend a 'Bond Girls' fashion show at London's Savoy Hotel.

13 September. Ringo holds a party for his son Zak's 21st birthday in the grounds of Tittenhurst Park. Paul and Linda McCartney are in attendance.

24 September. The second series of *Thomas The Tank Engine* begins transmission on the ITV network.

6 October. Ringo holds a press reception in Atlanta, Georgia, promoting the Brasserie, a new restaurant of which he is co-owner.

14 October. Ringo appears on an afternoon children's television programme with *Thomas The Tank Engine* creator the Rev. W Awdry.

27 October. The charity track 'You Know It Makes Sense' for the anti-heroin campaign is released as a 12" single in Britain.

24 November. The album *The Anti-Heroin Project: It's A Live-In World*, with a track by Ringo, is issued in Britain.

14 December. Ringo and Barbara take part in the fourth World Elephant Polo Championship in Nepal, representing Cartier jewellers. Their team was knocked out in the early stages and the Tiger Top Tuskers won the championship.

19 December. Ringo wins his case in the Court of Appeal in London against the decision in a High Court decree from April 1979 that additional payments of an extra $375,000 in alimony to his former wife should be backdated to 1976.

24 December. Channel Four repeats 'Blue Suede Shoes – Carl Perkins And Friends'.

1987

4 February. Ringo begins recording at the 3-Alarm Studios in Memphis, Tennessee for a proposed album with producer Chips Moman.

5 February. Ringo continues with his recording sessions in Tennessee.

25 April. Ringo resumes his recording sessions with Chips Moman in Memphis.

28 April. Ringo and Barbara host a party aboard the *Island Queen*, a riverboat in Memphis. A total of 254 guests attend, including country artist Charlie Rich and songwriter David Porter. A Memphis journalist who described Ringo as 'yesterday's news' wasn't invited! Ringo says, 'I've been in the game too long now to worry about what anyone's saying.' At the end of the evening Ringo joins Reba and the Portables on drums to perform several numbers

29 April. Bob Dylan visits Ringo's recording session at 3-Alarm Studios in Memphis.

1 May. An interview that Ringo had taped in Memphis is broadcast on *Entertainment Tonight*. Ringo denies a story, circulated by Donovan, that there was to be a joint project with the other former Beatles and Julian Lennon.

5 June. Ringo and George appear at the Prince's Trust Concert at Wembley Arena.

6 June. Ringo and George once again take to the stage on the second day of the Prince's Trust Concert

20 June. Highlights of the Prince's Trust Wembley Arena Concert with Ringo and George Harrison are screened on ITV in Britain.

4 July. A 21st birthday party is held for Island Records at Pinewood Film Studios. There is a jam session with Ringo, Andy Summers, John Martyn, Eric Clapton and Lee 'Scratch' Perry.

8 July. The second series of *Thomas The Tank Engine And Friends* is repeated on ITV each Wednesday from today for 13 weeks and is also repeated each Thursday.

14 August. The *Prince's Trust Concert 1987* album, on which Ringo and George appear, is released in Britain.

26 August. Ringo and Barbara dine at Le Dome restaurant in Hollywood.

31 August. BBC2 airs 'Bruce Willis – The Return Of Bruno', in which Ringo makes a cameo appearance.

13 September. HBO (Home Box Office), the American television channel, airs 'The Prince's Trust Concert'. It is repeated on 16, 19, 21 and 25 September.

26 September. Ringo and Barbara attend the official opening of the London Brasserie, situated in Peach Tree Center, a shopping mall in Atlanta, Georgia. Ringo, who has a half-share in the business, takes part in a jam session with Jerry Lee Lewis, Isaac Hayes and Jermaine Jackson.

27 September. Ringo and Barbara fly to Boston.

28 September. The episode in the *Legends Of Rock* series that focuses on Ringo is syndicated across America. Also screened are some pre-recordings Ringo made for *Showbiz Today* and *Entertainment Tonight*.

21 October. Ringo and George visit Paul at his Cavendish Avenue home in St John's Wood, London.

16 November. The home video of *Thomas The Tank Engine And Friends* with the initial 26 five-minute episodes is released in Britain.

18 December. Ringo, George and Elton John gather at Greenford Studios in London to record George's 'When We Was Fab'.

1988

18 January. The CD of Ringo's *Blast From Your Past* is released in America.

20 January. Ringo and George attend the third annual Rock And Roll Hall of Fame ceremony at the Waldorf Astoria Hotel in New York, where Mick Jagger inducts the Beatles. There is a jam session with Ringo, George Harrison, Mick Jagger, Bob Dylan and Bruce Springsteen. The proceedings are broadcast live in America on FM radio. Ringo and George supply the vocals for a rendition of 'I Saw Her Standing There'.

21 January. The TV shows *This Morning*, *Showbiz Today* and *Entertainment Tonight* all feature clips from the Beatles' induction ceremony.

24 January. MTV's *The Week In Rock* includes clips from the Beatles' induction ceremony with Ringo and George.

5 February. News is leaked that Ringo will appear in a TV situation comedy surrounding a rock-star widower who has to look after his children and maintain his career. He eventually rejects the project.

3 March. Both Ringo and George record an appearance on Michael Aspel's television chat show *Aspel And Co*, to be broadcast on 5 March.

24 March. Ringo and Barbara dine at the fashionable Chasen's restaurant in Beverly Hills.

8 May. *That'll Be The Day* is screened on the ITV network in Britain.

14 May. Paul McCartney's *Give My Regards To Broad Street*, which also features Ringo, is premiered on British television on the ITV network.

14 July. The appearances by Ringo and George Harrison on the Prince's Trust concerts at Wembley Arena in 1987 are included on the home video release by International Video Entertainment.

11 October. Ringo and Barbara fly to America for a six-week treatment for their problems with alcohol at a clinic in Tucson, Arizona.

18 October. *Stay Awake*, the album featuring Ringo's duet with Herb Alpert on the track 'When You Wish Upon A Star', is released in America.

24 October. The album *Stay Awake* is released in Britain.

25 November. Ringo and Barbara complete their treatment for their alcoholism and return to Britain.

1989

3 January. The American version of *Thomas The Tank Engine And Friends* is renamed *Shining Time Station*, and Ringo and Barbara attend the taping sessions at Travel Town Studios in Burbank, California.

9 January. At a press reception in Chicago, Ringo promotes *Shining Time Station*.

29 January. The Public Broadcasting System (PBS) in America begins screening the 20-part *Shining Time Station*, which Ringo narrates and appears in.

24 February. Rhino Records issue *Starr Struck: Ringo's Best 1976–1983* in America, which contain four tracks from the *Old Wave* album that had not been released in America before. *The Magic Christian* is also issued in America on laser disc and video.

5 March. Ringo records one line of a song at the Sarm West Studios in London for the single 'Spirit Of The Forest', to be released by Virgin on 5 June. Ringo is just one of a host of musicians who contribute to the recording.

22 March. Tom Petty shoots a promo video for his single 'I Won't Back Down' at Shepperton Studios in London. The band he has backing him on the video comprises himself, Ringo on drums, George Harrison, Jeff Lynne and Mike Campbell.

25 March. Ringo is one of the guests at Elton John's lavish (it cost £265,000) 42nd birthday party at the Bois de Boulogne restaurant in Paris.

27 March. At Abbey Road Studios, Ringo joins Buck Owens to record a new version of 'Act Naturally'.

20 May. The American World Music Awards is screened in Britain by ITV and includes Ringo presenting an award to singer Tanita Tikaram.

5 June. The charity single 'Spirit Of The Forest', which features some vocal work from Ringo, is issued as a 12" format in America. It is also released in Britain but in the 7" format.

7 June. Ringo and George Harrison attend Bob Dylan's concert at the NEC (National Exhibition Centre) in Birmingham.

13 June. Ringo attends Bob Dylan's concert at Les Arenas, Frejus, France – and joins him on stage for two numbers, 'Highway 61 Revisited' and 'Like A Rolling Stone'.

20 June. Ringo holds a press conference at the Palladium, New York, to announce a forthcoming solo concert tour. In the evening he appears on the *Late Night With David Letterman*, during which he reminisces about the Beatles and Ed Sullivan, because the Letterman show was filmed from the original theatre where the Beatles made their Sullivan debut. He also discusses his forthcoming tour and when asked when he'd last toured, says, '1966'. He points to the audience and adds, 'Before they were born'.

21 June. Ringo appears on the ABC TV show *Good Morning America* promoting his forthcoming tour.

23 June. Ringo and Buck Owens begin filming a promo for their 'Act Naturally' single, which is completed on 29 June. George Bloom directs and Ken Brown produces it.

4 July. 'Act Naturally' is issued in America and Ringo begins rehearsing with his new band, the first All-Starr Band.

7 July. Ringo celebrates his 41st birthday ay Morton's in Los Angeles with Barbara and her sister Marjorie. Actors Woody Harrelson and Bud Cort are also Ringo's guests and they bring along a home-made birthday cake.

21 July. The All-Starr Band rehearsals continue, this time at Los Calinas, Texas.

22 July. Ringo and Barbara attend a James Bond party at Le Bel Age Hotel in Hollywood.

23 July. Ringo and his All-Starr Band appear before an audience of 10,000 at the Park Central Amphitheater, Dallas, Texas following a 3½-hour sound check. Before the last number Ringo asked the audience, 'Well, what do you think so far?' and was answered by the crowd roaring his name.

24 July. Ringo appears on a live phone-in on the radio show *Rockline*.

25 July. Ringo and his All-Starr Band appear before an audience of 12,000 at the Poplar Creek Music Theater, Chicago. Billy Preston

replaces 'That's The Way God Planned It' with 'Nothing From Nothing'.

26 July. Ringo and his All-Starr Band appear before an audience of 7,000 at Deer Creek Amphitheater, Indianapolis. The local paper, the *Indianapolis News,* reports: 'It was everything a summer concert is supposed to be: good music, well performed and a lot of fun.'

28 July. Ringo and his All-Starr Band appear at Riverfest in Minneapolis.

29 July. Ringo and his All-Starr Band appear before an audience of 6,000 at the Alpine Valley Music Theater in East Troy, Wisconsin.

30 July. Ringo and his All-Starr Band appear before an audience of 6,500 at the Pine Knob Music Theater in Clarkston, Michigan. The *Detroit Free Press* reports: 'The mood on stage was warm, loose and collegial, resembling a basement jam session.'

31 July. Ringo and his All-Starr Band appear at the open-air Blossom Music Center, Cuyahoga Falls, Ohio.

2 August. Ringo and his All-Starr Band appear at Lake Compounce Amusement Park, Bristol, Connecticut. When introducing the 'No No Song' Ringo says, 'It means a lot more to me now than it did then.' Max Weinberg, former member of the E-Street Band, acts as guest drummer on some numbers.

4 August. Ringo and his All-Starr Band appear at the fully sold-out 8,000-seater Performing Arts Center, Saratoga Springs, New York.

5 August. Ringo and his All-Starr Band appear at the Garden State Arts Center, Holmdel, New Jersey. This date was added to the original itinerary. There is an audience of 6,900 and Paul Schaffer, bandleader from *Late Night With David Letterman,* guests on keyboards during the second set. The *New York Daily News* calls the band 'the travelling Ringo-buys' and comments that they will 'give you as good a time as you're going to find at a rock'n'roll concert all year'.

6 August. Ringo and his All-Starr Band appear at Bally's Grand Hotel, Atlantic City. The guest musician is Roy Bittan.

8 August. Ringo and his All-Starr Band appear before an audience of 14,000 at Merriweather Post Pavilion, Columbia, Maryland. Nils Lofgren's brother Tom guests on rhythm guitar.

9 August. Ringo and his All-Starr band appear at the Mann Music Center in Philadelphia, Pennsylvania. Max Weinberg is again a guest with the band.

11 August. Ringo and his All-Starr Band return to the Garden State Arts Center, Holmdel, New Jersey. Ringo and members of his band spend the day at Bruce Springsteen's house, during which they have a jam session. In the evening Springsteen joins them on stage and provides vocals for the final four songs: 'Get Back', 'Long Tall Sally', 'Photograph' and 'With A Little Help From My Friends'. Movie comedian John Candy also joins in, playing tambourine on 'With A

Little Help From My Friends'. Ringo's ex-wife Maureen and his son and daughter, Lee and Jason, are also in the audience.

12 August. Ringo and his All-Starr Band appear at Jones Beach Amphitheater, Wantaugh, New York. Paul and Linda McCartney are in attendance. The guest musician is Will Lee, bassist from *Late Night With David Letterman*.

13 August. Ringo and his All-Starr Band appear again at Jones Beach Amphitheater, Wantaugh, New York.

15 August. Ringo and his All-Starr Band appear before an audience of 12,500 at Great Woods Center, Mansfield, Boston, Massachusetts.

16 August. Ringo and his All-Starr Band appear at Kingston Concert Grounds, Kingston, New Hampshire.

18 August. Ringo and his All-Starr Band appear at the Memorial Auditorium, Buffalo, New York.

19 August. Ringo and his All-Starr Band appear at CNE, Toronto, Canada.

20 August. Ringo and his All-Starr Band appear at Castle in Charlevoix, Michigan.

22 August. Ringo and his All-Starr Band appear at Winnipeg, Manitoba, Canada. Ringo's injunction against Chips Moman's planned release of a Ringo album takes place in court and two of the numbers are played – 'Whiskey And Soda' and 'Can I Help' to indicate that Ringo's voice is substandard due to the fact that he'd been drinking alcohol.

23 August. In another added date, Ringo and his All-Starr Band appear at Saskatoon, Saskatchewan, Canada.

24 August. Ringo and his All-Starr Band appear at the Olympic Saddleroom, Calgary, Canada. Ringo is given a 30-day injunction in court preventing the release of the album by Chips Moman.

25 August. Ringo and his All-Starr Band appear at the Northlands Coliseum, Edmonton, Canada. An Oldsmobile commercial featuring Ringo and his daughter Lee is broadcast.

27 August. Ringo and his All-Starr Band appear at the PNE Pacific Coliseum, Vancouver, British Columbia, Canada.

29 August. Ringo and his All-Starr Band appear at the Cal Expo Amphitheater, Sacramento, another extra date.

30 August. Ringo and his All-Starr Band appear at the Aladdin Theater, Las Vegas, Nevada.

1 September. Ringo and his All-Starr Band appear at the Shoreline Amphitheater, Mountain View, California.

2 September. Ringo and his All-Starr Band appear at the Pacific Amphitheater, Costa Mesa, California.

3 September. Ringo and his All-Starr Band appear at the Greek Theater, Los Angeles. On 'The Jerry Lewis Muscular Dystrophy Telethon', Ringo's track 'Boys' is played.

4 September. Ringo and his All-Starr Band play the Greek Theater again. The concerts are recorded and filmed for future release.

2 October. *Act Naturally*, Buck Owens's album, which features his duet with Ringo on the title track, is issued in America.

12 October. A video clip of Ringo and his All-Starr Band performing, filmed at the Greek Theater, is shown at MIPCOM in Cannes, France.

23 October. Ringo flies to Japan for his first concerts there since he last appeared with the Beatles in 1966. He leads his All-Starr band on a seven-date concert tour in six major Japanese cities. UDO Artists promote the concerts.

26 October. Ringo holds a press conference in Tokyo to discuss his Japanese tour.

30 October. In the afternoon Ringo is interviewed for *11pm*, a Japanese TV show. Ringo and his All-Starr Band appear at the Rainbow Hall, Nagoya.

31 October. Ringo and his All-Starr Band appear at the Castle Hall, Osaka.

2 November. Ringo and his All-Starr Band appear at the Sun Plaza, Hiroshima.

3 November. Ringo and his All-Starr Band appear at the Kitakyushu Koseinenkin Hall, Kyushi.

6 November. Ringo and his All-Starr Band appear at the Nippon Budokan Hall, Tokyo.

7 November. Ringo and his All-Starr Band appear at the Nippon Budokan Hall, Tokyo.

8 November. Ringo holds a press reception in a Japanese Hotel. Ringo and his All-Starr band appear at Yokohama Arena, Yokohama.

9 November. Ringo and the members of his All-Starr Band set off in their different directions at the end of the Japanese tour.

15 November. Ringo appears in court in Atlanta, Georgia, to testify in his case against Chips Moman. A further injunction against the release of the album is granted.

1990

5 January. Ringo is granted another injunction at Fulton County Superior Court preventing Chips Moman from releasing the album. Ringo agrees to pay Moman $74,354 towards production costs, half of what Moman is seeking.

19 February. The Buck Owens album *Act Naturally*, with the singer's duet with Ringo on the title track, is released in Britain.

28 March. The tabloid newspaper the *Star* reports that Ringo, George and Paul have attended a birthday party for Elton John's wife.

12 April. Asteroids 4147–4150, originally discovered in 1983 and 1984, are named after each member of the Beatles.

15 April. A 90-minute special 'In Concert: Ringo Starr And His All-Starr Band' is screened in Britain on the satellite channel BSB. Filmed at the Greek Theater, Los Angeles, it features Ringo performing 'It Don't Come Easy', 'No No Song', 'Yellow Submarine', 'Photograph' and 'With A Little Help From My Friends'. Other artists perform 'Rocky

Mountain Way', 'The Weight', 'Will It Go Round In Circles', 'Quarter To Three' and 'Up On Cripple Creek'.

5 June. In Monte Carlo, Ringo is interviewed by Steffan Olander for a forthcoming Swedish radio broadcast to celebrate Ringo's 50th birthday.

7 June. The first two *Thomas The Tank Engine And Friends* home videos, with narration by Ringo, are issued in America.

14 June. Ringo and his All-Starr Band appear in concert at Le Zenith Indoor Arena in Paris.

20 June. Barbara Starkey appears on the BBC1 show *Wogan* during which she discusses the problems she and Ringo have had with alcohol.

21 June. Ringo records an interview with VH-1 in America.

30 June. *Ringo Starr And His All-Starr Band*, a videotaped film of their appearance at the Greek Theater, Los Angeles, in September 1989, is issued in America on laser disc.

15 July. The radio interview recorded on 5 June in Monte Carlo is broadcast on Chanel 3, a Swedish station, in a one-hour programme to celebrate Ringo's 50th birthday.

16 July. *Ringo Starr And His All-Starr Band,* recorded in Los Angeles, is issued as a home video in Britain, pruned to sixty minutes and missing the 'You're Sixteen' performance. The video of *Alice In Wonderland*, featuring Ringo as the Mock Turtle, is also issued in Britain.

18 July. Ringo and Barbara and George and Olivia Harrison attend the luncheon to launch the 'Romanian Angel' appeal at the Hyde Park Hotel in London.

23 July. The album *Nobody's Child: Romanian Angel Appeal* is released in Britain. It contains a contribution from Ringo.

24 July. *Nobody's Child: Romanian Angel Appeal* is released in America.

13 August. The 1975 film *Lisztomania*, which features Ringo as the Pope, is issued by Warner Home Video in Britain.

31 August. Ringo is in Dallas, Texas, attending the funeral of blues guitarist Steve Ray Vaughan, who died in a helicopter crash on 27 August.

10 September. *Thomas The Tank Engine And Friends*, featuring 17 of the stories narrated by Ringo, is issued in Britain by Video Collection International.

27 September. The home videos *Thomas And Turntables & Other Stories* and *Thomas Breaks The Rules & Other Stories,* with narration by Ringo, are issued in America.

8 October. The CD of *Ringo Starr And His All-Starr Band,* from the Greek Theater recordings, is issued in Britain.

12 October. The CD of *Ringo Starr And His All-Starr Band* is released in America, together with a bonus CD single.

1991

29 January. The home video of *Ringo Starr And His All-Starr Band* is released in America.

4 March. Ringo's 1973 album *Ringo* is issued on CD with three bonus tracks, 'It Don't Come Easy', 'Early 1970' and 'Down And Out'.

26 March. Ringo's 1978 album *Bad Boy* is issued on CD in America.

29 March. The film *King Ralph* opens in the UK. One of the numbers on the film soundtrack is 'Good Golly Miss Molly' a recording by Jeff Lynne with Ringo on drums. There is no soundtrack album release to accompany the film.

6 May. Ringo's 1973 album *Ringo* is issued on CD in America on Capitol/Apple CDP 795637.

31 May. Ringo joins Nils Lofgren on stage at the Roxy Club in Los Angeles playing drums on a version of the Beatles number 'Anytime At All'.

4 June. Chips Moman begins proceedings at the Georgia Supreme Court to seek the entire production costs of $162,600 for the unreleased Ringo album.

7 July. Ringo celebrates his 51st birthday by buying a new three-bedroom home in Beverly Hills, California, for $3.3m. He also spends $250,000 on a Mercedes-Benz that had been built for Liberace in the early 1980s.

26 July. Rykodisc issue a 23-track CD called *Steal This Disc 3*, which included Ringo's track 'Honey Don't'.

14 September. Ringo records the song 'You'll Never Know' in Los Angeles. Steve Dorff, who produced the number, also co-wrote the song with John Bettis. The track is to appear in the John Belushi film *Curly Sue*.

26 November. The soundtrack of the film *Curly Sue* is released in America, with Ringo's track 'You'll Never Know'.

27 December. *Curly Sue* is released in Britain.

1992

6 January. The soundtrack album *Curly Sue*, including Ringo's track 'You'll Never Know', is released in Britain.

28 February. Ringo announces the forthcoming release of his *Time Takes Time* album, the 'Weight Of The World' single and the forthcoming tours, saying, 'I'm coming back with a vengeance. I'm putting a band together and we know we're opening in Florida on the second of June.' When asked what the album sounded like he replies, 'The sound of the record goes to this tie,' pointing to a very colourful tie he was wearing.

2 April. Ringo holds a press conference at Radio City Music Hall in New York City to announce his new single, album, new band and concert dates.

3 April. Ringo appears on *The David Letterman Show* and also acts as a guest presenter at a Grammy Awards ceremony. Advance copies of his 'Weight Of The World' single are sent to American radio stations.

6 April. Ringo holds a press conference at the Dorchester Hotel in London. In the evening he attends the 'George Harrison and Friends' Natural Law Party concert at the Royal Albert Hall and watches the show from a private box. Then he comes on stage to join in for a performance on 'While My Guitar Gently Weeps' and 'Roll Over Beethoven'.

16 April. Ringo appears on the CNBC show *Real Life* in America.

19 April. In Aspen, Colorado, Ringo films an interview for a forthcoming television special 'The Making Of Sgt Pepper'.

21 April. Ringo acts as narrator for an animated tale in the Shelley Duvall *Bedtime* series on the American cable station Showtime.

5 May. Ringo appears on the American television show *Entertainment Tonight*.

9 May. Ringo appears as a guest on NBC's 'Dame Edna's Hollywood' and joins Dame Edna Everage in an unusual rendition of 'Act Naturally'. Dame Edna is, of course, Australian comedian Barry Humphries. When he appears, comedian/actor Robin Williams says, 'I know you. You played with Wings.'

16 May. Ringo begins filming a promotional video for 'Weight Of The World'.

17 May. Ringo completes the promo for 'Weight Of The World'.

18 May. The CNN *Showbiz Today* shows a clip of Ringo making his 'Weight Of The World' promo.

20 May. Ringo appears on *Entertainment Tonight* again.

22 May. Ringo and his All-Starr Band appear on the ABC TV show *In Concert '92*.

26 May. Ringo appears on the VH-1 television show *VH-1 To 1*.

27 May. Ringo is interviewed by Arsenio Hall on the television chat show *Arsenio* and also performs 'Weight Of The World' with his All-Starr Band.

28 May. A private party for Ringo and his All-Starr Band is held at Paramount Film Studios. A pre-recorded interview is also featured on the NBC television show *Today*.

2 June. Ringo and his All-Starr Band appear at the Sunrise Pavilion, Fort Lauderdale, Florida.

3 June. Ringo and his All-Starr Band appear again at the Sunrise Pavilion, Fort Lauderdale, Florida.

5 June. Ringo and his All-Starr Band appear at the Bayfront Pavilion in St Petersburg, Florida. He is also seen on the cable channel E!

6 June. Ringo and his All-Starr Band appear at the Blockbuster Pavilion, Charlotte, North Carolina.

7 June. Ringo and his All-Starr Band appear at the Chastain Park Amphitheater in Atlanta, Georgia.

9 June. Ringo and his All-Starr Band appear at the Riverbend Music Center, Cincinnati, Ohio.

10 June. Ringo and his All-Starr Band appear at the Blossom Music Center in Guyaboga Falls, Ohio.

12 June. Ringo and his All-Starr Band appear at the Deer Creek Music Center in Noblesville, Indiana. He is also the cover star of *Goldmine* magazine.

13 June. Ringo and his All-Starr Band appear at the Poplar Creek Music Theater in Hoffman Estates, Illinois.

14 June. The TV special 'The Making Of Sgt Pepper', featuring an interview with Ringo, is screened in Britain.

15 June. Ringo and his All-Starr Band appear at the Pine Knob Music Theater in Clarkston, Michigan.

16 June. Ringo and his All-Starr Band appear at the Kingswood Music Theater in Wonderland Park, Maple, Ontario, Canada.

17 June. Ringo and his All-Starr Band appear at Merriweather Post Pavilion in Columbia.

19 June. Ringo and his All-Starr Band appear at Radio City Music Hall in New York City.

20 June. Ringo and his All-Starr Band appear again at Radio City Music Hall in New York City.

21 June. Ringo and his All-Starr Band appear at Garden State Arts Center in Holmdel, New Jersey.

22 June. Ringo and his All-Starr Band appear at the Great Woods Amphitheater in Mansfield, Massachusetts.

23 June. Ringo and his All-Starr Band appear at Jones Beach Amphitheater in Wantaugh, New York.

25 June. Ringo and his All-Starr Band appear at the Marcus Amphitheater in Milwaukee, Wisconsin.

26 June. Ringo and his All-Starr Band appear at the Riverport Center, Maryland Heights, Missouri.

2 July. Ringo and his All-Starr Band appear at the Gothenburg All-Star Festival in Gothenburg, Sweden.

3 July. Ringo and his All-Starr Band appear at the Dalarock Festival in Hedemora, Sweden. Ringo's single 'Don't Go Where The Road Don't Go' was due to be released in America, but is cancelled, although it is issued in Germany with 'Everybody Wins' on the flip.

4 July. Ringo and his All-Starr Band appear at the Moelleparken in Malmo, Sweden.

6 July. Ringo and his All-Starr Band appear at the Empire Theatre, Liverpool. Highlights from this concert are to appear on the Disney Channel special 'Ringo Starr: Going Home' in April 1993.

7 July. Ringo and his All-Starr Band appear at the Hammersmith Odeon, London. In America Ringo is interviewed live by satellite on the CBS show *This Morning*.

8 July. Ringo and his All-Starr Band appear at Le Zenith, Paris, France.

10 July. Ringo and his All-Starr Band appear at the Stadtgarten in Hamburg, Germany.

11 July. Ringo and his All-Starr Band appear at the Tanzbrunnen in Koln, Germany.

12 July. Ringo and his All-Starr Band appear at the Unterfrankenhalle in Aschaffenburg, Germany.

13 July. Ringo and his All-Starr Band appear at the Montreux Jazz Festival in Montreux, Switzerland. Their performance is recorded and is issued as the album *Ringo Starr And His All-Starr Band Live From Montreux*, issued in Britain on 14 September 1993.

15 July. Ringo and his All-Starr Band appear at the Deutschlandhalle in Berlin, Germany.

17 July. Ringo and his All-Starr Band appear at the Pori Jazz Festival in Kirjurinluoto Park, Pori, Finland.

18 July. Ringo and his All-Starr Band appear at the Valby Idretspark in Copenhagen, Denmark.

19 July. Ringo and his All-Starr Band appear at the Lisbterg Fruespark in Arhus, Denmark.

20 July. Ringo and his All-Starr Band appear at the Belga Beach Festival at Belga Beach in De Panne, Belgium.

22 July. Ringo and his All-Starr Band appear at the Teatre Tenda in Brescia, Italy.

23 July. Ringo and his All-Starr Band appear at the Teatre La Versiliana in Marina Di Pietrasanta, Italy.

24 July. A proposed gig at Foro Iralico in Rome is cancelled.

1 August. Ringo and his All-Starr Band appear at Le Champs de Brionne Summer Music Theater in George, Washington.

3 August. Ringo and his All-Starr Band appear at Harvey's Hotel in Tahoe, California.

4 August. Ringo and his All-Starr Band appear at the Redwood Amphitheater in the Great American Amusement Park in Santa Clara, California.

5 August. Ringo and his All-Starr Band appear at the Concord Pavilion in Concord, California.

7 August. Ringo and his All-Starr Band appear at the California Mid State Fair in Paso Robles, California.

8 August. Ringo and his All-Starr Band appear at Camp Pendleton Marine Base in Oceanside, California.

9 August. Ringo and his All-Starr Band appear at the Pacific Amphitheater in Costa Mesa, California.

11 August. Ringo and his All-Starr Band appear at the Greek Theater in Los Angeles, California.

12 August. Ringo and his All-Starr Band appear again at the Greek Theater in Los Angeles, California.

13 August. Ringo and his All-Starr Band appear at the Desert Sky Pavilion in Phoenix, Arizona.

15 August. Ringo and his All-Starr Band appear at the Aquafest in Austin, Texas.

16 August. Ringo and his All-Starr Band appear at Riverfront Park in

Little Rock, Arkansas. *Ringo's Rotogravure* and *Ringo The 4th* are issued on CD in America.

18 August. Ringo and his All-Starr Band appear at the Starplex Amphitheater in Dallas, Texas.

20 August. Ringo and his All-Starr Band appear at the Ohio State Fair Celeste Center in Columbus, Ohio.

21 August. Ringo and his All-Starr Band appear at Freedom Hall at the Kentucky State Fair in Louisville, Kentucky.

22 August. Ringo and his All-Starr Band appear at the Iowa State Fair in Des Moines, Iowa.

24 August. Ringo and his All-Starr Band appear at the Star Lake Amphitheater in Pittsburg, Pennsylvania.

25 August. Ringo and his All-Starr Band appear at Finger Lakes Performing Arts Center in Canandaigua, New York.

26 August. Ringo and his All-Starr Band appear at the Saratoga Performing Arts Center in Saratoga Springs, New York.

27 August. The proposed gig for Ringo and his All-Starr Band at the Taj Mahal Casino in Atlantic City, New Jersey is cancelled, leaving Ringo free to appear with Joe Walsh at a charity concert at the China Club, New York City.

28 August. Ringo and his All-Starr Band appear at the Waterloo Village Amphitheater in Stanhope, New Jersey.

1 September. Ringo and his All-Starr Band appear at Fiddlers Green Amphitheater in Engelwood, Colorado.

2 September. Ringo and his All-Starr Band appear at the Park West Amphitheater in Park City, Utah.

4 September. Ringo and his All-Starr Band appear at Caesar's Palace in Las Vegas, Nevada.

5 September. Ringo and his All-Starr Band appear again at Caesar's Palace.

6 September. Ringo and his All-Starr Band complete their tour at Caesar's Palace. Harry Nilsson joins them on stage and performs 'Without You'. Ringo also appears on the 'Jerry Lewis Muscular Dystrophy Telethon' performing 'You're Sixteen'.

10 September. Ringo takes part in a comedy sketch on the 'MYV Music Video Awards Show'.

21 September. Ringo's single 'Don't Go Where The Road Don't Go' c/w 'Don't Know A Thing About Love' is released in Germany.

27 September. The documentary 'The Making Of Sgt Pepper' is screened on the Disney Channel in America.

29 September. Ringo travels to Liverpool to film further scenes for the Disney Channel special 'Ringo Starr: Going Home'.

8 October. Ringo, George and Paul have a business meeting at Paul's MPL offices.

20 October. A pre-taped appearance with Ringo is featured on the *Good Morning America* breakfast show. He appears with actor Dennis

Hopper and is promoting a three-day 'Sierra Tucson Ringo Starr Celebrity Weekend' to take place the coming weekend.

21 October. Ringo is interviewed by Arsenio Hall on the *Arsenio* chat show and also performs 'Don't Go Where The Road Don't Go' and 'Act Naturally'.

24 October. Ringo and members of his All-Starr Band appear at the three-day 'Sierra Tucson Ringo Starr Celebrity Weekend' at the McKale Center in the University of Arizona.

30 November. Ringo's album *Goodnight Vienna* is issued in Britain on a CD with three bonus tracks.

27 December. Ringo's 1991 appearance on *The Simpsons* is shown on Sky One in Britain.

1993

30 January. Ringo appears as a guest on *Late Night With David Letterman*.

20 March. Ringo and Barbara are spotted dining at the Cicada restaurant in Hollywood.

23 March. Ringo's album *Goodnight Vienna* is issued in America on CD.

28 March. Ringo appears on the 'Jimmy Stewart Relay Marathon' in Los Angeles.

16 April. Ringo joins Paul McCartney on stage at the 'Earth Day For The Environment' concert at the Hollywood Bowl. Paul announces him as 'Your friend and mine' and Ringo sings in the finale, 'Hey Jude'.

18 April. The Disney Channel special 'Ringo Starr: Going Home' is premiered.

24 April. Ringo plays drums in the group led by Don Was at Willie Nelson's Farm Aid Benefit at Ames Cyclone Stadium, Iowa. The group is called the New Maroons and also includes Neil Young, Willie Nelson, Bryan Adams, John Cooger Mellencamp and Bruce Hornsby and the Range. The Nashville Network TV channel videotapes the show.

23 June. Ringo makes another charity appearance with the New Maroons, this time for the Together For Our Children charity. It takes place at the Royce Hall, UCLA.

25 July. *Ringo Starr And His All-Starr Band Live From Montreux* is released in Japan on videocassette and laser disc.

7 September. Ringo films a guest appearance at Abbey Road for the ITV special 'Cilla – A Celebration'.

14 September. *Ringo Starr And His All-Starr Band Live From Montreux* is released in both Britain and America by Rykodisc.

23 September. The Spanish magazine *Hola!* features a colour spread of the wedding of Barbara's sister.

13 October. Ringo appears on the American television show *Today* to promote his *Montreux* album.

17 November. MPI home video issues *Live From Montreux*.

1994

11 January. Rhino Records releases *Max Weinberg Presents: Let There Be Drums*, a 3-CD celebration of rock drumming, with each CD covering a specific decade. Ringo's drumming isn't featured in the section on the 1960s because of licensing restrictions regarding Beatles recordings. He is found on *Vol 3 – The 80s*, when he performs 'Drumming Is My Madness' with Jim Keltner, from his 1981 album *Stop And Smell The Roses*. Weinberg, a drummer with acts including Meatloaf and Bruce Springsteen, was author of a book about rock drumming, *The Big Beat*.

15 January. Ringo's friend Harry Nilsson dies of a heart attack.

7 February. Ringo appears as one of the celebrity guests in the anti-drink initiative RAADD (Recording Artists Against Drunk Driving) that is launched at the American Music Awards. The campaign's theme song in the Beatles 'Drive My Car'.

4 May. Ringo presents the annual World Music Awards at Monte Carlo.

5 May. Ringo, George and Paul dine together at a vegetarian restaurant in Chiswick High Road, London.

8 June. Ringo, George and Paul, together with their wives, again visit the vegetarian restaurant in Chiswick High Road, London.

14 June. Ringo's 'Weight Of The World' is included on the sound-track CD *Getting Even With Dad* issued on Private Music 01005-82119-2.

22 June. Ringo, George and Paul, together with Jeff Lynne, attempt to work on a John Lennon demo of 'Now And Then' at Paul's East Sussex recording studio, the Mill.

23 June. Ringo, George and Paul continue their recording sessions at George's Friar Park Studios, FPSHOT.

22 August. Capitol Records' specialist label The Right Stuff releases CD versions of *Stop And Smell The Roses* and *Old Wave*.

27 August. Ringo's stepfather, Harry Graves, dies from pneumonia in Liverpool at the age of 87.

1 September. Harry Graves is buried at Huyton Cemetery in Liverpool, with Ringo in attendance.

6 September. Record company The Right Stuff reissue *Old Wave* on CD and cassette as a deluxe collectors' edition with previously unreleased tracks.

18 November. *Earthrise (The Rainforest Album)* is issued on Pyramid R2-71830. On it, Ringo sings one line of the song 'Spirit Of The Forest'.

30 November. Ringo is interviewed by satellite for the American ABC television show *Good Morning America*, during which he promotes the new release *The Beatles Live At The BBC*.

30 December. Maureen, Ringo's first wife, dies in hospital in America following a bone-marrow transplant.

1995

19 January. The episode 'Far Out Munsters' from the 1965 series of *The Munsters* is repeated on ITV in Britain. In the episode a group called the Standells perform 'I Want To Hold Your Hand' and 'Life's A Ringo'.

27 January. On BBC2's *Top Of The Pops 2* the promo for 'It Don't Come Easy' is screened.

6 February. Ringo, George and Paul are at Paul's studio, the Mill, to record 'Real Love'.

7 February. The three former Beatles continue recording 'Real Love' from the John Lennon demo disc.

17 February. Ringo and his All-Starr Band appear on the ABC television show *In Concert* in a pre-recorded segment.

20 March. Ringo, George and Paul continue recording at Paul's studio, the Mill.

21 March. The three former Beatles decide to abandon their efforts to record John Lennon's 'Now And Then'.

29 March. The three former Beatles are in Chiswick, London, viewing clips from the *Anthology* project.

31 March. Photographer Tom Hanley takes a photograph of Ringo, George and Paul together.

21 April. Ringo appears at the benefit for the Another Chance Foundation at the 14,000-seater Tucson Community Center.

15 May. Ringo, George and Paul return to the Mill studio.

16 May. Ringo, George and Paul finish recording 'Real Love'.

22 May. Ringo, George and Paul join George Martin at Abbey Road to listen to tracks for their forthcoming *Anthology* project.

24 May. Ringo films the American TV *Donahue* talk show. The audience ask him questions for an hour.

25 May. Ringo appears on *The Late Show With David Letterman* in the Ed Sullivan Theater where he'd appeared with the Beatles 31 years earlier. Before the show Ringo says to Letterman, 'What would you do if I sang out of tune, would you stand up and walk out on me?' Letterman says that he would and Ringo replies, 'Heartless bastard.'

26 May. Ringo begins rehearsing with his All-Starr Band in New York.

11 June. Ringo has further rehearsals with his All-Starr Band, this time in Los Angeles.

12 June. Ringo and Barbara arrive in Japan.

13 June. Ringo and his All-Starr Band hold a press conference in Tokyo.

14 June. Ringo and his All-Starr Band appear at Iwate Kenmin Kaikan in Morioka. The Fuji Television programme *Super Time* features a pre-recorded interview with Ringo.

15 June. Ringo and his All-Starr Band appear at Sendai Sun-Plaza in Sendai.

16 June. Ringo and his All-Starr Band appear at Niigata Telsa in Niigata.

18 June. Ringo and his All-Starr Band appear at Osaka Castle Hall, Osaka.

19 June. Ringo and his All-Starr Band appear at Kurashiki Shimin Kaikan in Kurashiki.

20 June. Ringo and his All-Starr Band appear at Hiroshima Kousel Nenkin Kaikan in Hiroshima.

22 June. Ringo and his All-Starr Band appear at Nagoya Century Hall, Nagoya.

24 June. Ringo and his All-Starr Band appear at Bay NK Hall in Uraysu.

26 June. Ringo and his All-Starr Band appear at the Nippon Budokan Hall in Tokyo.

27 June. Ringo and his All-Starr Band appear again at the Nippon Budokan Hall in Tokyo. The Japanese television station NHK-TV videotapes the show.

28 June. Ringo and his All-Starr Band appear at Hamamatu Kyouiku Bunka Kaikan in Hamamatu, the last date of the Japanese leg of their tour.

29 June. Ringo and Barbara leave Japan and fly to Detroit.

2 July. Ringo and his All-Starr Band appear at the Arch, St Louis, Missouri.

3 July. Ringo and his All-Starr Band appear at the Milwaukee Summerfest in Milwaukee, Wisconsin, one of America's largest music festivals, which runs for eleven days and has seven music stages, one comedy stage and an amphitheatre.

4 July. Ringo and his All-Starr Band appear at the Mall of America in Bloomington, Minnesota.

5 July. Ringo and his All-Starr Band appear at the Ravinia Festival Pavilion in Chicago, Illinois.

6 July. Ringo and his All-Starr Band appear at Highland Park in Illinois.

8 July. Ringo and his All-Starr Band perform two shows at the Star Plaza Theater, Merrillville, Indiana.

9 July. Ringo and his All-Starr Band appear at the Nautica Stage in Cleveland, Ohio.

10 July. Ringo and his All-Starr Band appear at the Pine Knob Music Theater in Detroit, Michigan. The *Donahue* show featuring Ringo is aired.

11 July. Ringo and his All-Starr Band appear at the First of America Stage in Acme, Michigan.

13 July. Ringo and his All-Starr Band appear at Radio City Music Hall in New York. The show opens with 'Don't Go Where The Road Don't Go', although 'Back Off Boogaloo' has now been dropped. Max Weinberg joins the group on stage for 'With A Little Help From My Friends'. Among the audience are Ringo's wife Barbara and her sister Marjorie, together with Lee Starkey, Zak's

wife, and their daughter Tatia Jane. Ringo appears on CBS TV's *This Morning*.

15 July. Ringo and his All-Starr Band appear at the Concord Hotel, Kiamesha Lake, in New York. They don't like the hotel and Ringo doesn't like his room, giving it to someone else and booking into another hotel. The air conditioning alternates between the ballroom and the dining room, but the hotel management won't have the air conditioning on in both places at once. This makes the ballroom hot and uncomfortable for both band and audience. During the encore three girls come on stage separately to give Ringo flowers and he kisses each of them in turn.

15 July. Ringo and his All-Starr Band appear again at the Concord Hotel, Kiamesha Lake, New York.

17 July. Ringo and his All-Starr Band appear at the Wolf Trap in Vienna, West Virginia.

18 July. Ringo and his All-Starr Band appear at the Garden State Arts Center in Holmdel, New Jersey. Max Weinberg, former member of Bruce Springsteen's E-Street Band, comes on stage for 'With A Little Help From My Friends'. As this is Springsteen's home state, the crowd begin chanting his name. Ringo also begins chanting, 'Bruce, Bruce, Bruce, Bruce. Oh, come out Bruce!' pointing to the side of the stage for an imaginary Springsteen.

19 July. Ringo and his All-Starr Band appear at the Harbor Lights Pavilion, Boston, Massachusetts before an audience of 3,350. When he introduces the second number, 'I Wanna Be Your Man' he comments, 'The next song I did with that other band I was in.' He introduces 'You're Sixteen' by saying, 'I'd like to do a number now for all the young girls in the audience . . . what is that, about ten young girls?'

21 July. Ringo and his All-Starr Band appear at Caesars in Atlantic City, New Jersey. The management insist that the group perform a shorter show than usual – probably because they want the people to spend more time in the casino. Jack Tempchen's set is cut from all the concerts at the hotel, and there were two shows per night. Ringo cuts three songs from his act: 'Don't Go Where The Road Don't Go', 'Closer To Home' and 'People Got To Be Free', which tightened the show to 90 minutes.

22 July. Ringo and his All-Starr Band appear again at Caesars with instructions to further cut the show. Apart from omitting the three numbers from the previous night, 'Boys' and 'No Sugar Tonight' are also cut from the repertoire. The set now lasts only 70 minutes. Noticing a couple with a little child, Ringo says, 'I see a lot of people with young children here. I wish my parents had brought me to see a show like this when I was young.' Their special guest for both shows is organist Paul Shaffer from *The Late Show With David Letterman*.

23 July. Ringo and his All-Starr Band make their final appearance at Caesars in Atlantic City, New Jersey.

25 July. Ringo and his All-Starr Band appear at the Warwick Music Theater in Warwick, Rhode Island. This is the first of three venues where the band played 'in the round'. The others are Wallingford and Latham. The stage actually turns as the group play and Ringo comments, 'This is the first time I've played one of these gigs where we keep moving. It's like constantly living in the present – there's always someone else!' The band now revert back to their full set. Instead of leaving the stage and then returning for an encore, Ringo decides to remain on stage telling the audience, 'What usually happens, you see, is we run off now, and you all get so excited that you want us back, and we run back! But of course, we can't run off here, we're "captured". So if you don't mind, just make the noise anyway.'

27 July. Ringo and his All-Starr Band appear at the Oakdale Theater in Wallingford, Connecticut.

28 July. Ringo and his All-Starr Band appear at the Starlite Music Theater, Latham, New York. This is another 'in the round' venue. There were to be two concerts this evening but, due to the stifling heat, the first show is cancelled.

29 July. Ringo and his All-Starr Band appear at the Melody Fair Theater in North Tonawanda, New York.

31 July. Ringo and his All-Starr Band appear at the Riverbend Music Center in Cincinnati, Ohio.

1 August. Ringo and his All-Starr Band appear at the Light Amphitheater in Pittsburgh, Pennsylvania.

3 August. Ringo and his All-Starr Band appear at the Orlando Centroplex, Orlando, Florida.

4 August. Ringo and his All-Starr Band appear at the Sunrise Musical Theater in Sunrise, Florida.

5 August. Ringo and his All-Starr Band appear again at the Sunrise Musical Theater in Sunrise, Florida.

7 August. Ringo and his All-Starr Band appear at the Chastain Park Amphitheater in Atlanta, Georgia.

8 August. Ringo and his All-Starr Band appear at the Palace Theater, Louisville, Kentucky.

9 August. Ringo and his All-Starr Band appear at the Van Braun Civic Center in Huntsville, Alabama.

11 August. Ringo and his All-Starr Band appear at the Arena Theater in Houston, Texas.

12 August. Ringo and his All-Starr Band appear at the Sunken Garden in San Antonio, Texas.

13 August. Ringo and his All-Starr Band appear at the Starplex Amphitheater in Dallas, Texas.

15 August. Ringo and his All-Starr Band appear at the Arizona Veterans Memorial Coliseum in Phoenix, Arizona.

16 August. Ringo and his All-Starr Band appear at Humphrey's in San Diego, California.

18 August. Ringo and his All-Starr Band appear at the Greek Theater, Los Angeles, California. Joe Walsh turns up following his tour with the Eagles and guests on 'With A Little Help From My Friends'.

19 August. Ringo and his All-Starr Band appear again at the Greek Theater in Los Angeles. Ringo's daughter Lee is present and visits Ringo backstage with her friends. Also in the audience are former Wings guitarist Laurence Juber and actor Tom Arnold.

20 August. Ringo and his All-Starr Band appear at the Concord Pavilion in Concord, California. Once again, 'Don't Go Where The Road Don't Go' has been dropped from the set list.

22 August. Ringo and his All-Starr Band appear at Pier 62/63 in Seattle, Washington. Ken Stringfellow from the Posies is in the audience. Ken had co-written 'Golden Blunders' on Ringo's *Time Takes Time* album. Initially he seems reluctant to appear as a guest on stage, but Ringo says, 'You going to come out, Ken, or are you going to hide? We're going to have a little help from Posie here.' Stringfellow then goes on stage and joins in 'With A Little Help From My Friends'.

23 August. Ringo and his All-Starr Band appear at Pier 62/63 in Seattle, Washington. It is to be the last date of the tour, as Ringo cancels the rest of the dates to rush to a London clinic where his daughter Lee is undergoing an operation to remove water from her brain.

24 August. Ringo and Zak return to England to see Lee in hospital.

16 September. Lee, having been released from hospital in London and returned to America, is rushed to a Boston hospital where a cancerous brain tumour is removed.

3 October. A photograph of Ringo, George and Paul, now often referred to as 'the Threetles', is published on the cover of the *Sun* newspaper.

20 November. Ringo appears on the American television show *Good Morning America* via satellite from his home in Monte Carlo as part of the promotion for the Beatles' *Anthology* project.

1996

14 January. A savage *Spitting Image* lampoon of Threetles Ringo, Paul and George is screened in Britain.

13 May. Ringo is videotaped with Paul performing the number 'Beautiful Night' at Paul's studios, the Mill.

30 June. Ringo appears alongside Willie Nelson at a charity concert in aid of schizophrenia at Peterborough, in Ontario, Canada.

24 November. The EMI double-album *The Live-In World Anti-Heroin Album* is issued in Britain, with two tracks by Ringo.

4 December. A clip of Ringo, George and Paul performing 'Blue Moon Of Kentucky', originally recorded at George's Friar Park Studio, is shown on the programme *Good Morning America*.

31 December. At a party held by Barbara's sister Marjorie, Ringo meets Dean Grakal, who suggests they get together with his songwriting partner Mark Hudson.

1997

15 April. Ringo begins rehearsing with his All-Starr Band at Studio City in Los Angeles.

19 April. Rehearsals continue in Los Angeles at the Center Stage in Studio City.

24 April. The *After Breakfast* show is broadcast, with a performance by Ringo and his All-Starr Band playing 'With A Little Help From My Friends'. The group end their rehearsals at Center Stage in Studio City one day early after it is decided to drop Dave Mason from the tour.

28 April. Ringo begins his tour with the fourth incarnation of his All-Starr Band, this time with an all-British line-up, at the Moore Theater in Seattle, Washington, before an audience of 1,400. The concert was originally due to take place at the Paramount Theater. Mark Rivera comments, 'It was the best opening night I've ever done in my life. We all felt that way.' Then he commented on the extended versions of the Cream and Frampton songs that had been used to replace the missing Dave Mason numbers, saying, 'Jack and Peter go "knob to knob". As Ringo says, it's just like with Cream. Jack's the kind of player that plays hard, then he plays harder. And Peter's playing better than he's ever played.'

29 April. Ringo and his All-Starr Band appear at the Hult Center for the Performing Arts in Eugene, Oregon. The concert was originally due to appear at the Silva Hall in Eugene.

30 April. Ringo and his All-Starr Band appear at the Arlene Schnitzer Auditorium in Portland, Oregon.

1 May. Ringo was to have been the main guest on *The Tonight Show With Jay Leno*, but drops out as it would mean nine days of straight work without a break.

2 May. Ringo and his All-Starr Band appear at the Concord Pavilion, San Francisco, California. Brooker performs 'A Whiter Shade Of Pale', which led Ringo to comment, 'I was on a few records that mattered in the Sixties, but this is one that mattered to me.' At the A&M Studios in Los Angeles, engineer Brian Scheubele begins mixing twelve songs from the first half of the Budokan Hall concert in Tokyo, Japan, for the forthcoming release *Ringo Starr And His Third All-Starr Band – Volume One*.

3 May. Ringo and his All-Starr Band appear at the Universal Amphitheater in Los Angeles, California. When Jack Bruce performs his 'Theme From An Imaginary Western', he dedicates it to the late Felix Pappalardi, the producer of Cream. After 'A Whiter Shade Of Pale', Ringo says, 'Enough of these oldies, now we're going to play something a little more modern – from 1974!' and then performs 'Photograph'. For the encore Ringo tells the audience, 'If you're good we might have a couple of special guests come and join us for this next one.' They are then joined on stage by Eric Burdon, Mark Farner and Timothy B. Schmit. Backstage in the amphitheatre's courtyard were a

number of celebrities – Jason and Lee, Ringo's kids, Jeff Lynne, Jim Capaldi, Carmine and Vinni Appice, Don Was and Gary Wright.

4 May. Ringo and his All-Starr Band appear at Humphrey's in San Diego, California.

5 May. Ringo and his All-Starr Band appear at the Mesa Amphitheater in Phoenix, Arizona.

7 May. Ringo and his All-Starr Band appear at Fiddler's Green Amphitheater in Denver, Colorado. Ginger Baker, former member of Cream, then living in Denver, joins the band in the performance of the Cream hit 'White Room'.

9 May. Ringo and his All-Starr Band appear at Rosemont Horizon in Chicago, Illinois.

10 May. Ringo and his All-Starr Band appear at the Riverport Amphitheater in St Louis, Missouri.

11 May. Ringo and his All-Starr Band appear at the State Theater, Minneapolis, Minnesota. When Gary Brooker plays the Procol Harum number 'Power Failure' he is joined by guest guitarist Leo Kottke.

13 May. Ringo and his All-Starr Band appear at Eagles Ballroom, Milwaukee, Wisconsin.

14 May. Ringo and his All-Starr Band appear at the Breslin Center, East Lansing, Michigan. As it is Jack Bruce's birthday, he is presented with a cake on stage and the band and the audience all sing 'Happy Birthday' to him.

16 May. Ringo and his All-Starr Band appear at Chastain Park, Atlanta, Georgia.

17 May. Ringo and his All-Starr Band appear at the Sunrise Theater, Miami, Florida.

18 May. Ringo and his All-Starr Band appear at Ruth Eckerd Hall in Tampa, Florida.

20 May. Ringo and his All-Starr Band appear at the Palace Theater, Myrtle Beach, South Carolina.

21 May. Ringo and his All-Starr Band appear at the Wolf Trap Farm Park For The Performing Arts in Vienna, Virginia. Nils Lofgren appears as a guest.

23 May. Ringo and his All-Starr Band appear at Billy Bob's Texas in Fort Worth, Texas.

24 May. Ringo and his All-Starr Band appear at the Lone Star Amphitheater in the Six Flag Fiesta amusement park in San Antonio, Texas.

25 May. Ringo and his All-Starr Band appear at the Six Flags Astroworld in Houston, Texas. Joe Walsh guests on 'Photograph' and 'With A Little Help From My Friends'.

28 May. Ringo and his All-Starr Band appear at the Bob Carpenter Center at the University of Delaware in Newark, Delaware. It is Gary Brooker's birthday, and he is also greeted with a birthday celebration on stage.

29 May. Ringo and his All-Starr Band appear at the I.C. Light Amphitheater in Pittsburgh, Pennsylvania.
30 May. Ringo and his All-Starr Band appear at the Pine Knob Amphitheater in Detroit, Michigan. The entire concert is videotaped and released in America as a home video, *Ringo Starr And His Fourth All-Starr Band,* on MPI home video on 28 July 1998. The video is 2 hours and 15 minutes in length and includes some backstage conversation.
31 May. Ringo and his All-Starr Band appear at the Rubber Bowl in Akron, Ohio, for the Veterans' Memorial Concert. This was part of the Salvation Army Veterans' Jam, and Aretha Franklin and Three Dog Night are also on the bill.
2 June. Ringo and his All-Starr Band appear at the Mohegan Sun Resort and Casino in Uncasville, Connecticut.
3 June. Ringo and his All-Starr Band appear at the PNC Bank Arts Center in Holmdel, New Jersey.
4 June. Ringo and his All-Starr Band appear again at the PNC Bank Arts Center. After the show the band are treated to a 'farewell and thank you' dinner.
5 June. Ringo and his All-Starr Band appear at the Harborlights Pavilion in Boston, Massachusetts.
6 June. Ringo and his All-Starr Band appear at the Resorts International in Atlantic City, New Jersey.
7 June. Ringo and his All-Starr Band appear at the Jones Beach Amphitheater in Wantaugh, New York. It is the last show of the tour and Ringo announces that he is going to 'let all of the boys do their solos'.
20 July. At the Whatinthewhatthe? Studios in Los Angeles, Ringo and his band the Roundheads continue recording for the *Vertical Man* album with the tracks 'What In The ... World', 'La De Da' and 'Mindfield'.
28 July. Ringo records the vocal for the track 'What In The ... World' in Los Angeles.
29 July. Ringo goes to the House of Blues in Sunset Strip, Los Angeles to watch his friend Joe Walsh perform.
30 July. At the Whatinthewhatthe? Studios Ringo records the vocals for the track 'Without Understanding'.
31 July. Joe Walsh turns up at the Whatinthewhatthe? Studios and adds the guitar track to the numbers 'What In The ... World', 'La De Da' and 'Mindfield'.
1 August. Ringo records another vocal for the 'Without Understanding' track in Los Angeles.
5 August. Recording continues on the *Vertical Man* album with the track 'Good News', which was originally known as 'Old Country Song'.
7 August. Lee Rocker, former member of the Stray Cats, drops into the Whatinthewhatthe? Studios to add his bass track to the 'Good News' number.

12 August. Blockbuster Video releases *Ringo And His All-Starr Band* as a home video in America, exclusively available at Blockbuster Music and Blockbuster Video.

29 September. At Paul McCartney's East Sussex studios, the Mill, Paul records backing vocals and bass for 'La De Da' and also another bass line for the track 'What In The . . . World'. Ringo, Mark Hudson, Dean Grakal and Geoff Emerick are also present.

15 October. Ringo and Barbara join Paul and Linda McCartney at Stella McCartney's fashion show in Paris. The string overdubs to 'I'm Yours' and 'King Of Broken Hearts' are added at AIR Studios in London.

27 October. Ringo films his appearance in the promo of Paul McCartney's 'Beautiful Night'.

1 November. Ringo returns to Los Angeles to continue work on the *Vertical Man* album.

3 November. Ringo records 'I Was Walkin'' at the Whatinthewhatthe? Studios in Los Angeles.

4 November. Ringo begins sessions on the number 'Puppet', originally called 'The Puppet Song'.

6 November. Ringo begins recording the track 'Sometimes'.

7 November. At the *Vertical Man* sessions Jeff 'Skunk' Baxter adds his steel guitar to the tracks 'Sometimes' and 'One'. Keyboards player Jim Cox also turns up to provide keyboards work on various tracks.

11 November. Jeff 'Skunk' Baxter adds piano to 'I Was Walkin'', 'La De Da' and 'Sometimes' at the Village Recorders Studio.

12 November. Overdubs for the *Vertical Man* album are put on tape at the Village Recorders Studio in Los Angeles.

13 November. At the Village Recorders Studio a huge choir of 46 friends and relatives of Ringo gather to provide backing vocals for the track 'La De Da'. They include his wife Barbara together with her daughter Francesca and sister Marjorie, producer Mark Hudson and his daughter Sarah, Nils Lofgren, Van Dyke Parks and his family, and Keith Allison, former member of Paul Revere and the Raiders.

14 November. Timothy B. Schmit and Dave Gibbs add their backing vocals to 'Puppet' and 'Sometimes'.

17 November. Aerosmith's Steve Tyler has flown in especially from Amsterdam to provide harmonica on the track 'Love Me Do'. He also plays harmonica on the track 'I Was Walkin''.

18 November. Ringo asks Steve Tyler to re-record his harmonica part for 'Love Me Do' to match the original recording.

19 November. Alanis Morissette drops into the Whatinthewhatthe? Studios and ends up providing a vocal for 'Drift Away'.

20 November. The latest artists to drop into the studio and add their contribution during the *Vertical Man* recordings are a gospel group based in Los Angeles called Sauce.

22 November. Channel Four in Britain screens an episode of the series *Brit Girls* featuring Cilla Black, which includes a contribution from Ringo.

25 November. Brian Wilson drops into the studio to add his voice to the 'Without Understanding' track and Christian Phillippe Quillici, Barbara's nephew, also sings on the track. Alanis Morissette also returns to the studio to provide backing vocals to 'Mindfield' and 'I Was Walkin".

30 November. Geoff Emerick flies into Los Angeles to begin work on the mixing of the *Vertical Man* album.

1 December. Mixing is completed on the track 'One' from the *Vertical Man* album, with Geoff Emerick working from the A&M Studios in Los Angeles.

2 December. Emerick completes mixing the 'Mr Double-It-Up' track.

5 December. Mixing is completed on the 'Everyday' track.

8 December. Mixing is completed on the 'I'm Yours' track.

11 December. Mixing is completed on the 'What In The ... World' track.

12 December. The announcement is made that Ringo has signed a record deal with Guardian Records, one of EMI's smaller labels, who will release the *Vertical Man* album.

16 December. Work is completed on the mixing of the 'Love Me Do' track.

18 December. Only days after Guardian Records has announced that it will be releasing *Vertical Man*, the new EMI president Ken Barry announces that he will be closing down the company's smaller labels. Guardian Records is one of them and Ringo no longer has a record company outlet.

22 December. George Harrison's overdubs for two of the *Vertical Man* tracks arrive in the post and Ringo gathers his group together to rush to the Village Recorders Studio to hear them.

1998

6 January. Mixing begins on the 'Mindfield' track for Ringo's *Vertical Man* album at A&M Studios in Los Angeles.

8 January. Mixing begins on the 'King Of Broken Hearts' track for the *Vertical Man* album, which includes George Harrison's overdubs.

11 January. Mixing begins on the track 'Drift Away' from the *Vertical Man* album.

16 January. Ozzy Osbourne adds his vocals to the 'Vertical Man' track.

17 January. Sax player Joel Peskin records his piece for the song 'Puppet' at A&M's Los Angeles studio.

23 January. The final mixing on the track 'Puppet' is completed.

29 January. Ringo gathers his friends together to listen to the *Vertical Man* album at A&M Studios. They include his wife Barbara, producer Mark Hudson, Geoff Emerick, the Roundheads, Jeff Lynne, Timothy B. Schmit, Gary Brooker and Peter Frampton.

17 February. Mark Hudson and Geoff Emerick fly to New York to supervise the mastering of the *Vertical Man* album. Hudson, together with Bruce Grakal, also meet up with Danny Goldberg of Mercury Records, who agrees to issue the album.

18 February. Greg Calbi at Masterdisc in New York is mastering the tapes.

11 March. Ringo and Barbara assist in the launching of a Marie Curie Daffodil Appeal for the cancer charity in Hyde Park, London, in a campaign to fund eleven specialist-care centres. Ringo comments, 'In the last couple of years, my ex-wife died of leukaemia, my daughter had a brain tumour, and it's a year to the day since Barbara's mother died of cancer. I thought it was about time I stood up and helped out.'

16 March. Ringo and Barbara are among the guests at the launch party for George Martin's *In My Life* album at AIR Studios in London.

8 April. Ringo begins rehearsing with his new band in Los Angeles.

11 April. Ringo and the Roundheads complete their rehearsals in Los Angeles.

13 April. Ringo is in Los Angeles to promote his *Vertical Man* album. He holds a press reception at Pacific Television Center in Culver City, California, mainly for the television media including CNN, E!, Fox News, MSNBC and ABC In Concert.

14 April. Ringo poses for photographer Harry Diltz for the centrefold of his *Vertical Man* album. He also holds a press reception for the newspaper and magazine media at the Wyndham Belage Hotel in West Hollywood.

17 April. Linda McCartney dies from cancer.

20 April. From their home in Monaco, Ringo and Barbara release a statement: 'Both Barbara and I would like to say how sorry we are. We were privileged to have known her – her positive courage through her illness was truly inspiring. We send all our love to Paul, Heather, Mary, Stella and James. It was a blessing that she was in our lives.'

23 April. Mercury Records ask Ringo to remove Steve Tyler's lead vocal from the 'Drift Away' track on the *Vertical Man* album due to their release of the *Armageddon* soundtrack, which features four Aerosmith tracks.

27 April. Ringo and the Roundheads begin a new set of rehearsals in London that last until 8 May.

2 May. Final mastering of the *Vertical Man* album begins at A&M Studios in Los Angeles.

9 May. Ringo and the Roundheads rehearse at S.I.R. (Studio Instrumental Rentals) in New York, where they also shoot footage for the 'La De Da' promo.

10 May. In New York Ringo shoots the promotional video for 'La De Da'. His plans to do it at Shea Stadium are shelved due to heavy rain and he films it on New York streets with the group Hanson and his daughter Lee.

12 May. Ringo and the Roundheads rehearse for the VH-1 show *Storytellers* at the Bottom Line Club in New York.

13 May. Ringo and the Roundheads perform their set for the VH-1 show *Storytellers* at the Bottom Line club, performing several numbers for the 45-minute show, including 'With A Little Help From My Friends', 'Back Off Boogaloo', 'Don't Pass Me By', 'It Don't Come Easy', 'Octopus's Garden', 'La De Da', 'King Of Broken Hearts' and 'Love Me Do'.

14 May. In the morning Ringo and his band videotape 'La De Da' at WABC Studios in New York for *Live With Regis And Kathie Lee*. Due to the death of Frank Sinatra, a planned interview with Ringo and Paul, pre-recorded at Paul McCartney's the Mill studio during the recording of *Vertical Man*, is postponed by *Entertainment Tonight*. The electronic press kit for *Vertical Man* is released to the media in America. Ringo videotapes three numbers, 'La De Da', 'Photograph' and 'With A Little Help From My Friends', for *The View*, an ABC Television show, with this edition called 'Ringo Invasion'.

18 May. *Entertainment Tonight* screens the pre-recorded interview with Ringo and Paul, originally scheduled for 14 May.

19 May. MTV Europe premieres the promo clip for 'La De Da'.

20 May. Ringo's pre-recorded performance of 'La De Da' with the Roundheads appears on the programme *Live With Regis And Kathie Lee*.

21 May. Ringo's pre-recorded performance appears on the ABC TV show *The View*.

22 May. Ringo and Barbara attend the auction for Elizabeth Taylor's Cinema Against AIDS charity at the Moulin De Mougins Restaurant in Cannes. First £60,000 is pledged for Ringo and Elton John to perform 'Great Balls Of Fire', then £90,000 is pledged for Ringo, Elton and Sharon Stone to perform 'Twist And Shout'. The TV show *Entertainment Tonight* screened excerpts from the performance.

24 May. Ringo leaves England for New York and an appearance on the *Donahue* show and *The Late Show With David Letterman*.

25 May. *Entertainment Tonight* screens Ringo's promo video for 'La De Da'.

28 May. Ringo and his All-Starr Band begin rehearsals at the York Theater, Vancouver.

31 May. The German TV show *Gute Nacht Gottschaulk* interviews Ringo and a clip of the All-Starr Band performing 'It Don't Come Easy' is shown.

1 June. Ringo's single 'La De Da' is sent to American radio stations.

8 June. Ringo and Barbara attend the memorial service for Linda McCartney at St Martin-in-the-Fields in London.

10 June. A radio special of *Vertical Man* is syndicated throughout the United States.

11 June. Ringo and his All-Starr Band pose for tour promo pictures and promo photographs by rock photographer Henry Diltz. Shots

taken in Ringo's Beverly Hills home include Ringo in his games room and on the diving board of his pool. Ringo is also shown giving the peace sign, with Diltz commenting, 'I have a collection of people making the peace sign.'

14 June. Ringo is at S.I.R. Studios in Hollywood where he videotapes 'Rocking With Ringo' for *Access Hollywood*, to be broadcast by NBC the following day.

15 June. In the morning Ringo and the Roundheads record *The Mark And Brian Radio Show*. In the evening Ringo appears on *The Tonight Show* and is interviewed by Jay Leno at the NBC Studio 3 in Burbank, California. He also performs 'La De Da' with the Roundheads.

16 June. Ringo arrives in New York to promote *Vertical Man*, which is released in America today. It is Ringo's first album in six years.

17 June. Ringo's pre-recorded appearance on Howard Stern's radio show *The View* is broadcast, in addition to a pre-recorded interview on *Larry King Live* and an Internet interview for AOL. Ringo and the Roundheads also record *Hard Rock Live* for VH-1 at the Sony Music Studios in New York. The television programme *The View*, which Ringo videotaped on 14 May, is broadcast by ABC TV in America.

26 June. Ringo appears on the Channel Four show *TFI Friday* and is interviewed by Chris Evans.

3 July. *Live With Regis And Kathie Lee* transmit the 14 May pre-recorded appearance by Ringo and the Roundheads.

4 July. *The ITV Chart Show* in Britain screens a clip of the 'La De Da' promo.

9 July. The American CNN show *Showbiz Today* screens a pre-recorded interview with Ringo. Ringo and the Roundheads performance for *Hard Rock Live* is mixed by Mark Hudson and Scott Gordon at the Village Recorders Studio in Los Angeles.

12 July. A pre-recorded interview with Ringo is featured on the VH-1 Europe show *Talk Music*. It is repeated twice in the next few days.

15 July. Ringo makes a live appearance on the *National Lottery Live* TV show from the BBC Television Centre in London and mimes to 'La De Da'.

19 July. The *Sunday Times* magazine features an article on Ringo entitled 'Rhythm 'n' Blues'. There is a quote from Ringo in which he says, 'I've never written my autobiography, because the publishers only want to know what happened in the Beatles. But I'm not interested in any of that. I was born very young and had a good life. End of story.'

21 July. Ringo travels to the Continent to meet the German and Finnish press to promote his forthcoming European tour.

23 July. An interview recorded on 21 July is broadcast on the German television channel ZDF's *Leute Heute*.

25 July. Ringo appears live on *The Steve Wright Show*, a BBC Radio 2 programme.

27 July. Mercury Records announce that they will not be releasing 'La De Da' as a single after all.

28 July. The home video *Ringo And His Fourth All-Starr Band* is released in America by PMI Video.

3 August. Part one of an interview with Ringo, taped on 17 June, appears on the American TV show *The Howard Stern Show* on the 'E!' channel.

6 August. Ringo and his All-Starr Band complete their tour rehearsals in London.

7 August. Ringo and his All-Starr Band open their concert tour at the Helsingin Jaahalli in Helsinki, Finland, on the opening date of their European tour.

8 August. Ringo and his All-Starr Band appear at the Festival in Zurich, Switzerland.

9 August. Ringo and his All-Starr Band appear at the Smukkeste Festivale in Skanderborg in Denmark.

12 August. Ringo and his All-Starr Band appear at the Freilichtbuehne in Killesburg, Stuttgart, in Germany.

13 August. Ringo and his All-Starr Band appear at the Theatreplatz in Chemnitz, Germany.

15 August. The concert at Luxembourg City in Luxembourg is cancelled due to a dispute with the promoter. A pre-recorded interview with Ringo appears on the German news channel N-TV, along with a clip of 'It Don't Come Easy' from their Theatreplatz concert.

16 August. Ringo and his All-Starr-Band appear at the Marktrock Festival in Leuven, Belgium. Ringo and the All-Starrs are the headliners and also on the bill are the Wailers, the Charlatans and Nick Rowe. Studio Brussels air a broadcast of 'It Don't Come Easy', 'Act Naturally', 'Show Me The Way', 'Sunshine Of Your Love', 'La De Da', 'All Right Now', 'So You Feel Like We Do', 'White Room', 'A Whiter Shade Of Pale' and 'With A Little Help From My Friends'.

18 August. Ringo and his All-Starr Band appear at Expo '98 in Lisbon, Portugal.

20 August. Ringo and his All-Starr Band appear at the Point Theatre in Dublin, Ireland.

21 August. Ringo and his All-Starr Band appear at the Shepherd's Bush Empire, London. Backstage, Ringo is interviewed for the *Today* show, an Australian Channel 9 programme. It is his only British appearance during the tour – a second concert that was to have taken place at the same venue the following day is cancelled.

22 August. *That'll Be The Day* is screened on Channel Four in Britain.

24 August. Ringo holds a press conference at the Rhythm & Blues Café in Moscow, Russia.

25 August. Ringo and his All-Starr Band appear at the Moscow Sports Complex in Moscow, Russia. This is the first time a former member of the Beatles has appeared in Russia.

26 August. Ringo and his All-Starr Band appear at the Jubilee Complex in St Petersburg, Russia, before an audience of 1,500.

27 August. Ringo's album *Vertical Man* drops out of the British charts after selling only 2,000 copies and reaching its highest position at No. 85.

28 August. Ringo and his All-Starr Band make the first of a series of appearances at the Sporting Club, Monte Carlo, where Ringo currently lives as a tax exile. They perform eight numbers during a shortened set.

29 August. Ringo and his All-Starr Band appear again at the Sporting Club, Monte Carlo.

30 August. Ringo and his All-Starr Band perform their third concert at the Sporting Club, Monte Carlo.

1 September. Ringo and his All-Starr Band appear at the Gruga Halle in Essen, Germany.

2 September. Ringo and his All-Starr Band appear at the Stadtpark Freilichbuhne in Hamburg, Germany.

3 September. Ringo and his All-Starr Band appear at the Museumhof in Bonn, Germany.

5 September. Ringo and his All-Starr Band appear at the Wintershall '98 Rock Extravaganza in Bramley, Kent, a fundraising event in aid of a lung cancer charity. Ringo topped the bill and Mike Rutherford joined him on stage for several numbers. Also on the bill were Roger Taylor of Queen, Rory Bremner, Bob Geldof and Mal Pope.

6 September. Ringo and his All-Starr Band return to America.

7 September. Former Beatles aide Derek Taylor, who has been suffering from cancer, dies in his sleep. Ringo and his All-Starr Band appear on the 'Jerry Lewis Muscular Dystrophy Telethon'.

27 September. The *News of the World* reveals that Kenny Hockley, Ringo's gardener, has been arrested for selling drugs from the greenhouse in the garden of Ringo's mansion.

10 October. Ringo appears on *Wetten Dass?* the German television show and mimes to 'La De Da'.

19 October. Ringo's album *Storytellers* is released simultaneously around the world by Mercury Records.

20 October. Ringo tapes an appearance on *Late Night With David Letterman* during which he performs 'Back Off Boogaloo' for the first time. He later appears at a signing at the Tower Records store in New York City, but will only sign copies of the *Storytellers* and *Vertical Man* CDs.

21 October. Ringo appears on the ABC TV show *Live With Regis And Kathie Lee* at WABC Television Studios in New York and with his Roundheads performs 'Back Off Boogaloo' and 'Photograph'. During the interview he plugs his *Storytellers* CD.

8 November. The VH-1 *Storytellers* appearance at the Bottom Line Club recorded on 13 May is premiered on VH-1 Europe.

19 November. Ringo's *Storytellers* performance is repeated on VH-1 in America.

18 December. Ringo and Barbara feature in a pre-recorded appearance on the Carlton TV programme 'A Capital Christmas', screened in the southern part of England.

20 December. VH-1 Europe repeats the Ringo performance in *Storytellers*.

1999

30 January. The Ringo Starr edition of *Hard Rock Live* is screened in America on VH-1.

11 February. Ringo appears on an Internet chat line for AOL prior to his All-Starr Band's tenth anniversary tour.

12 February. Ringo and his All-Starr Band appear at the Taj Mahal Casino in Atlantic City. The venue seats 3,300 and is approximately 80% full. Ringo wears a bright-red jacket, black shirt with stars in the centre, black trousers and Day-Glo painted trainers.

13 February. Ringo and his All-Starr Band appear again at the Taj Mahal Casino in Atlantic City. A drunken member of the audience keeps shouting out, 'Queen Of Broken Hearts.' Eventually Ringo says, 'You've been at the bar haven't you? It's actually "King Of Broken Hearts", but we're not going to do that one.'

14 February. Ringo and his All-Starr Band make their third concert appearance at the Taj Mahal Casino in Atlantic City. Ringo says, 'Happy Valentine's Day, everybody. Are there any little girls on the front row?' He then begins tossing sweets into the audience.

16 February. Ringo and his All-Starr Band appear at the Beacon Theater in New York City. Ringo also holds a press conference at New York's All-Star Café to promote the All-Starr Band's tenth anniversary tour. He confirms that Joe Walsh had left to rejoin the Eagles, saying, 'Joe called me one day and said he's in, then called and said he's out.' Discussing his Christmas album project, he says, 'It'll be very Christmassy – lots of bells, ding, ding, ding.'

17 February. Ringo and his All-Starr Band appear again at the Beacon Theater in New York City. Reviews aren't all that good; the *New York Times* reports that Ringo's charisma 'at least for a while, obviated the moments of musical gracelessness and the forced sense of good times that rippled through the music'.

19 February. Ringo and his All-Starr Band appear at the Mohegan Sun Casino in Uncasville, Connecticut

20 February. Ringo and his All-Starr Band appear again at the Mohegan Sun Casino in Uncasville, Connecticut.

21 February. Ringo and his All-Starr Band appear at the Westbury Music Fair in Westbury, New York.

22 February. Ringo and his All-Starr Band appear at the Jerome C. Shottenstein Center at the Value City Arena in Columbus, Ohio, a new basketball arena at the side of Ohio State University. When a fan hands Ringo a Stetson, he wears it throughout the show.

24 February. Ringo and his All-Starr Band return for a further concert at the Westbury Music Fair in Westbury, New York. The show takes place on a revolving stage at the 2,800-seat venue. Ringo asks, 'How many of you are here from the other show and never left?'

26 February. Ringo and his All-Starr Band appear at the Star Plaza Theater in Merrillville, Indiana.

28 February. Ringo and his All-Starr Band appear at the Park West in Chicago, Illinois, a 750-seat nightclub. Two girls sent a note requesting a drumstick and he went backstage and then gave them a pair. The local newspaper the *Sun Times* writes that the show was 'a blast, because everyone clearly had a jolly good time, and no one more than the host'.

1 March. Ringo and his All-Starr Band appear at the Palace Theater, Detroit, Michigan.

4 March. Ringo and his All-Starr Band appear at the Eureka Municipal Auditorium in Eureka, a 2,300-seater venue at which Ringo signs autographs from the stage for the first time.

5 March. Ringo and his All-Starr Band appear at the Konocti Harbor Resort and Spa in Kelseyville, California. They perform in the 1000-seater Joe Mazzola Classic Concert Showroom.

6 March. Ringo and his All-Starr Band appear again at the Konocti Harbor Resort and Spa. The local newspaper, the *Press-Democrat,* writes that the group 'revived each classic with plenty of heart and soul, proving their worth as ageless rockers with a relentless knack for playing live music'.

7 March. Ringo and his All-Starr Band appear at the Berkeley Community Theater in Berkeley, California, a 2,500-seater venue.

11 March. Ringo and his All-Starr Band appear at the Bank America Center in Boise, Idaho, before an audience of 3,800. (This was originally to have taken place on 14 March at the BSO Pavilion, Boise.)

12 March. Ringo and his All-Starr Band appear at the Dee Event Center in Weber Star University in Ogden, Utah, before an audience of 2,800.

13 March. Ringo and his All-Starr Band appear at the Joint in the Hard Rock Hotel and Casino in Las Vegas, Nevada, before an audience of 1,200.

14 March. Ringo and his All-Starr Band appear at 4th & B in San Diego, California, where the 1,500-seater venue was a complete sellout.

15 March. Ringo and his All-Starr Band appear again at 4th & B in San Diego.

18 March. Ringo and his All-Starr Band appear at the Universal Amphitheater in Los Angeles, California, before an audience of 4,500. He notices someone holding a sign with the name Pete Best on it and jokes, 'I see we have the Pete Best Fan Club here. That's the dead section – just kidding.' The band are joined on stage for two encores by

Joe Walsh, and Bruce Gary of the Knack also joins them on 'With A Little Help From My Friends'.

19 March. Ringo and his All-Starr Band appear at the Silver Legacy Casino in Reno, Nevada.

20 March. Ringo and his All-Starr Band appear again at the Silver Legacy Casino. The 1,500-capacity ballroom is sold out on both nights. The show is truncated to 75 minutes by dropping the numbers 'Shooting Star', 'Hammer In My Heart', 'Back Off Boogaloo', 'I Feel Free', 'I Wanna Be Your Man' and 'You're Sixteen'.

21 March. Ringo and his All-Starr Band appear in the South Shore Room at Harrah's Casino in Lake Tahoe, Nevada. The 800-capacity venue is sold out, despite the ticket price of $100. 'You're Sixteen' returns to the repertoire.

25 March. Ringo and his All-Starr Band appear at the Horseshoe Casino in Tunca, Mississippi, where there is a lower age-limit of 25 on admissions. The repertoire is returned to its full set and Ringo refers to the members of the audience as 'Tunisians'.

26 March. Ringo and his All-Starr Band appear at the Florida Theater in Jacksonville, Florida.

27 March. Ringo and his All-Starr Band appear at the 4,000-seater Sunrise Musical Theater in Fort Lauderdale, Florida, sponsored by the WMXJ Radio Show. They were originally booked for the 20,000-seater Lockhart Stadium, but the sales didn't match expectations, although the Sunrise show is a complete sellout.

28 March. Ringo and his All-Starr Band complete their tour at the Hard Rock Café in Orlando, Florida, a new 2,000-seater venue in Universal Studios Citywalk. Ringo tells the audience, 'I really love these guys and feel blessed to be able to work with these fantastic musicians – and to have worked with them all of these nights on this tour.'

29 March. Ringo and his All-Starr Band are due to appear on a two-hour show for the television programme *A&E* before a live audience at the Sony Music Studios in New York, but the event doesn't take place. An *A&E* spokesman says, 'It just didn't work out and we're not going to be airing it.'

5 April. Mark Hudson and Scott Gordon create a single edit of 'La De Da'.

24 May. Ringo, along with George Harrison and Jools Holland, attends the Chelsea Flower Show in London.

2 June. Ringo takes part in an Internet chat from Fort Lauderdale.

9 June. Ringo approves the 'La De Da' promo.

14 June. Ringo takes part in an Internet chat from Saratoga.

15 June. Ringo appears on the *Tonight* show.

17 June. Ringo appears on *The Larry King Show*.

18 June. The VH-1 programme *Hard Rock Live* featuring Ringo is screened in the States.

22 June. A clip of the rehearsal at the Bottom Line club is shown on *Entertainment Tonight*.

27 June. Ringo appears on the Kosovo Benefit charity concert 'Michael Jackson And Friends – What More Can I Give?' at the 80,000-capacity Olympic Stadium, Munich, Germany, performing 'Yellow Submarine' and 'With A Little Help From My Friends', backed by Jack Bruce and the Alan Parsons Project. Other artists included Michael Jackson and Stevie Wonder, while the classical concert in the evening features Luciano Pavarotti. The German television channel ZDF broadcasts the concerts.

29 June. Ringo takes part in an Internet chat from Denver, Colorado. 'La De Da' is officially premiered on VH-1's *Insomniac's Theater*.

4 July. The 'La De Da' promo has its British premiere on *The Chart Show*.

1 August. *Q* magazine features their readers' choice of the 100 greatest stars of the twentieth century. Ringo sits at No. 26 with the words, 'He's probably the best drummer in the world, if only because he treated his kit as a lead instrument while never playing a drum solo.' Also, 'Starr gave the Beatles a propulsive force that other bands lacked.'

19 October. Ringo's album *I Wanna Be Santa Claus* issued in the States.

2000

10 April. The movie *Candy* is released in America on DVD and video by Anchor Bay Entertainment Ltd.

2 May. Ringo holds a press reception at the Plaza Hotel, New York, to announce his forthcoming tour.

7 May. Ringo and his All-Starr Band begin rehearsals in Atlantic City, New Jersey. Ringo also takes part in an Internet chat.

12 May. Ringo and his All-Starr Band appear at the Trump Taj Mahal in Atlantic City, New Jersey.

13 May. Ringo and his All-Starr Band appear again at the Trump Taj Mahal.

15 May. Ringo and his All-Starr Band appear at the Mid-Hudson Civic Center in Poughkeepsie, New York.

16 May. Ringo and his All-Starr Band are at the Westbury Music Fair in Westbury, a Long Island venue in New York. It is a performance in the round with an audience of 2,800.

17 May. Ringo and his All-Starr Band appear again at the Westbury Music Fair.

18 May. Ringo records *The Late Show With David Letterman* at the Ed Sullivan Theater in New York.

19 May. Ringo and his All-Starr Band appear at the Mohegan Sun Center in Uncasville, Connecticut. *The Late Show With David Letterman* is broadcast. Apart from the interview, Ringo performs 'With A Little Help From My Friends'.

20 May. Ringo and his All-Starr Band appear again at the Mohegan Sun Center.

21 May. Ringo and his All-Starr Band appear at I Center in Salem, New Hampshire.

23 May. Ringo and his All-Starr Band appear at the Beacon Theater, New York. Andy Summers, former member of Police, joins the group for Jack Bruce's 'Theme From An Imaginary Western'. Max Weinberg joins the band for 'With A Little Help From My Friends'.

24 May. Ringo and his All-Starr Band appear at the State Theater in New Brunswick, New Jersey, a show that has been added to the itinerary. Due to a leak in the theatre roof, Ringo sings part of 'Raindrops Keep Falling On My Head'. Jack Bruce's son joins them on stage for 'With A Little Help From My Friends'.

26 May. Ringo and his All-Starr Band appear at the Norva in Norfolk, Virginia. This was Gene Vincent's home town and due to a request from a fan, Ringo sings a brief a cappella version of 'Be Bop A Lula'.

27 May. Ringo and his All-Starr Band appear at Tops Great American Rib Cook-Off & Music Festival in Cleveland, Ohio. This is a festival that runs from 25–29 May at Burk Lakefront Airport. Weird Al Yankovic is also co-headlining in Eric Carmen's home town.

28 May. Ringo and his All-Starr Band appear at the Riverport Amphitheater in Maryland Heights, Missouri. The concert was originally scheduled for 13 May, then 19 May, and finally moved to this date.

30 May. Ringo and his All-Starr Band appear at the Wolf Trap at the Filene Center in Vienna, Virginia.

31 May. Ringo and his All-Starr Band appear at the Gaylord Entertainment Center in Nashville, Tennessee, a concert that has been added to the original itinerary. Nashville Artists Pam Tillis, Kim Carnes, Tom Hanbridge and Sam Bush take the stage to join in the performance of 'With A Little Help From My Friends'. Jack Bruce performs 'Theme From An Imaginary Western' and is joined again by Andy Summers, former guitarist with Police.

1 June. Ringo and his All-Starr Band appear at the Horseshoe Casino in Robinsville, Mississippi.

3 June. Ringo and his All-Starr Band appear at Sunrise Musical Theater in Sunrise, Florida.

4 June. Ringo and his All-Starr Band appear at the Chastain Park Amphitheater in Atlanta, Georgia. Ringo has throat problems during the concert and the number 'I'm The Greatest' is dropped.

5 June. Ringo and his All-Starr Band are due to appear at the Iron City Light Amphitheater in Pittsburgh, Pennsylvania, but the concert is cancelled due to Ringo's illness. (A rescheduled concert at the venue is pencilled in for 2 July, but doesn't take place.)

7 June. Ringo and his All-Starr Band are due to appear at the Casino Rama in Rama, Ontario. This is the only Canadian date set for this tour, but it is cancelled due to Ringo's illness and isn't rescheduled.

8 June. Ringo and his All-Starr Band appear at the House Of Blues in Chicago, Illinois, following Ringo's bout of illness. 'I'm The Greatest' is dropped from this performance.

10 June. Ringo and his All-Starr Band appear at the Landmark Theater in Syracuse, New York.

11 June. Ringo and his All-Starr Band are due to appear at Freedom Park in Warren, Michigan, but the concert is relocated to the Pine Knob Music Theater in Clarkston, Michigan.

14 June. Ringo and his All-Starr Band appear at the Mountain Winery in Saratoga, California.

15 June. Ringo and his All-Starr Band appear once more at the Mountain Winery.

17 June. Ringo and his All-Starr Band appear at The Joint in the Hard Rock Hotel And Casino in Las Vegas, Nevada.

19 June. Ringo and his All-Starr Band are due to appear at the Sun Theater, Anaheim, California, but the concert is cancelled due to Ringo's continual throat problems.

20 June. A re-scheduled appearance at the Sun Theater is also cancelled due to Ringo's illness.

22 June. Ringo and his All-Starr Band appear at the House of Blues in West Hollywood, California. Guests who join them on stage include George Thorogood, former-Monkee Mickey Dolenz, Spencer Davis and Bruce Gary, drummer with the Knack.

23 June. Ringo and his All-Starr Band appear at the House of Blues again. One guest appears with them this evening, Bruce Gary of the Knack.

25 June. Ringo and his All-Starr Band appear at the first of two outdoor shows at Humphrey's By The Bay in San Diego, California, a 1,300-seater venue.

26 June. Ringo and his All-Starr Band perform their second outdoor concert at Humphrey's By The Bay and are joined on the number 'With A Little Help From My Friends' by Gary Pickett and Michael McDonald.

28 June. Ringo and his All-Starr Band appear at the Red Rocks Amphitheater in Morrison, Colorado. Ringo last appeared at this 9,600-seat venue in 1964 as a member of the Beatles.

30 June. Ringo and his All-Starr Band appear at the State Capitol Grounds in St Paul, Minnesota. During 'Yellow Submarine' Ringo mistakenly encourages the audience from 'Milwaukee' to join in with him.

1 July. Ringo and his All-Starr Band appear at the Summerfest at the Henry W. Maier Festival Park in Lake Michigan, although there are no solo spots during the performance and the band don't leave the stage prior to their encores. Ringo instructs the audience to 'visualise' them departing and leaving.

4 July. All-Starr Band concerts said to have been scheduled for today and tomorrow in Buenos Aires, Argentina, don't take place.

7 July. Ringo celebrates his 60th birthday. Perhaps 'celebrates' is not the best word to use. He says, 'I don't mind the other birthdays, but this one really gets up my nose.'

10 November. Ringo lights the bonfire at the Cranleigh Bonfire Event and also donates £5,000 to the charity.

16 December. Ringo and George Harrison attend the Christmas holiday gala show at the Cirque Du Soleil, Battersea.

2001

5 February. Eagle Records issues *Ringo Starr & His All-Starr Band – The Anthology . . . So Far.*

10 April. *Candy* is released on video and DVD by Anchor Bay in America. There is also a special limited edition of 16,000 'Candy Tin' DVD collector's cards.

1 August. Ringo appears on the Howard Stern radio show. He also makes a personal appearance at FYE in New York to sign copies of his CDs.

2 August. Ringo and his All-Starr Band appear on NBC's *Today* show.

30 November. Ringo makes a statement about the death of George Harrison: 'George was a best friend of mine. I loved him very much and I will miss him greatly. Barbara and I send our love and light to Olivia and Dhani. We will miss George for his sense of love, his sense of music and his sense of laughter.'

2002

16 March. Ringo and Barbara attend the annual Ball de la Rose in the Star Room of the Sporting club, Monte Carlo, Monaco. The ball is held in aid of the Princess Grace Foundation and Ringo and Marianne Faithfull perform, with Zak and Jason appearing in the backing band. Princess Stephanie is in the audience.

20 May. Ringo signs a new record deal with Koch Records.

20 June. Ringo and Barbara appear at the Cranleigh Carnival and Fun Day.

21 June. Beatles songs were performed by various artists in 'An Evening Of Beatles Music' at Cowdray House in East Sussex. The event is a concert for the Tibert House Trust and the White Lotus School in the Himalayas. Lulu performs 'Back In The USSR' and the other artists are Donovan with 'Julia' and 'Give Me Love', Dave Gilmour with 'Across The Universe', 'Revolution' and 'Long Long Long', Paul Carrack with 'It Won't be Long', Roger Taylor and Gary Brooker with 'Jealous Guy', 'I Feel Fine' and 'I Am The Walrus', Damon Hill with 'Come Together' and Bob Geldof sang a medley. Ringo ends the concert by performing 'Photograph', which he dedicates to George Harrison, 'Yellow Submarine', 'I Wanna Be Your Man', 'Boys' and 'With A Little Help From My Friends'. He is backed by his son Zak on drums, Ian McNabb on bass, Bernie Marsden on guitar, Peter Gordino on keyboard and Dave Caitlin on guitar.

22 June. Ringo and Barbara open a new gallery at the David Shepherd Wildlife Foundation, helping to raise money to support endangered mammals.
23 November. Barbara and Olivia Harrison are at the charity Christmas Dinner for the Tommy Campaign.
29 November. The 'Concert for George Harrison' tribute takes place at the Royal Albert Hall. Ringo is among the artists, who also include Paul McCartney, Eric Clapton, Ravi Shankar, Joe Brown, Jools Holland, Jeff Lynne, Tom Petty and Jim Keltner.
12 December. Barbara, together with Patti Boyd, joins Sarah, the Duchess of York in London to support the Chemical Dependency Charity.

2003

13 March. Ringo is on Jay Leno's *Tonight* show promoting his new album and his tribute to George Harrison, 'Never Without You'. He says that despite reports in the press he didn't join Paul McCartney at George Harrison's bedside in a New York hospital. He'd last seen George in Switzerland, six weeks before his death. He relates how he told George that he had to travel to Boston to see his daughter Lee, who was to undergo surgery. George, bedridden at the time, immediately said, 'Would you like me to go with you?'
14 March. Ringo appears on *E! News Live*.
17 March. The first of a two-part interview with Ringo on *Good Morning America* is broadcast – the second is shown on 18 March.
21 March. Ringo's appearance on CNN's *Morning With Paula Zahn* is scrapped due to the war in Iraq. Ringo's live appearance scheduled for *Good Morning Live* is also postponed for the same reason.
22 March. Ringo and the Roundheads perform a promotional set before the media at the Bottom Line club in New York. They play two new songs, 'Memphis In Your Mind' and 'Never Without You', plus a selection of past hits. VH-1 Classics presents a 'Ringo Rama Weekend'.
24 March. Ringo tapes an appearance on the American television show *Last Call With Carson Daly*, which is postponed until 1 April due to the Iraq war coverage. He discusses the Beatles *Anthology*, the Beatles' first visit to New York and the recording of 'Never Without You' and then performs that number and 'With A Little Help From My Friends' backed by the Roundheads. The *New York Post* also publishes an interview with Ringo in which he talks about his wife Barbara. 'I'm in love with that woman, and I'm blessed that she loves me. It's not like we're on cloud nine every day, we have our ups and downs. But overall it's great. All you have to do is remember why you're together in the first place, and you get through the rough times.' He also says, 'I love America, and Americans love me, I was blessed. America's always given me my due as one of the best drummers in the world.' On humour, he says, 'I've always been very quick with funny lines, it's my

character, but I have to watch that I don't live on that. Humour is a way to deflect things. I've used it to not deal with true emotions.' On the Beatles: 'God's love let us remember the good times, but if I thought they were all good times, I'd just be fooling myself. There were angry moments and disappointing moments. That's just what life is about. But look at what we did. I was a Beatle, and the music is still there today. It has held up. I'm proud to be a part of that. Back then I remember a woman holding up a baby and shouting to me, "His first words were 'yeah, yeah, yeah'." Is Britney singing anything the kids are learning today?' His interview on *Live With Regis And Kelly* was only shown in the Pacific time zone due to the launch of the war in Iraq.

25 March. Ringo appears on *The Conan O'Brien Show* and performs 'Never Without You'. He also appears on MTV's *TRL* and is a guest at New York's FYE to meet fans and sign copies of *Ringo Rama*.

26 March. Ringo appears on *The Daily Show* broadcast by Comedy Central.

1 April. Ringo appears on *Last Call* with Carson Daly.

9 April. Ringo performs 'Never Without You' on *Good Morning America*.

20 April. Clips of Ringo's performance at the Bottom Line club in New York, together with an interview, are broadcast on A&E's *Breakfast With The Arts*.

26 April. The KGSR Sunday night news premieres 'The Ringo Rama Radio Hour'.

19 May. Ringo and Barbara are at the Chelsea Flower Show to open a show garden – 'Octopuses Garden', designed by Marney Hall. It was designed to show awareness of the destruction of coral reefs. Cilla Black also turns up and says, 'I am an appreciator, a watcher. I do not have the green fingers but I do appreciate my own garden at home.'

22 May. Ringo donates a pair of his spectacles plus a signed photograph for the third annual 'Seeing The Stars' charity auction on Ebay in aid of the Discovery Fund for Eye Researchers.

3 June. Barbara, Francesca Gregorini and her actress friend Portia Rossi, are shopping in Bond Street, London.

7 June. A doodle by Ringo is auctioned for the Make A Wish Foundation at a masked ball at Blenheim Palace, Oxfordshire.

16 June. Ringo is a guest at Ravi Shankar's birthday celebrations.

18 June. Ringo is among the guests at an Indian themed party held by Heather as a surprise 61st birthday party for Paul. Other guests include Sir George Martin and Elvis Costello.

6 July. Ringo and Barbara attend the Cranleigh celebrity cricket match. The aim is to help raise funds for the building of a local hospital.

24 July. Ringo and his All-Starr Band begin their latest tour at Casino Rama, Toronto, Ontario, Canada.

25 July. Ringo and his All-Starr Band perform for a second night at Casino Rama in Toronto.

26 July. Ringo and his All-Starr Band appear at Darien Lake Six Flags Performing Arts Center, Darien Center, New York.

27 July. Ringo and his All-Starr Band appear at Fleet Boston Pavilion in Boston, Massachusetts.

28 July. Ringo and Barbara and Paul and Heather McCartney go to dinner together at the Four Seasons Hotel in New York.

29 July. Prior to his concert, Ringo holds a press reception at the Radio City Music Hall, New York City, New York, where he is appearing that night with the All-Starr Band.

30 July. Ringo and his All-Starr Band appear at the State Theater, Easton, Pennsylvania.

31 July. Ringo and his All-Starr Band appear at Mohegan Sun Casino, Uncasville, Connecticut.

1 August. While in New York, Ringo tapes his appearance on the *Good Morning America* television show.

2 August. Ringo and his All-Starr Band appear at Trump Taj Mahal, Atlantic City, New Jersey.

3 August. Ringo and his All-Starr Band appear at PNC Bank Arts Center, Holmdel, New Jersey.

5 August. Ringo and his All-Starr Band appear at Westbury Music Fair, Westbury, New York.

6 August. Ringo and his All-Starr Band appear again at Westbury Music Fair.

7 August. Ringo and his All-Starr Band appear at DTE Energy Music Theater, Detroit.

8 August. Ringo and his All-Starr Band appear at Van Andel Arena, Grand Rapids, Michigan.

9 August. Ringo and his All-Starr Band appear at Marcus Center For the Performing Arts, Milwaukee.

10 August. Ringo and his All-Starr Band appear at Soo Pass Ranch, Detroit Lakes, Minnesota.

12 August. Ringo and his All-Starr Band appear at Rosemont Theater, Rosemont, Illinois.

13 August. Ringo and his All-Starr Band appear at Chastain Park Amphitheater, Atlanta, Georgia.

15 August. Ringo and his All-Starr Band appear at the Grand Casino, Gulfport, Mississippi.

16 August. Ringo and his All-Starr Band appear at the Manaffay Theater, St Petersburg, Florida.

17 August. Ringo and his All-Starr Band appear at the Mizner Amphitheater, Boca Raton, Florida.

19 August. Ringo and his All-Starr Band appear at the Alico Arena, Florida Gulf Coast University, Fort Myers, Florida.

21 August. Ringo and his All-Starr Band appear at the Horseshoe Casino, Roberson, Mississippi.

22 August. Ringo and his All-Starr Band appear at Next Stage At Grand Prairie, Grand Prairie, Texas.

25 August. Ringo and his All-Starr Band appear at the Sandia Casino Amphitheater, Albuquerque, New Mexico.

26 August. Ringo and his All-Starr Band appear at the Amarillo Civic Center, Amarillo, Texas.

29 August. Ringo and his All-Starr Band appear at Harrah's Tahoe, Lake Tahoe, Nevada.

30 August. Ringo and his All-Starr Band appear at The Joint, Hard Rock Hotel, Las Vegas, Nevada.

31 August. Ringo and his All-Starr Band appear at Marymoor Park, Redmond, Washington.

2 September. Ringo and his All-Starr Band appear at Britt Festivals At Britt Pavilion, Jacksonville, Oregon.

4 September. Ringo and his All-Starr Band appear at the Villamontello Center for The Arts in Saratoga, California.

5 September. Ringo and his All-Starr Band appear at Dodge Theater, Phoenix, Arizona.

6 September. Ringo and his All-Starr Band are at the Universal Amphitheater, Universal City, California.

7 September. Ringo and his All-Starr Band are at Humphrey's, San Diego, California.

24 September. Ringo and Barbara attend the premiere of the *Concert For George* film on the Warner Brothers lot in Burbank, California.

Cilla

A BBC1 television series starring Liverpool singer Cilla Black, which was telecast live from the BBC Television Theatre in London. On 6 February 1968 Ringo became the first Beatle to make a solo musical performance. He also appeared in some comedy sketches, the first of which saw him acting as a ventriloquist with Cilla as his puppet, ending with an a cappella performance of the old British music-hall standard 'Nellie Dean'. Ringo and Cilla also performed a duet on the number 'Do You Like Me?' which had been penned by Herbert Darnlet in the early 1900s.

Ringo made a second appearance on the show on 1 October 1970, recording his appearance at the BBC Television Theatre in Shepherd's Bush, London. He sang a duet with Cilla, backed by a thirty-piece BBC orchestra, and performed a live version of 'Act Naturally'. Cilla also performed two Beatles numbers, 'Don't Pass Me By' in a duet with actor Richard Harris and 'Back In The USSR'. The theme song of the show was also Paul McCartney's composition 'Step Inside Love'. Stanley Holloway and John Clive were also on the 44-minute programme, which was aired on BBC1 on Saturday 13 February 1971.

Ringo received a fee of £750.

Cilla In Scandinavia

A television special filmed in Stockholm on 24 June 1971. Ringo was a guest on Cilla's show for the third time and sang 'It Don't Come Easy' on the peak of a mountain, to the sound of a 29-piece orchestra. He also sang 'The Snowman Song' with Cilla and Basil Brush (a popular hand puppet of a fox). Cilla, continuing a Beatles theme, sang 'Norwegian Wood', 'Drive My Car' and 'Step Inside Love'. The 45-minute programme was screened on BBC1 on Saturday 27 November 1971.

Clapton, Eric

Legendary guitarist Eric Clapton was George Harrison's closest friend and it was George who brought him in on a Beatles session to record the guitar solo in 'While My Guitar Gently Weeps'.

Clapton was born in Ripley, Surrey, on 30 March 1945 and joined various bands before teaming up with Ginger Baker and Jack Bruce in Cream. George Harrison composed the number 'Badge' for Cream to record, with Ringo giving him some help with the song.

He has appeared on a number of recording sessions with Ringo over the years, playing guitar on 'This Be Called A Song' on Ringo's 1976 album *Rotogravure* and also playing guitar on the 1983 album *Old Wave*.

During Clapton's wedding celebration party after he'd married George Harrison's former wife Patti, Ringo, George and Paul participated in a jam session, the nearest thing to a Beatles reunion.

Clapton also appeared with Ringo and George on Carl Perkins' TV special 'Blue Suede Shoes – A Rockabilly Session' in 1985 and performed with Ringo and George on the Prince's Trust Concert in 1987.

Ringo asked Eric to provide a guitar solo for 'Never Without You', his tribute to George on his *Ringo Rama* album.

Clemons, Clarence

An American musician born in Norfolk, Virginia, on 11 January 1942. In 1971 he began to work with Bruce Springsteen and became a member of the E Street Band. He also enjoyed a solo career and worked as a session musician. Clemons enjoyed an American Top 20 hit in 1986 with 'You're A Friend Of Mine'. He led various bands including the Red Bank Rockers, Clarence Clemons and Aja and Clarence Clemons and the Blues Crew.

In 1989 he became a member of the All-Starr Band, performing 'You're A Friend Of Mine' and 'Quarter To Three'.

Apart from being a musician, Clemons is also an actor and has appeared in films such as *Fatal Instinct* and *Bill And Ted's Excellent Adventure* and had a recurring role in the television series *Nash Bridges*.

The press release for the first All-Starr Band tour in 1989 included the following biography of Clemons:

'The Big Man on sax, also a gifted vocalist and a commanding talent, Clarence Clemons is a veteran of more than fifteen years with Bruce Springsteen and the E Street Band. He has a proven solo track record, with 'Rescue' and 'Hero' receiving critical raves, and has played on projects with Ian Hunter, Aretha Franklin, and Patti LaBelle.

'Born in Norfolk, Virginia, Clemons was reared in a devoutly religious family, and was given his first Pan American alto saxophone by his father when Clarence was a very young child. He continued playing in the high school jazz band and gradually switched to playing the tenor sax. Clemons attended Maryland State College with music and football scholarships, and began moonlighting with 'surf bands' around the Chesapeake Bay coast. When he moved to Philadelphia to play semi-pro football with the Newark Bears and then the Jersey Generals, he played with the Entertainers, met E Street Band bassist Gary Tallent, and finally Bruce Springsteen. Since then, Clemons has evolved as an integral part of the E Street Band, receiving accolades from fans, musicians, and musical organisations.

'Clarence's latest album, *A Night with Mr. C*, features many top names in the industry, and his role on tour with Ringo Starr and the All-Starr Band will once again prove that Clarence Clemons is one of the most accomplished, well-loved and well-respected sax players in musical history.'

Clarence is unlikely to be called to join another All-Starr Band line-up. Ringo invited him to join the 1995 All-Starr tour but he told Ringo that he wouldn't appear in Japan and was only willing to appear on a few dates. Ringo ended up hiring Mark Rivera instead.

Come On Christmas, Come On

The opening track on Ringo's 1999 Christmas album *I Wanna Be Santa Claus,* composed by Starkey/Hudson and Dean Grakal. It features Ringo on lead vocals, drums and percussion, Mark Hudson on bass, electric guitar, horn arrangement and backing vocals, Scott Gordon on harmonica and percussion, Pat Zicari on sax and Gary Burr, Sarah Hudson, Brett Hudson, Steffan Fantini, Marc Fantini, Kiley Oliver, Tess Whitehart, Dick Monda and the Xmas Files Singers on backing vocals. It is 3 minutes and 35 seconds in length.

Coochy-Coochy

A number Ringo recorded during his sessions in Nashville for the *Beaucoups Of Blues* album. Ringo wrote the number, but it was never used on the album; it was used as the flipside of the 'Beaucoups Of Blues' single in America, but wasn't released in Britain.

Cookin' (In The Kitchen Of Love)

The opening track of Side Two of *Ringo's Rotogravure*. John Lennon wrote this especially for Ringo. He also played piano in the studio in Los Angeles. Other musicians on the track were Danny Kortchmar and Mac Rebennack on guitars, Will Lee on bass guitar, Mac Rebennack on organ, King Errisson on percussion and Melissa Manchester and Duitch Helmer on backing vocals.

The number is 3 minutes and 40 seconds in length.

Cooler, The

When Ringo recorded his album *Stop And Smell The Roses*, Paul McCartney wrote and produced the numbers 'Private Property' and 'Attention', and produced the number 'Sure To Fall', which had been written by Cark Perkins, Quinton Claunch and Willian Cantrell.

It was Paul's idea to make a video of these three songs to use as a promotional video for the album. They filmed it from 13 to 15 January 1982 at Ewarts Studio in London. It worked out as an eleven-minute 'surrealist musical', directed by Godley and Crème, and it was entered in the Short Subject category at the Cannes Film Festival on 24 May 1982 and released in Britain as a support to the feature film *Grease 2*.

Ringo plays an habitual escapee who at the beginning of the film is caught and thrown into the cooler, a special solitary confinement cell. As his mental state deteriorates, he fantasises about his situation and his ambiguous relationship with the camp commandant, played by his wife Barbara Bach.

Paul McCartney appears three times in the film: as a prisoner, as Ringo's cowboy father and as the double-bass player in a country and western band. Linda McCartney plays a guard.

Cranleigh

A town in Surrey, England, where Ringo and Barbara bought a mansion in 1998 for £2 million. It was a seventeenth-century building with seven bedrooms, five reception rooms, four bathrooms, a lodge, a staff flat, two cottages, stables and several outbuildings.

Crawford, Marie

Formerly Marie Maguire. The Maguire family were neighbours of Elsie Starkey and her son Ritchie and were the ones who eventually introduced Elsie to her second husband, Harry Graves.

In June 1943 the Maguires moved into 10 Madryn Street in the Dingle area of Liverpool. Elsie and her son lived next door. Marie was four years older than Ritchie.

When Elsie went out to work it was Marie who would come in to look after Ritchie. Since he had suffered academically due to the length of time he'd spent in hospital, Marie would spend one hour, twice a week, reading to him and going over spelling lists with him. For helping Ritchie to learn to read, Elsie paid her 6d an hour.

When Ritchie was taken to hospital for another lengthy spell, Marie visited him there, bringing him a present that she thought he'd like, a drumming record, 'Bedtime For Drums' by Eric Delaney.

During the 1980s Marie, now Marie Crawford, became a Beatles guide in Liverpool.

Cruikshank, Robin

A furniture designer and former partner of Ringo. It was in 1966 that Cruikshank met Edward Heath, then Leader of the Opposition, who commissioned him to design furniture for his apartment. It was while there that he got to know the Beatles, who had just moved into their Apple offices in Savile Row, which was opposite Heath's apartment.

Apple Records head Ron Kass, husband of actress Joan Collins, asked Cruikshank to redesign his office. He was then commissioned to make furniture for John and Yoko's house, Tittenhurst Park, in Berkshire. He next began to make sculptures for George and Patti.

He says, 'I wasn't making a huge amount of money, but it was fun.'

Ringo then asked Cruikshank to do some work at his Hampstead home. Cruikshank recalls, 'He had designed some things himself, which he asked me to have made. This is how our friendship started. He bought into my little company and we changed the name to ROR (Ringo or Robin).'

The company then moved to the top floor of the Apple building.

'It was a wonderful time,' he remembers. 'Everyone was friendly. Elton John would often pop in at teatime and Marc Bolan was a regular visitor. And there were endless pretty girls, many of them camping on the steps of Apple.

'I went to all sorts of parties at Ringo's and George's homes and, with other musicians, they would often jam late into the night.'

Cruikshank married a Japanese pop singer, Chiyako. He worked with Ringo for seventeen years and the company exported furniture to America and designed for various celebrities ranging from Harry Nilsson to actor Christopher Plummer. Commissions came from the Sultan of Oman and they designed the interior of the head of state's guest palace in Abu Dhabi. Arab clients throughout the Middle East then gave them further work.

Cruikshank and his wife bought a small Caribbean island in 1987, fourteen miles off the Belize mainland.

Cryin'

Ringo co-wrote this number with Vini Poncia and it is featured on the *Ringo's Rotogravure* album. Sneaky Pete played pedal steel guitar on the track, which is 3 minutes and 17 seconds in length. Other musicians included Danny Kortchmar and Lon Van Eaton on guitars,

Cooker Lo Presti on bass guitar, John Jarvis on piano and Arif Mardin on electric piano.

It was included as the B side on the British-only single 'A Dose Of Rock 'n' Roll'.

Cummings, Burton

A Canadian musician born in Winnipeg on 31 December 1947. He joined the Guess Who, a group whose other members were Randy Bachman, Chad Allan, Bob Ashley and Garry Peterson, although there were a number of personnel changes later in their career. They had several hits, including 'These Eyes', 'Laughing', 'No Time', 'American Woman' and 'No Sugar Tonight'.

Cummings and Bachman (who became a member of the All-Starr Band in 1995) had their differences, resulting in Bachman leaving to form the Bachman-Turner Overdrive.

Cummings later turned solo and his 1979 album *Dream Of A Child* became the first Canadian album ever to go platinum.

Ringo brought him into the All-Starr Band in 1992 and he performed 'American Woman' and 'No Time' and is also found on the All-Starr album *Live From Montreux*.

Curly Sue

A 1991 film starring James Belushi. On 14 April 1991 Ringo recorded the song 'You Never Know', which was penned by Steve Dorff and Steve Bettis and produced by Peter Asher. The number appeared on the closing credits of the movie and also on the soundtrack album that was released in America on 26 November 1991 and in Britain on 6 January 1992. Among the musicians backing Ringo were the Posies, who had also recorded with him on the track 'Golden Blunders'.

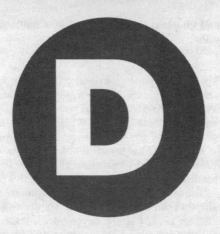

Danko, Rick Clare

The lead vocalist, bass guitarist and guitarist, born in Simcoe, Ontario, Canada, on 9 December 1943, who was one of the founder members of the Band. Rick left school at fourteen to become a musician and at the age of seventeen joined Ronnie Hawkins' backing band the Hawks as rhythm guitarist, before becoming bassist. Bob Dylan spotted the group's performance and hired them as his backing band for his 1965/66 world tour. The group changed their name to the Band and released the album *Music From Big Pink* in 1968.

After the Band split up following their 1976 farewell concert, Danko turned solo and issued his solo debut album in 1978. The Band reunited for a time in 1983.

Together with former Band member Levon Helm, Danko became part of the very first All-Starr Band in 1989, during which he performed 'Raining In My Heart' and 'Shape I'm In'. He also appeared on Ringo's 1973 album *Ringo* and is to be found on the Rykodisc album *Ringo Starr And His All-Starr Band,* the soundtrack of the 1989 tour, performing the Buddy Holly song 'Raining In My Heart'.

He died on 10 December 1999.

Darktown Skiffle Group, The

In 1958, when Eddie Miles decided to get married, the end of the Eddie Clayton Skiffle Group seemed inevitable. Ritchie Starkey wanted to continue playing and had offers from several other skiffle groups. He decided to take up the offer from the Darktown Skiffle Group. It was while he was a member of this outfit that he received an offer from Alan Caldwell to join his group the Texans. Although the Darktown changed to rock'n'roll, like most of the other Liverpool skiffle bands, and changed their name to the Cadillacs, Ritchie took up Caldwell's offer.

Davis, Pat

One of Ringo's first Liverpool girlfriends, Pat Davis was one of his 'steadies' while he was in his teens. She was educated at St Anthony of Padua Secondary School in Mossley Hill.

The blonde-haired Pat was Priscilla White's (better known now as Cilla Black) best friend and the two of them had ambitions to become hairdressers. She recalled, 'That meant finding someone to practise on, but neither of our mums would let us near their hair. The only woman we ever met who didn't mind us doing the practical work on her was Ringo's mother, Elsie Starkey. On Wednesday nights we went round to her house and she was the soul of patience. She let us bleach her hair and do terrible things to it, but she never once complained. She also gave us our tea – either boiled ham or spam and home-made cakes. Mrs Starkey was a fantastic lady.'

They used to meet at the Blue Angel club where Ringo and George Harrison would team up with Pat and Cilla.

The romance came to an end when Ringo met Maureen Cox, but they continued to be friends and she was one of the Ringo supporters, encouraging him on when he appeared with the Beatles for the first time at the Cavern club.

She later moved to London and worked for Polydor Records for a time, before marrying an American television executive and moving to New York.

De Paul, Lynsey

British singer/songwriter, real name Lynsey Rubin, who had several hits as a singer, including 'Sugar Me' and 'Won't Somebody Dance With Me'. As a composer she had fourteen of her songs in the British charts between 1972 and 1974. Spike Milligan used to call her 'Looney de Small' because of her diminutive size.

She went to Los Angeles in 1972 when the Fortunes took one of her songs, 'Storm In A Teacup', into the American Top 100. She then began a romance with the actor James Coburn. When she split with him and returned to London, her new boyfriend was Ringo.

At the time, in 1976, Ringo was a tax exile and was only allowed to remain in Britain for ninety days a year. The couple were seen everywhere together but, when his ninety days were up, Ringo left the country to return to his live-in lover Nancy Andrews in Los Angeles, and the romance with Lynsey was over.

However, during their relatively short time together there were a number of joint recording ventures, one of which occurred when Lynsey was producing a recording of veteran British singer Vera Lynn on the number 'Don't You Remember When' at the Marquee Studios in

London in 1976. She recalled, 'Ringo turned up to collect me from the studio, we put a tambourine in his hand for a photo-shoot and he ended up playing on the track.'

Lynsey's own single 'If I Don't Get You The Next One Will' was also inspired by Ringo. She says, 'We had arranged to go to dinner, and instead he slept through the evening in his offices, so the song relates to revenge.'

Lynsey also recorded at Ringo's own Startling Studios and said she had help from George Harrison: 'Ringo had a recording studio in his house, but he was not technologically minded at the time, insofar as he could not even turn on the equipment. George came to his house, which had written above the door 'This Is Not Here', and the three of us jammed from midnight to three o'clock in the morning. As we could not record on the proper deck, Ringo placed a little cassette player, driven by batteries, on a chair in between us all. Unfortunately, the batteries were running low, and the tape was slowing down as it recorded. When we played it back the result was that it sounded as if we were all getting faster and faster, and higher and higher in pitch. It was very funny, Ringo played drums, George the guitar, and I played piano.'

Dead Giveaway

The opening track on Side Two of the *Stop And Smell The Roses* album. Ringo and Ron Wood penned it. The number is 4 minutes and 26 seconds in length and features Ron Wood on guitar, acoustic bass and saxophones, Ringo on drums, Wilton Felder on electric bass, and Joe Sample and Greg Mathieson on piano.

Dear Santa

One of the numbers on Ringo's 1999 album *I Wanna Be Santa Claus*. It was penned by Starkey/Hudson/Dudas. Ringo is on lead vocals, drums and percussion, Mark Hudson on bass, percussion and backing vocals, Jim Cox on keyboards and string and horn arrangement, Scott Gordon on percussion, Dan Higgins on sax and Gary Burr on backing vocals. It is 5 minutes and 15 seconds in length.

Devil Woman

A track on the *Ringo* album, written by Ringo and Vini Poncia. Richard Perry and Klaus Voormann provided backing vocals. It is 3 minutes and 58 seconds in length. The number was also issued on the flipside of the hit single 'You're Sixteen'.

Dingle Vale Secondary Modern

Ringo first attended this school when he was eleven years old, although his primary school teachers hadn't allowed him to take the eleven-plus examination because they didn't believe he would pass it. He studied at

Dingle Vale until he was thirteen; he was then struck down with pleurisy and spent the next two years in hospital.

In a school report, one of the teachers, Mr S. Roberts wrote: 'A quiet, thoughtful type, although working rather slowly. Academic work will no doubt improve in time as he is trying to do his best.'

The school's physical training instructor, Mr Dawson, was to comment, 'He was always wanting to do the same things as the other boys, and I remember one incident which typifies this. It was during the middle of a PT lesson. All the class was jumping over the vaulting horse in the centre of the gym. When it came to Ringo's turn, he was obviously pretty doubtful whether he would get over the obstacle because he had never done it before. He ran up to it, jumped, and just managed to clear it. When he found that he had succeeded and not fallen flat, his face burst out in a really, broad satisfied grin.

'Recently the school put an old desk of Ringo's up for sale. We had thousands of girls queuing up to try and buy it. He has certainly helped to make Dingle Vale school famous.'

This final comment is interesting in the light of what Ringo had to say, after leaving the school without any qualifications. He needed to return to the school 'to get the certificate to prove I'd left. You needed that to get a job. They didn't even remember I'd been there.'

The name of the school was later changed to Shorefields Comprehensive School.

Discography
British 7" singles:

'It Don't Come Easy' c/w 'Early 1970', released in Britain on Apple R 5898 on 9 April 1971.

'Back Off Boogaloo' c/w 'Blindman', released in Britain on Apple R5944 on 17 March 1972.

'Photograph' c/w 'Down And Out', released in Britain on Apple R 5992 on 19 October 1973.

'You're Sixteen' c/w 'Devil Woman', released in Britain on Apple R 5995 on 8 February 1974.

'Only You (And You Alone)' c/w 'Call Me', released in Britain on Apple R 6000 on 15 November 1974.

'Snookeroo' c/w 'Oo-Wee', released in Britain on Apple R 6004 on 21 February 1975.

'Oh My My' c/w 'No No Song', released in Britain on Apple R 6011 on 9 January 1976.

'A Dose Of Rock 'N' Roll' c/w 'Cryin'', released in Britain on Polydor 2001 694 on 15 October 1976.

'Hey Baby' c/w 'Lady Gaye', released in Britain on Polydor 2001 699 on 26 November 1976.

'Drowning In The Sea Of Love' c/w 'Just A Dream', released in Britain on Polydor 2001 734 on 16 September 1977.

'Tonight' c/w 'Heart On My Sleeve', released in Britain on Polydor 2001 795 on 21 July 1978.
'Wrack My Brain' c/w 'Drumming Is My Madness', released in Britain on RCA 166 on 13 November 1981.
'Weight Of The World' c/w 'After All These Years', released in Britain on Private Music 115 392 on 18 May 1992.

5″ CD single:
'Weight Of The World'/'After All These Years'/'Don't Be Cruel', released on Private Music 665 392.

American 7″ singles:
'Beaucoups Of Blues' c/w 'Coochy-Coochy', released on Apple 2969 on 5 October 1970.
'It Don't Come Easy' c/w 'Early 1970', released on Apple 1831 on 16 April 1971.
'Back Off Boogaloo' c/w 'Blindman', released on Apple 1849 on 20 March 1972.
'Photograph' c/w 'Down And Out', released on Apple 1865 on 24 September 1973.
'You're Sixteen' c/w 'Devil Woman', released on Apple 1870 on 3 December 1973.
'Oh My My' c/w 'Step Lightly', released on Apple 1872 on 18 February 1974.
'Only You (And You Alone)' c/w 'Call Me', released on Apple 1876 on 11 November 1974.
'No No Song' c/w 'Snookeroo', released on Apple 1880 on 27 January 1975.
'It's All Down To Goodnight Vienna' c/w 'Oo-Wee', released on Apple 1882 on 2 June 1975.
'A Dose Of Rock 'N' Roll' c/w 'Cryin'', released on Atlantic 45-3361 on 20 September 1976.
'Hey Baby' c/w 'Lady Gaye', released on Atlantic 45-3371 on 22 November 1976.
'Wings' c/w 'Just A Dream', released on Atlantic 3429 on 26 August 1977.
'Drowning In A Sea Of Love' c/w 'Just A Dream', released on Atlantic 3412 on 17 October 1977.
'Lipstick Traces (On A Cigarette)' c/w 'Old Time Relovin'', released on Portrait 6-70015 on 17 April 1978.
'Heart On My Sleeve' c/w 'Who Needs A Heart', released on Portrait 6-70018 on 3 July 1978.
'Wrack My Brain' c/w 'Drumming Is My Madness', released on Boardwalk NB7-11-130 on 26 October 1981.
'Private Property' c/w 'Stop And Take The Time To Smell The Roses', released on Boardwalk NB7-11-134 on 11 January 1982.

'Act Naturally' c/w 'The Key's In The Mailbox' (Buck Owens), released on Capitol B-44409 on 24 July 1989.

'La De Da' c/w 'Everyday', released on Mercury MELP 195 in June 1998.

5″ CD single:
'Weight Of The World'/'After All These Years'/'Don't Be Cruel', released on Private Music 01005-81003-2 on 28 April 1992.

British albums:
Sentimental Journey, released on Apple PCS 7101 on 27 March 1970. The CD was issued on EMI CDPCS on 1 May 1995.

Beaucoups Of Blues, released on Apple PAS 10002 on 25 September 1970. The CD was issued on EMI CDPAS 10002 on 1 May 1995.

Tommy – The London Symphony Orchestra And Chamber Choir with Guest Soloists, released on Ode 99001 on 24 November 1972. The CD was issued on Castle ESSCD 029 on 26 November 1990.

Ringo, released on Apple PCTC 252 on 9 November 1973. The CD was issued on Parlophone CDP 7 95884 2 on 4 March 1991.

Goodnight Vienna, released on Apple PCS 7168 on 15 November 1974. The CD was issued on Parlophone CDEMS 1467 on 30 November 1992.

Blast From Your Past, released on Apple PCS 7170 on 12 December 1975. The CD was issued on EMI CD-PCS 7170 on 26 May 1987.

Ringo's Rotogravure, released on Polydor Deluxe 2302 040 on 17 September 1976.

Ringo the 4th, released on Polydor Super 2310 556 on 30 September 1977.

Scouse The Mouse, released on Polydor Super 2480 429 on 9 December 1977.

Bad Boy, released on Polydor 2310 599 on 16 June 1978.

Stop And Smell The Roses, released on RCA LP 6022 on 20 November 1981.

Old Wave, released in Germany on Bellaphon 260.16.029 on 16 June 1983 and in Canada on RCA DXL 1-3233 on 24 June 1983.

The Anti-Heroin Project – It's A Live-In World, released on EMI AHP LP 1 on 24 November 1986.

Recorded Highlights Of The Prince's Trust Concert 1987, released on A&M PTA 1987 on 14 August 1987. The CD was issued on A&M CDA 1987 on the same date.

Stay Awake – Various Interpretations Of Music From Vintage Disney Films, released on A&M AMA 3918 on 24 October 1988. The CD was issued on A&M CDA 3918 on the same date.

Ringo Starr And His All-Starr Band, released on EMI EMS 1375 on 15 October 1990. The CD was issued on EMI CZ 353 on the same date.

Music From The Motion Picture Curly Sue, released on Giant 7599 24439 2 on 6 January 1992.

Time Takes Time, released on CD on Private Music 262 902 on 29 June 1992.

For The Love Of Harry: Everybody Sings Nilsson, released on CD on Music Masters 65127 on 1 June 1995.

Vertical Man, released on CD on Mercury in August 1998.

VH-1 Storytellers, released on CD on Mercury 314 538 118-2 on 19 October 1998.

American albums:

Sentimental Journey, released on Apple SW 3365 on 24 April 1970. The CD was issued on Apple CDP 7 98615 2 on 15 August 1995.

Beaucoups Of Blues, released on Apple SMAS 3368 on 28 September 1970. The CD was issued on Apple CDP 8 32678 2 on 1 August 1995.

Tommy – The London Symphony Orchestra And Chamber Choir With Guest Soloists, released on Ode SP 99001 on 27 November 1972. The CD was issued on Rhino R2 71113 2 in June 1989.

Ringo, released on Apple SWAL-3413 on 2 November 1973. The CD was issued on Capitol CDP 7 95637 2 on 7 May 1991.

Goodnight Vienna, released on Apple SW-3417 on 18 November 1974. The CD was issued on Capitol CDP 7 80378 2 on 23 March 1993.

Blast From Your Past, released on Apple SW-3422 on 20 November 1975. The CD was issued on Parlophone CDP 7 46663 2 on 19 January 1988.

Ringo's Rotogravure, released on Atlantic SD 18193 on 27 September 1976. The CD was issued on Atlantic 7 82417-2 in August 1992.

Ringo The 4th, released on Atlantic SD 19108 on 26 September 1977. The CD was issued on Atlantic 7 82416-2P in August 1992.

Bad Boy, released on Portrait JR 35378 on 17 April 1978. The CD was issued on Epic EK 35378 on 26 March 1991.

Stop And Smell The Roses, released on Boardwalk NB1 33246 on 26 October 1981. The CD was issued on The Right Stuff T2-29676 on 20 September 1994.

Old Wave, released on CD on The Right Stuff T2-29675 on 6 September 1994.

Stay Awake – Various Interpretations Of Music From Vintage Disney Films, released on A&M SP 3918 on 18 October 1988. The CD was issued on A&M CD 3918 on the same date.

Starr Struck: The Best Of Ringo Starr, Vol 2, released on Rhino R1 70135 on 28 February 1989. The CD was issued on Rhino R2 70135 on the same date.

Ringo Starr And His All-Starr Band, released on Ryko Analogue RALP 0190 on 12 October 1990. The CD was issued on Rykodisc RCD 10190 on the same date.

Ringo Starr And His All-Starr Band (It Don't Come Easy), released on CD on Rykodisc RCD5 1019 on 12 October 1990.

Time Takes Time, released on CD on Private Music 01005-82097-2 on 22 May 1992.

Ringo Starr And His All-Starr Band Volume 2 (also known as *Live From Montreux*), released on CD on Rykodisc RCD 202664 on 14 September 1993.

For The Love Of Harry: Everybody Sings Nilsson, released on CD on Music Masters 01612-65127-2 on 9 May 1995.

Ringo Starr And His Third All-Starr Band Volume 1, released on CD on Blockbuster Exclusive 00010-52451 on 12 August 1997.

Vertical Man, released on CD on Mercury 314 558 400-2 on 16 June 1998.

Vertical Man Bonus Music, released on CD on Mercury MCEP 424 on 16 June 1998.

VH1 Storytellers, released on CD on Mercury 314 538 118-2 on 20 October 1998.

I Wanna Be Santa Claus, released on CD on Mercury 314 546 668-2 on 19 October 1999.

The Anthology . . . So Far, released on CD on Koch Records KOC-CD-8312 on 24 July 2001.

King Biscuit Flower Hour Presents Ringo And His New All-Starr Band, released on CD on King Biscuit KBCCD 143 on 6 August 2002.

Ringo Rama, released on CD on Koch on 25 March 2003.

Discover

A major American credit card company, which used one of Ringo's designs as a licence card. These are popular items with collectors in the United States. Ringo also appeared on television commercials in America promoting the card and part of the deal entailed Discover sponsoring his 1995 summer All-Starr Band American tour. They also featured Ringo's figurative painting of a face that he created for the Make-A-Wish Foundation in America. The painting was later auctioned for the charity at the Solomon R. Guggenheim Museum in New York on Wednesday 12 July 1995.

The cards were known as 'Private Issue' cards and there were three cards by celebrities featuring a painting by each. Apart from Ringo there was actress Jane Seymour and Olympian Florence Griffith Joyner.

When Ringo arrived at the auction he said, 'I believe everyone is an artist. Just let the creative juices flow.'

Among the celebrities attending the auction were John Entwistle, Randy Bachman, Billy Preston and Felix Cavaliere, who were members of Ringo's current All-Starr Band. Ringo's wife Barbara and daughter Lee were also present. Joyner's painting sold for $3,750, Seymour's for $25,000 and Ringo's for $33,000.

Don't Be Cruel

A number recorded during the *Time Takes Time* sessions, but not used on the album, although it was included on the 'Weight Of The World'

CD single and on the Japanese album release. It is 2 minutes and 7 seconds in length.

Don't Go Where The Road Don't Go
A track from the 1992 *Time Takes Time* album, written by Richard Starkey, Johnny Warman and Gary Grainger. It was produced by Don Was and engineered by Ed Cherney. Ringo was on lead vocals, drums and percussion, Mark Goldenberg on guitar, James 'Hutch' Hutchinson on bass, Benmont Tench on keyboards and Andrew Sturmer, Roger Manning, Doug Fieger and Berton Averre on backing vocals.

The number is 3 minutes and 22 seconds in length.

The extended format single was issued in Germany on 21 September 1992 on Private Music 74321 11369 2 as a 5" CD single with 'Everyone Wins' on the flip.

On the CD cover 'Everyone Wins' was called 'Everybody Wins'.

On the same day, in Germany, a 7" disc of 'Don't Go Where The Road Don't Go' was issued on Private Music 74321 11369 7 with 'Don't Know A Thing About Love' on the flip.

Don't Know A Thing About Love
A track from the 1992 *Time Takes Time* album, written by Richard Feldman and Stan Lynch. It was produced by Don Was and engineered by Ed Cherney. Ringo was on lead vocals, drums and percussion, Mark Goldenberg on guitar, James 'Hutch' Hutchinson on bass, Benmont Tench on keyboards and Roger Manning, Doug Fieger, Berton Averre and Andrew Sturmer on backing vocals. The number is 3 minutes and 50 seconds in length.

Don't Pass Me By
A track from the double album *The Beatles,* which Ringo had written in India.

The number was also included on the *VH-1 Storytellers* CD, which led Ringo to say, 'Well, "Don't Pass Me By" was the first song I'd written that we recorded. I'd written other songs but as I said in the *Storytellers* show, they were always other people's songs, I just rewrote the words. I used to say that I was rewriting Jerry Lee Lewis B sides.

'I remember writing it at the piano at my home in England. It's still magic when I write songs and get together with other musicians to record them.'

Previously Ringo had received partial credit for the *Rubber Soul* track 'What Goes On' and for 'Flying', the instrumental number on the *Magical Mystery Tour* release.

'Don't Pass Me By' was originally recorded by the Beatles on 5 June 1968 at Abbey Road Studios with Ringo on vocal, drums and piano, Paul McCartney on bass, John Lennon on acoustic guitar and tambourine and George Harrison on violin.

Donegan, Lonnie

The musician who, with 'Rock Island Line', sparked off the skiffle boom in Britain and inspired John Lennon to form the Quarry Men. He was a seminal influence on George Harrison and Paul McCartney, and inspired Ringo's early groups the Eddie Clayton Skiffle Group and the Darktown Skiffle Group.

When Adam Faith felt that British artists should help to participate in a comeback album for Lonnie, which he produced in 1978, Ringo was the only former member of the Beatles to participate.

The album was *Puttin' On The Style*, released in America on 9 January 1978 and in Britain on 27 January 1978. Ringo played drums on the tracks 'Ham 'N' Eggs' and 'Have A Drink On Me'. 'Ham 'N' Eggs' was also issued as the first single from the album on 3 February 1978.

Dose Of Rock 'N' Roll, A

The opening track of Ringo's 1976 album *Ringo's Rotogravure*. Composer Carl Grossman gave the number to Ringo and the musicians on the track included Peter Frampton, Danny Kortchmar and Jesse Ed Davis on guitars; Klaus Voormann on bass guitar; Mac Rebennack (Dr John) on keyboards; Randy Brecker and Alan Rubin on trumpets; Michael Brecker and George Young on tenor saxophones; and Lewis Delgatto on baritone saxophone.

The number is 3 minutes and 24 seconds in length.

'A Dose Of Rock 'N' Roll' was also issued as a single in Britain on Polydor 2001 694 on 15 October 1976, with 'Cryin'' on the flip. The record didn't chart.

It was issued in America on Atlantic 45-3361 on 20 September 1976, becoming Ringo's first Atlantic release. It reached No. 26 in the charts. 'Cryin'' was again on the flip.

Down And Out

The flipside of Ringo's October 1973 single 'Photograph', and written by Ringo. The number was included as a bonus track on the *Ringo* CD. It was produced by Richard Perry and included Gary Wright on keyboards.

Dr John

Dr John was born Malcolm John Rebennack in New Orleans, Louisiana, on 21 November 1940.

He performed his own Cajun Voodoo music, a combination of jazz, gospel, R&B and funk, and was also known as Mac Rebennack and Dr John the Night Tripper.

He contributed to Ringo's 1974 album *Goodnight Vienna*, his 1976 album *Ringo's Rotogravure* and his 1978 album *Bad Boy*. Together with Ringo he also appeared on Manhattan Transfer's album *Coming Out*.

Dr John's 1975 album *Hollywood Be Thy Name* has two photos of Ringo on the inner sleeve and Ringo is credited as 'Master of Ceremonies', because Dr John said that Ringo acted that part on a film to promote the album.

When he appeared as a member of the All-Starr Band he performed 'Iko Iko', 'Right Place, Wrong Time', 'Candy' and 'Such A Night'.

The press release for the first All-Starr Band tour in 1989 included the following biography of Dr John:

'Dr John is certainly one of modern music's most enduring characters, with over twelve albums chalked up since 1968. The trademarks that separate this artist from any other include his unmistakable, whiskey-cured voice, the distinctive ivory-stroking, and the richly textured releases that evoke images of backwoods magic. His brand new album, *In A Sentimental Mood*, is climbing the charts to success, proving his consistent popularity with international audiences.

'He's appeared on *David Letterman*, *Dolly Parton*, *Nashville Now*, *Sunday Night*, *B.B.King And Friends* and had his own one-hour special called "Lonesome Pine". Dr John has even penned soundtracks for films such as *Cannery Row*, *St Elmo's Fire*, *Bull Durham*, *Colours* and *Angel Heart*. His voice has graced television commercials, too, pitching for Thomas's English Muffins, the Milk Board, Popeye's Children, and American Express.

'Born Malcolm John "Mac" Rebennack in the fabled musical mecca of New Orleans, the Doctor began his career as a session guitarist, writer, and arranger around the time he was fifteen. Then, in '68, he launched his own legendary career with "Gris Gris", and went to work on collaborations with Eric Clapton, Mick Jagger, and Sonny and Cher. In 1973, Dr John hit the top of the charts with the Allen Toussaint-produced album, *In The Right Place*. His stylistic blends have laid the foundations for "swamp rock" and the World Beat explosion. Dr John's career takes another exciting turn as he begins touring with Ringo Starr and the All-Starr Band.'

Drake, Pete

An American pedal steel guitarist who George Harrison flew over to Britain to appear on his *All Things Must Pass* triple album. Ringo was also recording for the album and in conversation Drake suggested to Ringo, a C&W fan, that he should record a country music album. Ringo liked the idea and Drake offered to assist him, suggesting that he shouldn't record it in Britain but should go to Nashville where, he assured him, he could record the album in a couple of days. Ringo agreed and Drake went ahead and lined up a hundred country musicians for Ringo to choose from. When Ringo arrived a few days later, 21 musicians were chosen, Drake provided some production guidance and the album, *Beaucoups Of Blues*, was actually recorded in two days.

Drake died in 1988.

Dream

This track from *Sentimental Journey* was penned by Johnny Mercer and was an American million-seller for the Pied Pipers in 1945. George Martin arranged this version. It was recorded at Trident Studios, London, on 18 November 1969. It is 2 minutes and 41 seconds in length.

Drift Away

A track from the *Vertical Man* album. The number is 4 minutes and 10 seconds in length. Ringo provided vocals, rhythmatic guitar, percussion, tambourine and handclaps; Tom Petty and Alanis Morissette provided lead vocals, while Rose Stone, Lisa Banks, Ollie Woodson, Howard McCray and Christina Rasch provided backing vocals; Steve Cropper was on electric guitar; Steve Tyler was on drums; Steve Dudas was on bass and handclaps; Mark Hudson was on acoustic guitar, percussion, handclaps and backing vocals; John Cox was on B3 organ; and Scott Gordon was on percussion and handclaps.

Ringo, Steven Tyler and Alanis Morissette each sang a verse, the first, second and third respectively.

Drowning In A Sea Of Love

A single released in Britain on Polydor 2001 734 on 16 September 1977, with 'Just A Dream' on the flip. It failed to make an entry in the British charts. It was released in America on Atlantic 3412 on 18 October 1977 and also failed to reach the charts – and it became his last release on the Atlantic label.

Originally, 'Drowning In A Sea Of Love' was going to be the first release from the *Ringo The 4th* album, a sort of trailer to the album, issued in advance. However, in America the single 'Wings' c/w 'Just A Dream' replaced it. As that record failed to register, 'Drowning In A Sea Of Love' was then issued, but also failed to chart.

The song, penned by Kenny Gamble and Leon Huff, had originally been recorded by Joe Simon in 1971 and had been an American million-seller.

Ringo and Steve Gadd featured on drums, with Steve Spinozza on lead guitar, Don Grolnick on keyboards and Tony Levin on bass.

Arif Mardin produced the number, which is 3 minutes and 41 seconds in length.

Drumming Is My Madness

A track from the 1981 album *Stop And Smell The Roses*. It is 3 minutes and 28 seconds in length and was also issued as the flipside of the single 'Wrack My Brain'.

Apart from Ringo on drums, the other musicians were Jerry Jumonville on tenor saxophone, Bruce Paulson on trombone, Jim Gordon on baritone saxophone, Lee Thornburg on trumpet, Dennis

Budimar on guitar, Ritchie Zito on guitar, Jim Keltner on drums, Jane Getz on piano, Fred Tackett on guitar, Dennis Belfield on bass and Rick Riccio on flute.

The number was penned by Harry Nilsson and arranged by Van Dyke Parks.

Dylan, Bob

A major American artist who was admired by each of the Beatles. Initially it was John Lennon who was influenced by the folk artist, but over the years the closest association was that between George Harrison and Dylan.

Dylan was born Robert Zimmerman in Duluth, Minnesota, on 24 May 1941.

On the *Concert For Bangla Desh* recordings Ringo plays tambourine on the Dylan tracks 'A Hard Rain's Gonna Fall', 'Blowin' In The Wind', 'It Takes A Lot To Laugh, It Takes A Train To Cry' and 'Just Like A Woman'.

When Dylan embarked on his Rolling Thunder Revue, Ringo performed with him on the night of 24 January 1976 at the Houston Astrodome. Ringo also joined Dylan on stage at Les Arenes in Frejus, France on 13 June 1989 to play drums on 'Highway 61 Revisited' and 'Like A Rolling Stone'.

Ringo played drums on Bob Dylan's single 'Heart Of Mine' c/w 'Let It Be Me', released in Britain on CBS A1406 on 3 July 1981 to tie in with Dylan's British tour.

Early 1970

A number Ringo dedicated to his three fellow Beatles. George Harrison produced it and also played guitar and supplied backing vocals; Ringo played acoustic guitar, drums and piano. It became the flipside of 'It Don't Come Easy', Ringo's first solo chart single. It is 2 minutes and 18 seconds in length.

The title refers to the time when it was actually written. It was a time when Paul was suing the other three to dissolve the partnership.

Ringo referred to George as 'always in town, playing for you and me' and John being busy with Yoko but always willing to play with Ringo if asked. Paul, however, was on his farm in Scotland and Ringo wondered whether he would ever come out and play again, ending the song with the words, 'When I come to town, I want to see all three.'

Easy For Me

Harry Nilsson wrote this number for Ringo to record for his 1974 *Ringo* album. Lincoln Mayorga played piano and string arrangements were by Trevor Lawrence and Vini Poncia. Horn players were Trevor Lawrence, Steve Madaio, Bobby Keyes, Lou McCreery and Chuck Findley, and Richard Perry conducted.

It is 2 minutes and 17 seconds in length.

Ed Davis, Jesse

A native American Indian, born in Oklahoma, who was originally a member of Taj Mahal. He first met John Lennon while filming *The Rolling Stones' Rock 'n' Roll Circus* and George Harrison later added him to the *Concert For Bangla Desh* bill. Davis also did session work for a number of artists including B.B. King, Rod Stewart and Steve Miller.

He renewed acquaintances with both John Lennon and Ringo when he was in Los Angeles in 1973 and contributed to Lennon's *Walls And Bridges* and *Rock 'n' Roll* albums.

Jesse Ed Davis also contributed to Ringo's 1974 album *Goodnight Vienna* and his 1976 album *Rotogravure*.

He died of a drugs overdose at his home in Venice, California, at the age of 43 on 22 June 1988.

Eddie Clayton Skiffle Group, The

A skiffle group who formed in 1957 when Ritchie Starkey was working as an apprentice at H. Hunt & Sons. At the time he had no thoughts of taking up the drums as a career. He recalled, 'I remember my mum saying a neighbour was in a band and why didn't I have a go. I thought it was a jazz group – I was mad on jazz. When it turned out to be a silver band, playing in the park and sticking to the marches and all that, I chucked it in. I lasted just one night.'

His stepfather Harry Graves bought him a drum kit for £10 in London and brought it back by train.

Ritchie then got together with four other Hunts' employees, including his friend Eddie Miles. The band line-up was: Eddie Miles (using the name Eddie Clayton because he felt it sounded better than his own name), guitar/vocals; Ritchie Starkey, drums; Roy Trafford, tea-chest bass; John Dougherty, washboard; and Frank Walsh, guitar. They originally began playing during lunch breaks in the works canteen. Ritchie's grandfather then lent him £50 to put down as a deposit for a brand-new kit.

The group made their debut at the Peel Street Labour Club and became resident there, also initially appearing at Wilson Hall, Garston. They also appeared at the Cavern on Tuesday 31 July and Wednesday 4 December 1957. Their 1958 Cavern appearances were on 29 January, 7, 10, 16 and 23 February, and 8 and 28 March. They also appeared at various skiffle contests taking place at such venues as St Luke's Hall in Crosby.

Their nearest approach to a group uniform consisted of shirts in the same colour as their bootlace ties. The group was also to enjoy a residency at the Boys' Club meetings at the Florence Institute in Dingle.

Ritchie's mother, Elsie, was to recall in *Mersey Beat*: 'Ritchie joined the Eddie Clayton Skiffle Group with Ed Miles, the boy who lived next door, Roy Trafford and Johnny Dougherty – they all worked together in the same place. Eddie used to take his guitar to work every day. He was a smashing fellow – if ever a lad should have got somewhere he should have. I believe he's with Hank Walters and His Dusty Road Ramblers.'

The group disbanded because Eddie was getting married. Ritchie then went on to join the Darktown Skiffle Group.

Interestingly enough, Eric Clapton used the alias Eddie Clayton when he guested on the *Ringo* album.

Edmunds, Dave

A British musician born in Cardiff, Wales, on 15 April 1944.

He enjoyed a major hit in 1970 with 'I Hear You Knockin'' and charted again with his version of Elvis Costello's 'Girls Talk'. He was a member of Rockpile and the group appeared as part of Paul McCartney's Rockestra to perform the 'Rockestra Theme' at the Odeon, Hammersmith, on 29 December 1979.

Edmunds also found success as a record producer and has recorded numerous bands and artists including the Everly Brothers, Del Shannon, Status Quo, Dion, k.d. Lang and the Flamin' Groovies.

He appeared in *Stardust*, the sequel to *That'll Be The Day*. Ringo turned down the chance to appear in the movie, but both Ringo and Edmunds appeared in Paul McCartney's *Give My Regards To Broad Street* in 1984 and, along with Ringo and George Harrison, he appeared on the Carl Perkins special 'Blue Suede Shoes – A Rockabilly Session With Carl Perkins And Friends' in 1985.

Ringo invited him to join the All-Starr Band on tour in 1992 where he performed 'I Hear You Knockin'' and 'Girls Talk'; both numbers are to be found on the *Live From Montreux* album.

Elbert's Bad Word

A 15-minute animated tale in Shelley Duvall's *Bedtime Series* that was shown on the American cable station Showtime on 21 April 1992. Ringo provided the narration to the story.

Elizabeth Reigns

A track from the 2003 *Ringo Rama* album, 3 minutes and 37 seconds in length. A tribute to Queen Elizabeth II, although not particularly complimentary to Prince Charles with the words, 'God bless the Queen, if you know what I mean, we don't really need a king.' As a result, Ringo can be heard saying, 'Well, there goes the knighthood,' at the close.

Ringo was recording at his Rocca Bella Studio in England at the time, just prior to the Jubilee, when Dean Grakal asked him what ER meant. Dean then started on the song with Ringo protesting, 'I'm not going to sing about the Queen.'

Later the same year Ringo clarified his thoughts about British royalty in the *Sun* newspaper, commenting that the royal family should quit once Queen Elizabeth's reign ended. He said, 'Americans love them but I don't feel they're relevant any more. We don't need a king. I think it should all end with this Queen. The Queen Mother was well loved and I think that's ended now. If you go to the Palace to watch the changing of the guard you don't know if the Queen's in and no one even cares. Everyone's just going to see the pageant. So we can have the pageant without royals.

'There goes me knighthood. It doesn't bother me. I don't want to be a Sir. I want to be a duke or a prince. If they come through with that, I'll consider it.'

Empress, The
Public house in High Park Street, Liverpool 8, on the corner of Admiral Grove where Ringo lived. Ringo's mum worked there at one time and when Ringo recorded his album *Sentimental Journey* he decided to use a photograph of the pub on the cover, inserting pictures of his family members in the windows and one of himself standing outside the pub. The pub was later to place the individual Beatles' names above its doors.

English Garden
A track from the 2003 *Ringo Rama* album, 3 minutes and 17 seconds in length.

Entwistle, John
A British musician, born in London on 9 October 1944. Together with his school friend Peter Townshend, he formed a couple of bands in the 1950s and, with the addition of singer Roger Daltrey, they called themselves the Detours. Keith Moon was later to join them and they became known as the Who. He wrote a number of the group's songs including 'Boris The Spider', 'Fiddle About' and 'My Wife'. Ringo sang Entwistle's song 'My Wife' on the 1972 *Tommy* album.

In 1970 he became the first member of the Who to begin making solo recordings and he later formed a studio band called Rigor Mortis, prior to forming another band called John Entwistle's Ox.

Entwistle played on Ringo's *Old Wave* album in 1983 and also helped him to compose the song 'Everybody's In A Hurry But Me'.

Ringo invited him to join the All-Starr's for their official 1995 world tour, on bass guitar. At the time he said, 'I think I'd rather do five Ringo tours than one Who tour at the moment.' With the All-Starr's he performed 'Boris The Spider' and 'My Wife' – 'Boris The Spider' is to be found on the *Ringo Starr And His Third All-Starr Band Volume 1*.

It was while he was on tour with the Who in June 2002 that Entwistle died at the Hard Rock Hotel and Casino in Las Vegas, Nevada. He was on medication for a heart complaint.

Everybody's In A Hurry But Me
A track from the 1983 album *Old Wave*, penned by Richard Starkey, Joe Walsh, John Entwistle, Eric Clapton and Chris Stainton. This number arose from a jam session when Entwistle, Ray Cooper and Clapton dropped round to Startling Studios during the recording sessions. Ringo was on vocal rap and drums, Joe Walsh and Eric Clapton on guitars, John Entwistle on bass, Chris Stainton on piano and Ray Cooper on percussion.

Everyday
The first song recorded for the *Vertical Man* album at Mark Hudson's Whatinthewhatthe? Studios. It was originally titled 'My Love', but

Ringo pointed out that Paul McCartney had written a number with that title. It was decided that it wasn't suitable for the album and it was placed on the flipside of the 7″ disc of the 'La De Da' single.

Extended Versions: The Encore Collection

A ten-track CD of numbers recorded live during 2001 by Ringo Starr And His All-Starr Band, issued on BMG Special Products 75517465252 on 1 April 2003. The CD is 41 minutes and 41 seconds in length and the executive producers were Ringo Starr and David Fishof. The cover photograph was by Paul Natkin.

The tracks were 'Yellow Submarine', written by Lennon and McCartney, with Ringo Starr on lead vocals; 'Karn Evil 9', written by Keith Emerson and Greg Lake, with Greg Lake on lead vocals; 'It Don't Come Easy', with Ringo Starr on lead vocals; 'I Still Love Rock 'N' Roll', written and performed by Ian Hunter; 'Act Naturally', written by Johnny Russell and Vini Morrison with Ringo Starr on lead vocals; 'Photograph' by Starkey and Harrison with Ringo Starr on lead vocals; 'Love Bizarre', written by Prince and Sheila E and performed by Sheila E; 'With A Little Help From My Friends', written by Lennon and McCartney and performed by Ringo Starr; 'Everlasting Love', written and performed by Howard Jones; and 'Glamorous Life', written by Prince with Sheila E on lead vocals.

Ringo and his All-Starr Band comprised Ringo Starr on lead vocals, drums and percussion, Roger Hodgson on vocals, guitar and keyboard, Ian Hunter on vocals and guitar, Greg Lake on vocals and bass, Howard Jones on vocals and keyboard, Sheila E on vocals, acoustic guitar and percussion, and Mark Rivera on saxophone.

Eye To Eye

The opening track on the 2003 *Ringo Rama* album. It is 3 minutes and 17 seconds in length.

Farner, Mark

An American singer/guitarist born in Flint, Michigan, on 28 September 1948. He was a member of several bands and in 1968 became a founder member of Grand Funk Railroad, who became one of America's most successful heavy rock bands, selling out Shea Stadium in New York in 1971 and having major record success with their album. They also charted with the single 'I'm Your Captain' and topped the charts with 'We're An American Band', followed by another chart-topper, 'The Locomotion'. By that time they were just known as Grand Funk. They had a few more hit singles, including 'Some Kind Of Wonderful' and 'Bad Time', before disbanding.

Farner was invited to join the All-Starr's for their official 1995 world tour, during which he performed 'The Locomotion' and 'Some Kind Of Wonderful'.

On 3 May 1997 he was one of the guests who joined the All-Starr Band for their encore of 'With A Little Help From My Friends' at the Universal Amphitheater, Los Angeles.

Filmography

This is a selection of some of the films, TV shows and videos that Ringo has appeared in over the years.

Around The Beatles (1964)
A Hard Day's Night (1964)
What's Happening! The Beatles In The USA (1964)
Pop Gear (1965)
Help! (1965)
The Beatles (1965)
The Beatles At Shea Stadium (1965)

Tokyo Concert (1966)
Our World (1967)
Magical Mystery Tour (1967)
Yellow Submarine (1968)
Candy (1968)
The Beatles Mod Odyssey (1968)
The Magic Christian (1969)
Let It Be (1970)
Music! (1971)
200 Motels (1971)
Blindman (1971)
The Point (1971)
The Concert For Bangla Desh (1972)
Born To Boogie (1972)
That'll Be The Day (1973)
Ziggy Stardust And The Spiders From Mars (1973)
Son Of Dracula (1974)
Lisztomania (1975)
The 19th Annual Grammy Awards (1977)
The Beatles And Beyond (1977)
The Day The Music Died (1977)
Sextette (1978)
Ringo (1978)
The Last Waltz (1978)
I Wanna Hold Your Hand (1978)
The Kids Are Alright (1979)
Caveman (1981)
The Cooler (1982)
The Compleat Beatles (1982)
Princess Daisy (1983)
Ready, Steady, Go! Volume 1 (1983)
Bye Bye Star Club (1983)
Give My Regards To Broad Street (1984)
Thomas The Tank Engine And Friends (1984)
Alice In Wonderland (1985)
Water (1985)
Ready, Steady, Go! Volume 2 (1985)
Ready, Steady, Go! The Beatles Live (1985)
To The North Of Katmandu (1986)
Sun City/The Making Of Sun City (1986)
Rock 'n' Roll Goldmine: The Sixties (1986)
The Magic Years Volume 1 (1987)
The Magic Years Volume 2 (1987)
The Magic Years Volume 3 (1987)
Rolling Stone Presents Twenty Years Of Rock 'n' Roll (1987)
Imagine: John Lennon (1988)

Walking After Midnight (1988)
The 1960s: Music Memories And Milestones (1988)
The True Story Of Frank Zappa's 200 Motels (1988)
Shining Time Station (1990)
Shining Time Station Christmas: 'Tis A Gift (1991)
Secrets (1992)
MTV Video Music Awards 1992 (1992)
Fame In The Twentieth Century (1993)
The Beatles: The First US Visit (1994)
The Beatles Anthology (1995)
You Can't Do That! The Making Of A Hard Day's Night (1995)
The History Of Rock 'n' Roll Volume 3 (1995)
Beatles Diary, also known as *Alf Bicknell's Beatles Diary* (1996)
Really Big Show: Ed Sullivan's 50th Anniversary (1998)
Bring Me Sunshine: The Heart And Soul Of Eric Morecambe (1998)
The Beatles: Celebration (1999)
Hollywood Rocks The Movies: The Early Years 1955–1970 (2000)
Hendrix (2000)
The Beatles Revolution (2000)
Jazz (2001)
Wingspan (2001)
The Best Of Ringo Starr And His All-Starr Band So Far (2001)
VH1 Storytellers: Classics (2001)

In 1985 Ringo's personal manager John Hartmann explained that Ringo had taken the role in the *Alice In Wonderland* miniseries 'because he has put aside music and wants to become a prominent film actor. He's very, very serious about it.' Hartmann then said that Ringo was working on a film about a man who has silly phobias, such as a fear of peanut butter, a fear of turning left and so on. He was also considering the part of a gambler called 'Mr Continental' and was considering a biography of Morris 'Two-Gun' Cohen, an English-born General under Chiang Kai-Shek who Ringo actually physically resembled.

Ringo is unlikely to appear in any further movie roles. In 2003 he was asked if he had any further films or TV planned. He said, 'No. I've decided I'm just going to do music from now on. That's what I love. I'm a musician and that's all I want to be. I'm turning down everything else.'

Fishof, David

Major American promoter whose David Fishof Promotions Inc has presented over 4,000 musical events. He founded his New York Company to produce unique musical shows, which would appeal to audiences of all ages. In 1986 he launched the Monkees Reunion and in 2000 the Monkee Mania Tour, in addition to producing *The British Rock Symphony* album. He also created the Rock And Roll Fantasy

Camp, a camp in which adults who have always wanted to be rock stars can go along and mix with leading rock stars and attend seminars on music.

David was also the inspiration behind the All-Starr Band tours, promoting and organising them as well. David thought of Ringo and imagined a band built around him of well-known and respected musicians from the classic rock era. The idea was also to rotate the musicians to keep the band fresh and innovative on each of the different tours.

David recalled the time at the end of the 80s when he asked Ringo if he ever wanted to tour again. 'He said yes, so he got out his phone book, called some of his friends and the All-Starr concept was born.'

For The Love of Harry: Everybody Sings Nilsson

A tribute album to Harry Nilsson, released in America on 9 May 1995 on Musicmasters 65127-2. It contains the track 'Lay Down Your Arms' by Ringo and Stevie Nicks, which was recorded on 19 January 1995.

Frampton, Peter

A British guitarist, born in Beckenham, Kent, on 22 April 1950. He was something of a wizard on the guitar, gaining a reputation for his expertise by the age of ten, and appearing on the *Ready, Steady, Go!* TV show when he was only fourteen.

He was sixteen when he joined the Herd and nineteen when he was in Humble Pie. He also began session work and first met Ringo and George Harrison when he played on the Doris Troy sessions at Apple studios. He also played on George's *All Things Must Pass* triple album.

Peter recalled, 'I used to live around the corner from Ringo and hang out at his house when neither of us were busy.' He joined Ringo and George Harrison to play on Harry Nilsson's album *Son of Schmilsson* and also appeared in a scene of Ringo's film *Son Of Dracula*.

Ringo played drums on the tracks 'Alright' and 'The Lodger' on Peter's solo album *Winds Of Change* in 1972. Peter recalled that when he'd first asked Ringo if he would play on the record, Ringo said he'd like to hear the songs, so Peter went to his house and played them for him. He was pleased to say, 'He liked everything.'

Frampton returned the favour when he played on Ringo's album *Rotogravure* in 1976.

His album *Frampton Comes Alive* sold ten million copies and spawned the hit singles 'Show Me The Way', 'Baby I Love Your Way' and 'Do You Feel Like We Do'. He also starred in the 1978 film *Sergeant Pepper's Lonely Hearts Club Band*.

Ringo invited him to become a member of the All-Starr Band in 1997, during which he played 'Show Me The Way', 'Baby I Love Your Way', 'All I Want To Be (Is By Your Side)' and 'Do You Feel Like We Do'. He also performed 'Norwegian Wood'.

Friedman, Richard 'Kinky'

An outrageous country singer/songwriter, born in Chicago, Illinois, on 1 November 1944, although he has lived most of his life in Texas. He first recorded with the surf music band King Arthur and the Carrots in 1966 and then went on to lead a band called the Texas Jewboys, writing and recording numbers with them such as 'They Ain't Makin' Jews Like Jesus Anymore' and 'Ride 'Em Jewboy'.

When Ringo was appearing on Bob Dylan's Rolling Thunder Review in Houston, Texas, he met Friedman and agreed to be 'the voice of Jesus' on the 'Lasso From El Paso' track recorded at Cherokee Studios in Los Angeles.

Fury, Billy

The first major pop superstar from Liverpool. He became Decca Records' biggest-selling artist of all time, with 26 hits between 1961 and 1966 before ill health caused his early retirement from the music scene.

Fury was reared in the Dingle, the same area of Liverpool as Ringo, and attended St Silas's Junior School and Dingle Vale Secondary School, along with Ringo and Fury's best friend, Billy Hatton, who was later to become a member of the Fourmost.

Billy came out of retirement to appear with Ringo in a cameo role as Storm Tempest in the 1973 film *That'll Be The Day*. He died from a heart problem on 28 January 1983 at a time when he was in the process of recording a new album and had just had a new single enter the charts.

FYE Store

A record store in the Rockefeller Center at 1290 Avenue of the Americas in New York City. Ringo appeared there on 25 March 2003 to make an in-store appearance and sign copies of his *Ringo Rama* and *VH-1 Storytellers* albums. Fans began queuing the previous evening and the shop opened at 7 a.m. Ringo began the signing at 7 p.m. and would only sign copies of the two new CDs.

Gadd, Steve

The drummer who played on the *Ringo The 4th* album. Ringo began to enjoy playing alongside guest drummers when he played with Jim Keltner at the 'Concert For Bangla Desh' in 1970 and continued it through various albums, until he decided to change and become sole drummer on his 2003 *Ringo Rama*. He had been playing so much in recent years with his All-Starr Band that he felt he'd like to begin recording without a guest drummer.

Gartlan USA

An American company, based in New Jersey, that produces items for collectors. Ringo was licensed by the company to make a series of collectible items about himself, and in his home in Monte Carlo in December 1995 personally signed a 'Ringo' figurine based on the *Abbey Road* cover, which retailed at $350. On 25 April 1996 he spent four hours in a Los Angeles hotel signing 1,250 copies of 'All-Starr Collection' plates for Gartlan. There were also 1,000 hand-signed plates featuring Ringo in various stages of his career, which retailed at $225. Other items in the collection included a six-inch figure of Ringo on drums. There were 5,000 copies of this item, retailing for $150 each. There was an 8¼-inch plate, banded in 24-carat gold, which was limited to 10,000 copies at $29.95 each. An *Abbey Road* figurine was produced in an edition of 10,000, retailing at $49.95, and a 3¼-inch gold-banded mini-plate retailed at $14.95.

In 1999 Gartlan issued a new limited-edition pewter figurine of Ringo, limited to 500 pieces, each numbered and signed by Ringo, together with 50 sterling-silver plate-artists proofs and a smaller unsigned version limited to 5,000 copies.

Gibb, Maurice

The late member of the Bee Gees. Ringo and Maurice decided to collaborate on a project in the 70s, but it never came off. Ringo recalled, 'It was a little movie, actually, that we were working on. It was like *The Chase*. We had one camera between us and we'd chase each other all round the area in Britain where we were both living at the time. Then we went into the studio and I just overdubbed all the sound effects from the movie *Yellow Submarine*.'

Give My Regards To Broad Street

Paul McCartney's 1984 feature film, which also featured Ringo and Barbara Bach. Apart from playing drums on various numbers, Ringo appeared in several of the scenes. During a rendition of 'Eleanor Rigby', a dream sequence takes place in Victorian times as Paul, Linda, Ringo and Barbara picnic on a riverbank.

One of the numbers was 'Ballroom Dancing' and a special theatre set had been built in the studio. Paul commented, 'It was great that, we had the band on stage – John Paul Jones on bass, Ringo on drums, Dave Edmunds and Chris Spedding on guitars, Linda and me on piano, so we had that element, which was nice enough anyway.'

Golden Blunders

A track from the 1992 *Time Takes Time* album, written by Jonathan Auer and Kenneth Stringfellow. It was produced by Peter Asher and engineered by Frank Wolf. Ringo was on lead vocals, drums, percussion and tambourine, Robbie Buchanan was on keyboards, Waday Wachtel on guitar, Andrew Gold on acoustic guitar, guitar solo and backing vocals, Rob Glaub on bass, Peter Asher on tambourine and backing vocals, and Raven Kane, Rosemary Butler, Valerie Carter, Terri Wood, Carmen Twillie, Wendy Fraser, Stephanie Spruill, Andrea Robinson and Robbi Page on backing vocals. The number is 4 minutes and 6 seconds in length.

The number originally appeared on the 1990 album *Dear 23* by Seattle group the Posies.

Goodnight Vienna (album)

Richard Perry produced this album for Ringo during the summer of 1974 at the Sunset Sound and Producer's Workshop Studios in Los Angeles. The basic line-up of musicians was Ringo and Jim Keltner on drums with Klaus Voormann on bass. The total number of musicians appearing on the album was 25.

Roy Kohara designed the sleeve, which was the scene from the 1951 science-fiction film *The Day The Earth Stood Still* where Michael Rennie, as the alien Klaatu, steps forward from the entrance of his flying saucer, proceeded by the nine-foot robot Gort. On the sleeve Ringo's head was superimposed over Rennie's. The word 'Klaatu' also appeared on the sleeve. Two years later a Canadian group called themselves Klaatu and released an eponymous album that many people believed was the Beatles using another name – and it became a million-seller. The posters for Ringo's album also featured the words 'Klaatu Barada Niktu', which were instructions given to the robot to activate it.

The album was issued in Britain on Apple PCS 7168 on 15 November 1974 where it reached No. 24 in the charts. It was released in America on Apple SW 3417 on 18 November 1974 and reached No. 8 in the charts. It was re-released on Capitol SN-16219 in February 1981.

The tracks were: Side One: 'Goodnight Vienna', 'Occapella', 'Oo-Wee', 'Husbands And Wives', 'Snookeroo'. Side Two: 'All By Myself', 'Call Me', 'No No Song', 'Only You', 'Easy For Me', 'Goodnight Vienna (reprise)'.

A television commercial was filmed to promote the album. Shooting took place on Thursday 14 November 1974 on the roof of Capitol Records in Los Angeles, with Ringo dressed in a spacesuit. The commercial was produced by the Vidtronics Company and featured Ringo playing a drum with a marching band in the street. A flying saucer lands, captures him and takes him to the roof of the Capitol Building, where he is seen at the side of the saucer, waving.

To the background of the tracks 'Goodbye Vienna' and 'Only You', there is also a brief conversation between John Lennon and Ringo.

> John: Is that Ringo Starr advertising his new album *Goodnight Vienna* on Apple records and tapes?
> Ringo: It certainly is, John.
> John: My, you look so wonderful.
> Ringo: Thank you.

The commercial ends with them saying:

> John: *Goodnight Vienna* on Apple records and tapes.
> Ringo: Thanks John.
> John: It's a pleasure, Ringo.

Goodnight Vienna (song)

The opening track on the *Goodnight Vienna* album. John Lennon wrote this number especially for Ringo and he plays piano on the track. Backing vocals are by Clydie King, the Blackberries and the Masst Abbots and Billy Preston plays clavinet. It is 2 minutes and 33 seconds in length.

Goodnight Vienna (reprise)

The closing track on the 1974 *Goodnight Vienna* album, lasting 1 minute and 16 seconds. It is a different recording from the opening track, with John Lennon providing an introduction and the words 'OK, with gusto, boys. With gusto.'

Graves, Elsie

Ringo's late mother was born Elsie Gleave and was one of fourteen children reared in the Toxteth area of Liverpool. While working in a local bakery she met Richard Starkey and the couple were married in 1936, initially living with Elsie's parents at 59 Madryn Street, then moving into their own home at No. 9 Madryn Street, where their son Richard was born on 7 July 1940.

The marriage wasn't a happy one and lasted for only seven years, ending in divorce in 1943.

Ringo was only three when his father left the family home – Elsie was 29. He had only moved further up Madryn Street but continued to send a sum of money each week. However, it wasn't enough to support Elsie and Ritchie and they moved to a smaller house in nearby Admiral Grove. Elsie took on a job as barmaid, engaging relatives or friends to look after her son, who always referred to his mum as Elsie.

Ringo was to recall, 'Things were pretty tough for Elsie, as I've always called my mother. She tried to bring me up decently. We were poor but never in rags. I was lucky. I was her only child. She could spend more time with me.'

Elsie married Harry Graves in 1953, and when Ringo became famous he bought his mother and stepfather a new house in a fashionable area of Liverpool.

Graves, Harry

Ringo's stepfather, born in Romford in Essex. A painter and decorator, he moved to Liverpool to work for Liverpool Corporation and he first met Ringo's mother Elsie when Ringo was eleven, after being introduced to her by mutual friends, the Maguires.

Ringo immediately liked Harry and was pleased when Harry married his mother on 18 April 1953. He then referred to him as his 'stepladder'.

During a visit to Romford, Harry bought a drum kit costing just under £10 and lugged it by train all the way to Liverpool as a surprise present for his stepson. Harry also obtained a job for him at the engineering firm H. Hunt & Sons.

When Ritchie changed his name to Ringo Starr and said he wanted to turn professional – a summer season at Butlin's with Rory Storm and the Hurricanes meant he would have to abandon his job at Hunts – Harry and Elsie tried to persuade him against his decision.

When Ringo had success with the Beatles, as soon as he began to earn money he bought Elsie and Harry a bungalow in the Gateacre Park area of Liverpool.

Harry died of pneumonia on Saturday 27 August 1994 at the age of 87. Ringo and Barbara attended his funeral service at Huyton Cemetery on 1 September 1994.

Greek Theater

A 6,100-seater venue in Los Angeles where Ringo appeared with his All-Starr Band on 3 and 4 September 1989. The concerts were recorded and filmed for home video release, utilising two mobile 48-track machines from the Record Plant Studios. The director was Bill Szymezyk. The film was shown at MIPCIN in Cannes, France, on 12 October.

The All-Starr Band appeared at the venue again on their second and third tours.

Grossman, David

A singer/songwriter signed to Ring O' Records in 1975. His self-penned single 'I've Had It' c/w 'C'mon And Roll' was released in Britain only on Ringo O' 2017 103 on 14 November 1975.

The following year Grossman penned the number 'A Dose Of Rock 'N' Roll', which Ringo recorded on his *Rotogravure* album and which became Ringo's first hit single on the Atlantic label.

Happy Birthday John

A number Ringo recorded at Trident Studios, London, to celebrate John Lennon's thirtieth birthday on 9 October 1970, at the request of Yoko Ono. She was asking John's musical buddies to provide him with a musical tribute for his birthday. Stephen Stills, Billy Preston and Klaus Voormann backed Ringo.

Hard Day's Night, A

The reviews of this film suggested that Ringo had the potential to become a fine movie comedian.

Constantly badgered by Paul's 'grandfather' (played by Wilfred Brambell), Ringo gained the audience's sympathy. He literally stole the film during a number of sequences in which he wanders off by himself to the tune of 'Ringo's Theme', an orchestral arrangement by the George Martin Orchestra.

He wanders the London streets only to be spotted and pursued by a group of fans. He dodges into a shop, waits for the girls to go by, and then emerges dressed in an old mackintosh and peaked cap.

Ringo then nearly gets turfed into the murky waters of a canal when an old tyre knocks him over. A nine-year-old boy claims his 'hoop' and the two exchange words. They begin a friendly chat until the boy's mother calls him. Ringo walks on and enters a pub called, appropriately, the Liverpool Arms. He orders a lager and a sandwich, but isn't too pleased with the state of the latter. He moves around awkwardly and upsets some of the pub games that a number of hefty workmen are playing. Putting on a bold front, he picks up some darts and throws them at the board. Unfortunately, the first finds its way into a cheese sandwich, the second into a pint of beer and the third into the pub's parrot. Ringo is thrown out and encounters a policeman who has been keeping an eye on him for some time.

Ringo continues his stroll, noticing workmen who've been digging holes in the road. He spots a girl attempting to cross some puddles and lays down his mac for her in true Sir Walter Raleigh style. She smiles, steps on the coat – and then disappears from sight. The puddles had gathered in holes dug up by the workmen! One of the men is trying to help her when a young man comes along and thinks the workman is trying to accost his girl – it looks as if trouble is brewing. Ringo skips off – straight into the arms of a policeman. He is taken to the local police station, from where his fellow Beatles rescue him.

Hard Rock Live
A show Ringo and the Roundheads videotaped at the Sony Music Studios in New York on 17 June 1998. It was broadcast on VH-1 on 11 September 1998. The show was taped in front of a live audience of 150. The numbers broadcast were 'Photograph', 'La De Da', 'I Was Walkin'', and a medley of 'Love Me Do' and 'With A Little Help From My Friends'. A performance of 'Back Off Boogaloo' was omitted from the broadcast.

Hard Times
The opening track of Side Two of Ringo's 1978 album *Bad Boy*, lasting 3 minutes and 31 seconds. Peter Skellern wrote it.

Harry And Ringo's Night Out
In October 1974 Ringo and Mike Viners, president of Pride Records, financed a film project called *Harry And Ringo's Night Out*. It was filmed in Los Angeles and was based around Ringo and Harry Nilsson's wild nights in the Californian city, with a guest appearance by Keith Moon. It was intended to be a comedy with half live action, half animation, but the film remained uncompleted and was never released commercially.

Hatfield, Bobby
An American singer, born in Beaver Dam, Wisconsin, on 10 August 1940. He began singing professionally while at college and teamed up with another singer, Bill Medley. The duo then called themselves the Righteous Brothers and had a string of impressive hits in the 1960s including 'You've Lost That Lovin' Feeling', 'Unchained Melody', 'Ebb Tide' and 'Just Once In My Life'.

Medley left in 1971 and Hatfield continued the Righteous Brothers by teaming up with Jimmy Walker.

In 1971 Hatfield teamed up with producer Richard Perry, who was working on some recordings at the Apple Studios in London. Perry had arranged the title track for Ringo's *Sentimental Journey* album. Perry brought Hatfield to London for some recordings and asked Ringo if he would sit in on the session. He recalled, 'Ringo was great, he never turned me down, he sat in on the Hatfield session as a favour.'

The record was 'Oo-Wee Baby, I Love You', recorded at Apple Studios in January 1972 with Hatfield on lead vocals, Ringo on drums, Chris Stainton on keyboards, Klaus Voormann on bass and Bobby Keys on saxophone. It was issued in America as a single on Warner Bros WB 7566 in March 1972.

Have I Told You Lately That I Love You

Scott Wisemen wrote 'Have I Told You Lately That I Love You' and Foy Willing and the Riders of the Purple Sage originally recorded it. Elmer Bernstein arranged this version for Ringo's *Sentimental Journey* album. It is 2 minutes and 43 seconds in length.

Have You Seen My Baby

A number penned by Randy Newman and included on his *12 Songs* album. Ringo recorded the number at Sunset Sound Studios in Los Angeles in March 1973 and it is featured on the *Ringo* album. It is also known as 'Hold On'. Marc Bolan played guitar on the track, which he overdubbed at A&M Studios. The number is 3 minutes and 42 seconds in length.

Hayden, Charlie

A jazz musician who worked on Ringo's *Ringo Rama* album, playing upright bass on 'Imagine Me There'. He was to say about Ringo, 'He's really a great human being, you can see it in his taste of music. He listens to all different kinds of music, and that's why he's a great human being. He appreciates beauty.'

Heart On My Sleeve

This was Ringo's cover of the British May 1976 hit written and recorded by Benny Gallagher and Graham Lyle. It is 3 minutes and 19 seconds in length. It was issued as the flipside of the 'Tonight' single in Britain on Polydor 2001 795 on 21 July 1978. In America it was issued as an A side with 'Who Needs A Heart' on the flip, on Portrait 6-70018 on 6 July 1978. It proved to be another chart failure.

Helm, Levon

An American musician born in Marvell, Arkansas, on 28 May 1942. In 1958 he teamed up with Ronnie Hawkins and the two moved to Canada and joined four Canadian musicians. They eventually dropped Hawkins and became known as the Band, and Levon, who had been in and out of the line-up, became a permanent Band member in 1968.

When he was asked to join the All-Starr tour in 1989 he performed 'Up On Cripple Creek' and 'The Weight'.

The press release for the first All-Starr Band's tour in 1989 included the following biography of Levon:

'Being in the rock and roll stronghold for over twenty years, Levon Helm really *is* an allstar. As a founding member of the Band, Levon's career has soared since the 1968 Capitol release of *Music From Big Pink*. He sang lead vocals on such Band classics as 'Cripple Creek', 'The Night They Drove Old Dixie Down', 'The Weight' and 'Rag Mama Rag'. The Band's 1977 release 'The Last Waltz' was later made into a successful full-length motion picture.

'A well-respected drummer, harmonica, and mandolin player, Levon has also pursued a successful acting career, appearing in such films as *The Right Stuff*, *Coal Miner's Daughter* playing Loretta Lynn's father, *The Dollmaker* with Jane Fonda, *Best Revenge* with John Heard, *The Man Outside* and *Smooth Talk*.

'In a June 1, 1989 article about rockstars-turned-actors, the *Chicago Tribune* said, "Probably the best actor to emerge from the ranks of American rockers is the Band's drummer Levon Helm. If Helm ever burns out on the music business, this actor should have a rewarding career in the movies."

'Obviously, his upcoming tour with Ringo Starr proves that Levon Helm won't be burning out anytime soon.'

Hentschel, David

A British musician who originally began his musical career as a recording engineer at Trident Studios in London. In 1973 the studio bought a synthesizer and Hentschel became so skilled on the instrument that he was in demand to play synthesizer for a number of artists including Harry Nilsson, Carly Simon, Genesis, the Nice, Mama Cass and Jim Webb. He even contributed to Paul McCartney's *Red Rose Speedway* album.

Elton John's manager Gus Dudgeon introduced him to John Gilbert, who became his manager, and it was Gilbert who introduced him to Ringo at a time that he was seeking artists for his new Ring O' Records label.

Ringo wanted Hentschel to produce an instrumental version of his *Ringo* album. This became the first album release on Ring O' Records. Entitled *Sta*rtling Music*, it was issued in America on 17 February 1979 on Ring O' ST 11372 and in Britain on Ring O' 2320-101 on 18 April 1975. The tracks were: Side One: 'Devil Woman', 'Six O'Clock', 'Step Lightly', 'Oh My My', 'You're Sixteen (I)', 'You're Sixteen (II)'. Side Two: 'Photograph', 'Have You Seen My Baby', 'I'm The Greatest', 'Sunshine Life For Me (Sail Away Raymond)', 'You And Me (Babe)'.

The single 'Oh My My' c/w 'Devil Woman' was issued in America on 17 February 1975 on Ring O' 4030 and in Britain on 21 March on Ring O' 2017-101.

The musicians were David Hentschel on synthesizer and Ringo Starr and John Gilbert on finger snaps.

Hey Baby

A track from the *Ringo's Rotogravure* album, which was originally written by Margaret Cobb and Bruce Channel and provided Channel with a million-seller in 1962, when it topped the American charts and reached No. 2 in Britain. The Beatles also backed Channel on the bill of a Tower Ballroom promotion in New Brighton. Lon Von Eaton was on guitar, Cooker Lo Presti on bass guitar, John Jarvis played keyboards, Randy Brecker played trumpet, Alan Young, Michael Brecker and George Young played tenor saxophone, while Lewis Delgatto played baritone saxophone.

The number is 3 minutes and 10 seconds in length.

It was released as a single in Britain on Polydor 2001 699 on 26 November 1976, with 'Lady Gaye' on the flip, but didn't enter the charts. The single was issued in America on Atlantic 45-3371 on 22 November 1976 but only managed to reach No. 74 in the charts.

Hollywood Rocks The Movies: The Early Years (1955–1970)

A 2000 America television documentary lasting 145 minutes, directed by Edith Becker and Kevin Burns, with a narration by Ringo Starr.

Hopeless

A track on the 1983 *Old Wave* album, written by Richard Starkey and Joe Walsh and produced by Walsh. Ringo was on lead vocals, guitar and percussion, Joe Walsh on guitar and backing vocals, Mo Foster on bass, Gary Brooker on keyboards and Steve Hess, Mark Easterling and Patrick Maroshek on backing vocals. It is 3 minutes and 20 seconds in length.

Hopkins, Nicky

A British pianist, born in London on 24 February 1944. Hopkins was one of Britain's leading session musicians and played keyboards on the Beatles' 'Revolution' single. He also contributed to John Lennon's *Imagine*, *Walls And Bridges* and *Sometime In New York City*, George Harrison's *Living In The Material World*, *Dark Horse* and *Extra Texture*, Paul McCartney's *Flowers In The Dirt* and Ringo's *Ringo* and *Goodnight Vienna*.

He died in Nashville on 6 September 1994 after suffering from heart trouble and intestinal problems.

Horn, Jim

An appropriately named American musician who led the horn section on the 'Concert For Bangla Desh' and has worked with all four members of the Beatles during their solo careers.

He worked with Ringo in Los Angeles when Richard Perry was producing the album *Ringo* in 1973 and he was commissioned to write all the horn parts for it. He next worked with Ringo twenty years later on the *Time Takes Time* album in 1993.

Houston

The city in Texas where Ringo once wanted to emigrate to when he worked in a factory in Liverpool as a teenager.

He and his friend decided that they wanted to go to Houston and even went to the American Consulate to fill in the forms. Once they did that and took them back they were given another bundle of forms. They decided it was too much of a chore to fill them in, as it was very difficult to get into America in the 1950s. Ringo recalled, 'I was trying to immigrate to Houston, Texas, because Lightin' Hopkins, the blues player, lived there.'

Ringo finally managed to get to Houston when the Beatles appeared at the Sam Houston Coliseum there on 19 August 1965 and returned again with his All-Starr Band thirty years later on 11 August 1995.

Hudson, Mark

An American musician/songwriter/producer, born on 23 August 1951. He has produced a number of Ringo's albums, including *Vertical Man*, *I Wanna Be Santa Claus*, *Storytellers* and *Ringo Rama*. Mark has become an important partner to Ringo during recent years. They first met when Mark was called into the *Time Takes Time* sessions, produced by Phil Ramone, as vocal arranger.

Hudson, the uncle of actress Kate Hudson, was originally a member of the 1970s act the Hudson Brothers, a pop act who also appeared on television as a comedy team, and he later went on to produce records by artists such as Aerosmith, Harry Nilsson and Hanson, and to pen songs for Bon Jovi, Ozzy Osbourne, the Scorpions, Alice Cooper and Celine Dion. He was nominated for a Grammy for the Aerosmith song 'Livin' On The Edge'.

During a party for Barbara's sister Marjorie on 31 December 1996, Ringo met songwriter Dean Grakal, the son of his solicitor Bruce Grakal. They discussed songwriting and Dean suggested they get together with Mark Hudson as a songwriting team. Mark and Dean met Ringo at his Beverly Hills home and began songwriting together for material that was to appear on the *Vertical Man* album. The first number they composed together was called 'My Love', but Ringo told them that this was already the title of a Paul McCartney song, and they changed the name to 'Everyday'. They then recorded a demo of the song with guitarist Steve Dudas.

In February 1977 Ringo decided to employ Mark's services as a writer and producer and the following month, Ringo, Mark, Dean and Steve teamed up to begin recording at Hudson's Whatinthewhatthe?

Studios in Los Angeles. The studio was situated on the second storey above a Thai restaurant. The studio had been covered with photographs of the Beatles, but Mark was to recall, 'I had to take some down before Ringo came the first night, otherwise he would have thought I was a stalker!' They recorded 'Mr Double-It-Up' and 'One', the latter originally called 'All It Takes Is One'.

In February 2003, Hudson became Ringo's business partner in the formation of a new record label called Pumkinhead, which would be marketed and distributed by S Curve/EMI.

Hunter, Ian

Born on 3 June 1946 in Oswestry, Shropshire. Ian joined various bands, including the New Yardbirds, and backed several artists as bass guitarist, including Billy Fury. He joined Silence in 1969 – when they changed their name to Mott The Hoople they made their breakthrough with a version of David Bowie's 'All The Young Dudes' and went on to have seven hit singles and four hit albums. Hunter also wrote an acclaimed book *Diary Of A Rock 'n' Roll Star*. Over the years he has continued to join various bands and also release solo albums including his recent album *Rant*.

He was a member of the seventh All-Starr Band in 2001.

Husbands And Wives

A track from Ringo's 1974 album *Goodnight Vienna*. The number was originally written and recorded by Roger Miller in 1966. Richard Bennett provided an electric guitar solo, Tom Hensley played electric piano and Vini Poncia added harmony vocals.

It is 3 minutes and 29 seconds in length.

I Don't Believe You

A track from the 1992 *Time Takes Time* album, written by Andrew Sturmer and Roger Manning. Don Was produced it and the engineers were Ed Cherney and Rick Pekkonen. Ringo was on lead vocals, drums and percussion, Mikael Landau was on guitar, David Grissom on acoustic guitar, Roger Manning and Andrew Sturmer on acoustic guitars and backing vocals, James 'Hutch' Hutchinson on bass and Benmont Tench on piano and Hammond B3. The number is 2 minutes and 48 seconds in length.

I Keep Forgettin'

A track from the 1983 *Old Wave* album, written by Jerry Leiber and Mike Stoller, and produced by Joe Walsh. Ringo was on lead vocals and percussion, Joe Walsh on guitar, Mo Foster on bass, Gary Brooker on keyboards, Russell Kinkel on drums and Ray Cooper on percussion. It is 4 minutes and 21 seconds in length.

I Really Love Her

The brief closing track of the 2003 album *Ringo Rama*, on which Ringo plays drums, bass, acoustic guitar, electric and slide guitar. Looking through various albums, Ringo noticed ones in which the artist had played all the instruments on a particular track and felt he wanted to do that himself.

I Still Love You

This is a song originally written by George Harrison under the title 'When Every Song Is Sung'. There had been several unsuccessful attempts to record it by Cilla Black, Ronnie Spector and Leon Russell, so George altered the number, retitled it and gave it to Ringo. Lon Van Eaton played guitar, Klaus Voormann played bass guitar and Jane Getz played piano. The number is 2 minutes and 56 seconds in length.

When Ringo asked George to contribute a number to his 1976 *Ringo's Rotogravure* album, he asked if he could use the number as he'd originally played on the Cilla Black session and liked the number and was aware it hadn't been released.

Although George gave him the number to record he didn't like the result and he actually took legal action against Ringo because of it, but resolved it later the same year.

I Think, Therefore I Rock 'n' Roll

A track from the 2003 *Ringo Rama* album, lasting 3 minutes and 28 seconds. Ringo had the idea of including a Roy Orbison 'growl', so they phoned his widow, Barbara Orbison and she said posted them a CD, saying, 'I'm sending over a growl.'

I Wanna Be Santa Claus (album)

An album of Christmas numbers, some standards, others newly written (six covers and six originals, in fact). Work initially began at Ringo's home in Surrey in July 1998 where Mark Hudson and Ringo co-wrote two songs, 'Dear Santa' and 'Christmas Eve'. They taped the two numbers on 14, 15 and 16 September 1998 in England and worked on the recording sessions the following March in Los Angeles, beginning on 8 March at Whatinthewhatthe? Studios. There they recorded 'Rudolf The Red-Nosed Reindeer', 'Dear Santa', 'Little Drummer Boy' and 'Christmas Time Is Here Again' with Ringo, Hudson, Jim Cox and Steve Dudas. Work continued at different times of the year in Los Angeles and the UK at several different studios. It was completed in two final sessions at the Whatinthewhatthe? Studios on 8 and 9 September and the album was mixed at A&M Studios in Los Angeles and Sterling Sound in New York. The album was released in America on Mercury 314 546 668-2 in October 1999, although it wasn't issued in Britain.

The tracks were: 'Come On Christmas, Come On', 'Winter Wonderland', 'I Wanna Be Santa Claus', 'The Little Drummer Boy', 'Rudolph The Red-Nosed Reindeer', 'Christmas Eve', 'The Christmas Dance', 'Christmas Time Is Here Again', 'Blue Christmas', 'Dear Santa', 'White Christmas' and 'Pax Um Biscum (Peace Be With You)'.

Ringo was to part company with Mercury following the release of this album, which received virtually no promotion or publicity and therefore had extremely weak sales.

I Wanna Be Santa Claus (song)

The title track of Ringo's 1999 Christmas album in which he wishes he could be Santa Claus and would then bring Christmas cheer every day rather than just once a year. It was penned by Richard Starkey, Mark

Hudson and Dick Marda with Ringo on lead vocals, drums and percussion. Mark Hudson was on bass, acoustic guitar, keyboards, percussion and backing vocals, Steve Dudas on electric guitar, Jim Cox on keyboards and string arrangement, Scott Gordon on percussion, Dan Higgins on recorder and Timothy B. Schmit and Christina Rasch on backing vocals. It is 3 minutes and 46 seconds in length.

I Wanna Be Your Man
A track from the *Meet The Beatles* album on which Ringo takes lead vocal. Ringo also performed the number on stage between 1963 and 1966.

Although a Lennon and McCartney composition, it was mainly penned by Paul and John didn't have all that much confidence in the number. He was to comment, 'It was throwaway. The only two versions of the song were Ringo and the Rolling Stones. That shows how much importance we put on it. We weren't going to give them anything *great*, right?'

The number is a regular feature on the All-Starr tours.

I Was Walkin'
A track from the *Vertical Man* album lasting 3 minutes and 21 seconds. It was composed by Starkey/Hudson/Grakal. Ringo was on lead vocal, drums, keyboards, percussion and handclaps, with Paul McCartney and Alanis Morissette on backing vocals. Steve Cropper had an electric guitar solo, Steven Tyler was on harmonica and backing vocals, Steve Dudas was on electric guitar, Mark Hudson on bass, electric guitar, percussion and backing vocals, Jim Cox on piano, sax and synthesizer and Scott Gordon on percussion.

I'll Be Fine Anywhere
A track on the *Vertical Man* album that is 3 minutes and 41 seconds in length. Starkey/Hudson/Grakal/Dudas composed it. Ringo was on lead vocal, drums and percussion. George Harrison provided an electric guitar solo and also a slide guitar solo. Steve Dudas was on bass and electric guitar, Mark Hudson on electric guitar, acoustic guitar and backing vocals, and Jim Cox was on piano.

George Harrison had recorded a guitar track for the number and sent it to Ringo in Los Angeles by post. Ringo rushed to the studio to play the number and the studio engineer was to comment, 'You can hear it was a seemingly casually done track for George. He engineered it himself, and you can hear on the tape that he was at home, with people talking in the background.'

I'm A Fool To Care
This *Sentimental Journey* track is a country music number originally penned by Ted Daffan. It provided Les Paul and Mary Ford with a hit

in 1954 and John Barry with a million-seller version in 1961. Klaus Voormann arranged it for Ringo. It was recorded in Abbey Road's No. 2 studio on 11 February 1970 with mixing on 20 February and overdubs on 7 March. It is 2 minutes and 39 seconds in length.

I'm Going Down

A track from the 1983 *Old Wave* album, written by Richard Starkey and Joe Walsh and produced by Walsh. Ringo was on lead vocals, drums and percussion, Joe Walsh on guitar, Waddy Wachtel on guitar and harmonica, Mo Foster and Kenny Edwards on bass, Gary Brooker and Chris Stainton on keyboards, and Ringo, Barbara Bach, Joe Walsh, Gary Brooker and Mo Foster all contributing to the backing vocals. It is 3 minutes and 35 seconds in length.

I'm The Greatest

The opening track on the 1973 *Ringo* album.

John Lennon had originally taped a rough piano demo of the song at Tittenhurst Park in December 1970 as one of the numbers he intended recording himself. He thought about including it on the *Imagine* album, but didn't. He then forgot about the number completely until Ringo asked him for a number for his forthcoming solo album in 1973.

When John had originally penned the number it had been loosely autobiographical, with references to the Beatles' history and mention of Billy Shears, the character Ringo had played on the *Sgt Pepper* recording.

In April 1973 John arrived at the studio in Los Angeles and ran through the song with Ringo and Klaus Voormann. He acted as producer of that particular track. Soon after the session started there was a phone call to the control room. It was from George Harrison, who asked how Ringo's session was going. Richard Perry, the producer of the *Ringo* album, passed the phone over to John who said, 'Get over here and help me finish this bridge!'

George turned up within half an hour and the three ex-Beatles began to play together in a studio for the first time since January 1970. Interestingly enough, when Paul McCartney had walked out on the Beatles, there was a meeting in which they decided to carry on with Klaus Voormann replacing Paul on bass. However, they decided not to go ahead – but this track has all four of them on it, a sign of what might have been the sound if the Beatles had continued with Klaus instead of Paul.

John sang lead vocals and played piano himself until he was satisfied with the basic rhythm track. Ringo then used John's tapes as a guide when he recorded himself on lead vocal. John overdubbed a vocal harmony and George added lead guitar. Billy Preston then added some extra keyboard playing and the track was chosen to open the album.

The number is 3 minutes and 22 seconds in length.

I'm Yours

A track from the *Vertical Man* album that was composed by Starkey/Hudson/Nevin. Ringo provided lead vocal, Mike Nevin electric guitar, Mark Hudson acoustic guitar and celeste and George Martin provided the string arrangement.

The number was actually dedicated to Ringo's second wife Barbara and he commented, 'I feel exactly the same as I did when I saw Barbara at the LA airport eighteen years ago and fell in love with her. I am still in love with her. We tell each other we love each other every day. No matter how bad Tuesday night is, Wednesday we start afresh.'

Imagine Me There

A track from the 2003 *Ringo Rama* album, 3 minutes and 55 seconds in length, with jazz musician Charlie Hayden on upright bass and a guitar solo from Eric Clapton.

In A Heartbeat

A track from the 1992 *Time Takes Time* album, written by Diane Warren. Don Was produced it and Ed Cherney was the engineer. Ringo was on lead vocals, drums and percussion, Michael Landau and Mark Goldenberg on guitars, James 'Hutch' Hutchinson on bass, Benmont Tench on Hammond C3 and harmonica, Jamie Muhoberac and Robbie Buchanan on keyboards, and Brian O'Doherty, Brian Wilson, Roger Manning, Andrew Sturmer, Andrew Gold and Doug Fieger were on backing vocals.

In My Car

A track from the 1983 *Old Wave* album, penned by Richard Starkey/Joe Walsh/Mo Foster/Kim Goody and produced by Walsh. The musicians were Ringo on lead vocals and drums, Joe Walsh on guitar and backing vocals, Mo Foster on bass, Gary Brooker and Chris Stainton on keyboards, and Steve Hess, Mark Easterling and Patrick Maroshek on backing vocals.

The number is 3 minutes and 13 seconds in length.

'In My Car' was issued as a 7″ single in Germany on Bellephon 100.16.012 on 16 June 1983, with 'As Far As We Can Go' on the flip.

Instant Amnesia

A hard-rock track on the 2003 *Ringo Rama* album. Ringo commented that the track contains 'some of the best drumming I've ever played in the last ten, fifteen years'.

It is 5 minutes and 12 seconds in length.

It Don't Come Easy

A track recorded at Trident Studios in March and October 1970. George Harrison produced it. It had originally been recorded on 18

February 1970 at Studio Two at Abbey Road during the *Sentimental Journey* sessions when it was known as 'You Gotta Pay Your Dues'.

There were three versions of the number recorded, one of which included Klaus Voormann on bass and George Harrison on guitar, with another having Eric Clapton on guitar and Gary Wright on piano. The version released as a single was recorded on 8 March 1970 and featured Klaus Voormann on bass, Steven Stills and George Harrison on guitars, Ringo on drums and Ron Cattermole on saxophone and trumpet. It is 2 minutes and 59 seconds in length.

This was Ringo's first British solo single and it was issued in the UK on Apple R 5898 on 9 April 1971 with 'Early 1970' on the flip. It reached No. 5 in the *New Musical Express* charts.

It was actually Ringo's second single release in America, following 'Beaucoups Of Blues', and was issued on Apple 1831 on 16 April 1971 with the same flipside as in Britain. It reached No. 4 in the *Billboard* charts. Interestingly enough, it outsold the singles of his fellow ex-Beatles: John's 'Power To The People', Paul's 'Another Day' and George's 'Bangla Desh'.

There were two promotional films made. The first was based at Ringo's home in Sunny Heights and featured several of Ringo's media appearances, including *The Ed Sullivan Show*, clips from the film *Candy* and various home-movie clips of Ringo at his home playing with kittens, pulling faces at the camera and playing billiards. The other was filmed on a skiing holiday in April 1971, directed by Michael Hurll, and was shown on *Top Of The Pops* on 30 April 1971. This clip was repeated on the satellite channel UK Gold on 2 August 1993 on the *Top Of The Pops* re-run series.

Ringo is also heard performing the number on the *Concert For Bangla Desh* album, although he forgets the words in a few places on this live recording!

Jagger, Mick

Ringo played drums on a 1993 recording with Mick Jagger on lead vocals, Chris Stainton on guitar, Bill Wyman on bass and Leon Russell on drums. The number was '(Can't Seem To) Get A Line' c/w 'On You (Shine A Light)' which was said to be an early version of 'Shine A Light' found on the Stones' album *Exile On Main Street*. The track was eventually released on the reissue of the album *Leon Russell* in 1993.

Jerry Lewis Telethon

An annual American television charity broadcast hosted by comedian Jerry Lewis. Among many of Ringo's appearances on the show included the one that was broadcast on 3 September 1979. He teamed up with a number of other prominent musicians to perform three numbers. The other musicians were Bill Wyman on bass, Dave Mason on guitar, Doug Kershaw on fiddle, Todd Rundgren on guitar, Roger Powell on keyboards, Willie Wilcox on drums and Kasim Sulton on bass. The numbers they played were 'Money (That's What I Want)', 'Twist And Shout' and 'Jumping Jack Flash'.

Jingle Bell Rock

A three-hour radio special with Ringo as the host. It was a collection of Christmas rock'n'roll records in three sections, one for Motown, one for Phil Spector and one for the Beatles. The Beatles section featured 'Christmastime Is Here Again' by Ringo, 'Wonderful Christmastime' by Paul McCartney, 'Happy Xmas (War Is Over)' by John Lennon and some Beatles Fan Club Christmas messages from 1964.

The show was broadcast to 75 different radio stations throughout America in December 1999 and again in December 2000.

Incidentally, 'Jingle Bell Rock' was the title of a Bobby Helms hit.

John Lennon Scholarship Concert

A concert that took place in Liverpool on Saturday 5 May 1990. Both Ringo and Paul McCartney had decided to contribute, although neither was to appear in person that evening.

Each made a video contribution, shown on the side screens of the stage and also broadcast later that evening on British television on Channel Four.

The video by Ringo was of himself performing 'I Call Your Name', recorded on 22 March of that year, with him fronting a band comprising Joe Walsh, Jeff Lynne and Tom Petty on guitars and Jim Keltner on drums.

Jones, Howard

An English singer/keyboards player, born in Southampton, Hampshire, on 23 February 1955.

After leaving a music college in Manchester he became a piano teacher and then joined several bands. With money he received as compensation for an accident he bought a synthesizer, made a demo tape and was signed by WEA Records in 1983.

Jones first entered the British charts in 1983 with 'New Song' and topped the charts with his debut album *Human's Lib*. He had four Top 15 singles in 1984 and several Top 30 singles in the US.

He opened a vegetarian restaurant in New York, but within a year it burned down. When his 'In the Running' failed to chart in 1992, WEA dropped him. He initially thought his career was at an end, but decided to take his future into his own hands. In 1994 he produced a CD, *Working In The Backroom*, which he recorded at home and sold at gigs, eventually reaching sales of 20,000.

In 1996 he went out on the road performing acoustic tours and promoting a new album, *Live Acoustic America*, and later in the year began recording a new album, *Angels And Lovers*.

Ringo asked Howard to become a member of the seventh All-Starr Band and he toured with them in the summer of 2001.

Juke Box Jury

A popular British BBC1 television show, screened weekly in Britain during the 1960s and hosted by David Jacobs. There was an all-Beatles show on Saturday 26 October 1963 that was filmed from the stage of the Empire Theatre in Liverpool.

Ringo appeared on the show on 1 August 1 1964, having recorded it the previous week on 25 July.

Jacobs introduced Ringo as 'A gentleman known in the trade as Ringo Starr'.

Ringo was to comment, 'I'm not worried about what records they'll play. I'm OK judging records – just as long as I don't get carried away and get too outspoken.'

For the recording, Ringo's fellow judges were television celebrity Katie Boyle, comedian Ray Martine and actress Judy Cornwell.

The records reviewed were: 'Thinking Of You Baby', the Dave Clark Five; 'A Summer Song', Chad Stuart and Jeremy Clyde; 'Don't It Make You Feel Good', the Overlanders; 'It's For You', Cilla Black; 'Move It Baby', Simon Scott; 'I Wouldn't Trade You For The World', the Bachelors; and 'Not For Me', Sammy Davis Jr.

Just A Dream

A number penned by Ringo and Vince Poncia. It was issued as the flip-side of 'Drowning In The Sea Of Love' and was also used as the B side of the American single 'Wings'.

Although the A sides were taken from the *Ringo The 4th* album, 'Just A Dream' wasn't included on that release.

Produced by Arif Mardin, it is 4 minutes and 17 seconds in length.

Keltner, Jim

A session drummer who originally worked with Yoko Ono on her *Fly* album. He next met George Harrison at a Gary Wright session in London, resulting in some session work with George (on his *Living In The Material World* album, George had a line saying that information on the Jim Keltner fan club could be obtained if 'a stamped addressed elephant' could be sent) and then met John Lennon and played on 'Jealous Guy' and 'I Don't Wanna Be A Soldier, Mama' on the *Imagine* album. He appeared on *Walls And Bridges*, *Mind Games* and Lennon's *Roots* sessions and also appeared on the *Concert For Bangla Desh*.

His first sessions with Ringo were on the *Ringo* album in 1973, followed by *Goodnight Vienna* and *Ringo's Rotogravure* on which he and Ringo played drums on every track, with the exception of 'Las Brisas'. Keltner became Ringo's favourite drummer and they played double drums on a number of projects.

Ringo often recorded with a second drummer and it was usually Keltner. Ringo recalled, 'That started by accident because of the Bangla Desh concert which we played for George. Jim was there too. That was the first time I'd played with two drummers, and I just loved it so much. We did the *Ringo* album and *Goodnight Vienna* together. Then, when I went to New York to do the album *Ringo The 4th* that Arif Mardin produced, suddenly we had Steve Gadd around. I think there was a bit of a union situation as well in those days. You were allowed to sing, because no one else could do that for you, but I think there was something about taking a drummer's job away from an American musician.'

When Ringo decided on touring again he immediately contacted Keltner to join him in the first All-Starr Band.

The official biography contained in the programme for the 1989 All-Starr Band tour read:

'Session stars can be pretty pushy, egomaniacs: Jim Keltner is shy, nervous, and self-effacing. The wiliest, subtlest drummer in rock and roll is busier than ever, working on *Traveling Wilburys Volume 1*, Roy Orbison's *Mystery Girl*, Elvis Costello's *Spike*, *Get Rhythm* by Ray Cooder, George Harrison's *Cloud Nine*, John Hiatt's *Bring The Family*, Pink Floyd's *A Momentary Lapse Of Reason*, the Beach Boys' *Kokomo*, Richard Thompson's *Daring Adventures* and *Amnesia*, Tom Petty's *Full Moon Fever* and new albums by Maria McKee and Dave Edmunds . . . an amazing list that gets longer day by day.

'Born in 1942 in Tulsa, Oklahoma, he was christened "Jimmie Lee" into a family of drummers and bass players. At fifteen he was playing drums, giggling often and unlucratively until joining Gary Lewis and the Playboys. In '69 he played with Delaney and Bonnie and Friends, jamming with Jimmy Gordon and Jim Horn, and was then invited onto Joe Cocker's *Mad Dogs And Englishmen* tour. By 1971, Keltner had been asked to be in Derek and the Dominoes, played on five John Lennon albums, five George Harrison albums, and every Ry Cooder record but three. In 1979–1981, Keltner anchored Dylan's Christian tours.

'At 47, Keltner says he's hitting his stride only now.'

Keoghan, Phil

A reporter from the *Fox After Breakfast* show, who interviewed Ringo during his rehearsals with his new All-Starr band in April 1997.

Keoghan was obviously nervous during the interview and was stumbling over his questions. Ringo then sat him down on a box and gave him a sheet of lyrics, asking Keoghan, 'What's this?' '"Act Naturally"' said Keoghan. 'There you go,' said Ringo, 'Try it!'

Keys, Bobby

A well-respected saxophone player who Ringo had worked with on a number of projects in the early 1970s, including Keys' 1972 album on which Ringo, Eric Clapton, George Harrison, Dave Mason and Nicky Hopkins had also contributed.

Ringo signed him to his Ring O' Records in 1975 and released his single 'Gimme The Key' c/w 'Honky Tonk (Parts 1 & 2)'. It was released in Britain on Ring O' 2017 102 on 5 September 1975 and in America on Ring O' 4129 on 25 August 1975.

There was even a longer version issued to discos on Ring O' SPRO 8193.

The musicians on the single were Bobby Keys on horns and vibraslap, Steve Maddeo and Trevor Lawrence on horns, Spider Webb on drums, Jesse Ed Davis on guitar, Larry Von Nash on keyboards and Reggie McBride on bass.

Keys had appeared in a musical scene in Ringo's film *Son Of Dracula* and on the albums *Ringo* and *Goodnight Vienna*.

Khan, Aashish

An Indian musician and sarod player who contributed to George Harrison's *Wonderwall* soundtrack and to the Harrison-produced *Shankar, Family & Friends*. He recorded the number 'In Praise Of Lord (We Are All Children Of God)' at Trident Studios in London in late 1969 with Ringo, George Harrison, Eric Clapton and a keyboard player, although the song was never released.

King Biscuit Flower Hour Presents Ringo Starr, The

A live album issued in America by the syndicated radio network King Biscuit Flower Hour (No.7930188003-2) on 6 August 2002. It was recorded at the All-Starr concert at the Rosemont Theater, Chicago, on 22 August 2001.

The tracks were 'Photograph', 'Act Naturally', 'Logical Song', 'No One Is To Blame', 'Yellow Submarine', 'Give A Little Bit', 'You're Sixteen', 'No No Song', 'Back Off Boogaloo', 'Glamorous Life', 'I Wanna Be Your Man', 'Lucky Man', 'Take The Long Way Home', 'All The Young Dudes', 'Don't Go Where The Road Don't Go' and 'With A Little Help From My Friends'.

King Of Broken Hearts

A track from Ringo's *Vertical Man* album, written by Starkey/Hudson/Grakal/Dudas.

Ringo provided lead vocal, drums and percussion, George Harrison played slide guitar, Steve Dudas played electric guitar and acoustic guitar, Mark Hudson played acoustic guitar, keyboard, mellotron, percussion and was on backing vocals, John Baxter was on pedal steel guitar, Jim Cox on Wurlitzer and Graham Preskett provided the string arrangement.

Ringo recalled asking George Harrison to play on the track: 'He said he wasn't in the mood. Two weeks later I phoned him up from LA just to say hi and what are you doing? "Oh, I'm in the studio playing on the Dobro." I go, "Ooh, a Dobro would sound good on my album." So he goes, "Oh, all right, send it over then." I really wanted that slide guitar, it just blew me away.'

George Harrison then recorded a lead guitar overdub for this track and had sent it by post to Ringo. It arrived on the morning of 22 December, after Ringo had broken up from the recording sessions of *Vertical Man* for his European Christmas break, but he immediately gathered the members of his Roundheads and rushed to the Village Recorders Studio to listen to it. 'You're killing me, George,' Ringo said. 'You've got me crying, you bugger!'

George Martin also provided strings for this track. Geoff Emerick, the Beatles engineer, also worked on the track and commented, 'It's certainly the most energetic singing he's ever done.'

King, B.B.
The famous American blues guitarist, born Riley B. King on Itta Bene, Mississippi, on 16 September 1925.

In June 1961 he arrived in London to record the album *In London* with many notable British musicians, including Ringo, who played drums on a number of tracks.

Kirke, Simon
A British drummer, born in Shrewsbury, Shropshire, on 28 July 1949, whose first band was called the Maniacs. He joined Free in 1968 and later was a member of Bad Company. He has also appeared on recordings by a variety of artists including Jim Capaldi, Mick Jones, Mick Ralphs and Ron Wood.

He had just finished a tour with Bad Company when he received an invitation to join the fourth All-Starr Band on their 1995 tour.

Kirke then told his wife, 'It's a Beatle, I've got to go.'

He was asked back for the fifth All-Starr tour in 1999 and the sixth in 2000. He also appeared as a member of Ringo and the Roundheads.

Koch Records
Ringo signed with this record label in 2002 after he felt that Mercury Records hadn't done enough to promote *I Wanna Be Santa Claus*. Koch had previously released a live boxed set of his in 2001.

KROQ
A radio station in Pasadena, California, where Flo and Eddie (Mark Volman and Howard Kaylan, former members of the Turtles and Frank Zappa's Mothers Of Invention), had a late-night phone-in show. On Sunday 14 April 1974 an inebriated Ringo arrived with Keith Moon and uttered the word 'fuck' fourteen times at the beginning of his interview. As a result, Flo and Eddie and their producer were sacked and the Federal Communications Commission was asked to investigate Ringo's actions.

La De Da (promo)

The filming of the 'La De Da' promo began in London on Tuesday 5 May 1999 during rehearsals. The group was filmed playing on the roof of the rehearsal hall. Nicola Doring was the producer and it was directed by Nancy Bennett of Squeak Pictures who commented, 'The great thing about Ringo is he's a seasoned filmmaker, he knows what he wants. I think he's got a lot of hambone in him, too! He's one of the earnest, talented guys around. To share his passion for life is contagious.'

Further filming took place in New York on Sunday 10 May in a rainy Times Square. Ringo sat on a bench on the traffic island at 46th and Broadway, singing and holding an umbrella. Also on the set were Barbara and her son Gianni, her sister Marjorie and her son Christian Quilici, and Lee Starkey who, together with some fans, sat on the bench around Ringo and provided the chorus.

The video was completed on 6 June.

La De Da (song)

A track from the 1998 *Vertical Man* album on which Paul McCartney plays bass. It was recorded by producer Mark Hudson at Paul's home studio, the Mill in East Sussex. It is 5 minutes and 41 seconds in length and was composed by Starkey/Hudson/Grakal/Dudas.

Ringo provided lead vocal, drums, percussion and bongos. Paul McCartney and Steven Tyler were on backing vocals, while Joe Walsh was on electric guitar and provided a slide guitar solo and backing vocals. Mark Hudson was on bass, electric guitar, acoustic guitar and backing vocals, Steve Dudas was on electric guitar and acoustic guitar, and Jim Cox was on B3 organ. There were 43 others at the session who provided backing vocals.

La Motta, Stephanie

The daughter of world boxing champion Jake la Motta (portrayed by Robert De Niro in the film *Raging Bull*). Stephanie was born in New York in 1960.

She moved to London and first met Ringo when she was introduced to him at Tramp nightclub. She recalled, 'I didn't see anything but his big, beautiful, deep blue eyes.'

He asked Stephanie if she would go to Vienna with him the next day. She was initially unsure whether to accept, but then decided, collected her clothes and moved into Ringo's suite at the Dorchester Hotel.

They were booked into the Bristol Hotel in Vienna and were to meet up with Harry Nilsson.

After a few days in Vienna they next flew to Greece and she recalled that as they boarded the plane she told him, 'Say goodbye, Vienna, for this is where we fell in love.'

The two returned to London, but saw little of each other after that and Stephanie returned to New York, where she discovered that she had multiple sclerosis. Ten months later she returned to London and told her friend, Liverpool boxer John Conteh, that she had the disease. The two fell in love and became lovers. She met Ringo again down at Tramp, but their relationship was now over.

Stephanie has since continued to fight against the disease and has had further love affairs with Donny Osmond and Rod Stewart.

She was in a car accident in 1998 that, together with her illness, resulted in her having to be confined to a wheelchair, but her battle against the disease continues.

Lady Gaye

A number Ringo co-wrote with Vini Poncia. Clifford T. Ward was also cited as co-songwriter because the number was based on Ward's number 'Gaye'. Danny Kortchmar and Jesse Ed Davis played guitars, Klaus Voormann was on bass guitar, with Mac Rebennack on keyboards, George Devens on congas, Michael Breckner and Lou Marini on tenor saxophone and Lewis Delgatto on baritone saxophone.

The number is 2 minutes and 56 seconds in length and it was issued in Britain as the flipside of the 'Hey Baby' single released on 26 November 1976 on Polydor 2001 699.

Lancaster, Burt

The American film actor, who Ringo met in America. Lancaster said he'd send him some real guns. He sent Ringo a telegram in September 1977, 'Have not forgotten my promise to send your guns. Can you arrange import license so they can get by your customs. Burt Lancaster.'

Las Brisas
A number from the album *Ringo's Rotogravure*, which was co-written by Ringo and Nancy Andrews. Andrews was an American model he was dating at the time of the recording and the track features a mariachi band from a Mexican restaurant.

The number is 3 minutes and 33 seconds in length.

Last Waltz, The
In 1978 the Band made their farewell concert performance at San Francisco's famous Winterland ballroom. Martin Scorsese filmed the event as *The Last Waltz* – the running time was 101 minutes.

Ringo joined Bob Dylan and Ron Wood to accompany the Band on their rendition of 'I Shall Be Released'.

Other guest artists included Eric Clapton, Joni Mitchell, Neil Diamond, Muddy Waters, Van Morrison, Dr John and Emmylou Harris.

Lawrie, Billy
The brother of Scottish singer Lulu. He teamed up with Ringo in the early 1970s to write some songs together, including one called 'Where Are You Going' that remains unreleased. Ringo and Lawrie also penned 'Rock & Roller', which Lawrie recorded at Ringo's Startling Studios in May 1973 and included on his album release *Ship Imagination*.

Let The Rest Of The World Go By
J. Keirn and Ernest K. Ball wrote this number in 1918. Les Reed arranged it for Ringo's *Sentimental Journey* album. Recording began in Studio Two at Abbey Road on 12 February 1970 with overdubs completed on 18 February and mixing on 20 February. It is 2 minutes and 55 seconds in length.

Levin, Tony
A session guitarist who producer Arif Marden hired to work on the *Ringo The 4th* album in 1977. He later went on to work with John Lennon on the *Double Fantasy* album.

Lipstick Traces (On A Cigarette)
A number from the 1978 *Bad Boy* album, lasting 2 minutes and 59 seconds. It was originally written by Naomi Neville in 1962 and recorded by Benny Spellman, who had a minor hit with it. The number was announced as the first single from the album, to be issued on Polydor 2001 782 in June 1978 with 'Old Time Belovin" on the flip, although there seems little evidence that it was actually released.

It was released in America on Portrait 6-70015 on 18 April 1978, becoming Ringo's first single release for the Portrait label, but it failed to enter the charts.

Lisztomania

In 1975 Ringo appeared in a guest role as the Pope in Ken Russell's *Lisztomania*. He began filming at Shepperton Studios in Middlesex in February.

A critic was to comment at the time, 'Perhaps Russell's most audacious piece of *Lisztomania* casting is that of former Beatle Ringo Starr as the Pope. He visits Liszt (now an Abbe) in his monastic cell to tell him that Wagner has become possessed by the Prince of Darkness and orders Liszt to use his God-given musical powers to exorcise the devil in Wagner's soul.'

Lisztomania starred Roger Daltrey of the Who as composer and pianist Franz Liszt. In keeping with the pop-star treatment he gives to the life of this renowned musician, Russell cast Paul Nicholas as Wagner. The other stars were Sara Kestleman as Princess Carolyn and Fiona Lewis as Countess Marie.

Roy Baird produced the film with an original screenplay by Russell. It was a colourful, bizarre and irreverent approach to the work of two classical composers. A nice, iconoclastic touch, typical of Russell, was to allow Ringo to portray the Pope with a strong Scouse accent.

The film was premiered on 10 October 1975 in New York and on 13 November in London.

Little Drummer Boy, The

One of the numbers featured on Ringo's 1999 album *I Wanna Be Santa Claus*. It was penned by Harry Simeone, Henry V. Onorati and Katherine K. Davis. Ringo was on lead vocal, drums and percussion, Mark Hudson on electric guitar, percussion and backing vocals, Steffan Fantini and Mark Fantini on electric guitar and backing vocals, Steve Dudas and Ben Labi on electric guitar, Jim Cox on Wurlitzer and B3 organ, Scott Gordon on percussion, Bob Murphy, Ian Halliday, Roger Houth and Willie Cochrane on bagpipes, and Timothy B. Schmit on backing vocals.

Little Willow

A track from Paul McCartney's 1997 album *Flaming Pie* which was a tribute to Ringo's ex-wife Maureen following her death. Paul described it as a message to her and said, 'The morning I heard the news I couldn't think of anything else, as I wrote this to convey how much I thought of her. It's certainly heartfelt and I hope it'll help the kids. Instead of writing a letter, I wrote a song.'

Live At The BBC

A 1995 album of Beatles recordings from BBC radio shows in the 1960s. Ringo was the former Beatle chosen to promote the album and he appeared on a video press kit that was issued on 17 January of that year via satellite to television stations throughout America. An excerpt of Ringo's comments had already appeared on the American TV programme *Entertainment Tonight* on 12 January, and his comments from it had been published in the *New York Daily News* on 15 January.

On The Scene Productions had produced the kit and they had filmed Ringo in a London hotel in December 1994, with him wearing tinted glasses, a high-necked button-up white shirt, black vest and jacket and blue jeans.

Discussing the BBC tracks, Ringo said, 'I get excited listening to them because it is the band I was in. Everyone sort of gets to *Sgt Pepper* and they think that's what we were. You tend to forget we were a working band.'

Talking of his favourite tracks on the album, he said, 'I really like "I'll Be On My Way" – "A Shot Of Rhythm And Blues", which is an all-time classic. "Sure To Fall" has always been one of my favourites, even before I was in the band. "You've Really Got A Hold On Me", I think, is still a Beatles classic.'

Live-In World Anti-Heroin Album, The

A double album issued in November 1986 on AHPLP1 (album) and TC-AHPLP 1 (cassette) that was released to raise funds for Phoenix House, a charity for heroin recovery centres. The album featured two tracks by Ringo, his first new product for three years. He did a spoken intro about the horrors of heroin, saying, 'You know it makes sense,' and used references to the Beatles, 'Yellow Submarine' and the Blue Meanies. He was backed on the track by a woodwind-style instrument played by producer/composer Charles Foskett and Raymond Lamb.

The second track he made was called 'Naughty Atom Bomb' and was a comedy number taped at Ringo's Startling Studios in August 1986. It was produced by Charles Foskett, written by K. Craddock and C. Gibson and included contributions from Ringo's friends John Cleese, Michael Palin and Bill Oddie.

Zak Starkey and Paul McCartney's cousin Kate Robbins also had a track on the album.

Lofgren, Nils

An American singer/guitarist, born in Chicago, Illinois, on 21 June 1951. His first band was called Grin. He appeared on Neil Young's *After The Gold Rush* album and joined Young's band Crazy Horse. He appeared in the 1978 film *Sergeant Pepper's Lonely Hearts Club Band* and became involved in solo and session work before joining Bruce Springsteen's E Street Band.

Lofgren first met Ringo in 1985 when he was doing the *Born In The USA* tour with Bruce Springsteen. He met him through E Street Band drummer Max Weinberg, who had interviewed Ringo for his book on drumming.

It was Ringo's 45th birthday and they were both invited to a party at Tittenhurst Park. The party took place in the studio there; musicians began jamming and Lofgren was able to jam with Ringo. They had a chat together over drinks and Ringo gave him his card and told him to stay in touch. Lofgren began to ring him for a chat on a regular basis.

In 1989 Ringo called him and said, 'Nils, you know, I haven't toured without the Beatles. I'm putting together a band where it's a round robin and everybody plays. It's going to be my first tour, and I'd like you to be in the band.'

That was the first All-Starr Band in 1989, during which Lofgren performed 'Bein' Angry' and 'Shine Silently'. He was also asked to tour with Ringo again in 1992 during which he performed 'Shine Silently' and 'Walkin' Nerve'.

Lofgren wasn't able to join the All-Starr Band for their 1995 tour due to prior commitments, but he performed on several of the dates as the opening act.

The programme of the 1989 tour carried the following biography:

'Nils Lofgren is best known in recent years for his work as the featured guitarist and backup singer for Bruce Springsteen on the *Born In The USA* tour and *Tunnel Of Love* album and tour.

'Having recorded over seven solo records and four Grin albums along with contributing a core writing and performing role with Neil Young's Crazy Horse debut album and Neil's solo albums, Nils' collaborative efforts have given him tremendous credibility. More recently, in 1987, Nils was the featured guitarist on Lou Gramm's solo project and Steve Forbert's *Streets Of This Town* album in 1988. Nils also recently played at the 'Bridge benefit', which featured such artists as Crosby, Stills, Nash and Young, Tom Petty, Bob Dylan, the Grateful Dead and Tracy Chapman.

'The brash yet melodic rock 'n' roller's talent has long been treasured by album rock radio, celebrating Lofgren creations such as 'See What Love Can Do', 'White Lies', 'Night Fades Away', 'Beggar's Day', 'Keith Don't Go (Ode To The Glimmer Twin)' and 'I Came To Dance' as veritable anthems over the years.

'Despite all his heavyweight musical experience, Nils Lofgren's music could easily be mistaken for the debut of some fresh "wunderkind" (the tag often attached to the teenaged, Washington DC-based Nils in the early '70s). Bursting with tuneful vitality, welled-up emotion and pure commitment usually found only on an artist's extra-special first LP, Nils continues to show that he is one rock 'n' roll vet who hasn't lost the hunger.

'Nils Lofgren sees his strength "not as a poet but as a musician. If you just read my lyrics, something gets lost in the translation. There's something that happens with the beat, the chords and the music that says a lot more than I know to say with words. That's also why I don't do many interviews. I feel more comfortable letting my music speak for me."'

When Lofgren was appearing at the Roxy nightclub in Los Angeles on 31 May 1991, Ringo joined him on stage to play drums on a version of the Beatles number 'Any Time At All'. That same year Ringo had played drums on the 'Walkin' Nerve' track of Lofgren's Rykodisc album *Silver Lining*.

Ringo was also on the promo video for Nils Lofgren's single 'Valentine', shot in February 1991 in Los Angeles. Castle Communications issued it as a single in Britain on 22 April 1991.

Love First, Ask Questions Later
A track from the 2003 *Ringo Rama* album, lasting 4 minutes and 44 seconds. Ringo played acoustic guitar and jazz musician Grant Geissman played dobro.

Love Is A Many Splendoured Thing
A film theme from the popular movie of the same name starring William Holden and Jennifer Jones. Paul Francis Webster and Sammy Fain composed it, and the Four Aces had an American No.1 hit with the number.

Quincy Jones arranged the version for Ringo's *Sentimental Journey* album. Ringo overdubbed his lead vocal at A&M Studios in Los Angeles on 26 December 1969, although the final mix wasn't completed until 6 March 1970 at Abbey Road. It is 3 minutes and 4 seconds in length.

Love Me Do
The Beatles' first British single, penned by Paul McCartney.

When Pete Best had been sacked, Ringo travelled to Abbey Road Studios on Tuesday 4 September 1962 and recorded the number, which took fifteen takes. Engineer Norman Smith was later to reveal, 'I've a feeling that Paul wasn't too happy with Ringo's drumming, and felt that it could be better. He didn't make a good job of it.'

It was decided to re-record the number at the next session on 11 September. The producer at this session was Ron Richards, who was to say, 'We weren't happy with the drum sound on the original "Love Me Do", so I booked Andy White for the remake. I used him a lot at the time – he was very good.'

Ringo recalled that when he entered the studio, he was startled to see another drummer set up. He thought, 'They're doing a Pete Best on me.'

He was asked to sit in the control room while the recording went on. Richards felt sorry for him and asked him to play maraca on the B side of the record, 'P.S. I Love You'.

Strangely enough, when the single was released, the initial copies were of the first version, on which Ringo played. Copies of the Andy

White version were used on the *Please Please Me* album and on a single of 'Love Me Do' reissued in March 1976. Generally, there doesn't seem to be much difference between them as far as the drum sound is concerned.

Ringo also recorded a live performance of the number at the Bottom Line club in New York on 13 May 1998, which was released on the *VH-1 Storytellers* album. Ringo introduced it as 'the very first record that I didn't drum on'.

A new version was recorded for the *Vertical Man* album. The producer Mark Hudson told *Beatlefan* magazine: 'You remember the old story how Ringo didn't play on that session at first and the single was issued with a studio drummer, and how it's always been a kind of joking sore point with Ringo. So he did it. We rocked it. Rolling Stones on steroids.'

When Steven Tyler heard Ringo wanted him to play blues harp on this, he flew in from Holland. Hudson was former producer for Aerosmith.

Ringo was on lead vocals, drums, percussion and handclaps, Steve Dudas was on electric guitar and handclaps, Mark Hudson was on electric guitar, percussion, handclaps and backing vocals, and Dean Grakal and Scott Gordon were on handclaps.

It was recorded at the Whatinthewhatthe? Studios in Los Angeles, with Steven Tyler of Aerosmith on harmonica, performing a different harmonica arrangement.'

Ringo commented, 'I've always loved that song. I didn't get to play on the first one – I'll show the bastards!' He almost had second thoughts the next day, telling his musicians, 'It haunted me last night.' He had Steve Tyler re-record the harmonica to make it closer to the original.

As confirmation that Ringo doesn't even realise that it was his version of 'Love Me Do' that was originally released as the single, he told *Billboard* magazine in 1998 that he recorded it again for *Vertical Man* because he didn't perform on the version released as a single in the 1960s. 'I'm on the album version,' he said, 'and nobody can tell the difference, so it's not like Andy White was doing anything critical. But George Martin wasn't too happy with the drummers before me, shall we say. So when I was coming down, he didn't know anything about me. He wanted to play it safe, and he had Andy White ready for it.'

This shows how even a Beatle can forget the facts about events in which he was involved. George Martin didn't hire Andy White, Ron Richards did – and he didn't do it because of 'drummers before me' (referring, presumably, to Pete Best), but because he didn't like Ringo's drumming on 4 September. George Martin did know about Ringo before he hired Andy White because he'd already been at the recording at which Ringo had played on 'Love Me Do'.

Loves Of Harry: Everybody Sings Nilsson, The

A 23-track Harry Nilsson tribute album issued on Music Masters 65127 in 1995. On it Ringo duets with Stevie Nicks on a version of Nilsson's 'Lay Down Your Arms'. Al Kooper produced the album.

Lynch, Liam

An American musician, born in Kent, Ohio, on 5 September 1970, who sent a tape of one of his original songs to the Liverpool Institute of Popular Music and was enrolled as a pupil. He relocated to Liverpool and was one of a handful of students to receive personal lessons from Paul McCartney.

On initially meeting Paul he said, 'God, it's really great to meet you. I've been wanting to talk to you because I'm forming a Beatles cover band and I need someone to play Ringo. I know you really know the Beatles material and you can play drums. I don't know if you'd be into that.' A bemused Paul said, 'Watch it, lad!'

He returned to America and had a major hit with 'United States Of America', which was also issued in Britain. Ringo heard the number and asked someone to track him down, as he was seeking new acts for Pumkinhead Records, a label he had set up with Mark Hudson.

Ringo had no idea that Lynch had studied in Liverpool and had had individual lessons from Paul McCartney.

Lynch recalled, 'He was forming a label and asked me to be the first artist. He said, "I could come over there and set up me drums in your bedroom."'

He signed a production deal with Pumkinhead Records and his debut album *Fake Signs* was issued by S-Curve Records with Ringo appearing as a guest on two of the tracks, 'Cuz You Do' and 'Try Me'.

Lynch is the creator of the MTV show *Sifl And Olly* and is also a poet.

Lynne, Jeff

A British musician/songwriter/producer who was born in Birmingham, England, on 30 December 1947.

He was a member of Idle Race, then the Move before forming his acclaimed Electric Light Orchestra in 1972. The group had numerous hits including 'Evil Woman', 'Strange Magic', 'Mr Blue Sky' and 'Hold On Tight'.

Lynne turned mainly to production during the mid-1980s and was asked by George Harrison to help write and produce the number 'Zig Zag' for the film *Shanghai Surprise*. He then produced and played on George's *Cloud Nine* album.

Apart from George Harrison, among the artists produced by Lynne are Bob Dylan, Tom Petty, Brian Wilson, Roy Orbison and Del Shannon. He then joined the Traveling Wilburys along with Harrison, Dylan, Petty and Orbison.

He was one of the producers of Ringo's 1992 *Time Takes Time* album. He was to say, 'It was great to work with Ringo. He's one of my favourite drummers.' Lynne produced 'Don't Go Where The Road Don't Go', 'After All These Years', 'Don't Be Cruel' and the unissued 'Call Me'. He remixed all the songs he produced himself.

In 1994 Lynne was also asked to produce the Ringo, George and Paul recording of some John Lennon demos, resulting in the Beatles singles 'Free As A Bird' and 'Real Love'.

9 Madryn Street

The small terraced house in the Dingle district of Liverpool where Richard Starkey was born on 7 July 1940. His father Richard was 28 at the time and his mother Elsie was 26. He was born one week late at midnight, a month before the Luftwaffe began bombing the city, was delivered by forceps and weighed 10lb. The bombing began when Elsie was still in bed recovering from the birth and the couple nicknamed their son Ritchie.

In 1943 Elsie and her husband split up, with Richard Starkey moving into No. 59 Madryn Street. As Elsie didn't want to keep on bumping into her former husband, she swapped her house with a friend and moved into the nearby Admiral Grove.

Although it wasn't the house in which Ringo was reared, the fact that he was born there has attracted interest, although it became derelict.

In March 1977 it was bought at auction by Cliff Cooper, managing director of the World of Music shops, for £13,200. He bought it unseen and when visiting the property observed, 'It's in a terrible state. The ceiling is falling in and it's quite a sight, but it needs to get listed.' He then found that the cost of renovation would be £30,000. He referred to it receiving listed-building status from the National Trust.

Having bought the property, Cooper didn't seem to know what to do with it. He contacted the National Trust, who had recently purchased Paul McCartney's former home. They told him, 'The importance of 20 Forthlin Road was that it was the place where the Beatles came together in their formative years. We are not looking to get a set of four.'

Magic Christian, The

Ringo's first feature film, *Candy*, was based on a novel by Terry Southern, who was also the author of *The Magic Christian* on which Ringo's second solo movie was based (no wonder his *Goodnight Vienna* album had the phrase 'buy a Terry Southern book' among its sleeve notes).

Ringo had only appeared for about ten minutes in *Candy*, but he was given a co-starring role with Peter Sellers in this 95-minute British movie. It was filmed in colour and released in 1969 with an A certificate in the UK, the equivalent of a PG today. The director was Joseph McGrath, the producer was Denis O'Dell, and Terry Southern, O'Dell and Sellers wrote the screenplay based on Southern's book. The film's score was by Ken Thorne, while the theme song, 'Come And Get It', was written by Paul McCartney and performed by the Apple band Badfinger. Thunderclap Newman provided 'Something In The Air' and other songs featured in the film were 'Rock Of Ages' and Noel Coward's 'Mad About The Boy'.

Peter Sellers appeared as Sir Guy Grand, Ringo played Youngman Grand, Wilfred Hyde-White was the ship's captain and Patrick Cargill an auctioneer. The guest stars in the movie were Richard Attenborough, Leonard Frey, Laurence Harvey, Christopher Lee, Spike Milligan, Roman Polanski and Raquel Welch.

Although one reviewer wrote, 'Ringo Starr continues to exploit the melancholy wanderer's role he made his own in *A Hard Day's Night*,' Ringo didn't really have much to get his teeth into. His part had been specially written for the film (the character he played wasn't in the original book) and his role was mainly that of an observer, watching the various stunts, which Sellers sets up.

Ringo appears as Youngman Grand, the adopted son of the world's richest man, Sir Guy Grand. Sir Guy resolves to show Youngman the extent to which people are obsessed with money and the ends they will go to obtain it. He seeks to prove that 'everyone has his price'.

The lure of money encourages a traffic warden (Spike Milligan) to eat his own ticket and causes a snobby art gallery official (John Cleese) to sell him a Rembrandt. Before the man's horrified eyes, Sir Guy cuts out the nose in the painting, stating that he only collects Rembrandt's noses. He bribes the Oxford crew to lose the annual boat race against Cambridge and entices two beefy boxers to embrace each other in the ring during a bout. Money also persuades a famous Shakespearean actor (Laurence Harvey) to do a striptease in the middle of his soliloquy in *Hamlet*.

Sir Guy then takes Youngman on a cruise on the liner *Magic Christian*, where his education into man's greed continues. At one point a whip-wielding Raquel Welch shows him over the engine room of the ship, to discover that it is in fact a galley with topless females at the oars.

The grand finale of the film occurs back on dry land in London, where a giant vat has been filled with the most unspeakable detritus, including vomit, human excreta and pig's blood. Sprinkling it with money, Sir Guy stands back and watches as respectable businessmen brawl amid the unsightly mess.

In her review in *Films & Filming*, Margaret Tarratt commented, 'The surreal world of the *Goons* and the picaresque fantasy world of the Beatles are combined in an essential genial indictment of British capitalist society.'

The film received a royal world premiere on 12 December 1968 at the Odeon, Kensington, in the presence of Princess Margaret.

During the filming, Ringo and Peter Sellers became friends and they co-hosted a party at Les Ambassadeurs, a fashionable club in Hamilton Place, London.

Ringo also bought Sellers' house, Brookfields, from him.

Man Like Me, A
Originally sung by Ringo on the *Scouse Mouse* album under the title 'A Mouse Like Me'. Ringo adapted this Ruan O'Lochlain-penned number as the closing track on his 1978 *Bad Boy* album. It is 2 minutes and 29 seconds in length.

Manhattan Transfer
A band formed in New York City in 1969 that had numerous hits and won ten Grammy awards.

When Richard Perry was producing their *Coming Out* album in 1976 he approached Ringo. 'I asked him if he would play,' said Perry, 'and he's a great guy, and he never turned me down.'

Tim Hauser, founder member of Manhattan Transfer, recalled, 'Ringo and Jim Keltner produced a particular sound that was very unusual. Ringo played straight time, and Jim played time as well as fills. It had to do with the "flaming" that was produced by the simultaneity of their snares, coupled with their ability to get in the same groove. I personally loved it. That was the only time we played with Ringo. The session was done at Richard Perry's Studio 55 in Menlove Avenue in Hollywood. That studio was originally built in the 1940s for Bing Crosby as a convenience, as it was right next door to Paramount. It was the studio where he recorded "White Christmas".'

Ringo played the drums on the *Coming Out* tracks 'S.O.S' and 'Zindy Lou'.

Martin, Sir George
The Beatles' record producer. Ringo pre-recorded a version of 'Octopus's Garden' in December 1969 that was filmed for a BBC1 special on George Martin called 'With A Little Help From My Friends'.

Martin also produced Ringo's album *Sentimental Journey* and in 1998 contributed to Ringo's *Vertical Man* album.

Mason, Dave

A British musician, born in Worcester on 10 May 1944. He rose
to fame in Traffic, a group formed in 1967, and he later worked
with Delaney and Bonnie and Friends, and Fleetwood Mac. As a
session musician he has appeared with Mama Cass, the Rolling
Stones and Jimi Hendrix. He appeared on George Harrison's *All
Things Must Pass* album, then had solo hits, such as 'We Just
Disagree'.

Mason was due to become a member of Ringo's fourth All-Starr
Band in 1997, but there were problems with him turning up for
rehearsals and not agreeing to the musical policy. Ringo called a
meeting of the other members and there was a unanimous agreement to
begin the tour without him.

McLagan, Ian

A British musician, born in London on 12 May 1946. He was a
member of the Small Faces and the Faces and asked Ringo to
participate in his solo album *Troublemaker* in 1979. Ringo
appeared on the track 'Hold On'. McLagan also helped Ringo to
write the number 'Tonight', which was included on the 1979 album
Bad Boy.

Memphis In Your Mind

A rockabilly number from the 2003 *Ringo Rama* album, 3 minutes and
13 seconds in length. Ringo takes the opportunity to mention
'Heartbreak Hotel', Elvis Presley, 'Peggy Sue' and Roy Orbison's
growl. Ringo wanted to pay tribute to the seminal influence of
Memphis music on his teenage years, particularly the Sun Studios
artists such as Elvis and Jerry Lee Lewis.

Mercury Records

Ringo had three album releases with this American record company:
Vertical Man, *VH-1 Storytellers* and *I Wanna Be Santa Claus*. The first
two were released in 1998 the third in 1999.

Ringo split from Mercury Records in 2000. While in an Internet chat
on 29 June 2000 Ringo talked of Mercury's incompetence and he criticised them over his *I Wanna Be Santa Claus* album, saying, 'They
actually gave the Christmas album no support.' He added, 'We have
now parted company due to their incompetence, they let me go.'

He also talked about future recordings and said, 'I'm hoping to
record another studio album and I'm hoping Mark Hudson will
be involved and I'm hoping it will be on any label other than
Mercury.'

It was rumoured that several albums, apart from Ringo's, suffered
from lack of push from Mercury because they were adversely affected
by the merger between Universal and Polygram.

Mindfield

A track from the *Vertical Man* album, 4 minutes and 7 seconds in length. Starkey/Hudson/Grakal/Dudas composed it, with Ringo providing lead vocal, drums and percussion. The rest of the line-up was: Joe Walsh on electric guitar; Steve Dudas on electric guitar and acoustic guitar; Mark Hudson on bass, electric guitar, acoustic guitar, Wurlitzer and backing vocals; Jeff Baxter on pedal steel guitar; Jim Cox on B3 organ, cello and synthesizer; John Bergamo on tabla; and Steve Tyler and Alanis Morissette on backing vocals.

Missouri Loves Company

A country-style song, from the 2003 *Ringo Rama* album, 3 minutes and 32 seconds in length. Ringo recalled that the writing of the song was fairly quickly done once Dean Grakal had come up with the single line 'Missouri loves company', which, of course, is a pun on the phrase 'misery loves company'. Then Ringo thought of a travelogue around the States.

Moman, Chips

A producer who had a chance meeting with Ringo when they were both on holiday in the Bahamas and suggested recording an album together. In February 1987 they had sessions at Moman's 3-Alarm Studios, situated in a converted firehouse in Memphis. During his initial sessions the local *Memphis Commercial Appeal* newspaper published a piece by a journalist who referred to Ringo as 'yesterday's news'. This sparked a controversy in the publication during which 37 letters, both pro and con, were published.

Ringo returned to Memphis in April 1987 and continued to record at both 3-Alarm and the famous Sun Studios. While at Sun Studios he also filmed a video for one of the numbers. He recorded sixteen songs, twelve of them written specially for Ringo by different composers. He commented, 'We started with a couple of old rock'n'rollers, including "Ain't That A Shame",' which he said was a way of him getting to know the Memphis session musicians, who included guitarist J.R. Cobb, bassist Sam Shoup, keyboardist Jimmy Whitehead and drummers Gene Chrisman and Steve Mergen.

On 29 April Bob Dylan visited Ringo at the studio. Ringo was also interviewed by the *Memphis Commercial Appeal* and described his album as a rock'n'roll album, but one which didn't necessarily have the 'Memphis Sound'. He said, 'I don't know what that is. If I make an album in London, you don't call it a "London album". We are making an album with Memphis musicians. But once you hit the drum, you don't know if it's from Memphis or, you know, Canada.'

Ringo was to say, 'I'm singing real well. Chips is pulling things out of me.' He also said that Moman's wife Toni Wine was helping him with his vocals. He explained, 'because that's one area where I do get nervous. My game is drumming.'

On the sessions, he was to say that they were different from how he usually recorded. 'Usually we make the track, then you do the vocals. Here, you start right with the band, singing the song. And it's real hard sometimes to learn three songs in one day, to get it right. So you just do the best you can. You get to know it a bit, and you wing it.

'I tend to croon. Toni's great because she's an old rock'n'roller. She gets me out of crooning.'

Toni Wine commented, 'I've never seen a harder worker in my life than him. I mean, fourteen to fifteen hours straight.'

However, things weren't to work out on the project.

During his first All-Starr tour, on 24 July 1989, Ringo learned that Moman intended to release the album. Ringo claimed that his performance had been below standard due to the influence of alcohol and obtained a thirty-day restraining order from Judge Ralph Hicks at the Fulton County Supreme Court preventing Moman from releasing it. In court on 24 August two of the numbers from the album, 'I Can Help' and 'Whiskey And Soda', were played to the judge, who extended the ban on Moman issuing the album without Ringo's consent.

Ringo attended court in Atlanta, Georgia, on Wednesday 15 November 1989 to testify on the matter, pointing out that the recordings were below standard due to the large amounts of alcohol he had consumed. He also pointed out that no record label had been interested in releasing the album and that Moman had formed a label of his own called CRS because he wanted to issue the album to take advantage of Ringo's successful tour with his All-Starr band. The judge ordered a further injunction preventing the album's release. Another injunction was granted at Fulton County Superior Court on 5 January 1990 and Ringo was asked to pay $74,354 in production costs, which was only half of what Moman was seeking. Judge Clarence Carter also ordered that the tapes be handed over to Ringo.

On 4 June 1991 Moman went to the Georgia Supreme Court to begin proceedings seeking the full production costs of $162, 600, but was unsuccessful.

Monkey See – Monkey Do

A track from Ringo's 1978 album *Bad Boy*, 3 minutes and 35 seconds in length. It was penned by Michael Franks in 1975 and recorded by Melissa Manchester in 1977.

34 Montague Square

The ground floor and basement apartment that Ringo and Maureen moved into in 1965.

They hired Ken Partridge as their interior designer and he decorated the premises with purple watered-silk wallpaper, silk curtains and lead-streaked mirrors. Soon after Maureen gave birth to their son Zak, Ringo, Maureen and their new baby settled in Sunny Heights in

Weybridge, although he retained the Montague Square flat as his London base, and allowed friends to stay there.

In 1966 Paul McCartney actually used it as a small studio.

Ringo let the apartment to Chas Chandler, former bass guitarist with the Animals, on 6 December 1966 and he moved into the flat with his girlfriend Lotta, together with Jimi Hendrix and his girlfriend Kathy Etchingham.

When Chas and Jimi moved out, Cynthia Lennon's mother Lillian Powell moved in for a while. Then, when Cynthia discovered John and Yoko sleeping together at their Weybridge home, she moved into Montague Square with her mother for a while. Then she moved back to Weybridge while John and Yoko Ono moved into the flat.

On 18 October 1968 the police, led by Sergeant Norman Pilcher, raided the premises and alleged they found some cannabis resin. Lennon maintained their innocence, but said that he was told that if he pleaded guilty they wouldn't prosecute Yoko, who was pregnant at the time. He agreed and, as a result, had a major battle with the American authorities to obtain a green card due to the drugs conviction. Incidentally, Pilcher was later arrested and jailed when it was discovered that he actually planted drugs on people he wanted to arrest.

On 19 February 1969 Ringo received a writ from Bryman Estates, the superior landlords, for 'misuse of property' and they took civil proceedings against Ringo to prevent Lennon 'and other undesirables' from using the premises. Ringo was so upset that he sold the leasehold to the premises on 28 February 1969.

Monty Python

Famous British comedy team featuring Graham Chapman, John Cleese, Eric Idle, Terry Jones and Terry Gilliam (the only American member), whose *Monty Python's Flying Circus* show was made between 1969 and 1974.

Ringo appeared in one episode of the series called 'It's'.

Moon, Keith

Legendary drummer with the Who, born in London on 23 August 1947. He became a good friend of each member of the Beatles and is one of a number of friends sitting close to them during their performance of 'All You Need Is Love' on their 'Our World' special on 25 June 1967.

Keith was often referred to as 'Moon the Loon' and he used to call Ringo 'Bongo'.

When they were known as the High Numbers, the Who appeared on a bill with the Beatles at the Opera House, Blackpool, on 16 August 1964.

Moon was to become a close friend of Ringo and the association with the Who was also to become a link between them. Ringo, for instance, appeared in the Roger Daltrey film *Lisztomania* in 1975, and members of the Who were also to take an interest in Ringo's son Zak. John Entwistle produced tracks by Zak's early group Nightfly and Zak was eventually to become a member of the Who in 1996. Zak and Entwistle also joined Ringo's All-Starr Band on their tour of the US and Japan in 1995.

Ringo was also to sing two of the numbers on a recording of the Who's rock opera *Tommy*.

Moon once tried to join the Beatles. He bumped into them in a bar and said, 'Do you mind if I join you?' They told him to pull up a chair. 'No, I mean, do you mind if I *join* you?' There was a pause, then Ringo replied, 'We've already got a drummer, thanks.'

There was a friendship between the two drummers which matured and they did a lot of clubbing and socialising together. When celebrating Ringo's 35th birthday, Moon paid for a plane to write 'Happy Birthday Ringo' on the Los Angeles skyline, and the two wreaked such havoc that they both had their Playboy membership cards revoked.

In 1974, during John Lennon's 'lost weekend' in Los Angeles, Ringo was also in LA preparing to record the *Goodnight Vienna* album. John Lennon was recording his *Rock 'N' Roll* album and also producing Harry Nilsson's *Pussy Cats* album. Ringo, Moon, Lennon and Nilsson all moved into a house together and became involved in each others' recordings. It was Ringo who came up with a title for Moon's album – *Two Sides Of The Moon* and also contributed some drumming and dialogue to the album. He is found on the tracks 'Do Me Good', 'Move Over Ms L', 'Naked Man', 'Real Emotion', 'Solid Gold', 'Together' and 'Together Rap'.

The two of them also appeared together in a string of films – *200 Motels* in 1971, *Born To Boogie* in 1972, *That'll Be The Day* in 1973, *Son Of Dracula* in 1974, *Sextette* in 1978 and *The Kids Are Alright* in 1979.

The Kids Are Alright was a documentary covering the career of the Who, and during the film Ringo appeared in four sections of the movie in conversation with Moon.

The transcript of one of them is as follows:

Ringo: Well, I suppose all his friends have been here 'cause you know I'm only one of several. I've told you all about the mad things he's done in life, such as breaking up rooms, driving his car into swimming pools, driving his car into foyers. Well I'm not going to tell you about any of that, you know. I'm just here to tell you about the Keith I know and love.

What about the little singer, what's your opinion on him?

Keith: I think he does a damn good job out there. Personally, I mean, I wouldn't go out there up front with nothing to protect me but a small microphone. But he manages to revolve it so fast that when people do throw things he gets sort of desiccated egg and sliced tomatoes. I turn my cymbals up this way so that at the end of the night I have a salad mix. I sprinkle some salt, some Italian seasoning on it and that sort of really ends up my evening.

Ringo: Well Keith, we've heard you drink a lot; that's besides the point. If you could tell us, you know, how did you happen to join the Who, and if in fact that's what they were called when you joined?

Keith: I've just been sitting in for the past fifteen years. They never actually told me I was part of the band. I knew it by instinct.

Ringo: They have to ask you this – what do you think of Pete?

Keith: I love the man. He's one of my dearest friends. But I couldn't say that about Ringo. You know we have our moments and when we get together there are certain times . . . it's just something happens and I really don't know what it is – but there's that magic there.

Ringo: It's probably that we're drunk.

Keith: It could be that.

Ringo: Not drunk, teenyboppers.

Keith: No. Absolutely not, you Donny and Marie fans.

Ringo: Keith and me had a lot of medicine, you know, just a lot of medicine 'cause we're getting on now, we need our medicine.

Keith: Just see the age of this suit.

A single-sided 7″ promotional disc was issued to American radio stations to promote the film in 1979, 'The Kids Are Alright Radio Spots' on CR3926. On it, Ringo makes a 30-second announcement: 'Hello children! I'm Ringo. You know who I am and we know who they are – the Who. After fifteen years on the road the kids are all right. At Monterey, on Shindig, Top Of The Pops, Ready, Steady Go!, the Rolling Stones' Rock And Roll Circus and at Woodstock. The musical madness of the Who. "The Kids Are Alright", rated PG, Parental Guidance suggested.'

Moon never lived to see the release of it; he died of a mixture of prescription drugs and alcohol on 7 September 1978 following one of Paul McCartney's Buddy Holly Week celebrations at Peppermint Park.

Morissette, Alanis Nadine

A singer born in Ottawa, Canada, on 1 June 1974.

She dropped into the Whatinthewhatthe? Studios on 19 November 1997 during the Vertical Man recording sessions. Ringo was to say, 'We had this open-door policy, whereby if you dropped by while we were recording, you were going to be asked to be on the record.' As a result she recorded the vocal on the track 'Drift Away'.

Alanis returned to the studios on 25 November and provided backing vocals for the tracks 'Mindfield' and 'I Was Walkin''.

Mr Double-It-Up

A rockabilly track recorded for the *Vertical Man* CD, but not included on the British and American 13-track release. It was included on a 14-track German CD and was added as a bonus track, along with 'Everyday' on the Japanese CD.

Mark Hudson recalled that the title was actually a Ringoism. He said, 'I was remarking to him one day how good he is at double-tracking his vocals, something not everybody finds easy to do. He answered back, "Yeah, I'm Mr Double-It-Up," and that became the name of one of the songs. It was about a man who has two of everything.'

National Lottery Live, The

A BBC1 programme, which featured the National Lottery draw and also presented various artists performing their recent releases. On Saturday 15 July 1998 Ringo went to the Television Centre in White City to appear on the programme and mimed live to 'La De Da'.

Never Without You

A tribute to George Harrison. Although Ringo said it wasn't difficult writing a song about George, which appears on his 2003 solo album *Ringo Rama*, saying, 'I was happy to do it, because it was the best way I could do it – with a song,' he was also to admit that when he started writing the number he tried to widen it to a tribute to include other lost friends such as John Lennon and Harry Nilsson, but found it too messy and just concentrated on a tribute to George. Once he'd decided that the song was to be just about George he was then inspired to use some of the lyrics from George's songs such as 'Within You, Without You' and 'Here Comes The Sun'.

Ringo discussed the song in an interview about the album *Ringo Rama* with the *Toronto Sun* in 2003: 'We started the album last year in February, three or four months after he died, so it was to the fore that he'd gone. But where we started "We were young, it was fun ..." it automatically went to the group, to the Beatles. And then I was trying to put John Lennon in to say "Hello John", and Harry Nilsson. But it just got too messy and George was on my mind. So we decided, "Let's stop all this. Just make this for George." On all my records George has been on a track with that great guitar. It was always so emotional, his guitar. So who else could play the guitar? Eric. They were good friends. We're all good friends. So I asked Eric to play and he said "yeah".'

Clapton was also to play on another track on the album, 'Imagine Me There'.

Nice Way (a.k.a. You've Got A Nice Way)

A number penned by Steve Stills, which is included on the 1981 *Stop And Smell The Roses* album. Stills played lead guitar, with Ringo on drums, Mike Finnigan on piano and organ, Mike Stergis on rhythm guitar, Joe Lala on percussion and Harley Thompson on bass. The track is 3 minutes and 29 seconds in length.

Nicol, Jimmy

The drummer, born on 3 August 1939, who deputised for Ringo for a short period during the Beatles' 1964 world tour.

Ringo collapsed on 3 June 1964 during a Beatles photo session for the *Saturday Evening Post* and was rushed to University College hospital where he was diagnosed as having tonsillitis and pharyngitis, together with a temperature of 102 degrees.

Beatles manager Brian Epstein decided that the tour should go ahead and suggested that they find a substitute.

George Harrison protested at this, saying, 'If Ringo's not going then neither am I, you can find two replacements.'

He was overruled and their recording manager George Martin then suggested Nicol, who had played on a soundalike album of Beatles hits called *Beatlemania*. Nicol had also done some sessions for George Martin on recordings by Georgie Fame and the Blue Flames and Tommy Quickly.

Martin then phoned Nicol and arranged for him to rehearse with the Beatles at Abbey Road Studios at three o'clock that afternoon. Nicol recalled, 'I was having a bit of a lie down after lunch when the phone rang. It was EMI asking if I could come down to the studio to rehearse with the Beatles. Two hours after I got there I was told to pack my bags for Denmark.'

Nicol joined John, Paul and George in the studio and they rehearsed six numbers: 'I Want To Hold Your Hand', 'She Loves You', 'I Saw Her Standing There', 'This Boy', 'Can't Buy Me Love' and 'Long Tall Sally'.

An Australian journalist, Dick Hughes, was present at the rehearsals and said that Paul told him, 'This fellow is fine, but we just can't afford to be without Ringo at a real recording session, because the kids would always know that a record was one without him.'

Jimmy rehearsed with the Beatles the following day and made his debut with them at the Tivoli Gardens, Copenhagen.

Epstein was to comment, 'The difficulty was finding someone who looked like a Beatle and not an outcast. Yet Jimmy didn't have a Beatle fringe, so he began spreading a lotion on his hair, hoping it would stimulate the growth.' Jimmy was also given Ringo's actual suit to wear, although the trousers were too short for him.

The original repertoire was to have comprised eleven numbers, but it was decided to reduce it to ten by omitting 'I Wanna Be Your Man', the Ringo solo spot.

Following that first appearance, George had relented, commenting, 'Playing without Ringo is like driving a car on three wheels, but Jimmy has grasped our rhythm very quickly.'

It was decided to include Jimmy on all public appearances and press conferences.

Jimmy performed with the Beatles in Holland, Hong Kong and did four shows in Australia before Ringo returned to the fold in Melbourne, where there was a press conference with all five; a press photo of all five together was also taken.

Jimmy packed his bags and left for Essendon Airport without the opportunity of saying goodbye. He said, 'They were still asleep. I didn't think I should disturb them.' Brian Epstein, together with tour manager Lloyd Ravenscroft, accompanied Jimmy to the airport, where Brian presented him with a cheque and a gold Eternamatic wristwatch inscribed 'From the Beatles and Brian Epstein to Jimmy – with appreciation and gratitude'.

The high-profile image of being a Beatle didn't bring the expected offers and success that Jimmy had imagined. He didn't even get to meet them again although, with his group, he was on the same bill as the Beatles at the Hippodrome, Brighton on 12 July 1964. They never met that night – similar to when Pete Best was on some bills with the Beatles soon after he was sacked from the group, and they never met or greeted each other.

Even Jimmy's single 'Husky' c/w 'Don't Come Back' failed to register. Things got even worse and he was declared bankrupt on 29 April 1965 with only £50 to his name. He was to comment, 'Standing in for Ringo was the worst thing that ever happened to me. Up until then I was feeling quite happy turning over thirty or forty pounds a week. I didn't realise that it would change my whole life. I had half a million pounds worth of publicity and immediately I was offered three weeks at Blackpool standing in for Dave Clark at £350 a week. Everyone in the business said I couldn't miss. I was the hottest name there was. But after the headlines died, I began dying too. No one wanted to know me anymore; I borrowed from everyone and anyone.'

He was later to join the Swedish instrumental group the Spotnicks and while touring Mexico with them, married a Mexican Indian girl, Josephina.

The two returned to London penniless in 1987, but by 1996 they'd settled in a small flat in south London and Jimmy attempted to make a living as a carpenter.

Night And Day

A track from Ringo's first solo album *Sentimental Journey*. The Cole Porter number was first featured in the 1932 movie musical *The Gay*

Divorcee, when Fred Astaire and Claire Luce sang it. This arrangement was by Ringo and Chico O'Farrell.

It was recorded in Studio Three at Abbey Road on 27 October 1969 and mixed the same day.

The number is 2 minutes and 24 seconds in length.

Nilsson, Harry

Nilsson was born Harry Edward Nilsson in Brooklyn, New York, on 15 June 1941, although he was to spend most of his life in California, moving there in 1952. His August 1967 album *Pandemonium Shadow Show* contained the track 'You Can't Do That', also issued as a single, which contained titles of various Beatles songs in the lyrics. This tribute came to the attention of Beatles associate Derek Taylor, who was living in the west coast at the time. He sent a copy to Brian Epstein, saying of the singer, 'He is something the Beatles are.'

Nilsson was to win a Grammy award for his recording of 'Everybody's Talking' from the soundtrack of the film *Midnight Cowboy,* and he also topped the charts with 'Without You', a number penned by Pete Ham and Tom Evans of the Apple Records band Badfinger.

He was to form a particularly strong relationship with Ringo and John Lennon. Both Ringo and George Harrison contributed to his album *Son Of Schmilsson* under the pseudonyms Richie Snare and George Harrysong. Nilsson also contributed to Ringo's albums *Ringo, Goodnight Vienna, Ringo's Rotogravure* and *Stop And Smell The Roses.*

Nilsson and Ringo co-penned 'Party', which was originally scheduled for *Ringo's Rotogravure,* but remains unreleased.

In 1974 the soundtrack of *Son Of Dracula* was released, the film Ringo made that starred Nilsson as the vampire and Ringo as Merlin. A number from the soundtrack, 'Daybreak', on which Ringo and George Harrison play, provided Nilsson with his last hit.

Ringo and Nilsson made another film in 1974, *Harry and Ringo's Night Out,* although it was never released.

Nilsson next made a guest appearance in Ringo's promo video for the single 'Only You'.

Ringo was the best man at the wedding of Harry to Una and he became the godfather of their children.

When Lennon moved to Los Angeles with May Pang in his 'lost weekend' away from Yoko, he began recording an album with Phil Spector called *Rock 'N' Roll,* although Spector was to disappear with the master tapes. As Lennon remained in Los Angeles, he decided to produce a record with Nilsson called *Pussy Cats* and Lennon, Ringo, Nilsson and Keith Moon all moved into a house together. Their escapades could probably result in a film as wild as *Fear And Loathing In Las Vegas!*

Nilsson's next album was originally called *God's Greatest Hits*, but the title was changed to *Duit On Mon Dei*, with Ringo contributing to two of the tracks.

Harry Nilsson suffered a heart attack in 1993 from which he never fully recovered. He died in Los Angeles on 15 January 1994 at the age of 53.

Ringo played on his posthumously released 1995 album *The Harry Nilsson Anthology*.

No No Song

A track from the 1974 *Ringo* album, penned by Hoyt Axton, who gave the number to Ringo. Harry Nilsson provided backing vocals, Nicky Hopkins played electric piano and Jesse Ed Davis played guitar.

It is 2 minutes and 30 seconds in length.

It was issued as a single in America on Apple 1880 on 27 January 1975 and reached No. 3 in the charts, Ringo's seventh consecutive Top Ten entry. 'Snookeroo' was on the flip.

In Britain it was issued as the B side of 'Oh My My' on Apple R 6011 on 9 January 1976.

Occapella

A track from Ringo's 1974 album *Goodnight Vienna*. Penned by Allen Toussaint, the number was originally recorded by Lee Dorsey. Dr John played piano and backing vocals were by Jimmy Gilstrap, Joe Greene, Clydie King and Jimmy Hawkins.

It is 2 minutes and 50 seconds in length.

Octopus's Garden

A number written by Ringo, which was included on the *Abbey Road* album. When Ringo walked out of the recording sessions of *The Beatles* White album because Paul criticised his drumming, he took his family to Sardinia and they were lent Peter Sellers' boat. For lunch, the captain served them octopus, which Ringo refused to eat.

He then had a conversation with the captain, which inspired him to write the song. He commented that 'at the time I just wanted to be under the sea, too. I wanted to get out of it for a while.'

Ringo worked on the number with George Harrison while they were filming *Let It Be*. George was to say, '"Octopus's Garden" is Ringo's song. It's only the second song Ringo has written, mind you, and it's lovely. Ringo gets bored with just playing drums all the time, so at home he sometimes plays a bit of piano, but unfortunately he only knows three chords. He knows about the same on guitar, too. The song gets very deep into your consciousness, though, because it's so peaceful. I suppose Ringo is writing cosmic songs these days without even noticing it.'

The number was recorded at Abbey Road Studios on 26 April 1969, with overdubbing taking place on 29 April and 17 and 18 July.

Ringo managed to produce underwater sounds by blowing bubbles in a glass of water.

When Ringo and the Roundheads appeared at the Bottom Line club in New York and then recorded the VH-1 *Storytellers* series the next day, he included 'Octopus's Garden' in the repertoire.

He was to say, 'On every tour I do "Yellow Submarine", and I didn't really want to be doing too many novelty songs. I always felt it was just too much doing "Yellow Submarine" and "Octopus's Garden", so I chose "Yellow Submarine", because in all honesty it is the bigger song. I end the first half of my show every night with it.

'But when we were putting the set together for *Storytellers*, we didn't just want to do songs that were interesting, we also wanted ones with a story. And "Octopus's Garden" certainly had a story. During the White album, I left the Beatles, and went on holiday. We were lent this yacht and we ordered lunch and the guy presented us with octopus and French fries. And we thought, what the hell is that? The captain proceeded to tell me that octopuses actually go round the seabed "resting their head" and picking up shiny coral and stones and actually putting a garden around their cave. I just thought that was so beautiful and I happened to have a guitar there and wrote the song.'

Oh My My

The opening track of Side Two of the *Ringo* album, 4 minutes and 16 seconds in length.

It was also Ringo's final single on the Apple label, issued in Britain on Apple R 6011 on 9 January 1976. This number had already been a hit in America as the third single release from the *Ringo* album. It was issued in America on Apple 1872 on 18 February 1974 and became Ringo's fifth consecutive Top Ten hit, reaching No. 5 in the *Billboard* charts on 27 April 1974. 'Step Lightly' was on the flip.

The flipside of the British single was also a number that had already been a hit in America in its own right. 'No No Song' from the *Goodnight Vienna* album had reached No. 3 in the American charts.

Despite the fact that both numbers had been strong American hits, the single didn't chart in Britain.

Old Time Relovin'

A track from the 1978 album *Bad Boy*, 4 minutes and 16 seconds in length.

Old Wave

Ringo's ninth album, which was produced by Joe Walsh, former member of the Eagles. Jim Nipor was the engineer. It is 36 minutes and 57 seconds in length.

The cover was an early picture of Ringo that he had taken in a photo booth in Liverpool.

Walsh arrived in Britain to work with Ringo at Tittenhurst Park in February 1982 and the two began writing songs for the album together.

They started recording at Startling Studios in Tittenhurst Park, laying down seven of the instrumental tracks.

The core band for the sessions comprised Ringo on drums and percussion, Walsh on guitars and backing vocals, Mo Foster on bass, Gary Brooker doing most of the keyboard work, with occasional keyboard work by Chris Stainton.

At one point John Entwistle, Eric Clapton and Ray Cooper arrived at the studios and joined Ringo and Joe on a jam that turned into the number 'Everybody's In A Hurry But Me'.

On 19 March Walsh and Nipor returned to California, but came back to Startling Studios the following month to record Ringo's lead vocals between 19 and 23 April. Joe and Jim then mixed the tracks in Santa Barbara in August and the album was completed on 13 August.

The tracks were: 'In My Car', 'Hopeless', 'Alibi', 'Be My Baby', She's About A Mover', 'I Keep Forgettin'', 'Picture Show Life', 'As Far As We Can Go', 'Everybody's In A Hurry But Me' and 'I'm Going Down'.

Neil Bogart, Ringo's friend from Boardwalk Records, had died in 1982 and as a result there were various problems at Boardwalk, which meant that Ringo now found himself without a record company. RCA in Britain then rejected *Old Wave* and the album was not released in either America or Britain. It had a limited release in Germany on 16 June 1983 and a single from the album 'In My Car' c/w 'I'm Going Down' was also released there. On 24 June 1983 it was released in Canada on RCA DXL-1-3233 and other countries it was released in included Australia, Brazil, Mexico, New Zealand and Japan.

Four of the tracks finally saw an American release when they appeared on the CD *Starr Struck – Best Of Ringo Starr Vol 2* by Rhino Records on 24 February 1989.

There was also a promotional CD issued by Capitol in 1984 to promote their De-Luxe Collection edition reissue series. This comprised three tracks from *Old Wave* and three tracks from *Stop And Smell The Roses*. The *Old Wave* tracks were 'Be My Baby', 'In My Car' and 'She's About A Mover'. The *Stop And Smell The Roses* tracks were 'Wrack My Brain', 'Dead Giveaway' and 'Private Property'.

The Right Stuff/Capitol also issued a CD of *Old Wave* on 6 September 1994 with bonus tracks.

One

The opening track of the *Vertical Man* album, 3 minutes and 2 seconds in length. Starkey/Hudson/Grakal/Dudas penned it. Ringo performed lead vocals and played drums, bongos and percussion. The rest of the line-up was: Steve Dudas on bass guitar and electric guitar; Mark Hudson on electric guitar, acoustic guitar, keyboards and backing vocals; Jeff Baxter on pedal steel guitar; Jim Cox on B3 organ; and Scott Gordon on harmonica and percussion.

Only You (And You Alone) (promo)

The promo for 'Only You (And You Alone)' was directed by former *Top Of The Pops* director Stanley Dorfman, and continued with the science-fiction theme portrayed on the cover of the *Goodnight Vienna* album.

It was filmed around the Capitol Records building in Hollywood and opens with a flying saucer landing on the roof of the Capitol building. Harry Nilsson is sitting on the roof reading a paper in which there is a photograph of Ringo in a spacesuit. Ringo then appears at the door of the flying saucer wearing the silver spacesuit with a star-shaped mirror on his chest and wearing dark glasses while he sings the song. It ends with Ringo, Harry Nilsson, a robot and the saucer vanishing into the distance as a helicopter shot of the Capitol roof pulls away.

Only You (And You Alone) (song)

It was John Lennon who suggested that Ringo should record this number and assisted him in the recording by playing acoustic guitar. Harry Nilsson provided backing vocals and the other musicians participating were Ringo and Jim Keltner on drums, Billy Preston on electric organ and Jesse Ed Davis and Steve Cropper on electric guitars.

It was the first single released from the *Goodnight Vienna* album, but only reached No. 28 in the official British chart listings after it was issued in the UK on Apple R 6000 on 15 November 1974. It fared better in the American charts on its release there on Apple 1876 on 11 November 1974, reaching No. 6.

The number is 3 minutes and 22 seconds in length and 'Call Me' was on the flip. Buck Ram and Ande Rand had originally written the number for the Platters, whose 1955 version became a million-seller.

Ono, Yoko

John Lennon's second wife. John was always appreciative of the fact that Ringo didn't have a negative attitude towards Yoko, unlike the other Beatles, particularly George.

When John died it was Ringo who rushed to New York to offer his condolences face to face with Yoko. He was accompanied by Barbara Bach. When he entered the Dakota building he was initially told he couldn't take Barbara with him, but he insisted and both of them went to see Yoko.

Yoko wasn't invited to Ringo's wedding to Barbara. When asked in New York if she had been invited, she said, 'No. My way of taking it now is that, because of what happened to me, they felt intimidated about inviting me, because it was really not the right time to encounter people being happy. But it would have been nice to have been told about it.'

Oo-Wee

A track from Ringo's *Goodnight Vienna* album, which he co-wrote with Vini Poncia. Backing vocals were by Clydie King and the Blackberries, and Dr John played piano.

The number is 3 minutes and 40 seconds in length.

Our Show For Ringo

To coincide with the release of Ringo's *Goodnight Vienna* album in 1974, Graham Chapman, a member of the *Monty Python* team, and Douglas Adams, who was to become noted for his *Hitchhiker's Guide To The Galaxy* series, scripted 'Our Show For Ringo' (a.k.a. 'Goodnight Vienna') for American television, under the pseudonyms Nemona Lethbridge and Vera Hunt.

Sadly, the show was never filmed and both Graham and Douglas are no longer with us.

Graham was a prolific writer of comedy scripts for television, in addition to his work with *Monty Python*. He was born in Leicester on 8 January 1941 and died of throat cancer on 4 October 1989.

It was Michael Palin who originally created a character called the 'It's Man' for the *Monty Python* television series. The character was shabbily dressed and would struggle across difficult terrain before facing the camera, ready to make a statement – but he could invariably only ever manage to say 'It's . . .' before he was cut off and the opening titles began.

Python Graham Chapman explained, 'One day we decided to give the It's Man an opportunity to do more, finally to speak his piece, so at the end of show No. 28 we had Michael, dressed as the It's Man, come out on stage.

'The idea was that it was going to be his show, a chat show, and that he was finally going to be allowed to get the rest of this important sentence out, which had always been interrupted. Guests for this pretend chat show were going to include any famous people we could get.'

The Pythons initially approached John and Yoko, who agreed to appear, but they were involved in a car accident shortly after the offer was made and Ringo and Lulu agreed to appear instead.

Graham had originally met Ringo during the filming of *The Magic Christian*, the Peter Sellers/Ringo Starr film for which Graham wrote part of the script.

When Ringo appeared in the sketch, Graham recalled, 'This gave us the idea to maybe try to work with Ringo again later on, and so a few years later, Douglas Adams and myself wrote a special for Ringo, a part science fiction, part historical fiction story that loosely revolved around a few of Ringo's hit songs.'

In some ways it's a semi-promotional film for the *Goodnight Vienna* album, featuring a number of its songs: 'Snookeroo', 'No No Song',

'Husbands And Wives' and 'Goodnight Vienna'. Ringo's hit single 'You're Sixteen' was also to be featured.

More than a decade later, Graham was to comment, 'The script was never approved by any networks, or by cable TV, because I think that they thought it a bit rude and because, quite frankly, I don't think they understood it very much.'

The script is surrealistic and basically features Ringo, a narrator and a robot travelling in time and space. The robot is similar to the robot on the cover of the *Goodnight Vienna* album. The album cover itself was basically a still from the film *The Day The Earth Stood Still*. It showed Michael Rennie as the alien ambassador Klaatu with his protector, the robot Gort, standing at the opening of a flying saucer. On the album cover Ringo's head has replaced that of Rennie.

In the script, the robot grants Ringo the power to travel through space and time. He travels to ancient Rome, but in the garb of a slave. When a soldier begins to whip him he changes himself into a soldier. When he continues to be whipped he changes himself into Julius Caesar, just as Brutus and other senators are about to stab him. Eventually he finds himself travelling through space. One of the characters he encounters, Jack, was originally to have been played by Keith Moon. Ringo meets up with his double, Rinog Trars, who the robot had mistaken him for, and Ringo is able to transfer his recently acquired powers to him. The special ends with a scene similar to that of the album cover.

Elements of *Monty Python* and the forthcoming *Hitchhiker's Guide To The Galaxy* littered the script. Since the special was never filmed, Adams used some of the elements from the script in his novel *The Restaurant At The End Of The Universe*.

Owens, Buck

A country music singer, born Alvis Edgar Owens Jr in Sherman, Texas, on 12 August 1929. As Buck Owens he began to have a number of hit entries in the C&W charts, including 'Under Your Spell Again' and 'Excuse Me (I Think I've Got A Heartache)', with his biggest hit being 'Act Naturally'.

Ringo, always a country fan, recorded 'Act Naturally' with the Beatles in 1965. On 27 March 1989 he teamed up with Buck Owens at Abbey Road Studios in London to duet on the number that had become so strongly associated with both of them. The number appeared on Owens' *Act Naturally* album and was also issued as a single, with Ringo appearing on the music video to promote it.

Parkinson

A highly popular late-evening BBC1 chat show hosted by Yorkshire-born, ex-journalist Michael Parkinson.

Ringo and Barbara appeared on the show on Saturday 12 December 1981. Ringo was particularly amusing and drew a warm response from the audience. Liverpool comedian Jimmy Tarbuck, who had achieved fame during the Mersey boom in the mid-60s, was also a guest, as was Tim Rice. The show's finale was a hilarious jam session with Ringo on drums and Tarbuck, Rice and Parkinson joining in on the number 'Singing The Blues'.

Among the topics discussed by Ringo was a scene in *A Hard Day's Night* where he wanders along a towpath, his time with Rory Storm and the Hurricanes at Butlin's holiday camps, and working with actors such as Peter Sellers and Mae West.

He also discussed writing songs when he was in the Beatles, commenting, 'I used to write all these songs and I used to think, "Wow! I've written another song!" Then I'd go along where we'd be making another album, or something, and I'd say, "I've written this song." I would play them the song I had written and they would all be on the floor laughing, because I had usually rewritten another song, usually a Jerry Lee Lewis B side.'

Parkinson said, 'When the Beatles were recording you submitted a song? You all did? You all submitted songs when you were making an album?'

Ringo replied, 'Well, it was pretty difficult in the beginning because, even from the start, Lennon and McCartney were good writers.'

Parkinson commented, 'Not bad! Did you feel that was a bit daunting for you?'

Ringo answered, 'To say the least. It's like Emily Bronte. I don't even know what that means! It was a bit heavy, you know. "Well, I've got this, lads." And they'd say, "Well, we've got this: 'Yesterday'." So I'd say, "OK. We'll do yours."'

Parkinson In Australia

After several years hosting *Parkinson* for BBC Television, Michael Parkinson took up a lucrative Australian offer and proceeded to host a chat show down under.

The edition screened on 8 October 1982, recorded on 28 September, featured Ringo and Barbara Bach and Glen Sharrock, a former member of the Little River Band.

Ringo and Barbara were the first guests and appeared for the programme's full running time of one hour, being introduced with clips of the Beatles. The film clips were screened to the sound of 'Love Me Do', as it was the twentieth anniversary of its release in the UK.

The couple chatted, Ringo as witty as ever, with Barbara admitting that she'd never seen any of the Beatles' films. She also talked about her children. Parkinson persuaded Ringo to sing 'Honey Don't' with Sharrock and his band, but the former Beatle appeared ill at ease. However, when the group moved into 'Blue Suede Shoes' and then returned to 'Honey Don't', with Barbara joining them for a dance, Ringo had gained sufficient confidence to play drums.

Pax Um Biscum (Peace Be With You)

An original Christmas number that was included on Ringo's 1999 album *I Wanna Be Santa Claus*. It was composed by Starkey/Hudson/Scott Gordon. Ringo was on lead vocals, drums, Mellotron, synthesizer and percussion, with Mark Hudson on Mellotron, synthesizer, percussion recorders and backing vocals, Joe Perry on electric guitar, Scott Gordon on keyboard and synthesizer, Jim Cox on piano and string arrangement, Steve Dudas on percussion, Kalijut Bhamra on tabla and Marc Fantini, Steffan Fantini and Telsha Helgerson on backing vocals. It is 4 minutes and 46 seconds in length.

Perkins, Carl

A seminal influence on the Beatles and George Harrison in particular. Perkins was born in Lake County near Tiptonville, Tennessee, on 9 April 1932 and was to write and record the rock classic 'Blue Suede Shoes'. The Beatles were keen to help their idol and invited him to Abbey Road Studios on 1 June 1964 to witness them recording his song 'Matchbox', with Ringo on lead vocal. They were also to record two of his other songs, 'Honey Don't' (again with Ringo on lead vocal) and 'Everybody's Trying To Be My Baby'.

Both Ringo and George Harrison agreed to join his television special 'Blue Suede Shoes – A Rockabilly Session With Carl Perkins and Friends', which was originally broadcast in Britain on Channel Four on New Year's Day 1986. Ringo sang lead vocal on 'Honey Don't' and also played drums on several of the other numbers.

Perkins died on 19 January 1998.

Perry, Richard

A leading American record producer, born in Brooklyn, New York, in 1942. He studied at the University of Michigan before returning to New York where he began to produce records by such artists as Fats Domino and Captain Beefheart. Perry became a 'hot' name when he began producing Barbra Streisand, Carly Simon, Johnny Mathis and Harry Nilsson, and was then asked to produce Ringo's eponymous album *Ringo,* which was highly successful and spawned two chart-toppers, 'Photograph' and 'You're Sixteen'. He then went on to produce the follow-up album *Goodnight Vienna.*

In 1978 he formed his own company, Planet Records, which he sold to RCA in 1983. He continued to produce recordings by numerous artists including Rod Stewart, Syreeta, the Pointer Sisters and Julio Iglesias.

Petty, Tom

An American singer/multi-instrumentalist, born in Gainesville, Florida, on 20 October 1950.

He had major success in the 1970s with his band Tom Petty and the Heartbreakers, whose numerous hits included 'Refugee', 'Here Comes My Girl', 'I Won't Back Down' and 'You Don't Know How It Feels'. His 1989 album *Full Moon Fever* had a contribution from George Harrison and on the music video for the number 'Don't Back Down', Ringo played drums and Harrison acoustic guitar.

Petty also became a member of the Traveling Wilburys.

Petty, Jeff Lynne and Jim Keltner backed Ringo singing 'I Call Your Name', which was his contribution to the John Lennon Scholarship Concert held in Liverpool on 5 May 1990.

When Mercury Records requested that Ringo take off Steve Tyler's lead vocals for the *Vertical Man* track 'Drift Away' (they regarded it as competition to the new release of the soundtrack album *Armageddon,* which included four Aerosmith tracks), Ringo asked his friend Tom Petty to record a new vocal for the track. This took place on 2 May 1998. Petty recorded it at the Village Recorders Studio in Los Angeles while Ringo, Mark Hudson and Scott Gordon supervised from Abbey Road Studios in London via an ISDS telephone line.

Ringo played drums on 'To Find A Friend', a track from Petty's *Wildflowers* album He also played drums on 'Hung Up And Overdue' for the Tom Petty and the Heartbreakers soundtrack to the film *She's The One.*

Photograph

Ringo's third straight solo hit, which he recorded between March and July 1973 during the *Ringo* album sessions. Ringo and George Harrison penned the number and the musicians were George Harrison on 12-string guitar and harmony vocal, Ringo and Jim Keltner on drums, Nicky Hopkins on piano, Klaus Voormann on bass, Vini Poncia on acoustic guitar, Jimmy Calvert on acoustic guitar, Lon and Derrek Van Eaton on percussion, and Bobby Keyes on tenor sax.

It was released in Britain on Apple R 5992 on 19 October 1973 and reached No. 4 in the charts. 'Down And Out' was on the flip. It was issued in America on Apple 1831 on 16 April 1973 with the same flip-side and became Ringo's first American chart-topper.

Ringo was to recall that he and George completed the number on a yacht while they were at the Cannes Film Festival. He said, 'I wrote the melody and the lyrics for the first two verses and a chorus. And then George helped me on the last verse, so I could end the damn thing.'

Picture Show Life

A track from the 1983 *Old Wave* album, written by John Reid and John Slate, and produced by Joe Walsh. Ringo was on lead vocals, drums and percussion, Joe Walsh on guitar and backing vocals, Mo Foster on bass, Gary Brooker and Chris Stainton on keyboards, Waddy Wachtel on lead guitar, and Steve Hess, Mark Easterling and Patrick Maroshek on backing vocals. It is 4 minutes and 19 seconds in length.

Pieseckyj, Nina

The secretary to the landlord who rented Mark Hudson the room where he based his Whatinthewhatthe? Studios in Los Angeles. During the sessions for *Vertical Man*, Pieseckyj knocked on the door demanding $450 in back rent, which Hudson had forgotten to pay.

Ringo immediately asked her, 'Do you play an instrument?'

She was surprised by the question but answered, 'Yes, a cello.'

'Go get it,' said Ringo.

When she returned with her cello, Ringo got her to play it on the album's title track 'Vertical Man'.

Point, The

An animated film, written by Harry Nilsson and Norm Lenzer, about a little boy battling against discrimination.

Directed by Fred Wolf, the original telefilm was released with a narration by Dustin Hoffman. In April 1986, when it was issued in video format, Ringo recorded a new narration as the Hoffman one couldn't be issued on home video due to contractual difficulties.

Poncia, Vincent

A songwriter/producer/musician, born on 29 April 1942. He was originally a member of Tradewinds, and then began writing songs for a number of artists, including Elvis Presley. He co-wrote the major hit 'You Make Me Feel Like Dancing' with Leo Sayer.

He began assisting Ringo with his albums in 1973, performing as a musician on *Ringo*. The two began collaborating on songs and the *Goodnight Vienna* album included their compositions 'Oo-Wee' and 'All By Myself'. Poncia also appeared as a musician on several tracks. On *Ringo's Rotogravure*, Poncia and Ringo co-wrote 'Lady Gaye', based on a Clifford T. Ward single. On *Ringo The 4th*, all but four of the numbers were written by Ringo and Poncia, and Poncia also supplied backing vocals on some of the tracks. Poncia then produced Ringo's next album *Bad Boy* in 1978, on which he also collaborated with Ringo in writing some of the songs.

Postcards From The Boys

Brian Roylance, founder of Genesis Books, had been involved in many limited-edition books about the Beatles, particularly in collaboration with George Harrison and Derek Taylor. He has now published his first book with Ringo, *Postcards From The Boys*, and says, 'We've waited twenty years to publish a book by Ringo.'

It was published in 2004 in a limited edition of 2,500 copies, each copy signed by Ringo. The main core of the book is the quality facsimile reproduction of 53 postcards that John, Paul and George had sent to him over the years, with an explanation by Ringo of the messages on each card.

All Ringo's royalties are donated to a charity, the Lotus foundation, and Genesis will also contribute a sum from each book to the same charity.

Power To The People

A number penned by John Lennon. In 2000 Ringo recorded a version with Billy Preston for a projected movie on 1960s hippie Abbie Hoffman. Mark Hudson had the assignment and asked Ringo to record the track while he was in Los Angeles.

Preston, Billy

An American vocalist/keyboards player, born in Houston, Texas, on 2 September 1946.

He was raised in Los Angeles, California, and began his show-business career at the age of ten when he appeared in the film *St Louis Blues*. Little Richard hired him to play on his European tour in 1962.

The Beatles first met Billy in Hamburg that year when they were on the bill with Little Richard at the Star club and Billy was Richard's keyboards player. He and George Harrison became friends and, when

Apple was launched, George signed him up to the label. Preston also became the only musician to have his name attached to the Beatles when the 'Get Back' single was attributed to 'The Beatles with Billy Preston'. Both George and John Lennon also asked him to sit in on the sessions that resulted in the *Let It Be* album. Preston was to record two albums for Apple: *That's The Way God Planned It* in 1969 and *Encouraging Words* the following year, both produced by George Harrison, who also included Billy on his triple album set *All Things Must Pass* and invited him to appear on the Concert For Bangla Desh in 1970.

Preston then went on to record a number of solo albums for A&M records and had a series of Top 40 hits in America. He received a Grammy for 'Best Pop Instrumental' with his 'Outta Space' in 1972 and in 1974 had two chart-topping singles, 'Will It Go Round In Circles' and 'Nothing For Nothing'. In 1975 he wrote 'You Are So Beautiful' for Joe Cocker, which became Cocker's biggest solo hit, and he returned to the top of the charts in 1979 with his duet with Syreeta Wright, 'With You I'm Born Again'.

When the news came that he was to become a member of the first All-Starr Band he was asked how long it had been since he worked with Ringo. He said, 'It's been a long time. He used to work on my albums when I was on Apple. But the last time I worked with him was in 1973 on his album with 'Oh My My' and 'You're Sixteen' on it.

'We're all going to do some of our own songs as well as playing with Ringo. We'll be playing all of his hits.'

The press release for the first All-Starr Band tour in 1989 included the following biography of Billy:

'Singer/songwriter/keyboardist Billy Preston's legendary career spans three decades and is highlighted by a string of No. 1 records and collaborations with some of the most celebrated names in the music industry: Aretha Franklin, Sammy Davis Jr, Quincy Jones, Ray Charles, the Jackson Five, the Rolling Stones, Sly Stone, Barbra Streisand . . . and, of course, the Beatles.

'Today, Preston's concert performances exhibit the same high-energy feel and audience participation reaction that prompted superstars Mick Jagger, the fab four, and Little Richard to extend invitations to Billy to join them on vinyl, film and on the road.

'Born in Houston, Texas, Billy Preston credits his mother, singer/pianist Robbie Preston Williams, with his introduction to music while still a child. His musical genius was exhibited early on, and by the time he turned sixteen, Billy had already worked with such greats as Sam Cook and Little Richard.

'After initially signing with Vee-Jay Records, Preston moved to Capitol Records with the smash hit 'Sunny'. He proceeded to tour with the Beatles, and became universally regarded as 'the fifth Beatle', working with the group's *Let It Be*, *Abbey Road* and the White album, and on screen in *Let It Be*, *The Compleat Beatles* and *Sgt Pepper's Lonely Hearts Club Band*.

'Following the break-up of the Beatles, Billy worked with John and Yoko, George Harrison, and penned the chart-topping 'You Are So Beautiful', performed by Joe Cocker. Invited to be the opening act on the Rolling Stones' '74 tour, Preston remained with the band for three years. He went on to write and perform with the God Squad throughout Europe, showcasing an impressive array of old and new material.

'Billy Preston triumphantly returns to the touring circuit with Ringo Starr and the All-Starrs, further delivering his belief "in the message of life, in saying something positive", and does it with unmatched emotion and energy.'

On 18 August 1991 Preston was arrested at his Malibu home. A sixteen-year-old boy had reported that Preston had tried to assault him sexually after smoking cocaine and showing him sexually explicit pictures. He was charged with felony cocaine possession in addition to two misdemeanours involving pornography and maltreatment of children.

Preston said that it had all been a misunderstanding by the boy, who spoke little English and worked on Preston's farm as a day labourer. He said he did not use cocaine. Then he entered a plea to the charges in a Malibu municipal court hearing on 18 September. He asked to be able to attend a state drug programme and was released on $10,000 bail.

Ringo wanted him to provide the keyboards for his *Vertical Man* album, but he was in jail at the time.

Although David Fishof had originally mentioned that Billy would be in the 2000 All-Starr line-up, he didn't appear. When asked about it, Ringo said that Billy had done two tours with the All-Starrs and he'd recently recorded 'Power To The People' with him. Other people had mentioned that Billy wasn't available because of some legal difficulties he was involved with at the time.

Price, Jim

An American guitarist who conceived the All Occasion Brass Band, and who recorded the album *The Presence Of The Lord* at Olympic Studios, London in 1971. The credits thank Richard Starkey for his contribution and Ringo is credited as playing drums on the number 'Oh Lucky Day'. The album was released in America in 1974.

Price had taken part in the Delaney and Bonnie and Friends tour of Britain and Europe and appeared with them when they backed John Lennon at the UNICEF concert at the Lyceum, London.

Princess Daisy

An American television miniseries based on the novel by Judith Kranz. Originally a 4-part 200-minute drama, it was later edited down to a

100-minute home video release. The story concerned the daughter of a Russian prince and an American movie star who has to leave college to find a job in New York to pay the expensive medical bills for his sister's treatment. She becomes an internationally famous model.

In it Ringo portrayed a bisexual dress designer and Barbara his scheming lesbian wife. It was first screened by NBC in America on 6 and 7 November 1984.

Private Issue
Ringo has been painting since the 1960s and was originally encouraged to do so by his first wife Maureen when they lived in Sunny Heights in Weybridge.

Of his work he commented to an Associated Press reporter, 'I'm not good at figurative painting. If I paint you it'll never look like you. The people in my paintings, I call them "my people". Or it is very abstract. I don't use a brush, just paint out of the tube.'

'Private Issue' was a campaign in which Ringo, together with actress Jane Seymour and Olympic Gold medallist Florence Joyner, were asked to contribute an original painting of theirs to be sold at auction at the Guggenheim Museum in New York. The proceeds went to the Make-A-Wish Foundation, which helps terminally ill children. Ringo's painting fetched $33,000.

Private Music
The label that Ringo signed to in 1991. It was an American label which has specialised in 'new age' music but which wanted to expand into other areas of music. The announcement of the signing was made at the NARM (National Association of Radio Merchandisers) convention in San Francisco.

The label was only responsible for issuing one of Ringo's albums, *Time Takes Time*.

Private Property
A track from the 1981 *Stop And Smell The Roses* album lasting 2 minutes and 42 seconds. Paul McCartney wrote the number, produced it, played bass, piano and provided backing vocals. Other backing vocalists were Linda McCartney, Sheila Casey and Lezlee Livrano Pariser. Howie Casey, former leader of Derry & the Seniors, the first Liverpool group to go to Hamburg, was on sax.

It was issued as a single in America on Boardwalk NB7-11-134 on 13 January 1982, but failed to register in the charts.

Prodigy Service
An American online service on which Ringo was a guest on 25 May 1995. He didn't appear live, but questions were posted to him by subscribers to the service.

Q: You must be proud of your son Zak. Are you surprised that he followed in your footsteps and became a drummer?

Ringo: I am very proud of Zak, and I wasn't surprised by his interest. I gave him his first lesson when he was ten . . . and he's still waiting for the second!

Q: Do you miss not having Joe Walsh with you on tour this time?

Ringo: Joe couldn't make it this time because the Eagles got together, but I'm sure that he will pop up from time to time during our tour.

Q: What do you miss most about the Beatle?

Ringo: I miss hanging out with John, Paul and George.

Q: What's your favourite movie? What's your favourite album?

Ringo: *A Hard Day's Night*, and as for albums . . . there are too many to choose from.

Q: What was your proudest moment as a Beatle?

Ringo: It's hard to say . . . the Palladium, Shea, *Rubber Soul*, *Sgt Pepper*. It was all fabulous.

Q: Can you give us any tips on how to start a band? Who were your musical influences?

Ringo: Influences from childhood . . . Gene Autry and John Lee Hooker. Tips? Just get out there and play.

Q: How many All-Starr tours do you plan to do?

Ringo: When I planned to do this tour, I said that this was the last one, then everyone points out that I said that the last time. I plan to go on . . . as long as I can.

Q: How did 'Boogaloo' become a nickname for Paul, as in 'Back Off Boogaloo'?

Ringo: I didn't know it was a nickname for Paul . . . I was inspired to write that song by Marc Bolan of T. Rex. One night it was all 'Back off' and 'Boogaloo', and I went to bed that night and woke up with that song in my head in the middle of the night. It took me ten minutes.'

Q: Are there any plans for a new record?

Ringo: We'll be on tour until the middle of September, and then go on holiday. There are no plans for a record.

Q: Do you plan to write your autobiography? Who was the hardest act you ever had to follow?

Ringo: No plans to write a book. Roy Orbison, who we toured with.

Q: Are there many unreleased recordings by the Beatles we haven't heard?

Ringo: There aren't many, and whatever is unreleased will be out with the *Anthology*.

Q: Do you plan to do a reunion concert?

Ringo: No.

Puppet

A track on the *Vertical Man* album, 3 minutes and 21 seconds in length. Steve Cropper provided an electric guitar solo, Mark Hudson was on bass, electric guitar, acoustic guitar, banjo, percussion and backing vocals, Steve Dudas was on electric guitar, Jim Cox on B3 organ, Joel Reskin on sax, with Timothy B. Schmit and Dave Gibbs on backing vocals.

Pure Gold

A track from *Ringo's Rotogravure*. Paul McCartney wrote this especially for Ringo, and Paul and Linda also supply the backing vocals. Ringo shares the vocal with Vini Poncia and Lon Van Eaton plays guitar, Klaus Voormann bass, John Jarvis and Jane Getz keyboards and George Devens conga.

The number is 3 minutes and 13 seconds in length.

Ramone, Phil

A prominent record producer who had produced albums such as Bob Dylan's *Blood On The Tracks*, Billy Joel's *52nd Street* and Paul Simon's *Still Crazy After All These Years*. He also worked with Paul McCartney, Harry Nilsson and Elton John.

When Ringo decided to engage different producers to work with him on his 1992 *Time Takes Time* album, he had Ramone produce the tracks 'All In The Name Of Love' and 'Runaways' for him. He also assembled the musicians to play on the tracks; one of these was Mark Hudson, who later became Ringo's partner.

Ramone also produced a track called 'Love Is Going To Get You', which wasn't used on the album and Ramone commented, 'It was a great track, but it did not fit in with the character of the songs he did with Don Was and the other producers.'

Really Love You

A track from the *Flaming Pie* album that Ringo co-wrote with Paul McCartney. Ringo said, 'To be honest, I was a little bit surprised when I was getting the credit there. I just went down as a friend to do my bit. We didn't sit around as writers, we were just having fun.'

This was the first song to be credited McCartney/Starr and arose out of a jam after recording of the track began on 4 May 1996. Ringo played drums on the track and Paul was to comment, 'When I played it back to Ringo, he said, "It's relentless, it's relentless." He's a one with words!'

Recordings

Since leaving the Beatles, Ringo has recorded a vast amount of material. Following is a basic list of most of the recordings he has made in his post-Beatles days.

A

'A Dose Of Rock 'N' Roll', 'A Man Like Me', 'A Mouse Like Me', 'Act Naturally', 'Ain't That A Shame', 'Alibi', 'All By Myself', 'All In The Name Of Love', 'Angel In Disguise', 'As Far As We Can Go', 'Attention'

B

'Back Off Boogaloo', 'Bad Boy', 'Be My Baby', 'Beaucoups Of Blues', 'Blindman', 'Blue Christmas', 'Blue Suede Shoes', 'Blue, Turning Grey Over You', 'Boat Ride', 'Boys', 'Brandy', 'Bye Bye Blackbird'

C

'Call Me', 'Can She Do It Like She Dances', 'Can't Fight Lightning', 'The Christmas Dance', 'Christmas Eve', 'Christmas Time Is Here Again', 'Come On Christmas, Come On', 'Coochy-Coochy', 'Cookin' In The Kitchen Of Love', 'Cryin''

D

'The Dark End Of The Street', 'Dead Giveaway', 'Dear Santa', 'Devil Woman', 'Do You Like Me', 'Don't Be Cruel', 'Don't Blame It On Me', 'Don't Go Where The Road Don't Go', 'Don't Know A Thing About Love', 'Don't Pass Me By', 'Down And Out', 'Dream', 'Drift Away', 'Drowning In A Sea Of Love', 'Drumming Is My Madness'

E

'Early 1970', 'Easy For Me', 'English Garden', 'Elizabeth Reigns', 'Everybody's In A Hurry But Me', 'Everyday', 'Everyone Wins', 'Eye To Eye'

F

'Farther Down The Line', 'Fastest Growing Heartache In The West', 'Fiddle About', '$15 Draw', 'Freelance Lover'

G

'Gave It All Up', 'Going Down', 'Golden Blunders', 'Good News', 'Goodnight Vienna', 'Great Balls Of Fire', 'Gypsies In Flight'

H

'Happy Birthday Johnny', 'Hard Times', 'Have I Told You Lately That I Love You', 'Have You Seen My Baby', 'Heart On My Sleeve', 'Hey Baby', 'Hold On', 'Hopeless', 'Husbands And Wives'

I

'I Call Your Name', 'I Can Help', 'I Can See Clearly Now', 'I Changed My Mind', 'I Don't Believe You', 'I Got To Be Me', 'I Keep Forgettin'', 'I Know A Place', 'I Looked To The Left', 'I Love My Suit', 'I Really Love Her', 'I Think Therefore I Rock And Roll', 'I Wanna Be Santa Claus', 'I Wanna Be Your Man', 'I Was Walkin'', 'I Wouldn't Have You Any Other Way', 'I'd Be Talking All The Time', 'I'll Be Fine Anywhere', 'I'll Still Love You', 'I'm A Fool To Care', 'I'm The Greatest', 'I'm Yours', 'If I Had A Boat', 'Imagine Me There', 'In A Heartbeat', 'In My Car', 'Instant Amnesia', 'It Don't Come Easy'

J

'Just A Dream'

K

'King Of Broken Hearts'

L

'La De Da', 'Lady Gaye', 'Las Brisas', 'Lay Down Your Arms', 'Let The Rest Of The World Go By', 'Lipstick Traces (On A Cigarette)', 'Little Drummer Boy', 'Living In A Pet Shop', 'Lonely Weekends', 'Long Tall Sally', 'Loser's Lounge', 'Love Don't Last Long', 'Love First, Ask Questions Later', 'Love Is A Many Splendoured Thing', 'Love Is Gonna Get Ya', 'Love Letters', 'Love Me Do'

M

'Memphis In Your Mind', 'Mindfield', 'Missouri Loves Company', 'Misty Roses', 'Modulating Maurice', 'Money (That's What I Want)', 'Monkey See, Monkey Do', 'Mr Double-It-Up'

N

'Nashville Freakout', 'Nashville Jam', 'Naughty Atom Bomb', 'Nellie Dean', 'Never Without You', 'Night And Day', 'No No Song', 'Nonsense'

O

'Occapella', 'Octopus's Garden', 'Oh My My', 'Oh, Pretty Woman', 'Old Time Relovin'', 'One', 'One Way Love Affair', 'Only You (And You Alone)', 'Oo-Wee', 'Out On The Streets'

P

'Parole', 'Party', 'Party Doll', 'Pass It On', 'Pax Um Biscum (Peace Be With You)', 'Photograph', 'Piccadilly', 'Picture Show Life', 'Private Property', 'Puppet', 'Pure Gold'

R

'Real Man', 'Red And Black Blues', 'Rudolph The Red-Nosed Reindeer', 'Runaways', 'Running Free'

S

'S.O.S.', 'Scotch And Soda', 'Scouse's Dream', 'Sentimental Journey', 'She Makes Me Feel Good', 'She's About A Mover', 'She's So In Love', 'Shoo-Be-Doo', 'Silent Homecoming', 'Simple Life', 'Simple Love Song', 'Singing The Blues', 'Six O'Clock', 'Sneaking Sally Through The Alley', 'Snookeroo', 'Some Kind Of Wonderful', 'Something Wild', 'Sometimes', 'Spirit Of The Forest', 'Spooky Weirdness', 'Stardust', 'Stay Awake', 'Steel', 'Step Lightly', 'Stop And Take The Time To Smell The Roses', 'Stormy Weather', 'Sun City', 'Sunshine Life For Me (Sail Away Raymond)', 'Sure To Fall (In Love With You)'

T

'Tango All Night', 'Theme From *The Jeffersons*', 'This Be Called A Song', 'Three Ships In The Harbour', 'Time Takes Time', 'Tommy's Holiday Camp', 'Tonight', 'Trippin' On My Own Tears', 'Twist And Shout'

U

'Up The Tempo'

V

'Vertical Man'

W

'Waiting', 'Wake Up', 'Weight Of The World', 'What Goes Around', 'What I Knew Then', 'What In The ... World', 'What Kind Of Fool Am I', 'What Love Wants To Be', 'What'd I Say', 'When Every Song Is Sung', 'When You Wish Upon A Star', 'Where Did Our Love Go', 'Whiskey And Soda', 'Whispering Grass (Don't Tell The Trees)', 'White Christmas', 'Who Needs A Heart', 'Wine, Women And Loud Happy Songs', 'Wings', 'Winter Wonderland', 'The Wishing Book', 'With A Little Help From My Friends', 'Without Her', 'Without Understanding', 'Woman Of The Night', 'Wrack My Brain', 'Write One For Me'

Y

'Yellow Submarine', 'You Always Hurt The One You Love', 'You And Me (Babe)', 'You Belong To Me', 'You Can't Fight Lightning', 'You Don't Know Me At All', 'You Know It Makes Sense', 'You Never Know', 'You Were Great, How Was I', 'You Better Move On', 'You're Sixteen', 'You've Got A Nice Way'

Ringo also backed the various musicians of his All-Starr Band who presented their hits during Ringo's tours. As there were several All-Starr band albums, here are most of the tracks on which Ringo backed his musicians:

Randy Bachman: 'No Sugar Tonight', 'Takin' Care Of Business', 'You Ain't Seen Nothing Yet'.

Gary Brooker: 'A Salty Dog', 'A Whiter Shade Of Pale', 'The Angler', 'Conquistador', 'The Devil Came From Kansas', 'Homburg', 'Power Failure', 'Whiskey Train'.

Jack Bruce: 'I Feel Free', 'Sunshine Of Your Love', 'Theme From An Imaginary Western', 'White Room'.

Tim Cappello: 'Wiggle'.

Eric Carmen: 'All By Myself', 'Boats Against The Current', 'Go All The Way', 'Hungry Eyes'.

Felix Cavaliere: 'Good Lovin'', 'Groovin'', 'People Got To Be Free'.

Clarence Clemons: 'Quarter To Three', 'You're A Friend Of Mine'.

Burton Cummings: 'A Fool, A Fool, I Met A Fool', 'American Woman', 'Dream Of A Child', 'No Time', 'Stand Tall', 'These Eyes', 'Undun'.

Rick Danko: 'Raining In My Heart', 'The Shape I'm In'.

Dr John: 'Candy', 'Iko Iko', 'Right Place, Wrong Time', 'Such A Night'.

Dave Edmunds: 'Classical Gas', 'Crawling From The Wreckage', 'Girls Talk', 'I Hear You Knocking', 'I Knew the Bride (When She Used To Rock And Roll)', 'Lady Madonna'.

John Entwistle: 'Boris The Spider'.

Mark Farner: 'Closer To Home', 'The Locomotion', 'Some Kind Of Wonderful'.

Peter Frampton: 'All I Want To Be (Is By Your Side)', 'Baby I Love Your Way', 'Do You Feel Like We Do', 'Lines On My Face', 'Norwegian Wood (This Bird Has Flown)', 'Show Me The Way'.

Levon Helm: 'Up On Cripple Creek', 'The Weight'.

Simon Kirke: 'All Right Now', 'Shooting Star'.

Nils Lofgren: 'Bein' Angry', 'Believe', 'Just A Little', 'Shine Silently', 'Valentine', 'Walkin' Nerve'.

Billy Preston: 'Get Back', 'Nothing From Nothing'

Todd Rundgren: 'Bang The Drum All Day', 'Black Maria', 'Cliché', 'Hammer In My Heart', 'I Saw The Light', 'Love Of The Common Man', 'Mercy, Mercy Me', 'One World', 'There Goes My Inspiration', 'What's Going On', 'The Wheel', 'You've Got To Hide Your Love Away'.

Timothy B. Schmit: 'I Can't Tell You Why', 'Keep On Tryin''.

Joe Walsh: 'Desperado', 'The Friend Song', 'In The City', 'Indian Summer', 'Life In The Fast Lane', 'Look At Us Now', 'Meadows', 'Pretty Maids All In A Row', 'Rocky Mountain Way', 'Vote For Me', 'The Way I Am'.

Ring O' Records

Ringo formed a company called Beachport Co Ltd in 1970 and in 1973 formed a music publishing company, Wobble Music. The following year, on 28 June, he formed another company called Reckongrade Ltd and, in December of that year, he changed its name to Pyramid Records Ltd. On 4 April 1975 the formation of Ring O' Records was announced, together with a deal with Polydor Records, who issued the following press statement:

'Ringo was always the most business-minded of the Beatles, and was the only one of the Fab Four to make regular appearances at the Apple Headquarters in London's Savile Row. It wasn't only the Apple Scruffs (girls whose lives centred around the Apple company and the Beatles and who were immortalised by George in his song of the same name on the *All Things Must Pass* triple LP) that gave Ringo an incentive to turn up on time, but also the excitement which he found in being an integral part of the office, and in making decisions which affected the running of the company.

'So it wasn't too surprising that after several very successful solo albums which followed the break-up of the Beatles he should want to provide an outlet not only for his own creations, but also for the 'discoveries' that he had made whilst recording.

'The plans for the new label, called appositely "Ring O' Records" (please note the Irish spelling – it is very important) cater mostly for the happy-go-lucky type of music which Ringo himself records, and will concentrate mainly on singles rather than albums. It is to be a commercially minded enterprise, but keeping assured business success always firmly in mind.

'Curiously enough, the first product to appear on the label fits into neither of these categories, but is a sophisticated synthesized version of Ringo's album called simply *Ringo*. It is performed by David Hentschel, the wizard responsible for much of the synthesizer work on albums from such 'heavies' as Elton John, Paul McCartney, Nilsson and others. But then again, this recording points out the flexibility of the label and shows that it allows for a varied and exciting roster of international acts.'

Ring O' Records lasted in an active role for three years, during which a total of eleven artists were signed and fifteen singles and five albums were issued. Four further singles and three albums remained unreleased.

The artists signed to the label included: David Hentschel, Bobby Keys, Carl Grossman, Colonel, Graham Bonnet, Suzanne, Dirk and Stig, Johnny Warman, Stormer and Rab Noakes.

Ringo (album)

Ringo's third album, issued in Britain on Apple PCTC 252 on 9 November 1973, where it reached No. 6 in the charts. It was issued in America on Apple SWAL 3413 on 2 November 1973 and reached the No. 2 position.

It was recorded between March and July 1973, mainly at Sunset Sound in Los Angeles and Apple Studios, although there was some additional recording at Burbank Studios, Sounds Lab and Producer's Workshop, all in Los Angeles, and Abbey Road Studios.

Richard Perry produced it and the musicians who performed on the album were: Ringo Starr, lead vocals and drums; John Lennon, piano; George Harrison, guitar; Paul McCartney, mouth-sax solo, piano and synthesizer; Klaus Voormann, bass and upright bass; Billy Preston, organ and piano; Jim Keltner, drums; Marc Bolan, guitar; James Booker, piano; Milt Holland, percussion; Tom Scott, horns and saxophones; Nicky Hopkins, piano; Vini Poncia, acoustic guitar and percussion; Jimmy Calvert, guitar and acoustic guitar; Robbie Robertson, guitar; Levon Helm, mandolin; Rick Danko, fiddle; David Bromberg, fiddle and banjo; Garth Hudson, accordion; Steve Cropper, electric guitar; Chuck Findley, horns; and Tom Hensley, piano.

Within the gatefold sleeve was a 24-page book illustrated with 10 lithographs by Klaus Voormann. Tom Bruckner did the cover painting, which depicted a stage with a crowd of the musicians who appeared on the album.

The tracks were: Side One: 'I'm The Greatest', 'Have You Seen My Baby', 'Photograph', 'Sunshine Life for Me (Sail Away Raymond)', 'You're Sixteen'. Side Two: 'Oh My My', 'Step Lightly', 'Six O'Clock', 'Devil Woman', 'You And Me (Babe)'.

It was re-issued in Britain as a budget album on Music for Pleasure MFP 50508 on 27 November 1980 and in America on Capitol SN-16114 in October 1980.

'It Don't Come Easy' and 'Early 1970' were bonus tracks on the *Ringo* CD, issued in Britain on Parlophone CDP 7 95884 2 on 4 March 1991 and in America on Capitol CDP 7 95637 2 on 7 May 1991.

Ringo (television special)

A television special first screened in America on NBC on 26 April 1978, shortly before his *Bad Boy* album release. The film is a loose adaptation of Mark Twain's *The Prince And The Pauper* story (about a prince and a commoner who change places), written by Neil Israel and Pat Proffe.

It begins with George Harrison telling a press conference about two babies born at the very same moment in Britain: 'Remarkably, both children, though born of different parents, look exactly alike.'

One of the children was brought to America; the other remained in Britain and achieved fame as Ringo Starr. Ringo is in a car with four girls, as a motorcycle escort takes him past screaming fans. We hear him singing 'Back Off Boogaloo'.

George points out that fortune didn't smile on the other baby, who became known as Ognir Rats. We see Ognir selling maps outside Hollywood stars' homes. Some nuns ask him if he has maps to the homes of Jill St John, Susan St James, and Peter, Paul and Mary, then a carload of blond surfers call him a nerd and run over his sandwich board.

He daydreams about success, and then sets off for home, climbing into his room by ladder. His father (Art Carney), a 'cruel, vicious, mean' man, comes in and takes all his money off him, not even leaving him enough to take his girlfriend on a date that night.

Meanwhile, Ringo is in the studio playing drums. He takes a break and his manager Marty (John Ritter) tells him of the satellite concert, a forty-city tour, autographs to sign ... and the pressure is evident. Ringo says he needs some time to himself. Granted a few minutes break, he goes to the door and notices Ognir in the street. He calls him over and they begin to chat. To the tune of 'Yellow Submarine', they enter a fantasy sequence peopled by dancers in golden costumes.

Ringo talks Ognir into changing places with him and then sets off for Hollywood Boulevard, where he pays a youth a fistful of dollars in exchange for the loan of his car.

Ognir's girlfriend Markene (Carrie Fisher) spots Ringo and gets into the car. He sings 'You're Sixteen' to a scene which combines live action and animation (by Linda Taylor). Ognir's father sees them parked in the car, mistakes Ringo for Ognir and hauls him out, accusing him of stealing the vehicle. He locks him in his room and calls the police.

While in the room, Ringo watches the *Mike Douglas Show* and sees Ognir make a mess of it, knocking down a table, chairs and a mic and tapping away at the cymbals when he's supposed to play a number.

'He's going to ruin my reputation,' wails Ringo. He then crawls out of the window, but a policewoman (Angie Dickinson) is waiting for him and he's dragged off to the cop shop.

At the police station, two cops argue about the photographs Ringo's just had taken, which gives him the opportunity to escape. He bumps into Markene and tells her they must go to the concert. They rummage in some trash cans and he puts on a disguise.

Meanwhile, Marty has brought along a hypnotist (Vincent Price) to examine his client. The doctor puts Ognir into a trance and he imagines he is in a Hall of Fame with stars such as Roy Orbison, Johnny Ray, Jerry Lee Lewis, Chuck Berry, Elvis, Buddy Holly and Hank Williams. In a smoky tunnel, illuminated with laser light, Ognir sings 'With A Little Help From My Friends' and comes out of the trance believing he is Ringo.

He goes onto the stage, but the hypnotist makes an unconscious gesture, which brings him out of the trance, and he becomes Ognir again. The real Ringo arrives with Markene to save the day and he goes on stage to perform 'Heart On My Sleeve' and 'Hard Times'. The screen then darkens until a single star is illuminated. Ringo, dressed in white, walks on and sings 'A Man Like Me'. Backstage all is well and Ringo offers Ognir a job as his road manager.

The special was finally screened in Britain on Channel Four five years later on 2 January 1983.

Ringo And His New All-Starr Band

An album (lasting 73 minutes 58 seconds) recorded live at the Rosemont Theater, Chicago, on 22 August 2001. It was released by King Biscuit Flower Hour Records on Razor & Tie 79301 88003-2 on 2 August 2002.

The executive producers were Ringo and David Fishof, it was recorded, mixed and mastered by Glen Robinson and AFG Communications designed the cover.

The musicians were Ringo Starr, vocals, drums; Roger Hodgson, vocals, guitar, keyboards; Ian Hunter, vocals, guitar; Greg Lake, vocals, bass; Howard Jones, vocals, keyboards; Sheila E, vocals, drums, percussion; and Mark Rivera, saxophone.

The tracks were: 'Photograph', 'Act Naturally', 'Logical Song', 'No One Is To Blame', 'Yellow Submarine', 'Give A Little Bit', 'You're Sixteen', 'No No Song', 'Back Off Boogaloo', 'Glamorous Life', 'I Wanna Be Your Man', 'Lucky Man', 'Take The Long Way Home', 'All The Young Dudes', 'Don't Go Where The Road Don't Go' and 'With A Little Help From My Friends'.

Ringo In Nashville

The title of two 12″ discs that were auctioned at Sotheby's, London, on 27 August 1992. They were from the Mal Evans collection and the acetates were from Ringo's Nashville sessions of *Beaucoups Of Blues,* containing some alternative versions of the tracks, a different running order and a track that was recorded on 26 June 1970 but wasn't used, 'The Wishing Book'.

Ringo Invasion

The title of an appearance by Ringo and his band on ABC's *The View*, a programme hosted by Barbara Walters, Meredith Vieira, Star Jones and Joy Behar. On 14 May 1998 the band performed 'La De Da', 'Photograph' and 'With A Little Help From My Friends' live. On the last number the hostesses from the show provided backing vocals. The videotaping took place at the ABC Television Center in New York and was broadcast on 17 June 1998.

Ringo was backed by Simon Kirke, Jack Blades, Mark Hudson, Steve Dudas, Gary Burr and Jim Cox.

Ringo Or Robin Ltd

A company formed by Ringo in September 1970 with Robin Cruikshank to design furniture. It lasted until 1976.

Ringo Rama

A 13-track album issued on Koch Records 038 411-0 on 21 April 2003. It was a CD/DVD set in a slimline 2-CD case with an 8-page booklet and was Ringo's first studio album release since 1998. The CD

number was CD 038 412-2. The CD was re-released later in the year
with three bonus tracks that were originally recorded for a film.

The 'making of . . .' DVD is 41 minutes in length.

The musicians on the package were: Adam Ray, background vocals;
Barbara Starkey, background vocals; Charlie Haden, upright bass;
Christina Rumbley, background vocals; Cliff Downs, acoustic guitar;
Dan Higgins, clarinet, flute, sax; Dave Gilmour, guitar; Dean Grakal,
acoustic guitar; Eric Clapton, guitar; Gary Burr, acoustic guitar, background vocals, electric guitar, guitar; Gary Nicholson, 12-string
acoustic; Gary S. Grant, piccolo trumpet, trumpet; Grant Geissman,
dobro; Herb Pederson, banjo; Jack Blades, background vocals; Jay Dee
Maness, pedal steel guitar; Jim Cox, B3 organ, horn arrangements,
piano, string arrangements, Wurlitzer; John O'Shea, background
vocals; Mark O'Shea, background vocals; Mark Hudson, producer,
acoustic guitar, background vocals, bass, electric guitar, keyboards,
Mellotron, Wurlitzer (also cover illustration, photos); Mickey Raphael,
bass harmonica, harmonica; Nicole Renee Harris, background vocals;
Paul Santo, bass, electric guitar; Ringo Starr, acoustic guitar, background vocals, bass, drum, electric guitar, keyboards, lead vocals,
megamouth, percussion, slide guitar, producer, photos; Roy Orbison,
mercy growl (by permission of Barbara Orbison); Sarah Hudson, background vocals; Shawn Colvin, guest vocal; Sophia Sunseri, background
vocals; Steve Dudas, bass, electric guitar, guitar; Timothy B. Schmit,
background vocals; Van Dyke Parks, accordion; Victoria Shaw, background vocals; Willie Nelson, guest vocal.

The first single from the album was 'Never Without You', a tribute
to George Harrison featuring a guitar solo by Clapton. Ringo said,
'The song is my way to say – be remembered. I wanted Eric to come
and play that solo because I only wanted people on the track who
George knew and loved.'

Ringo, Mark Hudson and Gary Nicholson produced the album at
Ringo's Rocca Bella studio in England and Mark's Whatinthewhatthe?
Studios in Santa Monica.

The first 100,000 copies of the album, issued in America on Koch
KOC CD 8429, included a limited-edition bonus DVD which featured
over 49 minutes of interviews with Ringo and the Roundheads, and
footage of the recording sessions with Willie Nelson, David Gilmour,
Eric Clapton and Shawn Colvin at Mark Hudson's compact Los
Angeles studio and Ringo's unfinished studio in Britain.

The documentary was co-directed by Ringo, Mark Hudson and
Brent Carpenter and also features the lyrics for the songs.

On the album Ringo was backed by his Roundheads, plus several
guests, including Eric Clapton, Willie Nelson, David Gilmour, Van
Dyke Parks and Shawn Colvin.

The record company issued a special press release penned by David
Wild, which read:

KOCH ENTERTAINMENT PROUDLY ANNOUNCES THE MARCH 25 RELEASE OF RINGO STARR'S RINGO RAMA.

Ultimately what's the most impressive about Ringo Starr isn't what he's been, but rather who he is. And with his wonderfully infectious and intimate new album *Ringo Rama*, Starr and his close-knit team of collaborators have created a characteristically charming reflection of who Ringo Starr is in the present tense.

The man's great heart and soul, his wit and wisdom all come through loud and clear throughout *Ringo Rama*.

'There is a lot more of me in these songs,' Starr says. 'As time goes on, my personality is coming out more and more in the music. That's just what happens. On this album my drumming is more dynamic, I'm more to the front, I think I'm singing better and I believe we're writing better songs. All the touring helps because then you're keeping your chops up. I suppose I had a long time off and now I've had a long time on.'

A grown-up thrill ride, *Ringo Rama* lovingly and at times movingly celebrates yesterday and today. This is a song cycle that appropriately acknowledges the former Beatle's illustrious past but at the same time powerfully insists on the paramount important of living and loving here and now.

Ringo Rama would be a fine album without any of its back story. Yet coming from Starr, it feels in a sense like the album of a lifetime. Ever since cleaning up his own act at the end of the eighties, Starr started touring with his assorted All-Starr bands and recording a series of impressive albums that at long last made good on the tremendous promise of his early post-Beatles efforts.

'I had a great cycle with *Ringo* (1973) and *Goodnight Vienna* (1974) and then it all went downhill,' Starr admits. 'And then from the time of *Time Takes Time* (1992), we started climbing back up the hill. And since then they're all just getting better.'

The rock-steady drummer is excited to find himself in such a healthy and extended musical groove. 'I've said this over and over again, but I love being in a band,' Starr explains. 'And I love hanging out with a crowd of musicians. And that's what we are and that's what we do. We write them and we record them.'

For *Ringo Rama* the 'we' of which Starr speaks is a fine group of fellow travellers that includes producer Mark Hudson, and writer/players like Gary Burr, Dean Grakal, Steve Dudas, Jim Cox and Gary Nicholson. There are also some notable guest appearances from old friends like Eric Clapton, David Gilmour, Willie Nelson, Shawn Colvin, Timothy B. Schmit, Van Dyke Parkes and Charlie Haden.

The album was recorded largely at Starr's English studio, with a few tracks cut at producer Hudson's tiny studio in Los Angeles.

'I refuse to go into a so-called "real", stuffy studio anymore,'

Starr says. 'I like to see us all sweat together and feel the music together.'

Starr credits producer Hudson with helping to create an ideal atmosphere to work and play.

'Mainly we have a lot of laughs,' he explains. 'It's just a lot of fun working together. And we can shout at each other without us getting really hurt and leaving the room. Sometimes it gets a bit tense in the studio, but Mark brings a lot of love, a lot of musical talent and a lot of diplomacy within the group in terms of holding us together. We have a team and we hang out. And it just matters how many of us are in the room, how many write the song. It's whatever comes up at that minute. It's not all so pre-planned.'

The spontaneous, positive spirit at the heart of Starr's work since his days with the Beatles is very much in evidence on *Ringo Rama*, right from the aggressively peaceful first track 'Eye To Eye', with its opening allusions to Starr's own first solo smash, 1971's 'It Don't Come Easy'. Like several other tracks on the album, 'Eye To Eye' represents an impassioned cry for peace and love in tense, even traumatic times.

'To me "Eye To Eye" sounds like there's a war going on and we're trying to make it a war of love,' Starr offers. 'I know it's easy to say, but we're trying our best to see eye to eye because then the world would be a better place. With me, the mission all the time is the same – peace and love and four guys sitting around a room writing songs of love.'

Another standout on *Ringo Rama* is a love song of a different sort, 'Never Without You' – a luminous, deeply felt tribute to Starr's friend and former bandmate George Harrison. 'It was my way – with the help of Gary and Mark – to say how much George meant to me and how much he will be remembered,' he says softly. 'Gary Nicholson started that song, and Mark brought it over and we realised we could tailor it. George was really on my mind then. I actually tried to get George, John Lennon and Harry Nilsson all into that song. But it got too busy, so I thought I'm just going to do it for George.'

To play the moving guitar solo for 'Never Without You', Starr reached out to another guitar great and close friend of Harrison.

'I called Eric Clapton up and it was great to have him,' Starr says. 'Eric's on two tracks on the album, but I really wanted him on this song because George loved Eric and Eric loved George. I wanted Eric to come and play the solo because I only wanted people on the track who George knew and loved.'

Another major guitar player, Dave Gilmour of Pink Floyd fame, appears on the wryly philosophical tune 'I Think Therefore I Rock & Roll' and 'Missouri Loves Company'.

For the record, Starr points out that both of these legendary players were not only inspired but also convenient.

'We had a funny joke over here,' Starr recalls from his home in England, 'People would ask, "So who's on the record?" and we'd say, "Just a couple of local guys. You know, like Eric Clapton and Dave Gilmour." Because they do both live just around the corner.'

Certain [songs on] *Ringo Rama* – like 'English Garden' and 'Elizabeth Reigns' – reflect the album's British origins.

'"Elizabeth Reigns" was because when we were recording here the Queen's Jubilee was going on, and there was this big party where Paul played and lots of other bands too. And it was so in your face. And our American "cousins" who were staying with me at the time – namely everyone in the band on the record – were so excited about it all. Dean Grakal started the song. And because I thought they've had their day in all honesty myself, I had to put in that verse, "Six hundred servants/Use her detergents/Scrubbing the Palace floor". Elizabeth was the last of the great ones, and like the song says, "we don't really need a king".'

Even closer to home is 'English Garden', which references Ringo's beloved wife Barbara and even the family dog Buster. As befits an album created by a bunch of Brits and Americans, *Ringo Rama* also features songs with a decidedly American feel.

A lifelong country music lover – witness his classic cover with the Beatles of Buck Owens's 'Act Naturally' and his 1970 *Beaucoup Of Blues* album – Starr shines on the country-tinged 'Write One For Me' which features a strong vocal assist from the one and only Willie Nelson.

'That one was done long-distance because I was in England and Willie was touring America,' Starr explains. 'But I've met Willie time and time again, and he's a beautiful human being. He's a gentleman who's open to everything – an incredible man.'

The hilarious and lovely 'Missouri Loves Company' is an excellent, pun-filled road trip of a pop song.

'We love the double entendre of the thing,' Starr says with a warm laugh. 'For me I wanted it to be a kind of travelogue around America. America is still very romantic to me. Route 66 is very romantic to me too. That's sort of where I came into this thing with Chuck Berry.' And the King of Rock & Roll himself is name-checked in 'Memphis In Your Mind'.

'I Think Therefore I Rock & Roll' is another stirring testament to the importance of music in Starr's life.

'It's about rock'n'roll, the blues, just music really,' Starr explains. 'I love music. I still listen to it. I don't actually listen to that much of what's going on, though you can't doubt Coldplay. I love bands, but I'm not into all these bands from reality shows put together on TV. They haven't put in the time and the energy for it. That stuff is all a bit instant and it sounds a bit instant. In fact, you blink and you've missed them. I do love Eminem. I love that groove he always has and his writing has so much humour.'

Finally, just between friends, there's a bonus track at the end of *Ringo Rama*.

'We used to have quite a bit of those little tags on the Beatles albums,' Starr remembers. 'We'd throw a little something in. So I suppose it's part of that.'

This time around, Starr's parting shot of love and peace is the short but sweet 'I Really Love Her', which he recorded all on his own. 'Just one time in my career, I wanted to do it all,' he says, laughing. 'I'm tired of all my other mates doing everything. So I thought, "OK, I'm going to do it all." So that was a lot of fun for me.'

The inspired fun of *Ringo Rama* is likely to spread this summer when Starr takes the latest set of All-Starrs out on the road. 'We're going to live again this year,' Starr says. 'And I promised our promoter David Fishof that I'll play three new songs. So get ready.'

Koch Entertainment re-released *Ringo Rama* in a special Deluxe three-disc set on 11 November 2003. Their press release read:

'Koch Entertainment is pleased to announce the November 11 2003 re-release of *Ringo Rama*, Ringo Starr's first new studio album in over six years. Upon its release in March of 2003, the CD was universally hailed as one of the drummer's best studio albums in over two decades. *Rolling Stone* called it "his best work since 1973's hit-filled *Ringo*" and the *New York Post* proclaimed "Ringo's best album since the Beatles shattered".

'Hitting stores just one week prior to the Beatles' *Let It Be . . . Naked* release, *Ringo Rama* Deluxe has been upgraded to include: three new bonus tracks ('OK Ray', 'I'm Home' and a re-mixed/re-mastered version of 'Blink'), a full-fledged 40-minute interview disc hosted by Jody Denberg of KGSR/Austin and a 70-minute DVD which includes the original *Ringo Rama* sessions with Eric Clapton, David Gilmour, Timothy B. Schmit, Shawn Colvin, the Roundheads etc., plus 20 minutes of new footage from the making of the 'Never Without You' video with extensive commentary by the man himself. The aforementioned rarely seen video is also included here within and features a performance clip of Ringo and the Roundheads mixed in with classic Beatles footage in this moving tribute to George Harrison. Furthermore, *Ringo Rama* Deluxe will also feature completely revamped artwork and will come in a beautiful deluxe soft-digi-pack.'

Ringo Rama Land

A 41-minute DVD documentary on the making of the *Ringo Rama* album with Ringo, Mark Hudson and the Roundheads, plus guest stars such as Dave Gilmour, Eric Clapton and Willie Nelson. It showed them working on the album in Los Angeles and Ringo's home studio in England. It was co-directed by Ringo and Brent Carpenter and also features the lyrics to the songs.

Ringo Starr And His All-Starr Band – The Anthology . . . So Far

A three-CD set featuring highlights from the All-Starr Band from 1989 to 2000, issued by Eagle Records on EEECDO11 on 5 February 2001.

Disc One: 'It Don't Come Easy' (Ringo), 'No No Song' (Ringo), 'Iko Iko' (Dr John), 'The Weight' (Levon Helm), 'Shine Silently' (Nils Lofgren), 'Honey Don't' (Ringo), 'Quarter To Three' (Clarence Clemons), 'Raining In My Heart' (Rick Danko), 'Will It Go Round In Circles' (Billy Preston), 'Life In The Fast Lane' (Joe Walsh), 'Desperado' (Joe Walsh), 'Norwegian Wood' (Peter Frampton), 'Walking Nerve' (Nils Lofgren), 'Boris The Spider' (John Entwistle), 'You're Sixteen' (Ringo), 'Photograph' (Ringo).

Disc Two: The Really Serious Introduction (Ringo), 'I'm The Greatest' (Ringo), 'Don't Go Where The Road Don't Go' (Ringo), 'I Can't Tell You Why' (Timothy B. Schmit), 'Girls Talk' (Dave Edmunds), 'People Got To Be Free' (Felix Cavaliere), 'Groovin'' (Felix Cavaliere), 'Act Naturally' (Ringo), 'Takin' Care Of Business' (Randy Bachman), 'You Ain't Seen Nothin' Yet' (Randy Bachman), 'In the City' (Joe Walsh), 'Bang The Drum All Day' (Todd Rundgren), 'Black Maria' (Todd Rundgren), 'American Woman' (Burton Cummings), 'Weight Of The World' (Ringo), 'Back Off Boogaloo' (Ringo).

Disc Three: 'Yellow Submarine' (Ringo), 'Show Me The Way' (Peter Frampton), 'Sunshine Of Your Love' (Jack Bruce), 'I Hear You Knockin'' (Dave Edmunds), 'Shooting Star' (Simon Kirke), 'Boys' (Ringo), 'Baby I Love Your Way' (Peter Frampton), 'A Salty Dog' (Gary Brooker), 'I Feel Free' (Jack Bruce), 'All Right Now' (Simon Kirke), 'I Wanna Be Your Man' (Ringo), 'A Whiter Shade Of Pale' (Gary Brooker), 'Hungry Eyes' (Eric Carmen), 'All By Myself' (Eric Carmen), 'With A Little Help From My Friends' (Ringo).

Ringo Starr And His All-Starr Band – The Best So Far

A DVD issued by Aviva International in 2001. It begins with a short introduction by Paul McCartney and then Ringo takes over and says how much he enjoys the All-Starr tours and playing with such great musicians. The film contains highlights from tours between 1989 and 1997. Apart from the solo spot by Peter Frampton, Ringo appears on all the tracks, which are: 'Honey Don't', 'Iko Iko', 'The Weight', 'Photograph', 'Don't Go Where The Road Don't Go', 'Rocky Mountain Way', 'No No Song', 'Bang The Drum All Day', 'You're Sixteen', 'Yellow Submarine', 'I Wanna Be Your Man', 'Groovin'', 'You Ain't Seen Nothin' Yet', 'Boys', 'It Don't Come Easy', 'Sunshine Of Your Love', 'Norwegian Wood', 'A Whiter Shade Of Pale', 'All Right Now', 'Act Naturally', 'With A Little Help From My Friends'.

The end credits read: Executive Producers, Ringo Starr, David Fishof. Writers, Michael Drumm, Ringo Starr. Special thanks to Barbara Bach. Narrator, Paul McCartney.

Ringo Starr And His All-Starr Band, Volume Two – Live From Montreux

Ringo's second live album from his All-Starr Band. This time the line-up comprised Timothy B. Schmit, a former member of the Eagles and Poco, Burton Cummings, a former member of the Canadian band Guess Who, Dave Edmunds, Tim Cappello, Todd Rundgren, Zak Starkey, Joe Walsh and Nils Lofgren. It was recorded at the Montreux Jazz Festival on 13 June 1992, with Ringo announcing, 'I'm sure you'll remember me as an old jazz player.'

The tracks were: 'I'm The Greatest' (Ringo), 'Don't Go Where The Road Don't Go' (Ringo), 'Yellow Submarine' (Ringo), 'Desperado' (Joe Walsh), 'I Can't Tell You Why' (Timothy B. Schmit), 'Girls Talk' (Dave Edmunds), 'Weight Of The World' (Ringo), 'Bang The Drum All Day' (Todd Rundgren), 'Walking Nerve' (Nils Lofgren), 'Black Maria' (Todd Rundgren), 'American Woman' (Burton Cummings), 'Boys' (Ringo) and 'A Little Help From My Friends' (Ringo).

The press release from Ryko was headed 'Night Of A Thousand All-Starrs' and read:

> Ringo Starr and his lovable band of All-Starrs were the surprise hit of 1989's summer concert season. With more than a little help from his friends, Ringo delivered his own particular brand of nostalgic yet irreverent rock'n'roll to adoring audiences across the country. Back by popular demand, Ringo assembled a new line-up with a dream team of guitarists: Joe Walsh, Todd Rundgren, Nils Lofgren and Dave Edmunds. Rounding out the group were Burton Cummings on keyboards, Timothy B. Schmit on bass, Tim Coppella on sax, and Ringo along with his twenty-something son Zak Starkey pairing off on drums. Checking their egos at the stage door, this talented, if unlikely, band of who's who in rock turned every gig into a fun-loving, high-energy celebration, and were universally praised by critics and fans alike for their generous team-spirit and impassioned performances.
>
> Recorded on June 13, 1992 at the Montreux Jazz Festival, this disc captures 14 tracks of All-Starr excitement. Ringo anchors the set with five tracks, two from his 1992 Private Music release *Time Takes Time* ('Weight Of The World' and 'Don't Go Where The Road Don't Go'), two of his 'theme' songs ('Yellow Submarine' and 'With A Little Help From My Friends'), and one rare classic, 'Boys'.
>
> Joe Walsh contributes 'Desperado' and 'In The City', Timothy B. Schmit sings another Eagles hit, 'I Can't Tell You Why', and guitar legend Dave Edmunds performs his own hit 'Girls Talk' (penned by

Elvis Costello). Burton Cummings provides a rousing rendition of the Guess Who's 'American Woman', Nils Lofgren rocks out with 'Walking Nerve' (from his Rkyodisc solo album *Silver Lining*) and Todd Rundgren contributes his crowd-pleasing 'Bang The Drum All Day', as well as his classic 'Black Maria'. The album was produced by Ringo himself and mixed by veteran engineer Bruce Botnick, who counts all the Doors albums among his credits.

Like *Ringo Starr And His All-Starr Band* (RCD/RAC 10190), a recording from the 1989 All-Starr tour also on Rykodisc, Volume 2 is more than a tour souvenir. Ringo Starr And His All-Starr Band, Vol 2 captures a once-in-a-lifetime line-up of rock greats serving up memorable performances of some of rock's best-loved songs. Whether or not you made it to a show, here's a chance to relive a great party. As the *LA Daily News* noted in its concert review, 'Grown men aren't supposed to have this much fun!'

The two-hour home video release issued on MPI Home Video contained the whole concert and was released in America on 17 November 1993.

Ringo Starr And His Fourth All-Starr Band (home video)

A 135-minute video by Roccabella Inc, produced and directed by Peter M. Skorich, with Ringo and David Fishof as executive producers, was issued by MPI Home Video in 1998.

The video was taped on 30 May 1997 at Pine Knob Music Theater near Detroit and includes the complete show: 'It Don't Come Easy', 'Act Naturally', 'The Devil Came From Kansas', 'Show Me The Way', 'Sunshine Of Your Love', 'Shooting Star', 'Boys', 'Baby I Love Your Way', 'You're Sixteen', 'Yellow Submarine', 'Whaling Stories', 'Norwegian Wood', 'Theme From An Imaginary Western', 'Conquistador', 'I'm The Greatest', 'No No Song', 'I Feel Free', 'All Right Now', 'I Wanna Be Your Man', 'Do You Feel Like We Do', 'White Room', 'A Whiter Shade Of Pale', 'Photograph' and 'With A Little Help From My Friends'.

The band featured guitarist Peter Frampton, bassist Jack Bruce, keyboardist Gary Brooker, drummer Simon Kirke and Mark Rivera.

Ringo Starr And His Third All-Starr Band, Volume One

A live album of Ringo and his All-Starr Band performing at the Bodokan Hall, Tokyo, on 26 and 27 June 1995 during their tour of Japan, which was released on 12 August 1997 exclusively for Blockbuster Music and Blockbuster Video stores, with each store being supplied with between fifteen and twenty copies. Executive producers were Ringo and David Fishof, and David Scheuble mixed the CD.

There was a four-page booklet to go with the twelve-track album, and some dialogue between the songs.

The tracks were: 'Don't Go Where The Road Don't Go' (Ringo), 'I

Wanna Be Your Man' (Ringo), 'It Don't Come Easy' (Ringo), 'Locomotion' (Mark Farner), 'Nothin' From Nothin'' (Billy Preston), 'No Sugar Tonight' (Randy Bachman), 'People Got To Be Free' (Felix Cavaliere), 'Boris The Spider' (John Entwistle), 'Boys' (Ringo), 'You Ain't Seen Nothin' Yet' (Randy Bachman), 'You're Sixteen' (Ringo) and 'Yellow Submarine' (Ringo).

Ringo Starr Drive
One of the streets in Liverpool named after the Beatles.

Ringo Starr: Going Home
A Disney Channel documentary screened in America on 18 April 1993. It was a one-hour show filmed when Ringo was in Liverpool for a performance with his All-Starr Band.

The Disney press release read:

> **Ringo Starr Performs With His All-Starr Band And Gives A Tour Of Liverpool In *Ringo Starr: Going Home*.**

> **An Exclusive World Premiere, Airing April 18 At 9.00 (ET/PT) On The Disney Channel.**

> **The One Hour Special Will Feature Ringo Performing Nine Of His Greatest Hits.**

> *Ringo Starr: Going Home*, a one-hour retrospective special with a first-person look at the legendary drummer as he talks about his childhood in Liverpool, England, and his early days with the Beatles, will premiere Sunday, April 18, at 9.00 p.m. (ET/PT), exclusively on THE DISNEY CHANNEL. The program, which kicks off the premium cable network's 10th anniversary, also includes a homecoming and concert in Liverpool by Starr with his 'All-Starr Band', performing nine of the singer's greatest hits, both as a Beatle and a solo artist.

> In *Ringo Starr: Going Home*, Ringo gives his own tour of Liverpool, the city where he and the other Beatles grew up. His tour includes the homes he lived in as a child, his schools, and the venues where he first started performing as a teenager, including the Cavern and the famous Liverpool Empire, which is also where the concert was filmed.

The show opens with a performance of Ringo's 'I Was Great', mixed with childhood and teenage photos. Before he became a drummer, however, Ringo also worked as a waiter in the bar on a Welsh boat and as an apprentice engineer for the railroads. He claims he only took the job with the railways because he was very poor at the time and he thought they would give him a suit. 'I only got a hat, so you can imagine how disappointed I was.'

During his rendition of the Beatles' classic 'Yellow Submarine',

Ringo talks about how his early jobs added to his love of travel: 'I still have this craziness to be going places on boats and planes. I can sit in the garden and watch a plane go overhead and say, "I'd love to be on that".'

Ringo is joined by his son Jason, and stepfather, Harry, while he takes them on a tour of where he used to live and go to school. They visit Ringo's elementary school and he talks about the playground and the games he played with his young friends. As they stand outside the St Silas Infants School, Ringo happily declares, 'I was one of them, and in some ways, I still am.'

Ringo's other son, Zak, who performs as a drummer with his father's 'All-Starr Band', joins in the performances of Ringo's hits 'Boys' and 'Weight Of The World'. The Liverpool tour then continues with a walk past the Empress pub, famous for being featured on the cover of Ringo's first solo album, *Sentimental Journey*, and around the corner to his Admiral Grove home, where he lived from age 5 to 22. 'It looks the same,' notices Starr. 'It's probably 20-foot square and when I (turned) 21, we had 80 people in there. What a great birthday,' he remembers.

Now, at age 52, Ringo looks back over his musical career and his time in the limelight. 'It's just great,' he says, 'I've loved every night on stage. I love entertaining. That was my dream.' His enjoyment is clearly evident as he lends his vocal skills to a new rendition of his first No. 1 hit 'You're Sixteen', which hit the charts in 1973.

Now Starr is the drummer for his 'All-Starr Band', featuring such notable musicians as Dave Edmunds, Nils Lofgren, Todd Rundgren, and Joe Walsh on guitar, Timothy B. Schmit on bass guitar, Burton Cummings on keyboards, Timmy Capello, saxophonist, and Zak Starkey, Ringo's son, who is also on drums.

The next stop on the tour of Liverpool is at 9 Madryn Street, the house Ringo lived in until he was five years old. He describes his experience being bombed during World War II – diving under tables or into bomb shelters in the street. While taking a look at the rundown neighborhood, the concert footage picks up again with a song from Ringo's new album, *Time Takes Time*, called 'Don't Go Where The Road Don't Go'.

The performer then talks about his childhood illnesses, which forced him to live in the Royal Liverpool Children's Hospital for an entire year at age six. At 13, he also fell ill with tuberculosis, but as he says, 'It was in (the) hospital that I started to play drums.' Another personal insight into the life of Ringo comes with the celebration of his 52nd birthday with family and friends at a party given at the Adelphi Hotel in Liverpool, where he gets to reunite with his old childhood friends. Later that evening, Ringo dedicates his other No. 1 hit 'Photograph' to his family and friends, who are sitting in the audience.

One of the show's highlights is Ringo's visit to 'The Cavern', the famous subterranean Liverpool nightclub where the Beatles were first discovered. The original Cavern was turned into a parking lot years ago but the adjacent building is a near duplicate. Ringo talks in great detail about the old days, when he started out playing in skiffle bands and how he came to meet George Harrison, John Lennon and Paul McCartney, who invited him to join their band, after working with them as a part-time drummer. Ringo returns to the stage, closing his show with performances of the hit songs, 'Act Naturally', and his signature Beatles' tune, 'With A Little Help From My Friends'.

Produced and directed by Stanley Dorfman, *Ringo Starr: Going Home* is a Roccabella Inc. production, in association with THE DISNEY CHANNEL and Barron Management Ltd. Starr, David Fishof, and Hilary Gerrard are the executive producers.

Ringo Starr: Never Without You

A promotional CD, not available to the public, for the *Ringo Rama* album, including the Harrison tribute song 'Never Without You'. It was issued on Koch Records NOC-DS-8429 in April 2003.

Ringo Starr: 20th Century Masters: The Christmas Collection

A repackaging by Mercury/Universal of *I Wanna Be Santa Claus*, with new artwork. It was issued in America on 23 September 2003.

Ringo The 4th

Ringo's sixth album release, although he decided to regard it as his fourth solo album, dismissing *Sentimental Journey* and *Beaucoups Of Blues*.

It was issued in Britain on Polydor 2310 556 on 30 September 1977 and in America on Atlantic SO 19108 on 26 September 1977. Its highest placing in the *Billboard* chart was at No. 162. Incidentally, it was the only solo album by a former Beatle issued that year.

Ringo and Steve Gadd played drums. Other musicians included David Spinozza on lead guitar, Jeff Mironov and John Tropea on guitars, Don Grolnick on keyboards, Tony Levin on bass; Ken Bischel on synthesizer; Don Brooks on harmonica, Randy Brecker on trumpet, and Michael Brecker on tenor saxophone.

The backing vocalists were Vini Poncia, Jimmy Gilstrap, Luther Vandross, Melissa Manchester, Debra Gray, Robin Clark, David Lasley, Maxine Anderson, Marietta Waters, Brie Howard, Joe Bean, Dutch Helmer, Lynn Pitney, Arnold McCuller and Rebecca Louis. Arif Mardin produced the album, while the photographs on the sleeve, designed by John Kosh, were by Ringo's girlfriend Nancy Andrews.

Half of the songs were penned by Ringo and Vini Poncia.

The tracks were: Side One: 'Drowning In The Sea Of Love', 'Tango All Night', 'Wings', 'Gave It All Up', 'Out On The Streets'. Side Two:

'Can She Do It like She Dances', 'Sneaking Sally Through The Alley', 'It's No Secret', 'Gypsies In Flight', 'Simple Love Song'.

Ringo's Rock Riot

A TV series planned for the Showtime pay cable channel in America in 1987. No reasons were given why the project never went ahead, although Ringo had script approval and is likely to have rejected the scripts.

Ringo's Rotogravure

Ringo's first album on the Polydor label, issued in Britain on Polydor 2302 040 on 17 September 1978 and in America on Atlantic SD 18193 on 27 September 1976. It reached No. 28 in the American charts. Ringo recorded it during April and May 1976. Arif Mardin produced it.

Mardin had persuaded Ringo to ask the other three ex-Beatles to contribute material; John contributed 'Cookin'', Paul and Linda 'Pure Gold' and George 'I'll Still Love You'.

Ringo came up with the original idea for the sleeve, a close-up of his head with a magnifying glass in front of one eye. There was also a photograph on the back cover of the Apple door covered with graffiti. Some copies of the album came with a magnifying glass with which to see some of the graffiti slogans such as 'Give John A Green Card', 'Get Lost The Rollers, The Beatles Are The Best', 'We Love The Beatles', 'Keep On Rocking All Of You' and 'Long Live The Beatles'.

The tracks were: Side One: 'A Dose Of Rock 'N' Roll', 'Hey Baby', 'Pure Gold', 'Cryin'', 'You Don't Know Me At All'. Side Two: 'Cookin' (In The Kitchen Of Love)', 'I'll Still Love You', 'This Be Called A Song', 'Las Brisas', 'Lady Gaye', 'Spooky Weirdness'.

The title had been inspired by the 1948 film *Easter Parade* starring Judy Garland and Fred Astaire in which the word 'rotogravure' had been used. Ringo had seen the film three years previously and had enjoyed it.

A journalist asked Ringo how he'd managed to get contributions to the album from John, Paul and George. He replied, 'Well, Paul asked to write a song. I asked John and he worked on it and worked on it and eventually he came up with 'You Got Me Cooking'. You know he's really into that now – cooking! I also asked George to write one, but there was an old one of his that was never released by anybody that I always loved. I was on the session when it was recorded so, in the end, I asked him if instead of writing one could I have that old one? He said fine; it saved him a job. It's called 'I'll Still Love You', a big ballady thing.'

Ringo's Theme

An instrumental number that was performed by the George Martin Orchestra and included on the American release of the *A Hard Day's*

Night album. It was actually an interpretation of the number 'This Boy' and was played during the scene where Ringo is wandering along by a canal bank.

Ringo's Yellow Submarine – A Voyage Through Beatles Music

A series of 26 one-hour radio shows, all of which were pre-taped at Ringo's London home at Tittenhurst Park during April and May 1983. Ringo narrated his recollections of the Beatles years, accompanying the various records played.

Transmission of the series began on Saturday 4 June 1983. The final programme of the series took the form of a live phone-in programme from KLOS-FM in Los Angeles, with Ringo answering questions.

Rivera, Mark

An American musician who has been a regular part of the All-Starr Bands since 1995 (with the exception of 1999 when he was on tour with Billy Joel), playing saxophone with the outfit and also doubling as the group's musical director.

The Brooklyn-born Rivera attended the High School of Performing Arts in Manhattan and turned professional in 1967, backing numerous artists, including Billy Joel, Peter Gabriel, Simon and Garfunkel, and Hall and Oates.

Apart from the saxophone he is also a singer and plays guitar, keyboards, percussion, harmonica and flute.

He was a member of Etc, the group John Lennon formed to back him on the 'Salute To Sir Lew Grade' TV special.

It was George Travis, production manager of All-Starr shows, who introduced him to Ringo.

At the time Clarence Clemons was asked to take part in the 1995 All-Starr's tour but told Ringo that he didn't want to go to Japan and would only do a couple of dates. Ringo said, 'Well, I don't need you if you don't want to come out and do the tour,' and decided not to have a sax player in the group. Travis pressed him to listen to Rivera, but Ringo was initially adamant that he didn't want a saxophone player. Eventually, he bowed to the pressure and Rivera auditioned with the band.

Mark had been an enthusiastic follower of the various bands such as the Rascals and was so familiar with their music and that of the other musicians that Ringo became enormously impressed with his musical knowledge. When people asked advice about a musical part he began referring them to Mark, who then became the All-Starr's official musical director.

The job entails knowing the material of each of the artists, re-arranging the singer's parts if necessary, arranging for solos, rearranging the music to suit particular members and giving specific advice such as: 'OK, he can sing up to C, he can sing only up to G but he's got a great sound,' and so on.

It also involves helping to decide what the individual musicians should play, as each of them has had a number of hits and prefer some songs to others – Rivera has to go with what will make the best show. For example, with Eric Carmen he had to say that they shouldn't use the number 'Tonight', telling him, 'This is the All-Starr Band. It's not about what songs you like; it's about what songs sold the most records.' In the case of Ian Hunter, when he did certain numbers the audience didn't respond, but when he played 'All The Young Dudes' he brought the house down. Rivera also has to decide the best way certain numbers can be performed. For instance, with the complicated 'Karn Evil 9' he decided it should just be done with Greg Lake, Sheila E and Howard Jones, as the number had originally been written and performed by the trio Emerson, Lake and Palmer and he felt it should remain that way.

He continues to play with both the All-Starr Band and Billy Joel without any conflicts arising and is to be found on the albums *Ringo Starr And His All-Starr Band: The Anthology . . . So Far* and *Ringo Starr And His All-Starr Band*.

Rocca Bella Studios
Ringo's new studios in England. Once he teamed up with producer Mark Hudson, he made a lot of recordings in Mark's Whatinthewhatthe? Studios in LA and became comfortable in the tiny studios. He wanted to replicate it in Britain, so he had a similar studio built specially. Mark Hudson had hoped that Ringo would call it Whatinthewhatthe? East, but Ringo decided on Rocca Bella.

Rock 'N' Roll Fantasy Camp
A concept by David Fishof, who conceived Ringo's All-Starr Band tours. The idea was to hold a camp where participants could spend a week in a hotel learning to play guitar, play golf or listen to stories from classic rock musicians for $4,495.

'The Fantasy Camp' would feature famous musicians taking part in seminars and jam sessions and mixing with the adult attendees. Ringo took part in the first of two such Camps that took place in New York from 2 to 6 April 1997. Other musicians who appeared at the Camp were various members of his All-Starr Band, including Billy Preston, Joe Walsh, Felix Cavaliere, Nils Lofgren and Mark Farner.

The guests also received instruction in recording techniques, keyboards, drums and singing.

Rock And Roll Hall Of Fame
The Beatles were inducted into the 'Rock And Roll Hall Of Fame' on the third ceremony, which took place at the Waldorf Astoria Hotel in New York on Wednesday 20 January 1988.

Ringo and George attended, but Paul McCartney was conspicuous by his absence. Yoko Ono was also there, representing John Lennon.

Ringo began his speech by saying, 'You can sit down now, I'm going to be here for hours!' Later Ringo and George participated in a jam session with Bob Dylan, Bruce Springsteen, Mick Jagger and Mary Wilson of the Supremes.

Rockabilly Session – Carl Perkins And Friends, A

A television special to celebrate the thirtieth anniversary of Perkins's song 'Blue Suede Shoes'.

The session took place at Limehouse Studios in London on 21 October 1985 when Perkins's 'friends' included Ringo, George Harrison, Eric Clapton, Dave Edmunds, Rosanne Cash, Lee Rocker and Slim Jim Phantom.

There was an audience of 250, who included Ringo's wife Barbara, his son Jason and daughter Lee and his manager Hilary Gerrard.

Perkins had invited all three former Beatles to join him on the show and Ringo and George had agreed, but not Paul, which led Perkins to comment, 'All three just will not publicly play. There is a blockage there. There are some business reasons. And there are some reasons I don't know and the world doesn't know.'

The special was screened in Britain on Channel Four on New Year's Day 1986 and in America on 5, 10, 14, 20, 25 and 31 January 1986 on the Cinemax cable channel, a branch of HBO.

There was also a home video released, produced by Stephanie Bennett for Delilah Films and directed by Tom Gutteridge, which included backstage footage showing George Harrison and Ringo embracing.

Perkins opened the special playing 'Boppin' The Blues' and 'Cat Clothes'. Then he turns to Dave Edmunds and says they need a drummer. Edmunds says, 'Well, Ritchie's here,' and Ringo enters, dressed in his black shirt, pink tie and sunglasses. He then takes the lead on 'Honey Don't', just as he did on the Beatles recording. After the number he says, 'It's been a long time.'

Ringo and Carl are then joined on 'Matchbox' by Eric Clapton, and Ringo then leaves them as Perkins and Clapton duet on 'Mean Woman Blues'. Perkins then performs 'Turn Around'.

Johnny Cash's daughter Rosanne is introduced and Carl comments, 'I rocked this girl when she was a baby and I'd like to rock *with* her right now.' They then perform 'Jackson' together before Roseanne performs 'What Kinda Girl' solo.

George Harrison enters to perform 'Everybody's Trying To Be My Baby' and he next joins with Edmunds in backing Perkins on 'Your True Love'.

All his guests, including Ringo on tambourine, are then lined up for a medley of 'That's Alright Mama' and 'Blue Moon Of Kentucky'. This is followed by 'Glad All Over', 'Whole Lotta Shakin'' and 'Gone Gone Gone'.

The hour-long special ends with the assembled stars performing 'Blue Suede Shoes', with Ringo back on the drums and Harrison and Clapton providing guitar solos.

Rory Storm And The Hurricanes

Rory Storm and the Hurricanes were one of Liverpool's leading groups, often topping the bill above the Beatles.

Leader Rory Storm was called 'the Golden Boy' and 'Mr Showmanship'. His real name was Alan Caldwell, a former cotton salesman, who decided to form a skiffle group. On 13 March 1958, when he was eighteen, the 6ft 2in blond-haired singer opened the Morgue Skiffle Club in the basement at Balgownie, 25 Oakhill Road, Broadgreen. It was a large Victorian house, formerly a home for retired nurses, and could accommodate a hundred people. Groups began playing from 7.30 p.m. on opening night, including his own band, now called Al Caldwell's Texans, and the Quarry Men, who later evolved into the Beatles.

The police paid a visit on 1 April and the club was forced to close on 22 April. The Morgue had been open on Tuesdays and Thursdays. Incidentally, it was at the Morgue that George Harrison 'auditioned' for the Quarry Men and then became a member.

At one time George dated Iris Caldwell, Rory's sister, and he used to hang around 'Stormsville', hoping that Rory would let him join the Hurricanes, but Rory regarded him as being just a young kid. 'Stormsville' was an open house and Rory's mother Vi was always on hand to make cups of tea and bacon butties or chips for the numerous visitors, who included George, Paul McCartney, Jimmy Tarbuck, Bill and Virginia Harry and numerous others.

Rory travelled to London on 11 April 1958 for a cross-country running competition. While in London he played a jam session at Chas McDevitt's skiffle cellar, and as a result he arranged an appearance with his group the Texans on Radio Luxembourg on 30 April 1958 on the *Amateur Skiffle Club* programme playing 'Midnight Special'.

In January 1959 he changed the name of the group to the Raving Texans and their line-up comprised Al Caldwell (guitar/vocals), Johnny Byrne (guitar/vocals), Paul Murphy (guitar/vocals), Reg Hales (washboard) and Jeff Truman (tea-chest bass). Spud Ward, a former member of the Swinging Blue Jeans, took over from Truman on bass guitar and the group continued as the Raving Texans until July 1959.

By this time Rory had met Ritchie Starkey at a talent contest called '6.5 Special'. Ritchie had left the Eddie Clayton Skiffle Group and was playing with the Darktown Skiffle. Rory told him that he was looking for a drummer. Ritchie was interested in joining them and first appeared with the group on 25 March 1959 at the Mardi Gras in Mount Pleasant.

There were a number of changes to the group's name during 1959, first to Al Storm and the Hurricanes, then Jett Storm and the Hurricanes and finally, by the end of the year, Rory Storm and the Hurricanes. The new name came about after Caldwell and Byrne had appeared on a show with singer Rory Blackwell at Butlin's in August 1959.

On 11 October 1959 the Hurricanes entered a Carroll Levis 'Search For Stars' competition at the Empire Theatre, passing the various heats, and on Saturday 31 October Johnny was able to write in his diary: 'Played final and came 2nd out of 150 acts. Winner, singer, 26 points, Al Storm and the Hurricanes – 22 points (recount 16 points, but still second).'

During the group's first few years, Rory evolved several changes in stage wear and at one time they wore sunglasses and shirts with a palm-tree motif. They then donned red suits, with Rory wearing a pink suit, and Rory also got himself an Elvis-style gold lamé suit. When they appeared for their first season at Butlin's, Rory wore a turquoise suit and gold lamé shirt and the Hurricanes wore fluorescent suits.

The line-up now became Rory Storm (vocals), Johnny Byrne (rhythm guitar), Charles O'Brien (lead guitar), Wally Eymond (bass guitar/vocals) and Ritchie Starkey (drums). It remained that way until August 1962 when Ritchie became a member of the Beatles.

Despite changing the name from the Texans, Rory was obviously still fond of a Western theme – at the time there were numerous Western series on television. He decided to call Byrne 'Johnny Guitar', after the title of the 1954 Joan Crawford Western, Ritchie became Ringo Starr and Charles was renamed Ty after Ty Hardin, star of the *Bronco* series. Rory also thought that Lu Walters was a more suitable name for Wally.

Changing from a skiffle group to a rock'n'roll band caused problems at the Cavern club, where rock'n'roll was banned. In January 1960 the group were still including a number of skiffle songs in their repertoire and appeared at the Cavern on a bill with the Cy Laurie Jazz Band on Sunday 2 January. The following Saturday they were there again supporting the Saints Jazz Band and Terry Lightfoot's New Orleans Jazz Band.

On Sunday 10 January Cavern owner Ray McFall began his Liverpool Jazz Festival in an attempt to put Liverpool and jazz on the map. During that week top Trad bands such as Acker Bilk's appeared, together with modern jazz outfits, country music bands and skiffle groups. When Rory Storm and the Hurricanes appeared again on 17 January, on a bill with Micky Ashman's Jazz Band and the Swinging Blue Jeans, they began their set with 'Cumberland Gap'. Then they decided to switch to a rock'n'roll set and played 'Whole Lotta Shakin' Goin' On'. The jazz fans became furious and started pelting the group with copper coins. The Hurricanes continued the show but were drowned out by a booing audience. When they came offstage, a furious McFall fined them six shillings (30p) for daring to play rock'n'roll music. The group were able to collect all the coins off the stage, which more than compensated for the fine.

Lu Walters' voice produced a contrast to Rory's and he performed numbers such as 'Fever', 'Let It Be Me', 'Summertime', 'Beautiful Dreamer' and 'Mailman'. Rory performed numbers such as 'Brand New Cadillac', 'I'll Be Your Hero', 'Roll Over Beethoven', 'Down The Line', 'Dr Feelgood' and 'Whole Lotta Shakin' Goin' On'. Johnny duetted on 'Since You Broke My Heart' with Lu and played the instrumental 'Green Onions'.

The group appeared at the Liverpool Stadium on 3 May 1960 on the bill with Gene Vincent. This was the show that aroused Larry Parnes' interest in Liverpool groups and led to the Wyvern club auditions. Rory actually turned up at the auditions, not to perform, but just to have his photo taken with Billy Fury! In May the group were offered a summer season at Butlin's in Pwllheli in the Rock 'n' Calypso Ballroom, from July to September.

Despite the Butlin's offer of £25 each per week, some members of the group had to consider the risks they were taking in becoming fully professional. Ritchie was the most reluctant member: he was an apprentice at the time, and didn't want to go to Butlin's, but Rory convinced him.

It was during this period that Rory insisted on Ringo having his own five-minute spot, 'Starrtime', during which he sang numbers such as the Shirelles 'Boys' and 'Alley Oop'.

£25 was a huge sum in those days and years later Johnny Guitar was to recall, 'We had to decide whether to stay at home with our routine jobs or whether to throw them in and turn professional. Ringo was very much against it. He was serving an apprenticeship at Henry Hunt's, making school climbing frames. We persuaded him, when we told him of all the women that would be "available". The Stormy Tempest character that Billy Fury played in the film *That'll Be The Day* was based on Rory, but they got one thing wrong, there were far more women than that.'

At the Wyvern club auditions, which were nominally held to find a backing group for Billy Fury, but were really to find backing bands for various solo acts managed by Larry Parnes, Rory Storm and the Hurricanes didn't audition because Rory was the lead singer and didn't want his band to become a backing group to someone else. However, with his thirst for publicity, he turned up at the audition and had himself photographed with Billy Fury, looking as much the star as Fury himself.

The Hurricanes were local agent Allan Williams' first choice for a group when he wanted to send a Liverpool band to the Kaiserkeller in Hamburg to replace Derry and the Seniors, but as they were committed to Butlin's he sent the Beatles instead.

Back at Butlin's, the act began to shape up far more professionally and they were playing for sixteen hours a week.

Rory and the Hurricanes played at Butlin's, Pwllheli, in 1960. In 1962 they were at Butlin's, Skegness, where the highlight of their week was the weekly rock show in 'Europe's First Air-Conditioned Theatre' (in big letters over the proscenium arch in the Butlin's theatre).

In October 1960 Rory Storm and the Hurricanes were off to Hamburg, replacing Derry and the Seniors at the Kaiserkeller. They were paid more than either the Seniors or the Beatles.

They were billed above the Beatles and alternated with them on the daily twelve-hour stretch, which the groups had to play. Each band did ninety minutes on and ninety minutes off. They also received a certificate from Bruno Koshmider, the Kaiserkeller owner, praising them on their performance. Johnny Guitar was to comment, 'It was like getting a school report. We were very pleased. The Beatles never had one.'

It was during this eight-week season, on Saturday 15 October 1960, that the recording session took place at the Akustic Studio. Three of Wally's ballads were recorded: 'Fever', 'September Song' and 'Summertime'.

Rory also sang at the Top Ten club, accompanied by Tony Sheridan.

Back in England, Rory Storm and the Hurricanes became the star band on the first Beat night at the Orrell Park Ballroom in March 1961.

When local promoter Sam Leach decided to publicise Mersey groups in the London area in order to give top agents the opportunity of seeing them perform live, he booked a series of Saturday evenings at the Palais Ballroom, Aldershot. The first, on Saturday 9 December, featured the Beatles. The planned advertisement for the gig didn't appear in the local paper and eventually only 18 people turned up. Rory Storm and the Hurricanes appeared the following week and drew an audience of 210.

At one time Ringo considered joining the Seniors, but on 30 December 1961 he left for Germany to back Tony Sheridan at the Top Ten club in Hamburg, enticed by the lure of a large fee, a flat and the use of a car. However, he found Sheridan's eccentric style of performing too hard to cope with (he'd often change songs in the middle of a performance without telling his backing band) and returned to the Hurricanes. While he was absent from the group, Derek Fell from the Blackpool group the Executioners replaced him.

In 1962 Rory Storm and the Hurricanes toured American bases in France and appeared at a club in Marbella, Spain, before their season at Butlin's in Skegness. One of their bookings was for a one-month season at an American base in Fontenet, where they had to be accompanied by a female vocalist. They took Vicki Woods, who'd appeared regularly in Liverpool clubs in a double act with her mother. The group performed from 7.00 to 10.45 each night, with four fifteen-minute breaks. It was also during this year that Lu left the group for a while to join the Seniors.

During the 1962 Skegness season, Ringo received a letter from Kingsize Taylor offering him £20 a week if he would join them in Germany as a replacement for Dave Lovelady, who was leaving the Dominoes to complete his studies. Ringo agreed. Then, one day, John Lennon and Paul McCartney turned up at the holiday camp and offered Ringo £25 a week if he'd join them. The extra £5 sealed it and Ringo agreed to become a Beatle as from August 1962.

Johnny Guitar says that John and Paul turned up at ten o'clock one morning and knocked on their caravan door, saying they wanted Ringo to join them. Rory told them that the Hurricanes couldn't work without a drummer and they hadn't finished their season. Paul told him that Brian Epstein said that they could have Pete Best. Rory went to Liverpool but Pete Best was too upset to join the Hurricanes. Rory then returned to Skegness and used relief drummers, one of whom, Anthony Ashdown, was an actor.

Once Ringo left the band, the Hurricanes fell into a pattern of losing drummers on a regular basis. In the 23 May 1963 issue of *Mersey Beat* Virginia Harry wrote in her 'Mersey Roundabout' column:

'Hurricanes drummer Brian Johnson is joining Mark Peters and the Silhouettes. Says Brian: "Any drummer who wants to get anywhere should join the Hurricanes. Young drummers will find the group an ideal training ground – I have improved tremendously since joining them – and look how their former drummers have fared: Ringo Starr is now with the Beatles and Gibson Kemp is with Kingsize Taylor and the Dominoes."'

On 2 January 1964 *Mersey Beat* ran a story called 'The Ghost Of Ringo Haunts This Group':

Virtually every night of the week, Rory Storm and the Hurricanes perform at venues in the North. But something seems to be missing. Rory, Ty, Lu and Johnny seem to swing together, but the drummer always seems to be the odd one out.

It has been this way since August 1962 when Richard Starkey left the group.

Says Rory: 'Ringo was with us for more than four years. When the group first started, only ourselves and the Blue Jeans were known on the Mersey scene – we were the first rock group to do the rounds.'

At the time Ringo was a member of the group, the Hurricanes were regarded as one of Merseyside's leading outfits, and in the first *Mersey Beat* poll they were placed fourth.

'During the four or five years Ringo was with us he really played drums – he drove them. He sweated and swung and sung.

'Ringo sang about five numbers a night, he even had his own spot – it was called 'Ringo Starrtime'. Now he's only a backing drummer. The Beatles' front line is so good he doesn't have much to do. This is not the Ringo Starr who played with us.

'When Ringo first joined the Hurricanes (we were called the Raving Texans then) he didn't have any rings and we just called him Ritchie.

'During our first year at Butlin's we all chose fancy stage names and that's when he became Ringo Starr.'

Since August '62 the group has had a great deal of bad luck as far as finding a suitable replacement is concerned. Drummers from Preston, Newcastle, London and numerous Merseyside musicians have occupied the drum seat with the group – yet Ringo's place remains vacant.

Gibson Kemp, Brian Johnson, Keef Hartley, Ian Broad, Trevor Morais – the names of the drummers who have appeared with the Hurricanes continues to lengthen.

Without a suitable regular drummer the group can't practise or rehearse, and they can't regain the enthusiasm they once had.

But whatever happens, Liverpool's 'Golden Boy' has been on the local scene for seven years – and he'll be around for some years to come.

Keef Hartley joined the Hurricanes in August 1963. He'd formerly been with Preston's Thunderbeats. Then he joined Freddie Starr and the Midnighters, later leaving Liverpool to join the Artwoods and then John Mayall's Bluesbreakers.

Rory Storm and the Hurricanes appeared on scores of bills alongside the Beatles, particularly at the local ballrooms and town halls, ranging from Lathom Hall and Litherland Town Hall to Hambleton Hall and Knotty Ash Village Hall. Initially they were the bill-toppers, then they shared bills, then they were billed second to the Beatles. Several books about the Beatles seem to be under the impression that the Beatles got to know Ringo only in Hamburg, but they were appearing at the local 'jive hives' together and knew each other well.

Rory Storm and the Hurricanes remain a Liverpool legend and there have been no fewer than three stage plays about Rory. Cilla Black has said, 'Rory Storm and the Hurricanes was the first group I sang with.'

Drummer Dave Lovelady of the Dominoes said, 'One night at St Luke's Hall was an absolute sensation. Rory Storm came in with Wally, who had got the first bass in Liverpool. There was always a bass on American records, but we'd never seen one, and here was Wally with a Framus four-string bass guitar. The groups crowded round in amazement, and when they opened with 'Brand New Cadillac', this deep-booming sound was tremendous.'

In the first *Mersey Beat* poll, Rory Storm and the Hurricanes received more votes than any other group. Bill and Virginia Harry disqualified a number of the entries because they were all written in green ink and posted from the same place at the same time, which meant that the Beatles became No. 1 instead and the Hurricanes were placed fourth. The following year they had dropped to the No. 19 position. This was probably due to the fact that they were absent from Liverpool for most of the year with their season at Butlin's, their tour of American bases in France and their spell in Hamburg.

As befitted his local status, Rory was featured regularly in *Mersey Beat*. There were photographs of him leaving hospital with nurses after breaking a limb at a gig, signing autographs for fans at the airport, leading the *Mersey Beat* soccer team and so on.

He was also renowned for his exuberant stage act. At a 'Beat & Bathe Show' at New Brighton swimming baths on August Bank Holiday 1963, attended by 1,600 people, he twisted his way to the high-diving board, stripped to his trunks and climbed to the top board, diving as he finished the song. In January 1964, during an appearance at the Majestic Ballroom, Birkenhead, he scaled one of the columns from the stage to the balcony, slipped and fell thirty feet, fracturing his leg, necessitating a short stay at Broadgreen Hospital. While performing at New Brighton Pier, he climbed on to the roof of the Pavilion, started twisting, and fell through the glass skylight! During one of his shows at the Majestic he played five-a-side football with a team from the ballroom, the Top Rank Ravers – the result was a five-all draw!

Once he'd decided to become a singer, Rory turned professional with total dedication. He changed his name to Rory Storm by deed poll, christened the family home in Broadgreen 'Stormsville' and, when some members of his band couldn't play lunchtime sessions at the Liverpool Jazz Society because they had jobs, he formed Rory Storm and the Wild Ones to perform during lunch hours.

A superb athlete, apart from being an exceptional swimmer (he once swam the 12½-mile length of Windermere in the Lake District) and golfer (he would go round Allerton golf course dressed only in shorts and golf shoes), he was captain of the *Mersey Beat* soccer team and also ran for the Pembroke Harriers.

When A&R men began to take an interest in Liverpool in 1963, Rory and the group were among the number of bands who recorded for Oriole's two *This Is Mersey Beat* albums, and Oriole also released a single 'Dr Feelgood' c/w 'I Can Tell' in December 1963. The mobile unit recorded them in primitive conditions at the Rialto Ballroom and they missed the opportunity of proper recording facilities in a studio. However, for some reason the major record companies overlooked them, perhaps because they lacked a manager.

Rory actually approached Brian Epstein and asked him to manage them, but he refused. Later on, Arthur Howes, the promoter of the Beatles' tours, took over as their manager, but he was based in London and they remained in Liverpool.

It seemed that their luck had changed in 1964, when Rory met Epstein at the Blue Angel club one evening and Epstein agreed to personally record the group. This was a coup and they travelled to London, where Brian produced their record at IBC Studios. They selected the number 'America' from the musical *West Side Story*. As Rory explained in *Mersey Beat*:

'We first heard this number when we played in Spain. Everyone seemed to be playing it. We liked it a lot and when we came back to Liverpool we did our own arrangement and added it to our repertoire. We shortened it, used some of our own words and it goes down a bomb!

'At the recording session we played one number after another to Brian Epstein. He kept saying "No" until we played this and then he gave an emphatic "Yes".'

The B side was the old Everly Brothers number 'Since You Broke My Heart', with the vocals handled by Lu and Johnny.

The session lasted for fifteen hours and other numbers they performed were 'Ubangi Stomp' and 'I'll Be There'. Among the session singers were Rory's sister Iris and her husband Shane Fenton. Ringo also attended the session.

'America' was released by Parlophone on 20 December 1964, but didn't reach the charts. Epstein only ever recorded one other band, the Rustiks.

Ringo offered his support to his old group and gave them further chances to record, but they didn't take them. Ringo said that he'd fix for them to record whenever they wanted to, but Rory couldn't be bothered finding new material and seemed content to just play rock-'n'roll standards. Perhaps he didn't really want to make the big time. His sister Iris said, 'He was happy to be the King of Liverpool: he was never keen on touring, he didn't want to give up running for the Pembroke Harriers ... and he'd never miss a Liverpool football match!'

For a time they were joined by Vince Earl, former leader of bands such as the Zeros and Talismen. Then, in 1967, Ty Brien collapsed on stage and was rushed to hospital. There were complications resulting from a recent appendicitis operation and he died at the age of 26.

The group then broke up for a short time, before Rory and Johnny tried to revive it with three new members, but it didn't work out.

After his group had split up Rory became a disc jockey in Benidorm and Amsterdam – a strange profession for a man with a noticeable stutter. He also acted as a DJ at the Silver Blades ice rink in Liverpool.

It was while in Amsterdam that Rory received the news that his father had died. He returned to Liverpool to console his mother, Vi, but neither recovered from the shock. Rory was suffering from a chest condition and took sleeping pills to ease it.

On 28 September 1972, both Rory and his mother were found dead in Stormsville. Their deaths remain a mystery, although Shane Fenton, his brother-in-law at the time, commented: 'Rory became very ill. He had a chest condition, which meant he couldn't breathe properly. He found it difficult to sleep so he'd take his pills with a drop of Scotch, which doped him completely. At the postmortem it was established that he hadn't taken enough pills to kill himself. It had been nothing more than a case of trying to get some kip, but because he was so weak, his body couldn't handle it. He died in the night and his mother found him. She must have felt that she'd lost everything. I think she took an overdose, but I'm convinced that Rory didn't. When you've known somebody long enough, you know whether they're going to do it or not. The whole thing was an accident.'

No member of the Beatles attended Rory's funeral. When asked about this, Ringo said, 'I wasn't there when he was born either.'

Rory was only 32 years old.

Rory Storm and the Hurricanes were to become Liverpool icons, affectionately remembered on Merseyside but virtually unknown outside the area. They were the classic group who didn't make it, the favourite local group with the golden-boy singer who were left behind when the recording moguls trawled the Mersey scene.

Johnny Guitar became an ambulance driver. In the 1990s he joined Mersey Cats, a group of original Mersey bands who perform in aid of local charities, and he launched his own band, Johnny and the Hurricanes. Tragically, he died of motor neurone disease in August 1999 at the age of 59. Lu Walters formed a group called Combo, with guitarist Brian Griffiths, and later became a psychiatric nurse, while Vince Earl found success as a comedian and later became one of the stars of the television series *Brookside*.

Roundheads, The

The title Ringo gave to his band while recording the *Vertical Man* album in 1997. They were made up of various members from his All-Starr Bands and made their live debut during a promotional appearance before the media at the Bottom Line club in New York at 11 p.m. on 22 March 2000 prior to filming a VH-1 *Storytellers* programme and recording the following day. It was a 35-minute set and the Roundheads comprised Mark Hudson, Gary Burr and Steve Dudas on guitar, Mark Hart on keyboards, Matt Bisonette on Hofner bass and Greg Bisonette on drums. The songs performed were: 'With A Little Help From My Friends', 'Back Off Boogaloo', 'Don't Pass Me By', 'It Don't Come Easy', 'Octopus's Garden', 'Photograph', 'La De Da', 'King Of Broken Hearts', 'Love Me Do' and 'With A Little Help From My Friends (reprise)'.

Ringo didn't want to tour as Ringo and the Roundheads because he felt happier in the All-Starr atmosphere of being part of a band with everyone doing their solo spots – he didn't want an outfit in which he was to be the highlight all of the time.

Rudolph the Red-Nosed Reindeer

One of the Christmas standards that Ringo featured on his 1999 album *I Wanna Be Santa Claus*. Ringo was on lead vocals, drums and percussion, Mark Hudson on bass, acoustic guitar, electric guitar, percussion and backing vocals, Steve Dudas on acoustic guitar and electric guitar, Jim Cox on keyboards and horn arrangement, Scott Gordon and Christina Rasch on percussion, and Dan Higgins on saxophone. It is 2 minutes and 24 seconds in length.

Runaway

A track from the 1992 *Time Takes Time* album, written by Ringo and Johnny Warman, and produced by Phil Ramone. Ringo was on lead vocals, drums and percussion, Neil Stubenhaus on bass, Michael Thompson and Jeff Baxter on guitars, Jeffrey Vanson on keyboards and song arrangement, and Mark Hart, Craig Copeland, Naomi Star, Darlene Koldenhoven, Kathryn Coller and Mark Warman on backing vocals.

Rundgren, Todd

An American musician born in Philadelphia on 22 June 1948. He formed a group called the Nazz, whose hits included 'Open My Eyes' and 'Hello It's Me'. He later went solo, his first album *Runt* resulting in a Top 20 single 'We Gotta Get You A Woman'. Other singles included 'I Saw The Light', 'A Dream Goes On Forever' and 'Real Man'.

As a session man he appeared with numerous artists included Cheap Trick, Grand Funk Railroad, Meat Loaf, the Tubes and Patti Smith.

Ringo brought him into the 1992 All-Starr's tour, during which he performed 'Bang The Drum All Day' and when the group appeared in Liverpool he performed an acoustic version of 'You've Got To Hide Your Love Away'. Ringo often called him 'Mr Wacky' or 'Toddy' on stage.

He was also a member of the fifth All-Starr Band in 1999.

Russell, Leon

An American musician, born Claude Russell Bridges in Lawton, Oklahoma, on 2 April 1941. He toured with Delaney and Bonnie and Friends and on Joe Cocker's *Mad Dogs And Englishmen* tour.

For his debut album, the eponymous *Leon Russell* in 1969, he had contributions from Ringo and George Harrison, who both recorded their parts at Olympic Studios in London

Rykodisc

During his solo career, Ringo appeared on several different labels. Rykodisc issued his CD *Ringo Starr And His All-Starr Band* and the limited-edition CD *Ringo Starr And His All-Starr Band (It Don't Come Easy)* in America, both in October 1990. They were also to release *Ringo Starr And His All-Starr Band, Volume Two, Live From Montreux* in September 1993.

Scouse The Mouse

A concept by actor Donald Pleasence that resulted in an album and was intended to be adapted for animation, the latter being dropped due to a strike at the BBC.

The album was issued in Britain on Polydor 2480 429 on 9 December 1977 and comprised fifteen tracks, eight of which featured Ringo.

He starred as Scouse the Mouse, the story of which begins in the window of a pet shop in Liverpool where all the animals – dogs, cats, birds and fish – can speak a language called animo, which human beings can't understand. A little boy buys him, takes him to his home and places him in a cage. The mother is making a traditional dish called Scouse and they decide to name the white mouse after that.

From his position in the cage Scouse watches television and slowly begins to learn English. A musical family called the Jollys particularly appeal, and they entertain and inspire him. When the family go to bed at night Scouse pretends to be a singer.

At Christmas the young boy leaves the door to Scouse's cage open and the mouse escapes into a tiny hole in the wall where he meets a brown mouse called Bounce. The two, from their position in the wall, continue to watch the Jollys on television.

Scouse declares that he will go out into the world in his bid to become famous, although Bounce is content to remain behind. The white mouse is able to scramble aboard a ship, the QE2. He goes into a cabin where a little girl is lying on the bed. She thinks he is a dream. When he speaks to her in English she asks him if he'd like some clothes and shows him all her dolls. He picks a yellow jacket and a pair of trousers. Her parents come in and he realises she is Holly Jolly and he has come across his idols, the Jollys. They are charmed by him and take him for a walk along the deck, where he is introduced to the captain. On hearing that Scouse can sing, the Captain invites him to perform at the ship's concert. He also introduces him to the ship's cat Geoffrey.

Scouse triumphs at the concert and is invited to Geoffrey's table. Geoffrey suggests they go to the discateque. When they arrive there the cats surround Scouse, pick him up and throw him out of a porthole. As he still has his British Airwaves bag, he is able to float above the waves until saved by a sympathetic seagull, Louey, who picks him up and takes him back to the QE2 where he is reunited with the Jollys. He then arrives in New York, ready to embark on his new adventure in show business.

Ringo was Scouse, Adam Faith was Bounce, Barbara Dixon was Molly Jolly, Michael Golden was Mr Jolly/Captain, Ben Chatterly was Olly Jolly, Henry Wolf was Little Boy/Geoffrey the Cat, Miranda Pleasence was Holly Jolly (although the singing voice for the character was provided by Lucy Pleasence), Ruby Wax was the American Lady, Donald Pleasence was the narrator and Polly Pleasence was Polly Jolly. The story was written by Donald Pleasence and the album was produced by Hugh Murphy at Berwick Street Studios in London.

Pleasence also co-wrote most of the songs with Roger Brown. Ruan O'Lochlainn also contributed to some of the songs.

The eight numbers sung by Ringo were 'Living In A Pet Shop', 'Scouse's Dream', 'Running Free', 'Boat Ride', 'Scouse The Mouse', I Know a Place', 'S.O.S.' and 'A Mouse Like Me'.

Ringo later changed 'A Mouse Like Me' to 'A Man Like Me' and included it on his 1978 album *Bad Boy*.

The other songs were 'Sing A Song For The Tragopan', 'Snow Up Your Nose For Christmas', 'America (A Mouse's Dream)', 'Scousey', 'Passenger Pigeon', 'Caterwaul' and 'Ask Louey'.

Sellers, Peter

A British screen comedian, born 8 September 1925 in Southsea, England. He first came to prominence as a member of the Goons, a zany, anarchic comedy group in which he starred with Spike Milligan, Harry Secombe and Michael Bentine in a radio show much loved by the individual members of the Beatles. Sellers also shared the same recording manager as the Beatles, George Martin. When the group heard that Martin had recorded *Songs For Swinging Sellers*, they were impressed. The Beatles film director Dick Lester had also filmed Sellers and the Goons in *The Running, Jumping And Standing Still Film*.

Sellers became a good friend of the Beatles and presented them with their Grammy awards on the Tavern set of *Help!* in 1965. He also recorded parodies of 'Help!' (Sellers had originally been offered the film *Help!* but had turned it down), 'A Hard Day's Night' and 'Can't Buy Me Love' and appeared on their 'The Music of Lennon and

McCartney' television special performing his version of 'A Hard Day's Night', dressed as Richard III and performing the number as if it were a Shakespearean verse. His single of the number on Parlophone R 5393 reached No. 14 in the British charts in December 1965.

Peter sold his Brookfields house to Ringo and in January 1969 they began filming *The Magic Christian* together.

The two used to play practical jokes, such as knotting together the belts of coats belonging to the film crew. When one of Ringo's friends visited the set he couldn't figure out why there were so many sniggers, until he discovered that a variety of objects, including match boxes and empty cigarette packets, had been taped to his back.

A promotional album for the film was made, issued in America on Commonwealth United Records, which contained interviews with Ringo, Sellers and author Terry Southern.

Ringo and Peter hosted a joint party at the end of filming at the fashionable Les Ambassadors club in London. Paul and Linda and John and Yoko were among the guests, who also included Roger Moore, Michael Caine, Spike Milligan, Christopher Lee, Sean Connery and George Peppard.

When Ringo left the Beatles during the recording of *The Beatles* album, he spent time on Sellers's yacht, where he wrote 'Octopus's Garden'. On *The David Frost Show* on 6 December 1969, Ringo and Sellers performed a duet singing 'Octopus's Garden'.

Sellers died of a heart attack in May 1980.

Sentimental Journey (album)

Ringo's first solo album. He decided to record a number of old standards he'd remembered from his childhood, after first discussing the songs with his mother and stepfather. He originally thought of calling the album 'Ringo Starrdust'.

He began recording it in September 1969 and recorded further sessions during November and December of that year, finishing it off in February 1970.

George Martin produced the album and he used his George Martin Orchestra and had the arrangements for each song prepared by different well-known musicians or composers.

Richard Polak took the photographs featured on the album and the cover sports a shot of Ringo's Liverpool local, the Empress pub in High Park Street. A picture of Ringo is superimposed in front of the pub and the heads of his relatives appear in the windows.

The tracks were: Side One: 'Sentimental Journey', 'Night And Day', 'Whispering Grass (Don't Tell The Trees)', 'Bye Bye Blackbird', 'I'm A Fool To Care', 'Stardust'. Side Two: 'Blue Turning Grey Over You', 'Love Is A Many Splendoured Thing', 'Dream', 'You Always Hurt The One You Love', 'Have I Told You Lately That I Love You', 'Let The Rest Of The World Go By'.

It was issued in Britain on Apple PCS 7101 on 17 March 1970 and reached No. 15 in the *NME* chart. In America it was released on Apple SW 3365 on 24 April 1970 and entered the Billboard chart at No. 51 on 16 May after selling 500,000 copies. It rose to the position of No. 22 and remained in the Top 30 for five weeks.

It was reissued in America as a budget album on Capitol SN-16218 in February 1981.

Sentimental Journey (song)

'Sentimental Journey' was penned by Bud Green, Les Brown and Ben Homer and was originally an American chart-topper – for nine weeks! – for Doris Day, becoming her first major hit record.

It was the opening track on Ringo's album of that name, his first solo album venture. He recorded the number on 14 January 1970 at Olympic Studios, London, and the mixing was done at Abbey Road Studios on 20 February 1970. The track is 3 minutes and 25 seconds in length.

Richard Perry arranged the number for Ringo's album and was later to produce two more of Ringo's albums.

Although no singles were issued from *Sentimental Journey*, Ringo actually made a promotional film of this track on 15 March 1970 at the Talk Of The Town in London. It was directed by Neil Aspinall and produced by John Gilbert. Ringo mimed and danced to the number, supported by a group of dancers and backing vocals from Madeline Bell, Marsha Hunt and Doris Troy. The promo was screened on *Frost On Sunday* in Britain and *The Ed Sullivan Show* in America.

Sextette

Mae West's last film in 1978 provided Ringo with another cameo role. The legendary actress played Marlo Manners, an American sex goddess who has just wed husband number six, Sir Michael Marrington (Timothy Dalton). She reclines in a London suite, meeting her various lovers and ex-husbands, revealing that she has made a cassette tape of her memoirs. Various factions seek to locate the tape to discover if it contains any secrets – her latest husband turns out to be one of Britain's leading special agents – but it all ends happily.

Ringo appears as Laslo Karozny, a European movie director and one of Marlo's ex-husbands. Other stars included Tony Curtis as Alexei Karansky and veteran actors Walter Pidgeon and George Raft.

Ken Hughes directed the 91-minute film.

Ringo was to recall, 'I thought it would be fantastic to play with Mae, just to see what the legend was really like, but on the very first day of shooting I got uptight. I felt completely left out of things. But by the end of the second day I would have stayed on as long as she wanted me. She's old enough to be my grandmother, so it's sort of embarrassing to say, but she's bloody attractive. And Mae's no Garbo. Mae doesn't want to be alone!'

Shaffer, Paul

Canadian musician, born in Thunder Bay, Ontario, on 28 November 1949.

He has been involved with numerous American shows such as *Saturday Night Live* and *Late Night With David Letterman*. On the latter show he was leader of The World's Most Dangerous Band. When the show was renamed *The Late Show With David Letterman* Shaffer's group underwent a name change to the CBS Orchestra.

Shaffer recorded an album, *The World's Most Dangerous Party*, in 1993, produced by Todd Rundgren, in which there was a vocal contribution from Ringo on the track 'Mysterious Ways'. Shaffer also introduces Ringo at the end of the track 'Running Down The House' saying, 'Do you want to sit in with the band?' Ringo replies, 'Love to.'

She's About A Mover

A track from the 1983 *Old Wave* album, written by Doug Sahm and produced by Joe Walsh. Ringo was on lead vocals, Joe Walsh on guitar and backing vocals, Freebo on bass and tuba, Sherwood Ball and Kal David on guitars, Peter Bunetta on drums, Bruce McPherson on organ, Sam Clayton, Joe Lala and Jocko Marcellino on percussion, Garrett Adkins on trombone, Lee Thornburg on trumpet and David Woodford on saxophone. It is 3 minutes and 54 seconds in length.

Sheila E

Sheila Escoved, vocalist/drummer, was born in San Francisco on 12 December 1959. She began her career at seventeen and appeared in her father's band Azteca and also with artists such as George Duke and Herbie Hancock.

She was discovered by Prince in 1983 and he arranged for her to sign with Warner Brothers records, penning the title track to her 1984 debut album *Sheila E In The Glamorous Life*, resulting in the hit single 'Glamorous Life'. Sheila then toured with Prince as the opening act on his *Purple Rain* tour in 1984/5 and had another major hit with 'Hold On' on Prince's Paisley Park label.

She has also been a session musician on records for a host of major artists including Lionel Richie, Diana Ross, Marvin Gaye, Stevie Nicks, Don Was and Herbie Hancock.

Sheila joined Ringo in the seventh and eighth All-Starr bands in 2001 and 2003.

Shepherd's Bush Empire

The London venue where Ringo and his All-Starr Band made their single British appearance during their 'Second British Invasion' European tour on Friday 21 August 1998.

The theatre had sold out so quickly that there was talk of Ringo performing an additional concert at the venue the following night, but it didn't happen.

Ringo came on stage to perform 'It Don't Come Easy' in an orange and red paisley patterned shirt and his sunglasses – giving his standard peace sign. After performing 'Act Naturally' he introduced the members of his band – Peter Frampton, Jack Bruce, Gary Brooker, Simon Kirke and Mark Rivera.

The repertoire only featured two numbers from his latest *Vertical Man* album: 'La De Da' and 'Love Me Do'.

Ringo was interviewed backstage for the *Today Show*, an Australian Channel 9 programme.

Shining Time Station

The name of the American version of *Thomas The Tank Engine And Friends*. The programmes had been remade for US television. In addition to the narration, Ringo also contributed an appearance as Mr Conductor, trick camerawork reducing him to a height of eighteen inches.

The first twenty episodes of *Shining Time Station* were aired on the PBS network from 3 January 1989. When promoting the series that year Ringo commented, 'I love to appear and disappear at will and being miniaturised. That's the magic in the show. It's great to be eighteen inches again.'

In August 1991 PBS announced that Ringo was to be replaced as Mr Conductor for a new twenty-episode series of the show. Quality Family Entertainment, the producers of the show, said that Ringo was unavailable for the new series, which was to begin filming in October. The role was taken over by comedian George Carlin and Quality Family Entertainment said that it was likely that Ringo would also be replaced as narrator of the British episodes.

Shining Time Station Christmas: 'Tis A Gift

A special Christmas edition of the children's programme, released in 1990 and featuring Ringo as Mr Conductor.

Sierry Tucson Hospital

The hospital in Tucson, Arizona, that Barbara and Ringo attended during their battle against alcoholism. They arrived in America to undergo an extensive six-week treatment at the clinic. It was generally known that the couple had been having drinking problems for some time. George Harrison was to comment, 'I'm really glad he's sorting out his problems. Ringo's a lovely bloke and a great mate.'

The couple had to become involved in domestic work at the hospital, which included doing the laundry and cleaning ashtrays.

The treatment proved successful.

In May 2000 Ringo discussed this period with interviewer Tony Perkins for the ABC programme *Good Morning America*, although these comments didn't appear in the two-part show when it was aired.

He told Perkins about what he and Barbara went through: 'Well, we helped each other. We helped each other the other way, and we're still helping each other this way. I mean, it's brilliant that we both found ourselves in the gutter – not really the gutter, but, you know, down on the floor. And we both are now climbing the ladder to daylight.'

Simon, Carly

An American singer, born in New York City on 25 June 1945. Her major hit was 'You're So Vain' in 1972. She was married to singer James Taylor.

When Richard Perry recorded her 1975 album *Playing Possum*, Ringo played drums on the track 'More and More'.

Carly sang the theme tune 'Nobody Does It Better' for the James Bond film *The Spy Who Loved Me*, which featured Ringo's future wife, Barbara Bach.

Simpsons, The

Ringo was featured in 'Brush With Greatness', the second-season episode of the popular animated series, numbered 7F18 and first screened in America on 11 April 1991.

Homer's wife Marge is rooting around the attic when she comes across some old paintings of hers. This inspires her interest in art once again and she enrols in a painting class with Professor Lombardo at Springfield Community College. She gains in confidence and enters her work in the Springfield Arts Fair and wins first prize, which results in multimillionaire Mr Burns commissioning her to paint a portrait of him. She finds Mr Burns to be an ugly man and paints him with all his flaws. As a result, this humanises him in the eyes of the local population and he regards the portrait as a success.

Ringo appears as himself in the subplot. In 1966 Marge, a Beatles fan, had sent Ringo a fan letter. We now see Ringo settled in his castle in England, determined to answer every letter sent to him, with the help of his butler Weatherby. He has reached the year 1966 and sends an answer to Marge, saying that they do have French fries in England, only they call them chips. Marge has asked Ringo what he thinks of her portrait of him and he says it's 'gear'.

When Homer hears that Marge had a schoolgirl crush on Ringo he is jealous. He makes the comment, 'Who's the moptop with the big Schnozz?'

The Ringo portrait turns up in other episodes. In episode 9F21 Marge has Ringo's portrait in her swap/meet stall. The Ringo portrait is seen again in episode 4F02 (Season 8). There is also a portrait of Ringo seen on the wall at Pimento Grove when Troy McClure takes Selma there for dinner.

In episode 9F11 (Season 4), Homer is seen eating a cookie in the shape of Ringo's head and in episode 2F02 (Season 6), Lisa compares

Sideshow Bob's reputation to Krusty the Clown as 'Ringo to his rest of the Beatles'.

Singing Rebels Band, The

The name of a fictitious band in the 1985 HandMade film *Water*, which starred Michael Caine. George Harrison was executive producer of the film and wrote the song 'Freedom' for it. In one scene the group called the Singing Rebels Band perform the number in a club. They comprised Ringo, George, Eric Clapton and Scottish comedian Billy Connolly. Connolly recalled, 'The song was recorded at George Harrison's house and Eric Clapton turned up to hear us record and ended up playing on the recording.'

Six O'Clock

A track from the *Ringo* album that had been specially written for him by Paul and Linda McCartney. Paul and Linda recorded it in London and sent the tapes to Ringo in Los Angeles. Paul played piano and synthesizer and arranged the strings and flutes. It is 4 minutes and 4 seconds in length.

Snookeroo

Elton John and Bernie Taupin wrote this number for Ringo for his 1974 album *Goodnight Vienna*. Elton played piano, with Robbie Robertson of the Band on guitar, James Newton Howard on synthesizer and vocal backing by Linda Lawrence, Clydie King and Joe Greene.

It is 3 minutes and 23 seconds in length.

The single version is one second longer. It was issued in Britain on Apple R 6004 on 21 February 1975, with 'Oo-Wee' on the flip and became Ringo's first single not to enter the British charts. In America it was issued on Apple 1880 on 27 January 1975, but only as the flipside of 'No No Song', which reached No. 3 and became his seventh consecutive Top Ten American hit.

Son Of Dracula (film)

A film produced by Ringo in 1972 at a personal cost of $800,000. The original title was 'Count Downe' and it starred Harry Nilsson as the vampire Count Downe, with Susannah Leigh providing the romantic interest as Amber, Dennis Price as Frankenstein and Ringo as a 200-year-old Merlin the magician. The director was Freddie Francis, veteran of the Hammer movies, and J. Fairbank wrote the script.

Commenting on the movie, Ringo said, 'I just think that if Dracula were around today he would be into rock. We've got the whole family in this one – Frankenstein, the Mummy, Dracula, the Wolf Man, and me as Merlin. On 'Count Downe' I went through everything – casting, meetings with actors, electricians, the lot. I wanted to make the film in England because it's easier to learn at home.'

He also said, '*Son Of Dracula* has a great premise, which is that Drac takes the cure and marries the girl. I'm using all the elements: the Wolf Man, Frankenstein, Merlin, just the whole gang. It's like a non-musical, non-horror, musical-musical, comedy-comedy.'

Talking about the casting of Harry Nilsson, he said, 'The freaky thing was that I asked him to do it without knowing that he'd done a Drac photograph for the cover of the album I'd been playing on with him. So it seemed right.'

The movie tells how Count Downe, the son of Dracula, is due to become the king of the Netherworld. However, several hours before he takes up this throne, he falls in love with a girl named Amber. She returns the feeling and they get married.

It was Apple's fifth full-length movie, was filmed between August and October 1972 and was premiered in Atlanta, Georgia almost two years later on 19 April 1974.

The film didn't prove successful – yet a few years later another Dracula spoof in which the vampire gets the girl, *Love At First Bite*, proved to be a smash hit.

Son Of Dracula (soundtrack)
The soundtrack to the film Ringo produced starring Harry Nilsson as Count Downe. Excerpts from Ringo's dialogue in the film are included on the disc, along with Nilsson's 'Daybreak' with Ringo on drums and George Harrison on cowbell and 'At My Front Door' with Ringo on drums. Other tracks included 'Count Downe Meets Merlin And Amber' and 'It Is He Who Will Be King'. The album was issued in America on 1 April 1974 on RAPPLE APL 10220, signifying a merging of Harry's RCA label with Apple. The album was released in Britain on 24 May 1974.

Songs Lennon And McCartney Gave Away, The
An album issued in Britain on EMI NUT 18 in April 1979. This is a compilation of Lennon and McCartney numbers recorded by various artists. The opening track is 'I'm The Greatest', by Ringo.

Songwriting
Ringo always seemed to find songwriting difficult. He felt he could write lyrics, but not music, because every time he came up with a number, the other members of the Beatles recognised that the music always seemed to be a copy of something already recorded by someone else.

With the Beatles he managed to compose 'Don't Pass Me By', 'Octopus's Garden' and 'What Goes On'.

He recalled that with his early solo records he could only really come up with two verses and a chorus and would always give it to George to help him with the third verse. At the time he could only play three chords on a guitar.

In 1964 Bill Harry suggested to George Harrison that he should try to write songs with Ringo as a balance to the Lennon and McCartney team. George told him, 'I almost did a number with Ringo. He was playing my guitar and I had the tape on, so we tried something. We played it back fast and we had a song.'

Whatever the song was, no name was mentioned and it was never recorded – but it's interesting to see that after the Beatles break-up George and Ringo did collaborate on some songs together.

During his solo years Ringo began to gain more confidence as a songwriter, beginning with his 1970 composition 'It Don't Come Easy' which sold two million copies globally.

He also composed the flipside of the record 'Early 1970', a tribute to his fellow Beatles. Both sides of his next major chart single 'Back Off Booglaloo' c/w 'Blindman' were composed by him and he collaborated with George Harrison on his third million-selling single 'Photograph', composing the flipside 'Down And Out' himself.

His only solo composition on the *Ringo* album was 'Step Lightly', but an important step was his collaboration with Vincent Poncia on the numbers 'Oh My My' and 'Devil Woman'. Ringo seemed to work well with collaborators and teamed up with professional songsmith Poncia, a former member of Tradewinds. Tradewinds were described in their press release as 'a four-strong group from Providence', although they really only comprised the songwriting team of Poncia and Peter Anders.

Ringo was also to pen 'Call Me', the flipside of the 'Only You' single.

He teamed up with Poncia again for the *Goodnight Vienna* album on which the two wrote 'Oo-Wee' and 'All By Myself'.

Ringo's collaborations with Poncia on *Ringo's Rotogravure* included 'Cryin' and 'Lady Gaye', the latter adding a credit to Clifford T. Ward as they based it on his hit single 'Gaye'. The album also saw his collaboration with his live-in girlfriend Nancy Andrews on the song 'Las Brisas'.

Ringo and Poncia wrote 'Just A Dream', included as the flipside of the 'Drowning In The Sea Of Love' single. On his next album *Ringo The 4th*, all but four of the songs were composed by Ringo and Poncia: 'Gypsies In Flight', 'Wings', Give It All Up', 'Out On The Streets', 'It's No Secret' and 'Simple Love Song'.

Poncia actually produced Ringo's next album *Bad Boy* and collaborated with Ringo on the numbers 'Who Needs A Heart' and 'Old Time Relovin''.

The teamwork with Ponica was over by the time Ringo recorded his 1981 album *Stop And Smell The Roses* on which he collaborated with Harry Nilsson on 'Stop And Take The Time To Smell The Roses' and with Ron Wood on 'Dead Giveaway'.

For his ninth album, *Old Wave*, which was produced by his musician friend Joe Walsh, he collaborated on 'In My Car' with Walsh, Mo

Foster and Kim Goody, who were all musicians contributing to the album. Ringo was to continue this system of acknowledging the musicians' contributions on numbers by sharing songwriting credits with them. Other tracks were 'Hopeless', 'Alibi' and 'I'm Going Down' by Ringo and Joe Walsh and 'Everybody's In A Hurry But Me' by Ringo, Walsh, John Entwistle, Eric Clapton and Chris Stainton.

In 1992, for his first new album in ten years, *Time Takes Time*, Ringo collaborated on 'Don't Go Where The Road Don't Go' with Johnny Warman and Gary Grainger and on 'After All These Years' and 'Runaways' with Johnny Warman, a former artist on Ringo's own Ring O' Records.

By the time of the *Vertical Man* release he had formed a close partnership with producer/songwriter Mark Hudson. Mark had also written songs with Dean Grakal, son of his and Ringo's lawyer, and the three often collaborated. Eleven of the songs on *Vertical Man* were penned by various combinations of Ringo, Hudson, Grakal and Steve Dudas. All four wrote 'One', 'What In The . . . World', 'Mindfield', 'King Of Broken Hearts', 'Vertical Man', 'La De Da', 'I'll Be Anywhere' and 'Puppet'. Ringo, Hudson and Grakal penned 'I Was Walkin'' and 'Without Understanding' and Ringo, Hudson and Mark Neven penned 'I'm Yours'.

On his Christmas album *I Wanna Be Santa Claus*, two of the numbers were written by Ringo and Mark Hudson: 'Dear Santa' and 'Christmas Eve'.

The 2003 album *Ringo Rama* saw Ringo being involved as a songwriter on every track. From the days of the Beatles, when he had no confidence in writing, he matured and developed until he now had the confidence to rely entirely on his own songwriting talents, albeit with his close collaborators.

The main writers were Ringo, Hudson, Grakal and Steve Dudas on 'Eye To Eye', 'Missouri Loves Company', 'Instant Amnesia' and 'Memphis In Your Mind'. The other tracks were 'Never Without You' by Ringo, Hudson and Guy Nicholson, 'Imagine Me There' by Ringo, Hudson and Gary Burr, 'I Think Therefore I Rock'n'Roll' by Ringo, Hudson, Grakal and Paul Santo, 'Trippin' On My Own Tears' by Ringo, Hudson, Grakal and Burr, 'Write One For Me' and 'What We Want To Be' by Ringo, Hudson and Burr, 'Love First, Ask Questions Later' by Ringo, Hudson, Grakal and Burr, 'Elizabeth Reigns' and 'English Garden' by Ringo, Hudson, Burr, Dudas and Grakal and 'I Really Love Her', a brief one-minute love message to Ringo's wife Barbara penned by Ringo and Mark Hudson.

Southern, Terry

The American author who co-wrote *Candy* with Mason Hoffenberg. Initially the book was considered too explicit to be published in America and was first issued by the Olympia Press in Paris. Eventually it was published in America where it became a bestseller.

The novel was to provide Ringo with his first solo film role.

Southern also wrote *The Magic Christian*, which was first published in 1958. This provided Ringo with his second solo screen role (although his character wasn't in the actual novel, but written especially for the film version) and he co-starred with Peter Sellers.

Southern is one of the figures on the *Sgt Pepper* cover, and when Ringo's album *Goodbye Vienna* was issued, it had the words 'Buy a Terry Southern book' included in the sleeve notes.

Southern died in 1995 at the age of 71.

Spirit Of The Forest

A record made by Sting in 1989 to raise funds for the benefit of the world's rain forests. Ringo sang on the record and also made an appearance in the promotional video.

Spooky Weirdness

The closing track of *Ringo's Rotogravure*, a number which was ad-libbed in the studio and is only 1 minute and 24 seconds in length.

St Silas Infants School

Ringo was enrolled at the school at the age of five, but missed a lot of his schooling due to continual ill health.

Stardust

This track from *Sentimental Journey* was a number penned by Hoagy Carmichael in 1927. There had been several versions that were million-sellers and there have been more than 1,100 versions of the song (it could have been called gold dust!). Paul McCartney made this arrangement for Ringo.

Recording began at Wessex Sound Studios on 7 November 1969 and Ringo completed the vocals on 14 November. It is 3 minutes and 16 seconds in length.

Starkey, Barbara Bach

Ringo's second wife, who was born Barbara Goldbach in Queen's, New York, on 27 August 1947. Her father, an Austrian Jew, was a New York cop and her mother was an Irish Catholic. On leaving school at the age of sixteen she became a model and the following year shortened her surname to Bach. (Incidentally, Barbara was at Shea Stadium to see the Beatles in 1965.) She was a very successful model with the Eileen Ford Agency, and when she was seventeen was sent to Rome on a modelling assignment for *Seventeen* magazine. While there she met and fell in love with an Italian businessman eleven years her senior called Augusto Gregorini; they married when she was eighteen.

She was approached in the street to appear on a television show and then Italian director Franco Rossi asked her if she would appear in his television film of *The Odyssey*.

She then began her film career and her filmography is: *The Adventures of Ulysses* (1969), *Un Peu De Soleil Dans L'eau Froide* (1971), *Mio Tarantola Del Ventre Nero* (1972), *I Predatori Si Muovono All Alba* (1973), *Paolo Il Caldo* (1973), *Il Maschio Ruspante* (1973), *Street Law* (1974), *Legend Of The Sea Wolf* (1974), *Stateline Motel* (1975), *The Spy Who Loved Me* (1977), *Ecco Noi Per Esempio* (1977), *The Mask Of Alexander Cross* (TV movie, 1977), *Force 10 From Navarone* (1978), *The Humanoid* (1979), *Island Of The Fishmen* (1979), *Jaguar Lives!* (1979), *The Great Alligator* (1979), *Up The Academy* (1980), *The Unseen* (1981), *Caveman* (1981), *The Cooler* (a promotional film with Ringo and Paul and Linda McCartney, 1982), *Give My Regards To Broad Street* (1984), *To The North Of Katmandu* (1986), *The James Bond Story* (television, 1999).

Barbara and Augusto were separated in 1975 and she moved back to America. She was divorced in 1978.

Following her success as one of the most popular Bond girls in *The Spy Who Loved Me*, she was the subject of an exclusive pictorial feature in the June 1977 issue of *Playboy* magazine. Her romance with Ringo began when they starred together in *Caveman* in February 1980. In the film it was Shelley Long and not Barbara who 'got her man'.

Soon after the filming was complete, Ringo and Barbara flew to Britain. On 19 May they were involved in a road accident when their car spun out of control, smashed into two lampposts and ended up somersaulting and landing on its back. Ringo dragged Barbara from the wreckage.

She was later to say, 'He believes that if we could survive that together, we can survive anything. We then decided to make sure we were never apart again. He's the nicest, kindest, funniest and most sensitive man I've ever met.'

The couple were taken to Queen Mary's Hospital in London – Barbara had injuries to her back and Ringo to his leg. They left hospital and stayed the night at the Dorchester Hotel before flying to Los Angeles – with Ringo proposing on the flight over.

A few days after they arrived in Los Angeles Ringo announced to the press that they'd be getting married. He said, 'She's a beautiful, sexy, funny and warm-hearted person.'

The couple arrived at Marylebone Register Office by taxi. Joseph Jevons, who had officiated at Paul and Linda's marriage at the same venue, married them there on 27 April 1981. David and Elizabeth Emmanuel, who were making Princess Diana's wedding dress for her marriage later that year, made Barbara's wedding dress.

Present at the ceremony were Paul and Linda McCartney, George and Olivia Harrison, Elsie and Harry – Ringo's mother and stepfather,

Harry Nilsson, Ray Cooper, Neil Aspinall and Derek Taylor. Terry O'Neill, who had flown in from New York especially for the occasion, took the official photographs.

Ringo had had two fragments of glass from their May 1980 car crash set into the two star-shaped gold wedding rings.

The reception took place at Rag, a club in Mayfair, with seventy guests in attendance. A jam session took place at the club with Ringo on teaspoon percussion with Ray Cooper, George on guitar and Paul and Nilsson alternating on piano. The session included 'All You Need Is Love', 'I Saw Her Standing There' and 'Lawdy Miss Clawdy'.

Several months after the wedding there were rumours in the media that their marriage was in crisis. They were so upset by the false rumours that Ringo phoned the *Sunday Mirror* newspaper saying that the stories were nonsense. He said, 'Barbara is here with me now and I'm telling you in front of her that I am deeply in love with her and we are very much married – now and for always!' The story detailing Ringo's phone call was published in the *Sunday Mirror* on 21 March 1982.

Barbara retired from films and became involved in a number of charity functions, which included 'Fashion Aid' and the 'Romanian Angel Appeal'. The latter was a charity set up by Olivia Harrison to aid the orphans in Romania and she enlisted the help of Barbara and Yoko Ono. Barbara was to say, 'It's made such a difference. In one orphanage I visited, the walls have been cheerfully painted with flowers and the alphabet and there were sinks and toilets.'

Barbara also worked with Olivia on another charity, 'Parents For Safe Food' and in 1991 she and Patti Boyd set up a free clinic for addicts.

In 1993 she received a Masters Degree in Psychology from UCLA.

Starkey, Elsie

See Graves, Elsie

Starkey, Jason

Ringo and Maureen's second son. Jason was born at Queen Charlotte's Hospital, London, on 19 August 1967.

Little has ever been reported about him, unlike information available on Zak and Lee. Although he is a musician, he has never enjoyed the success that Zak has.

Jason has had two brushes with the law, the first for stealing a car stereo in 1986 and the second for possessing cannabis in 1989.

He now lives in London and in the late 1990s he was appearing in a pub band.

Starkey, Lee Parkin

Lee is Ringo and Maureen's only daughter. Parkin was added to her name as it was the reintroduction of a former Starkey family name.

She was born at Queen Charlotte's Hospital in London on 11 November 1970.

Lee left King Alfred's School, Hampstead, without any qualifications and then tried her luck at drama school, but didn't like it and abandoned that to enter a beauty school, to learn all about make-up. Although she received a diploma there, she said she didn't like that school or possible career either, and for a time had a stint working at Tower Records megastore in London.

She became the co-owner with Christian Paris of a boutique in Portobello Road, then moved to Los Angeles after her mother had remarried. She dubbed herself a 'professional party-giver and tequila-drinker' and talked her business partner into relocating the boutique, called Planet Alice, in LA. There was an official opening of the boutique, situated on Melrose Avenue, with Ringo and Barbara and Maureen and her husband Isaac attending. It closed after a year, but Lee remained in Los Angeles for a career as a fashion designer.

When Ringo was touring with his All-Starr Band in 1995, her brother Zak was also on the road with them and she attended a number of the concerts, including the one that took place on 19 August at the Greek Theater, Los Angeles. She returned to England a few days later but fell ill and was taken to a London clinic. Ringo cancelled the rest of the tour and, with Zak, flew to London to be at Lee's side. She was suffering from hydrocephalus, which is fluid on the brain, and an operation was necessary to drain the fluid away. Fortunately, the operation was a success.

Ringo was to say, 'She had been feeling unwell and the next thing, she was here. I came as soon as I heard. We were desperately worried, but she is going to be all right. She is out of danger now. Lee had the operation on Friday, and is now up and about. The best thing was to see her walking around.'

Commenting about cancelling several of the tour dates, he said, 'We have cancelled the tour. Family is more important, isn't it?'

Lee left the hospital and returned to America but then was rushed to a Boston hospital for further surgery on 16 September, where a cancerous brain tumour was removed. It was of a rare but curable type and was removed completely. Lee was then released from hospital the following Wednesday.

However, in 2001, at the age of 31, she fell ill again and returned to Boston for treatment. She had a second operation when it was discovered that the cancer had recurred.

Ringo was at the hospital on 20 October and then returned to his home in Monte Carlo.

Fortunately, the tumour left and she is fine now.

Starkey, Zak

Ringo's eldest son, born to his first wife Maureen at Queen Charlotte's Hospital in London on 13 September 1965.

Ringo and Maureen had an agreement. If the baby was a girl, then she would choose the name. If the baby was a boy, the choice would be Ringo's. He decided on Zak, a name he wished he'd been called himself when he was a youth. He said, 'It's a nice strong name and it can't be shortened – that was something I didn't want at all.'

Zak has now developed into an acclaimed drummer in his own right, despite his father's reticence about him following in his own footsteps. Ringo once said, 'I won't let Zak be a drummer,' although he did buy his son a drum kit for his ninth birthday.

Ringo only ever gave Zak one drum lesson, then told him that as he'd been self-taught Zak should listen to records and play along with him. To help him appreciate music Ringo hired a piano teacher for Zak.

When the Beatles split, Zak was only five years old. However, being the son of such a famous father was not easy for him, and by the age of fifteen he experienced serious drinking problems, which were so extreme that at one time Ringo kicked him out of their home at Tittenhurst Park. When Ringo and Maureen were divorced, this caused Zak to resent his father even more and he blamed Ringo for the break-up of the marriage.

At the age of 19 he married 24-year-old Sarah Menikides, keeping the wedding on 24 January 1985 secret, even from his parents.

Reconciliation occurred when Zak and Sarah had a baby daughter, Tatia Jayne, who was born on 7 September 1985. Zak recalled the moment when Ringo saw his granddaughter for the first time, saying, 'The look of joy on his face is one I'll never forget.'

Of his drumming, Zak recalls, 'I persuaded my Dad to give me my first lesson when I was ten years old. Dad taught me a few simple rhythms. He told me if I was really serious I should learn by playing along to records wearing a pair of headphones.'

Zak's drumming hero was not his father, but Keith Moon of the Who, a group who inspired him. He said, 'I was mad about them. As a kid I used to dream that one day I might join the band. I asked for a load of their albums for my ninth birthday. *Quadrophenia* was my favourite. I used to play along to it, from start to finish, over and over again.'

Discussing Moon, he said, 'I thought of him as a mate rather than an adult. He gave me an enormous drum kit when I was twelve. It was a big white set which was featured on one of the Who album covers. He used to encourage me a great deal.'

Over the years he formed a number of bands, including Next, Nightfly and Ice, and also became a session musician on records by artists such as Bobby Womack and Roger Daltrey.

He always regarded Keith Moon as his favourite drummer, over Ringo, and said, 'My old man's a good timekeeper but I've never thought of him as a great drummer.'

When Moon died he said, 'It was really hard to take in. He was my hero as well as a close family friend and suddenly he was gone.'

In 1979 he teamed up with John Entwistle, the Who's bass guitarist, in a group called Rock and in 1984 joined Roger Daltrey on world tour.

At the age of 29 he became a member of the Who and said, 'It was a dream come true.' He followed in the footsteps of the legendary Keith Moon, who actually taught him how to play and commented, 'I've been a Who fanatic since I was nine years old, so it's amazing to play with them, they are the best rock'n'roll band in the world.'

He'd been with the Who for six years when he played a charity gig with them at the Royal Albert Hall on 27 November 2000 with Ringo, George Harrison, Damon Hill, Mick Jagger, Jimmy Page and Martin Scorcese among the celebrities in the audience.

Ringo had included him as a drummer with his All-Starr Band on their tours in 1992 and 1995, but he missed another opportunity to tour with his father because he was touring America with the Who at the time.

For a time in the early1990s he moved to Los Angeles and shared a house with his brother Jason and sister Lee.

Discussing his father, Zak said, 'I've always been proud of my dad. He's come through a lot over the years and he's a better person now than he ever was. He's still very much a Northerner in attitude, always straightforward and down to earth. He believes in getting on with life. We're very much alike in those ways – that and our noses! Dad brought us up to believe that if we wanted something we should go out and work for it.'

After his mother Maureen contracted leukemia, Zak donated some of his bone marrow to save her, but she died following the operation in December 1994.

The following year Zak moved back to England with his wife and daughter and in September 1995 formed a band called Face with Ronnie Thomas, Gary Nuttall and Danny Burton.

Starrstruck: Ringo's Best – Volume Two – (1976–1983)

A compilation album issued on Rhino Records on 24 February 1989 on R11G 70135. The cassette version was R41G 70135 and the CD R21S 70135.

Ringo's initial compilation of hits had been *Blast From Your Past* in 1974, which was really a selection of hits from his 'golden years' (hence the reference to 'Volume Two'). The Starrstruck compilation was basically the 'best of the rest'. There were tracks from his *Old Wave* album, which had never been released in the States, and contributions from each of the individual Beatles.

The cover shot was one that was originally intended to be the cover for the unreleased *Can't Fight Lightning*, an album that was eventually altered and retitled *Stop And Smell The Roses*.

The titles were: Side One: 'Wrack My Brain', 'In My Car', 'Cookin' (In The Kitchen Of Love)', 'I Keep Forgettin'', 'Hard Times', 'Hey! Baby'. Side Two: 'A Dose Of Rock 'N' Roll', 'Private Property', 'Can She Do It Like She Dances' 'Heart On My Sleeve', 'Sure To Fall (In Love With You)', 'She's About A Mover'.

The CD contained four bonus tracks: 'Attention', 'Who Needs A Heart', 'Hopeless' and 'You Belong To Me'.

Stay Awake

An album project by American producer Hal Willner that featured celebrities singing songs from Walt Disney films. On it, Ringo sings 'When You Wish Upon A Star'. The A&M album was issued in America on 18 October and in Britain on 24 October 1988.

Step Lightly

A track from the *Ringo* album, which Ringo had written, his only solo composition on the album. Ringo tap dances while Steve Cropper plays electric guitar..It is 3 minutes and 14 seconds in length.

Stewart, Eric

An American singer/songwriter who was the opening act of the 1997 All-Starr Band's American tour, providing a twenty-minute acoustic set. David Fishof said that the artist had been recommended to them; they listened to his tape, liked it, then forwarded it to Ringo. Ringo also approved and agreed to him becoming the opening act.

As the 1997 tour featured an all-British All-Starr Band, he is not to be confused with Eric Stewart, the former member of 10cc.

Stills, Stephen

An American singer/songwriter born in Dallas, Texas, on 3 January 1945. He unsuccessfully auditioned for the Monkees and his songs were recorded by the Mojo Men and Buffalo Springfield. In 1967 he became a member of Crosby, Stills, Nash and Young.

It was during the Doris Troy recording sessions at Apple that Ringo first met Stills and the two became good friends. When Ringo moved into Tittenhurst Park in December 1969, Stills bought Ringo's previous home, Brookfield, in Elsted, Surrey. It was at Brookfield that Stills composed the song 'Johnny's Garden'.

Ringo was also to become a guest musician on several of Stills' solo tracks, including 'To A Flame', 'We Are Not Helpless' and 'As I Come Of Age', the latter song crediting 'English Richie' on drums.

Stills also contributed to Ringo's *Stop And Smell The Roses* album.

Stop And Smell The Roses

Ringo's ninth album, which includes contributions from George Harrison and Paul McCartney. John Lennon had given the song 'Life

Begins At 40' to Ringo for the album, but although it was recorded, it wasn't used. The producers included Paul McCartney, George Harrison, Harry Nilsson, Steve Stills and Ron Wood. A dedication to his former Beatle colleagues appears on the sleeve: 'Thanks to My Three Brothers.'

Ringo said, 'Barbara got me out of bed to make this album.' In fact, the original title was due to be 'Can't Fight Lightning', a number Ringo had written for Barbara after they had been almost struck by lightning.

It was his first album since 1978, and was issued in Britain on RCA RCALP 6022 on 20 November 1981 and in America on Boardwalk NB1-33246 on 27 October 1981. Although it was voted 'Worst Record Of the Year' in America, it managed to reach No. 98 in the charts.

When it was initially released in America it was also issued in a limited edition that contained a 'scratch and sniff' sleeve to enable buyers to 'smell the roses'. It was originally to have been distributed in America on CBS Records (using the 'Can't Fight Lightning' title) in April 1981, but Ringo had a disagreement with the label and looked for another recording outlet, finally signing with Boardwalk in America and RCA in Britain.

Ringo recorded part of the album at the Super Bear Studios in Paris during a ten-day session in July 1981.

Paul McCartney wrote and produced 'Private Property' and 'Attention' and also played bass, piano, percussion and backing vocals. He also played on the track 'Sure To Fall'. George Harrison wrote and produced 'Wrack My Brain', on which he also played guitar and supplied backing vocals. George also played lead guitar on 'You Belong To Me'.

The tracks were: Side One: 'Private Property', 'Wrack My Brain', 'Drumming Is My Madness', 'Attention', 'Stop And Take The Time To Smell The Roses'. Side Two: 'Dead Giveaway', 'You Belong To Me', 'Sure To Fall (In Love With You)', 'Nice Way' and a new version of 'Back Off Boogaloo'.

Capitol Records reissued it as a CD on their specialist label The Right Stuff (CAP 29676) on 22 August 1994 with five bonus tracks. The first was 'Can't Fight Lightning', produced by Paul McCartney. The other bonus tracks were 'Wake Up', 'Red And Black Blues', 'Brandy' and an alternative take of 'Stop And Smell The Roses'.

Stop And Take The Time To Smell The Roses
The closing track of Side One of Ringo's 1981 album *Stop And Smell The Roses*. It is 3 minutes and 7 seconds in length. Ringo and Harry Nilsson penned the number and Nilsson also produced it.

Stormy Weather
A number Ringo recorded for his *Sentimental Journey* album that didn't make it to the final listing. He recorded it at Wessex Sound

Studios on 6 November 1969. It has since turned up on bootleg releases.

Story Of Frank Zappa's 200 Motels, The
A 1988 home video documentary, directed by Frank Zappa, in which Ringo appeared.

Sun City
A campaign called 'Artists Against Apartheid' was launched by Steven Van Zandt in 1985, with one of his aims being to discourage artists from appearing in South Africa's famous resort Sun City. He gathered a number of leading musicians to contribute to an album called *Sun City* and they included Ringo and his son Zak, who drummed on backing tracks, recording them at Ringo's Startling Studios. They also appeared on the promotional video, and in the liner notes is a photo of Ringo and Zak taken by Barbara Bach.

Sunny Heights
The name of the Tudor-style house that Ringo bought in St George's Road, St George's Hill, Weybridge, in 1965 for £37,000. He spent a further £40,000 refurbishing it.

The property had a large garden, which had a playhouse in a tree. It overlooked St George's Golf Course, but Ringo said he had no intention of joining the golf club.

It was situated in an area known as 'the stockbroker belt' and Ringo had bought it on the advice of the Beatles financial advisor Walter Stracht. John Lennon had also bought a house in the area and it was then referred to as 'the Beatle belt'.

Unlike John, Ringo decided not to have a swimming pool, but he did have a bar installed, which he called the 'Flying Cow'. In his miniature pub he displayed a cowboy holster that had been presented to him by Elvis Presley.

He had a large garage in which were installed three cars – a Mini Cooper, a Facel Voga and a Land Rover.

Ringo and Maureen loved pets and Sunny Heights was also home to two Airedale dogs – Daisy and Donovan – a white poodle called Tiger and nine cats.

Sure To Fall (In Love With You)
A track from the 1981 *Stop And Smell The Roses* album that was written by Carl Perkins, Quintin Claunch and William Cantrell, and was a number the Beatles performed on stage early in their career. Paul McCartney sang on the track and Lloyd Green played guitar, with Lawrence Juber on electric guitar and bass. It is 3 minutes and 40 seconds in length.

Take It Away (promo)
The promo for a Paul McCartney number that was filmed at EMI's Elstree Studios in Boreham Wood on 23 June 1982 and proved a treat for members of the Wings Fun Club, who were invited along for the session. Directed by John McKenzie, the film featured Paul (bass), Eric Stewart (lead), George Martin (electric piano), Ringo and Steve Gadd (drums), Linda McCartney (tambourine) and a horn section.

Tassone, Chris
A Ringo Starr lookalike who often appears at Beatles conventions. When he attended a benefit in Canada to raise money for Ronnie Hawkins, whose son is schizophrenic, the media believed he actually was Ringo, and the story that Ringo had attended the benefit appeared in the press around the world.

Taupin, Bernie
An English lyricist, born in Sleaford, Lincolnshire, on 22 May 1950. He became immensely successful as Elton John's songwriting partner. In 1976, when he had split temporarily from Elton, he recorded an album that contained a vocal duet with Ringo on the Buck Owens song 'Cryin' Time'. Ringo also contributed illustrations to his book *The One Who Writes The Words For Elton John* in 1976.

Tavener, John
A British classical composer/conductor who was signed to the Apple label. Ringo was assigned to look after Tavener's work for Apple Records and participated in the recording of the album *The Whale* in 1970, singing on the recording, which was made at the Church of

St John the Evangelist in London, and also adding noises and percussion. He was present at the entire recording of Tavener's second album *Celtic Reunion*, made the following year.

Ringo also included some of Tavener's music on the soundtrack of his *Son Of Dracula* film.

Television Commercials

Over the years Ringo has appeared in a number of television commercials, which have proved quite lucrative for him.

In December 1986, while on holiday in the Bahamas with Barbara, Ringo made three thirty-second commercials for Sun Country Coolers. They were aired in March 1987 on primetime network TV and on daytime TV.

In 1995 he appeared on American television promoting Pizza Hut and Discovery credit cards.

He has also appeared in various commercials for Japanese products. The first was for Simple Life, which produced five sixty-second ads with Ringo, beginning with one featuring a saucer-shaped spaceship that lands in a field. A group of children then attack it with missiles, including American footballs. Ringo pops out his head to say, 'Hello. To all Japanese people: I came here to talk about the Simple Life and also to talk about my friend who was last seen here on your wonderful green planet.' He ends with a voice-over: 'Talking Simple Life'. The second commercial featured him as an inventor on a beach, fiddling around with a machine, which comes to life. Four children admire his machine and he says, 'Just finished,' and looks into the camera to say, 'Talking Simple Life'. In the next commercial he is sitting at a piano in a field with a circular object spinning above him. A group of people appear and wave at him and Ringo waves back saying, 'Hello.' He then points to the sky and says, 'Look at that.' The fourth ad sees him with children again and also a donkey called Roobat. They walk up a hill towards the saucer-shaped spaceship, which then takes off. The final ad is mainly a repeat of the first.

In April 1996 Ringo promoted Ringo Suttar, a Japanese fruit drink. Ringo is Japanese for 'apple'. Ringo was paid £500,000 for one line of dialogue involving two days work in Vancouver, Canada. Janet Thomas of Tokyo Front line, who arranged the deal, said, 'Ringo wasn't too keen on doing the ad until the half-million-pound price tag was attached. It was easy work. Two days in Vancouver with first-class flights home.'

Tempchen, Jack

The singer/songwriter who was the opening act on Ringo Starr and the All-Starr Band's 1995 American tour. He was booked to appear by David Fishof. Tempchen opened the show, with 'Slow Dancing', a former hit for Johnny Rivers, and some songs he had written for the Eagles, including 'Already Gone' and 'Peaceful Easy Feeling'.

That'll Be The Day

One of the best British rock musicals ever made, although the sound-track mainly comprised American rock numbers from artists of the late 50s such as Little Richard, Bobby Vee, Dion, the Everly Brothers and Jerry Lee Lewis – a selection chosen by Keith Moon and Neil Aspinall.

Ray Connolly, a Liverpudlian writer based in London who had inter-viewed the Beatles on a number of occasions, wrote the screenplay. The 91-minute colour film was directed by Claude Whatham and produced by David Putnam and Sandy Lieverson.

The story follows the fortunes of a youth growing up in the late 50s and early 60s who turns to music. It provided Ringo with what is, arguably, his finest screen performance. It's a relatively brief role, and Ringo only spent ten days filming it, but the character of Mike, a teddy boy who works in a fairground, suited him ideally.

The lead character is Jim Maclaine, played by David Essex, and the story begins in 1958 in a town where Jim lives with his mother. The boy's father had deserted the family when Jim was a small boy but Jim still recalls how his father used to take him out for walks in the park. In some ways, these scenes are reminiscent of the early life of John Lennon.

Jim eventually leaves home and finds work in a fairground where he meets Mike; a Jack-the-lad with greased hair and sideburns. The two share a flat, date girls together and become firm friends. While at a holiday camp they watch a rock band called Stormy Tempest and the Typhoons (which must have brought back memories for Ringo of his days at Butlin's holiday camp with Rory Storm and the Hurricanes).

Tempest is portrayed by the late Billy Fury, who was in the same class at school as Ringo; his drummer in the film is Keith Moon.

At the fairground, Jim notices Mike having an argument with a youth. Mike has fiddled the boy out of his change on one of the amuse-ment rides. Later that evening the youth and his friends beat Mike up badly, an assault witnessed by Jim. Instead of helping his friend, Jim runs away.

The film was premiered on 12 April 1973 and was successful enough to spawn a sequel, *Stardust* (1975), in which Ringo was once again offered the part of Mike. For some reason Ringo turned down the role, even though it was much meatier than in the first film. The part of Mike was taken by Adam Faith, who received a great deal of critical acclaim for the role.

In *Stardust* Mike, saddled with a limp because of his beating in the previous film, becomes road manager for Jim's group the Stray Cats (early scenes in a cellar club in which the group are dressed in black leather, mirror the Beatles' early performances). Mike remains with Jim through his days of superstardom and eventual decline until he extracts a degree of revenge for the earlier betrayal.

In the late 70s a real-life rockabilly band took the name the Stray Cats and enjoyed a degree of success.

This Be Called A Song

A track on the *Ringo's Rotogravure* album, 3 minutes and 13 seconds in length. Eric Clapton and Lon Van Eaton played guitar, Jane Getz played piano and Robert Greenidge played steel drum.

Thomas The Tank Engine

The children's television series of *Thomas The Tank Engine* had its origins in the 1940s when an Anglican vicar, the Rev. W. Awdry, began to create stories for his son Christopher, who was ill in bed at the time. The first *Thomas The Tank Engine* book was published in 1945. Rev. Awdry wrote 26 books and his son Christopher later took over, writing six more.

Britt Alcroft became the producer of the television series that first appeared on British television as *Thomas The Tank Engine And Friends* in 1984.

Producer Alcroft had originally visited Ringo at Tittenhurst Park in November 1983 to discuss the possibility of him narrating the series. Ringo initially declined it, as he felt children were more interested in subjects such as dinosaurs. He eventually agreed and signed a contract in December 1983 to narrate 26 5-minute episodes of the show. He was also given shares in the character. The first series was broadcast on the ITV network on 9 October 1984.

When the series was adapted for children's television in America for the PBS network under the title *Shining Time Station*, Ringo also narrated and, in addition, appeared as a miniature Mr Conductor.

Thomas, Guthrie

An American folk musician, born in Wichita Falls, Texas, on 6 January 1952. He actually adopted the name because he took it from his two heroes, Dylan Thomas and Woody Guthrie.

He first met Ringo while taping a Hoyt Axton television special in Los Angeles and gave Ringo a copy of his album *Sittin' Crooked*. Ringo was so impressed with the record that he contacted Capitol Records and persuaded them to sign him up. Ringo and Guthrie then became good friends and the folk artist was a regular visitor to Ringo's Los Angeles home.

Ringo couldn't play on Thomas's first Capitol album as he was working on something else, but he agreed to contribute to the second album *Lies And Alibis*, playing drums on the tracks 'Band Of Steel', 'Good Days Are Rollin' In' and 'Ramblin' Cocaine Blues'.

'Band Of Steel' was a number Ringo had written that he'd intended to use on his *Beaucoups Of Blues* album, but he gave it to Guthrie instead.

Ringo also contributed to the album *Hobo Eagle Thief* and Thomas was to say, 'One of the nicest people I ever met in the business, and certainly the most generous, was Richard Starkey.'

Three Ships In The Harbour

A number penned by Ringo. In 1998 he recalled, 'I've got a song that I wrote called "Three Ships In The Harbour" and it has forty-three verses. And at one time I gave it to Harry Nilsson to edit and he got it down to I think ten or eleven verses. But I still haven't recorded it, of course. Sometimes the day you write one isn't the day you need to record it. But you can record it later, so maybe one day "Three Ships In The Harbour" will be out there.'

Tigrett, Maureen Cox Starkey

Ringo's first wife, born Mary Cox in Liverpool on 4 August 1946.

Ringo met her in 1962 when she was sixteen. A convent-educated girl, she trained as a manicurist. She was an assistant hairdresser at the Ashley Du Pre salon in Liverpool. Soon after he joined the Beatles she and a friend chased him as he was getting out of his car and asked for his autograph. Maureen also wrote down his number plate and said she remembered the number for the rest of her life. Ringo next saw her at the Cavern and he asked her for a dance.

Due to the success of the Beatles, they began to see less of each other and by late 1964 Ringo had settled in London while Maureen remained in Liverpool. The media then began to print stories of a romance between Ringo and a model called Vicki Hodge.

Ringo was taken to University College Hospital in London on Tuesday 1 December 1964 for a tonsillectomy. Maureen caught a train to London to be at his side, taking him some ice cream. When he left hospital the couple spent Christmas together and in mid-January Maureen told him that she was pregnant.

One evening, during a visit to the trendy Ad Lib club, a slightly tipsy Ringo got down onto his knees and proposed.

They were married at Caxton Hall Registry office in London on Thursday 11 February 1965. The registrar who conducted the ceremony was Mr D.A. Boreham. Beatles manager Brian Epstein was best man and George Harrison and John and Cynthia Lennon were in attendance, although Paul McCartney was on holiday in Tunisia with Jane Asher.

Also present were Ringo's mother and stepfather and Maureen's mother and father.

The ceremony was a simple one that took place at 8 a.m. (the register office had opened two hours earlier than usual to avoid the expected crowds). The wedding breakfast took place at Epstein's house and the couple then enjoyed a short honeymoon in Brighton at the home of the Beatles' solicitor, David Jacobs.

The two then moved into a Montague Square flat, before buying a house, Sunny Heights, in Weybridge, Surrey, when their first child Zak was born on 13 September 1965. Their second son Jason was born on 19 August 1967 and their daughter Lee on 11 November 1970.

Maureen never called him Ringo, saying, 'Ringo just seems funny, his name is Ritchie.' Ringo used to say that Maureen's eyes had hypnotic power; he once made a twenty-minute colour film discussing one of Maureen's eyes.

They divorced on 17 July 1975, with Ringo admitting to adultery with American actress Nancy Andrews.

Ringo and Maureen remained good friends and he was very generous, granting an immediate settlement of £500,000, buying her a £250,000 house in Little Venice, London, and continuing with financial support for several years afterwards.

Her second marriage was to Isaac Tigrett, co-founder of the Hard Rock Café group. They married on 27 May 1989 in Monte Carlo, the only guest from the Beatles days being Cynthia Lennon. Following the wedding the couple flew off to Egypt for their honeymoon. Their daughter Augusta Burton Tigrett was born in 1987.

Maureen was living in Beverly Hills, California by 1994 and had been suffering from leukemia. She was being treated with chemotherapy at the Fred Hutchinson Cancer Research Center in Seattle, Washington. Her condition worsened towards the end of the year and doctors advised a bone-marrow transplant. Her eldest son Zak was the donor, but the operation was a failure and there were complications. Maureen died on 30 December 1994. Ringo was devastated.

Ringo was to say, 'We had always been friendly because of our children, but we had just started to be friends again when she was struck down. We were right at her bedside when she died. I feel blessed that I was there.'

Time Takes Time

This album was released on 2 May 1992 on Private Music 262 902, a relatively small label. Ringo went with the Private Music label because they seemed to be the only ones willing to take a chance with him. For this album he decided to play drums on every track and also to have multiple producers. He selected four: Don Was, Jeff Lynne, Peter Asher and Phil Ramone, giving his reason as, 'because it's been so long for me that I didn't really know any producers I wanted to go with for the whole record. So I figured I'd try a few people.'

He also had a number of guest artists, who included Tom Petty, Brian Wilson, Harry Nilsson, Mike Campbell and Andrew Gold.

The record lasts for 40 minutes and 6 seconds and the cover illustration was by Mark Ryden, a designer whose cover designs range from Michael Jackson to the Red Hot Chili Peppers. It was Ringo's tenth album release of new material. Recording began in March 1991 and was mainly completed by September of that year, although the final parts were completed in February 1992.

Time Takes Time was a mix of new songs he had written with former Ring O' Records artist John Warman, plus some outside material. The

recordings with Jeff Lynne included a cover of 'Don't Be Cruel', a
Lynne composition 'Call Me', and a Starr-Warman song 'Don't Go
Where The Road Don't Go'.

With Phil Ramone he recorded 'All In The Name Of Love', one of his
own songs, and 'Runaways', a version of 'All In The Name Of Love'
penned by Jerry Williams.

The Peter Asher productions were 'Thank You For Being A Friend'
by Andrew Gold, a cover of the Posies hit 'Golden Blunders', and
'Angel In Disguise', which Paul McCartney provided and Ringo added
new verses to.

With Don Was he recorded Diane Warren's 'In A Heartbeat', with
Brian Wilson on backing vocals, and 'Weight Of The World' with
Jellyfish on backing vocals. The Was sessions had Benmont Tench of
the Heartbreakers on keyboards, Mark Goldenberg, former member of
the Cretonnes on guitar and Hutch Hutchinson from Bonnie Raitt's
band on bass.

Ringo said, 'I haven't been this happy with an album since *Ringo* in
1974. It's time I stretched.' Despite the optimism, the record didn't
chart.

There were three outtakes: 'Call Me', 'Love Is Going To Get You' by
Phil Picket and the McCartney/Starkey number 'Angel In Disguise'.

The official Private Music press release for the album read:

'It all comes down to what you crucify/You either kiss the future
or the past goodbye'.

Thus sings Ringo Starr in 'Weight Of The World', the first rock-
'n'roll single from his long-awaited album *Time Takes Time*,
Ringo's debut release on Private Music and his first studio collection in nearly a decade.

'It's time I stretched,' he says about all of the choices on *Time
Takes Time* – a triumphant project involving no less than four
prestigious producers – which was recorded in Los Angeles over
the past year. Five songs were produced by Don Was, two by Phil
Ramone, two by Jeff Lynne and one by Peter Asher.

'I don't want to play it safe. I feel I've moved on in my life, and
I wanted that to show on the album.'

Indeed, it 'shows' . . . starting with the ingredients of 'Weight Of
The World' ('a great title' he observes). Ringo's emotionally
moving vocal delivery . . . that unmistakable, splendid musicality
of his drumming . . . the complementary backing vocals of Jellyfish
. . . stellar session players . . . even newcomer songwriter Brian
O'Doherty (who co-wrote the song with Fred Velez) participated
in the arrangements . . . all produced by Don Was (and mixed by
Bob Clearmountain) . . . 'Weight Of The World' is a performance
of integrity.

'We didn't know it would be the single when we started,' reports

Ringo. 'It turned out so well. But I don't know anyone who can predict a single going on. It's only when you record it that you get that feeling.'

And there is no short supply of 'feeling' on this recording, as exemplified by the three songs co-written by Ringo himself.

'Don't Go Where The Road Don't Go' might be the closest representation of an autobiographical composition, strong and rock-steady: 'When you wake up from a bad dream to the howling of a lonely night/You feel the walls come closing in like the victim of a one-way fight/I don't remember many yesterdays, I left a lot of things undone/Now I'm back and I'm here to say, I'm looking after number one/Oh! Don't go where the road don't go'.

'After All These Years' has a tough, rock groove, again with a hint of the first person: 'Travelling the world in a rock'n'roll band/It's in my blood, it's in my blood/Oh but you know it's good to get back home'.

'"Runaways" has a sci-fi sound, with cold, city effects. It's about the kids who run to Hollywood and run to London. They leave home because their parents don't understand them. But, when they get there, it's a very hard place to be. It's worse than what they left behind. They are the young homeless,' Ringo concludes.

The songs he interprets – the Posies-penned 'Golden Blunders', the Jellyfish original 'I Don't Believe You', Jerry Lee Williams's 'All In The Name Of Love' and 'Don't Know A Thing About Love' by Richard Feldman and Heartbreaker Stan Lynch – present another fresh aspect of the superstar singer-drummer's work.

Ringo's summary is very direct. 'I just feel I'm a different person than I was, so that's what's coming out. That's how I'm writing. And, that's also how I'm performing. It's a bit more *real*.'

'In A Heartbeat' is a poignant example of the musicians that came out to support Ringo. Pop-hits songwriter Diane Warren wrote it, Brian Wilson arranged and sang the five-part harmony, Benmont Tench is on the Hammond B3.

In fact, the album is chock-full of supporters. In addition to the aforementioned, there are: guitarists Waddy Wachtel, Andrew Gold, Mark Goldenberg and Jeff 'Skunk' Baxter, Harry Nilsson, Bonnie Raitt's bassist Hutch Hutchinson, Mark Hudson, and more.

Don Was says, 'He is the leading and most musical drummer to influence generations of musicians. If there is a central theme to the album, it's this: "Here is a great musician and a really emotional singer, doing songs in his style." It's a Ringo Starr album.'

Ringo confides, 'I haven't been as happy with an album since the solo album, my *Ringo* album in 1974.' And with a knowing laugh, he says, 'For me, this album feels good . . . I like what it says . . . and it's in my range!'

Don't miss the soon-to-be 'famous three-minute ending' on the album's final track, complete with karmic title, 'What Goes Around (Comes Around)'.

Tittenhurst Park
Ringo bought this property from John Lennon in September 1973. The 300-year-old estate in Sunningdale, Berkshire, close to Ascot, was surrounded by 70 hilly acres of heath and the house itself contained seven main bedrooms, three reception rooms, large kitchen regions, staff quarters and guest cottages.

John had bought the property for £150,000 in 1967 and had numerous additions made, including an artificial lake in the grounds, a swimming pool, sauna and snooker room.

He also built an eight-track recording studio in the former chapel, which he called Ascot Sound.

John put it on the market when he decided to remain in America and within two weeks Ringo had made an offer – he bought the mansion on 9 September 1973 and he moved into the property with Maureen and their three children almost immediately.

He renamed the recording studio Startling Studios and apart from using it to record in himself, also rented it out for private hire.

Ringo eventually moved out in 1979, selling the property to Sheikh Zayed bin Sultan-Nahyan, ruler of Abu Dhabi, for $9 million. The Sheikh then spent £55 million renovating it. During the alterations the workmen destroyed Startling Studios and threw all the large collection of master tapes and films into a skip. They also removed wall paintings that John Lennon had executed because 'they didn't fit in'.

To The North Of Katmandu
A British film, released in 1986. It was directed by Terence Ryan and starred Barbara Bach, Ringo Starr and Billy Connolly.

Tommy
The famous rock opera by Pete Townshend of the Who. Lou Reizner decided to produce an album with the London Symphony Orchestra with guest soloists.

Ringo was given the part of Uncle Ernie on the album, which was recorded at Olympic Studios, London, between March and September 1972. Ringo recorded his vocals there and performed 'Fiddle About' and 'Tommy's Holiday Camp' on the two-album set, which was issued in Britain on Ode 99001 on 24 November 1972 and in America on Ode SP 99001 on 27 November 1972. It reached No. 5 in the American charts but didn't have much impact in Britain.

Tonight

Due to either very poor sales or possibly the abandonment of the release of a 'Lipstick Traces (On A Cigarette)' single in Britain, Polydor rushed out this track from the *Bad Boy* album on Polydor 2001 795 on 21 July 1978. Lasting 2 minutes and 50 seconds, it was Ringo's last single on the Polydor label. 'Heart On My Sleeve' was on the flip.

Too Much To Lose

A March 1989 single by Jan Hammer, released in Britain by MCA Records. Ringo, Jeff Beck and Dave Gilmour appeared in the promotional video.

Tours

When comparing his tours with the Beatles to his All-Starr Band tours, Ringo says, 'I can't remember sleeping properly for more than four hours at a stretch in the old days but it's far better now. In the Sixties there were always very big places to perform in, no real contact with the audience, a lot of fun to do in some ways, but very little proper sound from the speakers and an awful lot of high-pitched screeching from the fans.'

The Beatles tours usually saw them do short sets, sometimes only half an hour at a time, with a specific set of numbers. In fact, due to the brevity of their tour performances, Pete Best actually appeared on stage performing with the Beatles for a greater number of hours than Ringo did.

Ringo's first post-Beatles tour didn't take place until 1989. Prior to that he had made numerous one-off appearances with a number of other major artists. It was eventually tour promoter David Fishof who persuaded him to embark on his own tour, which was called Ringo Starr's All-Starr Band. The format of this tour was one Ringo continued to follow – lining up various star musicians to join him, beginning the show with some of his own hits, having his guests perform some of their strong hits and ending the show with the classic 'With A Little Help From My Friends', during which additional surprise guests would join in.

The musicians he assembled for his first All-Starr Band were Billy Preston and Dr John on keyboards, Joe Walsh and Nils Lofgren on guitars, Rick Danko on bass, Levon Helm on percussion, Jim Keltner on drums and Clarence Clemons on sax. Danko and Helm were from the Band and Clemons from the E Street Band.

Rehearsals began at S.I.R. Studios in Los Angeles on 5 July 1989 and then moved to Dallas, Texas, for a week before the tour opened on 23 July 1989. Ringo spent some time with vocal coach Nate Lam during the rehearsal period and Lam was described in the tour programme as 'throat mechanic'.

Before the tour, Ringo announced, 'I've changed my attitude towards life, and my way of living. And I wanted to work again. I wanted to do what I do best. What do I do? I'm a drummer. I'm a singer and an entertainer; I'm not just a Beatles personality.'

The tour was sponsored by Diet Pepsi, who dubbed it a 'Tour for All Generations'.

It was Ringo's first tour since the Beatles played in America in 1966 and was officially announced at a press conference on 20 June, which was broadcast live on the Westwood Radio Network. Ringo briefed the conference from the Palladium in New York and announced that the band would be called Ringo and the All-Starrs. The tour's musical director was Billy Preston.

It was said that Ringo was to receive $75,000 for each show, although the agreement was that if the ticket sales didn't go well, the tour would be cancelled. Fortunately, the tour virtually sold out in advance.

The tour band, with the exception of Keltner and Dr John, were assembled for the press conference, which was attended by around a hundred journalists and photographers.

A ponytailed Ringo announced that it was his appearance at the Prince's Trust concert the year previously that had given him the urge to tour again. 'It really gave me the sort of idea that I'd like to go on the road. And David Fishof came to see me with this idea because Pepsi went to him. And then I thought, "Well, who would I like to go out with?" And this is them.'

Ringo had previously been reticent about touring and when he was asked what had changed his mind he said, 'I think what changed my thinking was sobering up. You know, and thinking what do I do? And what I do is I'm a musician first and an entertainer.'

He said he wasn't apprehensive about going on the road again, 'Show business is my life. No, I'm really excited about it. It can be fun and we can have a real good time. And it's not as crazy as it used to be so I won't be so hectic and so mad.'

When asked why he was taking such a big band on the road, considering that there had only been four of them in the Beatles, he replied, 'The stages got bigger. I think it's more fun, you know, the way we're trying to put this act together. Besides, everyone being great musicians, everyone's a vocalist as well, so I can have fun playing the drums behind Joe and behind Nils, Rick or anybody who's in the band. And they can have fun playing behind me.'

Commenting on the fact that he would be playing drums on the tour he said, 'Yes, I'm a drummer. I will be drumming. With Levon, of course, and Jim Keltner. I'm the drummer so I want a crowd of drummers with me. Let's have fun.'

He was asked if he intended to tour Europe and replied, 'This morning was the first time we've all met together. We've got plenty of time to talk things over now and see what we all want to do, because these are all qualified musicians. I'm not like the leader. I'm just the name in front.

'I can't see us not having a load of fun on this tour and enjoying ourselves, and then it's up to the boys if they want to roll it over and carry it on.'

The tour opened with a thirty-minute set by New Orleans artist Mason Ruffner, who was introduced as 'Having been personally selected by Ringo Starr to open the show'.

The first part of the show featured: 'It Don't Come Easy', 'No No Song' and 'Yellow Submarine' by Ringo, 'Such A Night' (a Dr John performance although he changed this to 'Iko Iko' from the 6 August show), 'The Weight' by Levon Helm, 'Shine Silently' by Nils Lofgren, 'Will It Go Round In Circles' by Billy Preston, 'Act Naturally' and 'Honey Don't' by Ringo, 'You're A Friend Of Mine' by Clarence Clemons, 'The Shape I'm In' by Rick Danko, 'Life In The Fast Lane' by Joe Walsh and 'Back Off Boogaloo' (which was changed from 6 August to 'I Wanna Be Your Man').

Following the interval, the show recommenced with 'Desperado' by Joe Walsh, 'Raining In My Heart' by Rick Danko, 'Up On Cripple Creek' by Levon Helm, 'Boys' by Ringo, 'Bein' Angry' by Nils Lofgren, 'Candy' by Dr John, 'Right Place, Wrong Time' by Dr John, 'Quarter To Three' by Clarence Clemons, 'Rocky Mountain Way' by Joe Walsh, 'Nothing From Nothing' by Billy Preston and 'Photograph' by Ringo. There were two encores, 'You're Sixteen' and 'With A Little Help From My Friends'.

The tour itinerary was:

23 July	Park Central Amphitheater, Dallas, Texas
25 July	Poplar Creek Music Theater, Hoffman Estates, Illinois
26 July	Deer Creek Music Center, Noblesville, Indianapolis
28 July	Riverfest, Minneapolis, Minnesota
29 July	Alpine Valley Music Theater, East Troy, Wisconsin
30 July	Pine Knob Music Theater, Clarkston, Michigan
31 July	Blossom Music Center, Cuyahoga Falls, Near Cleveland, Ohio
2 August	Lake Compounce Amusement Park, Bristol, Connecticut
4 August	Performing Arts Center, Saratoga Springs, New York
5 August	Garden State Arts Center, Holmdel, New Jersey
6 August	Bally's Grand Hotel, Atlantic City
8 August	Merriweather Post Pavilion, Columbia, Maryland
9 August	Mann Music Center, Philadelphia, Pennsylvania
11 August	Garden State Arts Center, Holmdel, New Jersey
12 August	Jones Beach Amphitheater, Wantaugh, New York
13 August	Jones Beach Amphitheater, Wantaugh, New York
15 August	Great Woods Center, Mansfield, Massachusetts
16 August	Kingston Concert Grounds, Kingston, New Hampshire
18 August	Memorial Auditorium, Buffalo, New York

19 August	CNE, Toronto, Canada
20 August	Castle in Charlevoix, Michigan
22 August	Winnipeg, Canada
23 August	Saskatoon, Saskatchewan, Canada
24 August	Olympic Saddledome, Calgary, Canada
25 August	Northlands Coliseum, Edmonton, Canada
27 August	PNE Pacific Coliseum, Vancouver, Canada
29 August	Cal Expo Amphitheater, Sacramento
30 August	Aladdin Theater, Las Vegas
1 September	Shoreline Amphitheater, Mountain View, California
2 September	Pacific Amphitheater, Costa Mesa, California
3 September	Greek Theater, Los Angeles
4 September	Greek Theater, Los Angeles

The All-Starr Band then toured Japan:

30 October	Rainbow Hall, Nagoya
31 October	Castle Hall, Osaka
2 November	Sun Plaza, Hiroshima
3 November	Kitakyushu Koseinenkin Hall, Kyushi
6 November	Nippon Budokan Hall, Tokyo
7 November	Nippon Budokan Hall, Tokyo
8 November	Yokohama Arena, Yokohama

Ringo formed a new All-Starr Band for his North American and European tour in the summer of 1992:

The set comprised Ringo performing 'I'm The Greatest' and 'No No Song', Burton Cummings with 'No Time', Dave Edmunds with 'Girls Talk', Joe Walsh with 'Look At Us Now' (he changed to 'Rocky Mountain Way' on 26 June), 'I Can't Tell You Why' by Timothy B. Schmit, 'Shine Silently' by Nils Lofgren, 'Bang The Drum All Day' by Todd Rundgren and 'Don't Go Where The Road Don't Go' and 'Yellow Submarine' by Ringo. Following the intermission, Timothy B. Schmit opened with 'Keep On Tryin'' followed by Tim Cappello with 'Wiggle', Todd Rundgren with 'Black Maria', Joe Walsh with 'In The City' (which he replaced with 'Vote For Me' on 8 August), 'You're Sixteen' and 'Weight Of The World' by Ringo, 'Walkin' Nerve' by Nils Lofgren, 'I Hear You Knocking' by Dave Edmunds, 'American Woman' by Burton Cummings and 'Boys' (which was added to the repertoire on 28 June) and 'Photograph' by Ringo. The encores were 'Act Naturally' and 'With A Little Help From My Friends'.

The tour itinerary was:

2 June	Sunrise Pavilion, Fort Lauderdale, Florida
3 June	Sunrise Pavilion, Fort Lauderdale, Florida
5 June	Bayfront Pavilion, St Petersburg, Florida
6 June	Blockbuster Pavilion, Charlotte, North Carolina

7 June	Chastain Park Amphitheater, Atlanta, Georgia
9 June	Riverbend Music Center, Cincinnati, Ohio
10 June	Blossom Music Center, Guyaboga Falls, Ohio
12 June	Deer Creek Music Center, Noblesville, Indiana
13 June	Poplar Creek Music Center, Hoffman Estates, Illinois
15 June	Pine Knob Music Theater, Clarkston, Michigan
16 June	Kingswood Music Theater in Wonderland Park, Maple, Ontario, Canada
17 June	Merriweather Post Pavilion, Columbia
19 June	Radio City Music Hall, New York City
20 June	Radio City Music Hall, New York City
21 June	Garden State Arts Center, Holmdel, New Jersey
22 June	Great Woods Amphitheater, Mansfield, Massachusetts
23 June	Jones Beach Amphitheater, Wantaugh, New York
25 June	Marcus Amphitheater, Milwaukee, Wisconsin
26 June	Riverport Amphitheater, Maryland Heights, Missouri

The next leg of the tour was in Europe:

2 July	Gothenburg All-Star Festival, Gothenburg, Sweden
3 July	The Dalarock Festival in Hedemora, Sweden
4 July	Moelleparken, Malmo, Sweden
6 July	Empire Theatre, Liverpool, England
7 July	Hammersmith Odeon, London, England
8 July	Le Zenith, Paris, France
10 July	Stadtgarten, Hamburg, Germany
11 July	Tanzbrunnen, Cologne, Germany
12 July	Unterfrankenhalle, Aschaffenburg, Germany
13 July	Montreux Jazz Festival, Montreux, Switzerland
15 July	Deutschlandhalle, Berlin, Germany
17 July	Pori Jazz Festival, Pori, Finland
18 July	Valby Idretspark, Copenhagen, Denmark
19 July	Lisbterg Fruespark, Arhus, Denmark
20 July	Belga Beach Festival, De Panne, Belgium
22 July	Teatre Tenda, Brescia, Italy
23 July	Teatre La Versiliana, Marina Di Pietrasanta, Italy

During the European tour the group were videotaped and recorded at the Montreux Jazz Festival for future release on record and video. The group then returned to the US to complete the tour, although Todd Rundgren was absent on the dates for Engelwood and Park City and Joe Walsh didn't appear on the Caesar's Palace shows:

1 August	Le Champs de Brionne Summer Music Theater, George, Washington
3 August	Harvey's Hotel, Tahoe, California
4 August	Redwood Amphitheater in the Great American Amusement Park, Santa Clara, California

5 August	Concord Pavilion, Concord, California
7 August	California Mid State Fair, Paso Robles, California
8 August	Camp Pendleton Marine Base, Oceanside, California
9 August	Pacific Amphitheater, Costa Mesa, California
11 August	The Greek Theater, Los Angeles, California
12 August	The Greek Theater, Los Angeles, California
13 August	Desert Sky Pavilion, Phoenix, Arizona
15 August	Aquafest, Austin, Texas
16 August	Riverfront Park, Little Rock, Arkansas
18 August	Starplex Amphitheater, Dallas, Texas
20 August	Ohio State Fair Celeste Center, Columbus, Ohio
21 August	Freedom Hall, Kentucky State Fair, Louisville, Kentucky
22 August	Iowa State Fair, Des Moines, Iowa
24 August	Star Lake Amphitheater, Pittsburg, Pennsylvania
25 August	Finger Lakes Performing Arts Center, Canandaigua, New York
26 August	Saratoga Performing Arts Center, Saratoga Springs, New York
28 August	Waterloo Village Amphitheater, Stanhope, New Jersey
1 September	Fiddlers Green Amphitheater, Engelwood, Colorado
2 September	Park West Amphitheater, Park City, Utah
4 September	Caesar's Palace, Las Vegas, Nevada
5 September	Caesar's Palace, Las Vegas, Nevada
6 September	Caesar's Palace, Las Vegas, Nevada

In 1995 Ringo formed a third All-Starr Band for tours of Japan and North America. The new band rehearsed in Vancouver from 28 May to 9 June. The original planned line-up included Clarence Clemons and Nils Lofgren of the E Street Band, but they dropped out to begin summer recording and a tour with Bruce Springsteen. The final line-up included Zak Starkey on drums, Mark Farner of Grand Funk Railroad and Randy Bachman of Guess Who and the Bachman-Turner Overdrive on guitars, John Entwistle on bass, Billy Preston and Felix Cavaliere of the Rascals on keyboards and Mark Rivera of Billy Joel's band on saxophone.

The repertoire comprised 'Don't Go Where The Road Don't Go', 'I Wanna Be Your Man' and 'It Don't Come Easy' by Ringo, 'The Locomotion' by Mark Farner, 'Nothing For Nothing' by Billy Preston, 'Taking Care Of Business' by Randy Bachman, 'People Get Ready' by Felix Cavaliere, 'Boris The Spider' by John Entwistle, 'Boys' by Ringo, 'You Ain't Seen Nothing Yet' by Randy Bachman, 'You're Sixteen' and 'Yellow Submarine' by Ringo, 'My Wife' by John Entwistle, 'Honey Don't' and 'Act Naturally' by Ringo, 'Groovin'' and 'La Bamba' by Felix Cavaliere, and 'Photograph', 'No No Song' and 'With A Little Help From My Friends' by Ringo.

When the group arrived in Japan they held a press conference. During the tour Japanese television began screening a number of commercials Ringo had made for the soft drink Ringo Suttar. His appearance at the Budokan Hall was almost 29 years after he'd originally appeared there with the Beatles. The second Budokan concert was filmed by the Japanese station NHK-TV and screened on the *JST Show*.

The tour itinerary was:

14 June	Iwate Kenmin Kaikan in Morioka
15 June	Sendai Sun-Plaza in Sendai
16 June	Niigata Telsa in Niigata
18 June	Osaka Castle Hall in Osaka
19 June	Kurashiki Shimin Kaikan in Kurashiki
20 June	Hiroshima Kousel Nenkin Kaikan in Hiroshima
22 June	Nagoya Century Hall in Nagoya
24 June	Bay NK Hall in Uraysu
26 June	Nippon Budokan Hall, Tokyo
27 June	Nippon Budokan Hall, Tokyo
28 June	Hamamatu Kyouiku Bunka Kaikan in Hamamatu

The tour then moved to America:

2 July	The Arch, St Louis, Missouri
3 July	The Milwaukee Summerfest, Milwaukee, Wisconsin
4 July	Mall of America, Bloomington, Minnesota
5 July	Ravinia Festival Pavilion, Chicago, Illinois
6 July	Highland Park, Illinois
8 July	The Star Plaza Theater, Merrillville, Indiana
9 July	Nautica Stage, Cleveland, Ohio
10 July	Pine Knob Music Theater, Detroit, Michigan
11 July	First Of America Stage, Acme, Michigan
13 July	Radio City Music Hall, New York City, New York
14 July	Bud Light Amphitheater, Harvey's Lake, Pennsylvania
15 July	The Concord Hotel, Kiamesha Lake, New York
17 July	The Wolf Trap, Vienna, West Virginia
18 July	The Garden State Arts Center, Holmdel, New Jersey
19 July	Harbor Lights Pavilion, Boston, Massachusetts
21 July	Caesars, Atlantic City, New Jersey
22 July	Caesars, Atlantic City, New Jersey
23 July	Caesars, Atlantic City, New Jersey
25 July	Warwick Music Theater, Warwick, Rhode Island
27 July	Oakdale Theater, Wallingford, Connecticut
28 July	Starlite Music Theater, Latham, New York
29 July	The Melody Fair Theater, North Tonawanda, New York

31 July	Riverbend Music Center, Cincinnati, Ohio
1 August	Light Amphitheater, Pittsburgh, Pennsylvania
3 August	Orlando Centroplex, Orlando, Florida
4 August	The Sunrise Musical Theater, Sunrise, Florida
5 August	The Sunrise Musical Theater, Sunrise, Florida
7 August	Chastain Park Amphitheater, Atlanta, Georgia
8 August	The Palace Theater, Louisville, Kentucky
9 August	Van Braun Civic Center, Huntsville, Alabama
11 August	The Arena Theater, Houston, Texas
12 August	The Sunken Garden, San Antonio, Texas
13 August	The Starplex Amphitheater, Dallas, Texas
15 August	The Arizona Veterans Memorial Coliseum, Phoenix, Arizona
16 August	Humphrey's, San Diego, California
18 August	The Greek Theater, Los Angeles, California
19 August	The Greek Theater, Los Angeles, California
20 August	Concord Pavilion, Concord, California
22 August	Pier 62/63, Seattle, Washington
23 August	Pier 62/63, Seattle, Washington

The rest of the tour was immediately cancelled when it was discovered that Ringo's daughter Lee had been rushed to an intensive care unit in a London clinic. Ringo and Zak flew over to be at her side.

The cancelled dates were:

25 August	The Reno Hilton Amphitheater, Reno, Nevada
26 August	The Star Of The Desert Amphitheater, Apple Valley, California
28 August	Humphrey's, San Diego, California
29 August	The MGM Grand, Las Vegas, Nevada
31 August	The MGM Grand, Las Vegas, Nevada
1 September	The MGM Grand, Las Vegas, Nevada
2 September	The MGM Grand, Las Vegas, Nevada
3 September	The MGM Grand, Las Vegas, Nevada

1997 saw an All-British line-up for the fourth All-Starr Band tour of America in April, May and June, promoted by David Fishof. It comprised Ringo on drums, Dave Mason on guitar, Peter Frampton on guitar, Jack Bruce on bass, Gary Brooker on keyboards and Simon Kirke on drums. The only American musician in the band was saxophonist and percussionist Mark Rivera, who also acted as the tour's musical director. Zak Starkey was touring with the Who at the time, so was unable to join the ensemble, which is why Ringo sought out Kirke, a former member of Free and Bad Company.

Incidentally, Ringo slightly changed his image for this tour, ridding himself of his ponytail in favour of close-cropped hair. He gave his usual peace sign to the audience when he appeared and performed with his Ludwig drum kit, which had the image of a moon and a star representing himself and Barbara.

The tour sponsor was Glade, who manufacture fresh-air products. They organised contests, sweepstakes in radio stations, merchandising displays in stores and offered a CD sampler 'Classic Sensations', which included All-Starr-era tracks and tracks such as 'Only You' from the *Goodnight Vienna* album.

Rehearsals began at the Center Stage in Studio City on 15 April and were to last until 25 April. Musical Director Rivera had listed his song suggestions and Ringo had told him, 'Let's try to throw some curves at them.' However, he decided to retain the successful formula they had, which Ringo describes as 'all the songs you know and love'.

It was also decided to use the acoustic solo break, which had been popular on the last All-Starr tour. Gary Brooker, Peter Frampton, Jack Bruce and Dave Mason, individually or in pairs, would perform their personal favourites, with two of the artists performing a number each night, which would be rotated throughout the tour with the other members.

An example is what happened on the first night when the musicians used their extended spot to play some of their favourites. Jack Bruce played 'Theme From An Imaginary Western', Gary Brooker played 'A Salty Dog' and 'The Angler' and Peter Frampton played 'Norwegian Wood'.

Rock photographer Henry Diltz took the tour photos of the band, although there was to be a last-minute change.

On 24 April a late decision was made to drop Dave Mason from the group. No reason was given, but Mark Rivera did point out the problem of 'musical differences', although there was talk that Mason was turning up late for the rehearsals.

Mason was to have performed on 'Only You', 'I Know', 'Feeling Alright' and 'We Just Disagree', all of which were scrapped from the repertoire and replaced by extended version of Cream's 'White Room', 'Sunshine Of Your Love' and Frampton's 'Do You Feel Like We Do'.

The set list for the tour was finally decided on:

First set: 'It Don't Come Easy' and 'Act Naturally' by Ringo, 'The Devil Came From Kansas' by Gary Brooker, 'Show Me The Way' by Peter Frampton, 'Sunshine Of Your Love' by Jack Bruce, 'Shooting Star' by Simon Kirke, 'Boys' by Ringo, 'Baby I Love Your Way' by Peter Frampton and 'You're Sixteen' and 'Yellow Submarine' by Ringo.

Second set: 'Conquistador' by Gary Brooker, 'I'm The Greatest' and 'No No Song' by Ringo, 'I Feel Free' by Jack Bruce, 'All Right Now' by Simon Kirke, 'I Wanna Be Your Man' by Ringo, 'Do You Feel Like We Do' by Peter Frampton, 'White Room' by Jack Bruce, 'A Whiter Shade Of Pale' by Gary Brooker and 'Photograph' by Ringo. The encore was 'With A Little Help From My Friends'.

The opening act was Eric Stewart (not to be confused with the former member of 10cc), an American singer/songwriter who performed a twenty-minute acoustic set. Although he didn't appear on every show during the tour, he performed on approximately 90% of the dates.

The itinerary was:

28 April	Moore Theater, Seattle, Washington
29 April	Hult Center, Eugene, Oregon
30 April	Arlene Schnitzer Auditorium, Portland, Oregon
2 May	Concord Pavilion, San Francisco, California
3 May	Universal Amphitheater, Los Angeles, California
4 May	Humphrey's, San Diego, California
5 May	Mesa Amphitheater, Phoenix, Arizona
7 May	Fiddler's Green, Denver, Colorado
9 May	Rosemont Horizon, Chicago, Illinois
10 May	Riverport Amphitheater, St Louis, Missouri
11 May	State Theater, Minneapolis, Minnesota
13 May	Eagles Ballroom, Milwaukee, Wisconsin
14 May	Breslin Center, East Lansing, Michigan
16 May	Chastain Park, Atlanta, Georgia
17 May	Sunrise Theater, Miami, Florida
18 May	Ruth Eckerd Hall, Tampa, Florida
20 May	Palace Theater, Myrtle Beach, South Carolina
21 May	Wolf Trap Farm Park, Vienna, West Virginia
23 May	Billy Bob's, Fort Worth, Texas
24 May	Six Flags, San Antonio, Texas
25 May	Six Flags, San Antonio, Texas
28 May	Bob Carpenter Center, Newark, Delaware
29 May	I.C. Light Amphitheater, Pittsburgh, Pennsylvania
30 May	Pine Knob Amphitheater, Detroit, Michigan
31 May	Rubber Bowl, Akron, Ohio
2 June	Mohegan Sun Resort and Casino, Uncasville, Connecticut
3 June	PNC Bank Arts Center, Holmdel, New Jersey
5 June	Harborlights Pavilion, Boston, Massachusetts
6 June	Resorts International, Atlantic City, New Jersey
7 June	Jones Beach Amphitheater, Wantaugh, New York

Ringo had formed a group, the Roundheads, to support him on the *Vertical Man* and *VH-1 Storytellers* CDs, although instead of taking the Roundheads on tour, he decided to continue the theme of an All-Starr Band. The fourth incarnation were to play 18 dates in 16 European cities in what was referred to as 'The Vertical Tour'.

Rehearsals began in London and ended on 6 August 1998 with a rehearsal show.

The musicians in the All-Starr Band were Gary Brooker, Jack Bruce, Peter Frampton, Simon Kirke and Mark Rivera.

The set list began with 'It Don't Come Easy' and 'Act Naturally' by Ringo and followed with 'Whiskey Train' by Gary Brooker, 'Show Me The Way' by Peter Frampton, 'Sunshine Of Your Love' by Jack Bruce, 'Shooting Star' by Simon Kirke, 'Boys' by Ringo, 'Baby I Love Your Way' by Peter Frampton, 'Love Me Do' (with Scott Gordon on harmonica) and 'Yellow Submarine' by Ringo, 'A Salty Dog' by Gary Brooker, 'All I Want To Be (Is By Your Side)' by Peter Frampton, 'Theme From An Imaginary Western' by Jack Bruce, 'Conquistador' by Gary Brooker, 'I'm The Greatest', 'No No Song' and 'La De Da' by Ringo, 'I Feel Free' by Jack Bruce, 'All Right Now' by Simon Kirke, 'I Wanna Be Your Man' by Ringo, 'Do You Feel Like We Do' by Peter Frampton, 'White Room' by Jack Bruce, 'A Whiter Shade Of Pale' by Gary Brooker and 'Photograph' by Ringo. The encore was 'With A Little Help From My Friends'.

Apart from the different personnel Ringo selected to be in the All-Starr Bands, another feature of the tours is that guest artists invariably turn up to take part in the encore of 'With A Little Help From My Friends'. The special guests who turned up to appear on stage during this tour included Mark Farner, Timothy B. Schmit, Eric Burdon, Ginger Baker, Leo Kottke, Joe Walsh and Max Weinberg.

Ringo became the first member of the former Beatles to appear in Russia when he performed in Moscow on 25 August. The European leg of the tour was as follows (a planned 15 August concert in Luxembourg was cancelled due to a dispute with the promoter):

7 August	The Helsingin Jaahalli in Helsinki, Finland
8 August	The Festival, Zurich, Switzerland
9 August	Skanderborg Festivale in Skanderborg, Denmark
12 August	Reilichtbuehne, Killesburg Stuttgart, Germany
13 August	Theatreplatz, Chemnitz, Germany
16 August	The Marktrock Festival in Leuven, Belgium
18 August	Expo '98, Lisbon, Portugal
20 August	The Point, Dublin, Ireland
21 August	Shepherd's Bush Empire, London
25 August	Moscow Sports Complex, Moscow, Russia
26 August	The Jubilee Complex, St Petersburg, Russia
28 August	The Sporting Club, Monte Carlo
29 August	The Sporting Club, Monte Carlo
30 August	The Sporting Club, Monte Carlo
1 September	Gruga Halle, Essen, Germany
2 September	Stadtpark, Hamburg, Germany
3 September	Museumshof, Bonn, Germany
5 September	The Wintershall '98 Rock Extravaganza, Kent, England

In 1999, to celebrate the tenth anniversary of the All-Starr Band, Ringo and David Fishof gathered a fifth line-up of musicians to join Ringo on a tour of North America, each member being a veteran of previous All-Starr tours. They were: Gary Brooker, Jack Bruce, Simon Kirke, Todd Rundgren and Tim Cappello. Joe Walsh was initially approached but had to pull out because he was joining the Eagles tour. Originally, a week in South Africa with concerts in Cape Town and Johannesburg was mooted for early March, but it was decided to replace them with further US dates.

The set list was: 'It Don't Come Easy' and 'Act Naturally' by Ringo, 'Whiskey Train' by Gary Brooker, 'I Saw The Light' by Todd Rundgren, 'Sunshine Of Your Love' by Jack Bruce, 'Shooting Star' by Simon Kirke, 'Boys', 'Love Me Do' and 'Yellow Submarine' by Ringo, 'Conquistador' and 'A Salty Dog' by Gary Brooker, 'Hammer In My Heart' by Todd Rundgren, 'I'm The Greatest', 'No No Song' and 'Back Off Boogaloo' by Ringo, 'I Feel Free' by Jack Bruce, 'All Right Now' by Simon Kirke, 'I Wanna Be Your Man' by Ringo, 'Bang The Drum All Day' by Todd Rundgren, 'White Room' by Jack Bruce, 'A Whiter Shade Of Pale' by Gary Brooker and 'Photograph' by Ringo. The encores were 'You're Sixteen' and 'With A Little Help From My Friends'.

The itinerary was:

12 February	The Taj Mahal Casino, Atlantic City, New Jersey
13 February	The Taj Mahal Casino, Atlantic City, New Jersey
14 February	The Taj Mahal Casino, Atlantic City, New Jersey
16 February	The Beacon Theater, New York City, New York
17 February	The Beacon Theater, New York City, New York
19 February	Mohegan Sun Casino, Uncasville, Connecticut
20 February	Mohegan Sun Casino, Uncasville, Connecticut
21 February	Westbury Music Fair, Westbury, New York
22 February	Schottenstein Center, Columbus, Ohio
24 February	Westbury Music Fair, Westbury, New York
26 February	The Star Plaza Theater, Merrillville, Indiana
28 February	Park West, Chicago, Illinois
1 March	Palace Theater, Detroit, Michigan
4 March	Eureka Municipal Auditorium, Eureka, California
5 March	Konocti Harbor Resort and Spa, Kelseyville, California
6 March	Konocti Harbor Resort and Spa, Kelseyville, California
7 March	Berkeley Theater, Berkeley, California
11 March	The Bank America Center, Boise, Idaho
12 March	Dee Event Center, Ogden, Utah
13 March	The Joint, Las Vegas, Nevada
14 March	4th & B, San Diego, California
15 March	4th & B, San Diego, California
18 March	The Universal Amphitheater, Los Angeles, California

19 March	The Silver Legacy Casino, Reno, Nevada
20 March	The Silver Legacy Casino, Reno, Nevada
21 March	Harrah's Casino, Lake Tahoe, Nevada
25 March	The Horseshoe Casino, Tunica, Mississippi
26 March	The Florida Theater, Jacksonville, Florida
27 March	The Sunrise Musical Theater, Fort Lauderdale, Florida
28 March	Hard Rock Café, Orlando, Florida

The next tour, with the sixth All-Starr Band, saw a number of veterans and one newcomer, Eric Carmen, former member of the Raspberries. He replaced Billy Preston, who was currently involved in legal problems. Two other proposed musicians didn't appear in the final line-up: Ray Davies, leader of the Kinks and Billy Squier, a 1980s rocker. The other All-Starr's comprised Dave Edmunds, Mark Rivera, Simon Kirke and Jack Bruce.

The tour was sponsored by Century 21 and was known as the 'Connections' tour. Rehearsals began in Atlantic City and the press launch on 2 May took place at the Plaza Hotel, New York.

The set list was: 'It Don't Come Easy' and 'Act Naturally' by Ringo, 'Hungry Eyes' by Eric Carmen, 'I Hear You Knocking' by Dave Edmunds, 'Sunshine Of Your Love' by Jack Bruce, 'Shooting Star' by Simon Kirke, 'I Wanna Be Your Man', 'Love Me Do' and 'Yellow Submarine' by Ringo. The solo spots were 'Classical Gas' and 'Lady Madonna' by Dave Edmunds, 'Theme From An Imaginary Western' by Jack Bruce, 'Boats Against The Current' by Eric Carmen. The show continued with 'Go All The Way' by Eric Carmen, 'I'm The Greatest', 'No No Song' and 'Back Off Boogaloo' by Ringo, 'I Feel Free' by Jack Bruce, 'All Right Now' by Simon Kirke, 'Boys' by Ringo, 'I Knew The Bride (When She Used To Rock And Roll)' by Dave Edmunds, 'White Room' by Jack Bruce, 'All By Myself' by Eric Carmen and 'Photograph' by Ringo. The encores were 'You're Sixteen' and 'With A Little Help From My Friends'.

The itinerary for the 2000 tour of North America was as follows:

12 May	Trump Taj Mahal, Atlantic City, New Jersey
13 May	Trump Taj Mahal, Atlantic City, New Jersey
15 May	Mid-Hudson Civic Center, Poughkeepsie, New York
16 May	Westbury Music Fair, Westbury, Long Island, New York
17 May	Westbury Music Fair, Westbury, Long Island, New York
19 May	Mohegan Sun Center, Uncasville, Connecticut
20 May	Mohegan Sun Center, Uncasville, Connecticut
21 May	I Center, Salem, New Hampshire
23 May	Beacon Theater, New York
24 May	State Theater, New Brunswick, New Jersey
26 May	Norva, Norfolk, West Virginia
27 May	Tops Great American Rib Cook-Off and Music Festival, Cleveland, Ohio

28 May	Riverport Amphitheater, Maryland Heights, Missouri
30 May	Wolf Trap, Filene Center, Vienna, West Virginia
31 May	Gaylord Entertainment Center, Nashville, Tennessee
1 June	Horseshoe Casino, Robinsville, Mississippi
3 June	Sunrise Musical Theater, Sunrise, Florida
4 June	Chastain Park Amphitheater, Atlanta, Georgia
8 June	The House of Blues, Chicago, Illinois
10 June	Landmark Theater, Syracuse, New York
11 June	Pine Knob Music Theater, Clarkston, Michigan
14 June	Mountain Winery, Saratoga, California
15 June	Mountain Winery, Saratoga, California
17 June	Hard Rock Hotel And Casino, Las Vegas, Nevada
22 June	The House of Blues, West Hollywood, California
23 June	The House of Blues, West Hollywood, California
25 June	Humphrey's By The Bay, San Diego, California
26 June	Humphrey's By The Bay, San Diego, California
28 June	Red Rocks Amphitheater, Morrison, Colorado
30 June	State Capitol Grounds, St Paul, Minnesota
1 July	Summerfest, Henry W. Maier Festival Park, Lake Michigan

The line-up for the 2001 tour featured Sheila E, Roger Hodgson, Ian Hunter, Greg Lake and Howard Jones. The itinerary was:

26 July	Casino Rama, Rama, Ontario
27 July	Molson Center, Montreal, Quebec
28 July	Freedom Hill Amphitheater, Sterling Heights, Michigan
29 July	The Harv At Mountaineer Racetrack, Chester, West Virginia
1 August	Jones Beach, Wantagh, New York
2 August	Mohegan Sun, Uncasville, Connecticut
3 August	The Today Show, New York City, New York
4 August	Fleet Boston Pavilion, Boston, Massachusetts
5 August	Riley Music Center, Manchester, Vermont
7 August	Meadowbrook Park Amphitheater, Gilford, New Hampshire
10 August	The Taj Mahal, Atlantic City, New Jersey
11 August	Harbor Center Pavilion, Portsmouth, Virginia
13 August	Chastain Park, Atlanta, Georgia
14 August	Broward Park Arts Center, Fort Lauderdale, Florida
15 August	USF Sundome, Tampa, Florida
16 August	Horseshoe Casino, Tunica, Mississippi
18 August	Billy Bob's Texas, Fort Worth, Texas
19 August	Frontier City/Six Flags, Oklahoma City, Oklahoma
21 August	Fox Theater, St Louis, Missouri

22 August	Rosemont Theater, Rosemont, Illinois
23 August	Minnesota State Fair, Saint Paul, Minnesota
25 August	Fiddler's Green, Engelwood, Colorado
27 August	Schnitzer Concert Hall, Portland, Oregon
28 August	Chateau Saint Michelle, Woodinville, Washington
30 August	Chronicle Pavilion, Concord, California
1 September	Rio Hotel, Las Vegas, Nevada
2 September	San Diego State University Open Air theatre, San Diego, California

Ringo's eighth All-Starr Band in 2003 comprised: Paul Carrack from Squeeze and Mike and the Mechanics on vocals/keyboards; Colin Hay from Men At Work on vocals/guitar; Sheila E on drums/percussion; Mark Rivera on saxophone; and John Waite from the Babys and Bad English on bass guitar.

The itinerary was:

24 July	Casino Rama, Rama, Ontario, Canada
25 July	Casino Rama, Ramaz, Ontario, Canada
26 July	Darien Lake Six Flags Performing Arts Center, Darien Center, New York
27 July	Fleet Boston Pavilion, Boston, Massachusetts
29 July	Radio City Music Hall, New York City, New York
30 July	State Theater, Easton, Pennsylvania
31 July	Mohegan Sun Casino, Uncasville, Connecticut
2 August	Trump Taj Mahal Atlantic City, New Jersey
3 August	PNC Bank Arts Center, Holmdel, New Jersey
5 August	Westbury Music Fair, Westbury, New York
6 August	Westbury Music Fair, Westbury, New York
7 August	DTE Energy Music Theater, Detroit
8 August	Van Andel Arena, Grand Rapids, Michigan
9 August	Marcus Center For the Performing Arts, Milwaukee
10 August	Soo Pass Ranch, Detroit Lakes, Minnesota
12 August	Rosemont Theater, Rosemont, Illinois
13 August	Chastain Park Amphitheater, Atlanta, Georgia
15 August	Grand Casino, Gulfport, Mississippi
16 August	Manaffay Theater, St Petersburg, Florida
17 August	Mizner Amphitheater, Boca Raton, Florida
19 August	Alico Arena, Florida Gulf Coast University, Fort Myers, Florida
21 August	Horseshoe Casino, Roberson, Mississippi
22 August	Next Stage At Grand Prairie, Grand Prairie, Texas
25 August	Sandia Casino Amphitheater, Albuquerque, New Mexico
26 August	Amarillo Civic Center, Amarillo, Texas
29 August	Harrah's Tahoe, Lake Tahoe, Nevada

30 August	The Joint, Hard Rock Hotel, Las Vegas, Nevada
31 August	Marymoor Park, Redmond, Washington
2 September	Britt Festivals At Britt Pavilion, Jacksonville, Oregon
4 September	Villamontello Center for The Arts, Saratoga, California
5 September	Dodge Theater, Phoenix, Arizona
6 September	Universal Amphitheater, Universal City, California
7 September	Humphrey's San Diego, California

Tribute Records

Following the Beatles amazing impact on America in 1964 a shoal of 'tribute' records were issued. Apart from ones about the Beatles in general, virtually every record about an individual Beatle was about Ringo. Few people realise that, initially, Ringo was the most popular member of the Beatles in America.

The records included 'Where Did Ringo Go?' (the Beatle Bugs), 'What's Wrong With Ringo?' (the Bon Bons – who later changed their name to the Shangri-Las), 'Ringo, Ringo' (Daws Butler – the voice of Huckleberry Hound), 'Ringo Pt 1/Pt 2' (Carl and the Haircuts), 'Ringo Comes To Town' (Chug and Doug), 'Ringo' (Bob Dean), 'R (Is for Ringo)' (Tina Ferra), 'Ringo-Deer' (Gary Ferrier), 'A Tribute To Ringo Starr (The Other Ringo)' (Larry Finnegan), 'Ringo's Walk' (Joey and the Classics), 'Ringo Did It' (Lee Veronica and the Moniques), 'Like Ringo' (Dick Lord), 'Ringo Boy' (Dori Peyton), 'Minuet For Ringo' (Viv Prince – drummer with the Pretty Things), 'My Ringo' (the Rainbows), 'Ringo's Jerk' (Ron Ringo), 'Ringo' (the Starlettes), 'Ringo Ringo' (Terri Darlene), 'Ringo Bells' (Three Blonde Mice), 'Ringo Dingo, Here Comes Ringo' (the Tributes), 'Ringo' (the Weekends), 'Go Go With Ringo' (the Whippets), 'Ringo, I Want To Know Your Secret' (Pay Wynter) and 'Ringo For President' (the Young World Singers).

There was even a compilation called *The Beatles Tribute Album*. The tracks were: 'We Love You Beatles' (the Carefrees), 'A Letter From Ringo' (Casey Kasem), 'Ringo For President' (the New World Singers), 'Boy With The Beatles Hair' (the Swans), 'The Beatles Barber' (Scott Douglas), 'Beatlemania Blues' (the Roaches), 'Christmas With The Beatles' (Judy and the Duets), 'The Other Ringo' (Larry Finnegan), 'Little Beatle Boy' (the Angels), 'Bring Back My Beatles' (the Detours), 'Ringo Bells' (Three Blonde Mice), 'A Letter To The Beatles' (the Four Preps), 'Treat Him Tender Maureen' (Angie and the Chicklettes), 'My Boyfriend's Got A Beatles Haircut' (Donna Lyne) and 'Interview With The Fab Four' (Harv Moore).

Trippin' On My Own Tears

A track from the 2003 *Ringo Rama* album, 3 minutes and 31 seconds in length. Country rock vocalist Shawn Colvin provided backing vocals.

200 Motels

This 98-minute colour film, released in 1971, was described as a 'fantasy opera'. Filming began at Pinewood Studios on 1 February 1971.

The movie saw Ringo in a dual role, portraying both Larry the Dwarf and Frank Zappa.

200 Motels was issued by Warner Bros and produced by Jerry Good and Herb Cohen, with a story and screenplay by Frank Zappa. Tony Palmer actually directed the movie, although it was reported that he wasn't too pleased with the result. His credit read: 'Visuals directed by Tony Palmer'.

Ringo's chauffeur Martin Lickert also got a part in the movie. He was told there were auditions for the role of a bass player. He attended, said he played bass, and got the part. Actor Theodore Bickel also appeared as the evil Rance Mohamets and Keith Moon played a nun who overdoses on Mandrax.

The movie's 'band-on-the-road' theme was set in a mythical town called Centreville. The Mothers of Invention arrive in Centreville and find it an extremely strange place to be in – at one end of town there is a concentration camp where an orchestra lives!

Ringo arrived on the set with a beard, but he cut most of it off, leaving just a goatee, for his part as Zappa.

He completed his role on 5 February. The 95-minute film was edited down from 24 hours of videotape. It was premiered in New York on 10 November 1971 and in London on 16 December 1971 at the Classic Cinema, Piccadilly Circus, although it never received proper distribution in Britain.

Tyler, Steve

Leader of Aerosmith. His former producers included Adrian Barber, former member of legendary Liverpool group the Big Three and Mark Hudson, who became Ringo's producer and business partner.

Hudson had co-written 'Livin' On The Edge' for Aerosmith and when Ringo heard it, he told him, 'I really like that song. It's kind of Beatley. Maybe we should get together and write something some day.'

When Hudson was producing the *Ringo Rama* album he contacted a lot of celebrated musicians, many of whom contributed to the album.

He phoned Tyler, who was in Amsterdam, and told him that Ringo wanted to record 'Love Me Do'. Tyler asked, 'Who's playing the harmonica?' and Hudson replied, 'You are, if you can get here on time.'

Tyler was in the studio within two days and provided the harmonica on Ringo's re-recording of the song.

Valentine

A track on the 1991 album *Silver Lining* by Nils Lofgren. Ringo played drums on the promotional video for the track, filmed in February 1991 in Los Angeles. Castle Communications issued the number as a single in Britain on 22 April 1991.

Van Eaton, Lon and Derrek

Singer/songwriter brothers who were born in Trenton, New Jersey, Lon on 12 March 1948 and Derrek on 12 August 1950.

They sent a tape of their material to Apple and were signed to the label on 15 September 1971. George Harrison produced their first single 'Sweet Music' and they began work on their debut album. Unfortunately, Apple was being downsized at the time and was soon to become merely a label specifically concentrating on Beatles products.

Ringo played drums on their song 'Another Thought' and on a couple of other tracks that remain unreleased.

When the brothers moved to Los Angeles they contributed to the *Ringo* and *Goodnight Vienna* albums. Lon played on Ringo's 1976 album *Rotogravure* and the 1977 album *Ringo The 4th*. He was also a member of Ringo's Roadside Attraction, a band Ringo assembled for his *Bad Boy* album and the television special 'Ringo'.

The brothers recorded for Portrait records in 1978 and Ringo played on one of the tracks, 'Get Happy'.

Vertical Man (album)

The recording of Ringo's first studio album in seven years began in February 1997 and lasted until May 1988. The recordings took place at the Whatinthewhatthe? Studios, A&M Studios and Village

Recorders in Los Angeles, and the Mill, AIR Studios, Abbey Road Studios, FPSHOT and Sarm Hook End Studios in Britain.

The title 'Thanks for Comin'' was originally considered, but the new title came from a set of quotations in a book belonging to Barbara's daughter Francesca.

The album was produced by Mark Hudson (former member of the Hudson Brothers) and Ringo and was mixed by Geoff Emerick, former engineer on Beatles recordings.

Ringo was to comment, 'If you listen to the album you can hear it evolve. It started very, very simple and it gets ... complicated is the wrong word, but more interesting as it goes on. That's how it happened and I've never had so much fun.'

Commenting on the recordings in the Whatinthewhatthe? Studios he said, 'We were not in a "real" studio, but it is a real studio. The drums were in a cupboard, and in that cupboard one day we had Steve Tyler, Steve Cropper, Mark Hudson, Steve Dudas on guitar, and myself in an eight-foot room and it was fun. The whole atmosphere was like that all the way through. There were no red lights and there was no big glass surrounding me.'

Discussing the various artists who appeared as guests, Ringo said, 'The thing is, we had this open-door policy. If you walked in the door you were asked to play. We didn't organise anything. Alanis Morissette came to say hello, it was like there was no struggle, there was an absolute pause waiting for her. We just happened to be doing that track so I just said to her, "Would you like to sing on this?" and she said "yes" which was great. Steven was phoning from all over Europe, he wanted to come and have fun with us.

'Of course, we went to England to get Paul on. I just felt his bass playing, and his singing and harmonising on the track would work. And I always feel, if I ever do a record, I like to have him on it, and I like George on it. George, yet again, plays one of his most moving guitar solos on "King Of Broken Hearts".'

Discussing the album's theme, he said, 'There's one line I think which encapsulates this album: "Let's all get well together." That's sort of what the album is about. It's called *Vertical Man* because I was reading this huge book of quotes that my stepdaughter Francesca won at school. I was flipping through it and I saw this quote: "Let's hear it for the Vertical Man, there's always so much praise for the horizontal one." And I thought, "That's a really cool thing, let's hear it for now, not for later."

'A lot of players I'm with, thank God, we're all still vertical. For a few of us it was touch and go for a while. We've lost so many great players through the years and we're still standing, as Elton John says.

'I'm a grateful human being and the album talks somewhat about that. I do feel that we should all get well together. I think we should have an understanding about love and peace. I'm trying to promote that now. If there is a message – I don't particularly like messages, because everybody takes whatever they take from whatever – that's what this album is about. It's called *Vertical Man*. Enough said, really.'

Seventeen tracks were recorded, thirteen of which were used on the album. Thirteen of the recorded numbers were co-written by Ringo, Mark Hudson, Dan Grakal and Steve Dudas.

Paul McCartney and Ringo appeared on two tracks together, 'La De Da' and 'What In The … World', which were recorded by Mark Hudson at Paul's home studio, the Mill in East Sussex. George Harrison recorded his guitar parts for 'King Of Broken Hearts' and 'I'll Be Fine' at his FPSHOT Studios at Friar Park and sent the overdubs to Ringo by post. George Martin scored the strings for 'King Of Broken Hearts'.

On 12 December 1997 it was announced that a deal had been made with Guardian Records, a subsidiary of EMI Records, to release *Vertical Man* on 21 April 1998 on Guardian A2-23702. Guardian had been a label set up to release new produce by high-profile names such as Ray Davies of the Kinks and Ringo, but EMI decided to drop the idea. Mercury Records then announced that they would release *Vertical Man* on 16 June.

Nine hundred copies of a promotional CD were pressed which included the Steve Tyler version of 'Drift Away'.

The CD received its world broadcast premiere on *The Album Network*, hosted by disc jockey Alan Ladd over five days from 10 to 14 June 1988.

It was issued in America on 16 June 1998 and in Britain on 3 August.

The tracks were: 'One', 'What In The … World', 'Mindfield', 'King Of Broken Hearts', 'Love Me Do', 'Vertical Man', 'Drift Away', 'I Was Walkin'', 'La De Da', 'Without Understanding', 'I'll Be Fine Anywhere', 'Puppet', 'I'm Yours'.

The four tracks recorded but not used were: 'Sometimes', 'Mr Double-It-Up', 'Everyday' and 'Good News'.

Best Buy, the American retail chain, had a special offer of a sampler single containing three of these numbers available to those customers who pre-ordered. The supply was limited to twenty copies per store.

Following its release in Britain it sold poorly and only reached a disappointing No. 85 in the charts. A spokesman commented, 'He is obviously more than a little disappointed with the sales. Ringo put a lot of time and effort into the album and there was an array of talent on it too. But clearly this wasn't enough. It seems the public just didn't like it and it shows that not everything connected to the Fab Four is going to be popular and profitable.'

Vertical Man (song)

The title track from the *Vertical Man* album, composed by Starkey/Hudson/Grakal/Dudas.

It is 4 minutes and 42 seconds in length. Ringo was on lead vocal, drums, Mellotron, synthesizer strings and percussion, Ozzy Osbourne was on backing vocals, Mark Hudson was on bass, electric guitar, piano, Mellotron, synthesizer strings and provided the string arrangement and backing vocals. Nina Pieseckyj was on cello, and Sarah Hudson, Barbara Vander Linde and John Goodman on backing vocals.

VH-1 *Storytellers*

A series for the music channel VH-1 that featured big-name artists performing their favourite tracks and telling stories about the origins of their songs.

Ringo and the Roundheads' appearance on 13 May 1991 was recorded and issued as a CD.

The performance took place at Sony Music Studios on West 54th Street, New York.

VH-1 executive producer Bill Flanagan introduced the group to the audience and they began by performing 'With A Little Help From My Friends'. Ringo then revealed that the original line of the first verse was: 'Would you stand up and throw a tomato at me', which resulted in him saying, 'I'm not singing that!'

The next song was 'It Don't Come Easy'. Ringo said that he co-wrote this song with George Harrison, although he went uncredited. Commenting that George was 'into spiritual things' he said, 'So we got to the last verse and he was saying "God . . ." "No, George, *I* don't sing about God, *you* sing about God," I told him. So George said, "Oh, Hare Krishna." "No, I don't sing about Hare Krishna," I told George. "Well, how about Peace?" So we settled on the word Peace.'

Ringo next played drums on 'I Was Walkin'' and then went to the keyboard to introduce 'Don't Pass Me By'. Mark Hudson asked him to tell another story and Ringo said, 'This was the first song that was ever written by me and put on record when I was in that "other band".' He said that although he'd written other songs before, the other members of the Beatles wouldn't do them because of his tendency to rewrite existing songs without realising it. 'I'd just rewrite, you know, "I Did It My Way" and I'd change it into something, and they'd be rolling on the floor saying, "Oh, he's written another one."'

'Back Off Boogaloo' was next and Ringo explained that he'd heard the phrase from Marc Bolan and one evening after having dinner with Bolan he found himself repeating the phrase in his sleep, this time with a catchy tune. He kept the melody in his mind while he searched the house for a tape recorder. The one he found had no batteries, but as he began looking for batteries the tune began to turn into 'Oh, the shark, babe, has such teeth dear.'

'I was saying, "No! Not 'Mack The Knife!'" commented Ringo.'

The next song was 'King Of Broken Hearts' and Ringo said the song was written by four guys. 'Get any four guys writing a song, it's all sob stories.'

For 'Octopus's Garden' he told the story of falling out with the other members of the Beatles and going to Sardinia, where he wrote the number.

Discussing the next song, 'Photograph', he said that it came to him after George complained about Ringo always playing guitar in the key of E, the only key Ringo knew. George then taught him how to play the C chord when they were on holiday, so Ringo wrote 'Photograph' as an exercise.

He played drums on 'Love Me Do' while Scott Gordon played harmonica. The show then ended with the usual 'With A Little Help From My Friends'.

When it was aired by VH-1 on Sunday 28 June, three songs were dropped from the show – 'I Was Walkin'', 'Photograph' and 'What In The . . . World.' It was premiered in Britain on 8 November. Mercury Records issued *Ringo Starr – VH-1 Storytellers* simultaneously around the world on 20 October on CD, featuring all the tracks from the performance: 'With A Little Help From My Friends', 'I Was Walkin'', 'Don't Pass Me By', 'Back Off Boogaloo', 'King Of Broken Hearts', 'Octopus's Garden', 'Photograph', 'La De Da', 'What In The . . . World', 'Love Me Do' and 'With A Little Help From My Friends (reprise)'.

A home video version was also issued by Mercury Records on 10 November.

Voormann, Klaus

A German artist/bass guitarist, born in Berlin, who befriended the Beatles when they first performed in Hamburg in 1960. He later became bass guitarist with the Liverpool band Paddy, Klaus and Gibson prior to joining Manfred Mann.

Klaus played bass on several of Ringo's recordings, including the albums *Ringo*, *Goodnight Vienna* and *Ringo's Rotogravure*. He played bass on the hit singles 'It Don't Come Easy', 'Photograph' and 'Back Off Boogaloo', in addition to playing sax on the latter track.

Klaus was also a trained artist and designed the cover of the Beatles *Revolver* album, for which he received a Grammy award, and also the cover of George Harrison's *Wonderwall* album.

For the *Ringo* album he created ten lithographs illustrating each of the songs and they were packaged with the 24-page lyric book that came with the album. Klaus later went on to design the covers for the *Beatles Anthology* CDs.

When Paul sought the dissolution of the Beatles, it was rumoured that Klaus was initially considered as his replacement.

He was a member of John Lennon's Plastic Ono Band and the recordings he was on with John included the singles 'Cold Turkey', 'Instant Karma', 'Power To The People', 'God Save Us' and 'Whatever Gets You Thru The Night' and the albums *Plastic Ono Band – Live*

Peace In Toronto 1969, John Lennon/Plastic Ono Band, Imagine, Walls And Bridges and *Rock 'N' Roll.*

For George Harrison he appeared on the single 'My Sweet Lord' and the albums *All Things Must Pass, The Concert For Bangla Desh, Living In The Material World, Dark Horse* and *Extra Texture (Read All About It).*

In the 1970s Klaus moved to Los Angeles and was to live there for eight years, during which time he did sessions for several artists including Ringo, Carly Simon, Billy Preston and Harry Nilsson. Klaus introduced Ringo to Harry Nilsson and co-composed a number with Ringo that was intended as the title song for the film *Blindman*, although it wasn't used in the final print.

Klaus stopped working for Ringo in the late 1970s when Ringo had drink and drug problems. In an interview about this in the magazine *Beatlefan* he recalled, 'I love him. He's fantastic. But I had terrible experiences in Los Angeles with him where he really got out of hand. I could go to him whenever I wanted but so could every other idiot. The place was full of people shoving drugs down him and stuff. It was just awful. He was very discouraged and he actually lost his, for some years, lost his integrity.

'You could really rely on him, he was this rock, he was there for you and if he said something, he meant it and even though he sometimes was a little silly, you could really believe in him. When he said, "I'm gonna do this for you," he would do it. And then suddenly, for a while, that changed and he was not so nice.'

Waite, John

A British singer/songwriter who became bass guitarist and lead singer with the Babys and Bad English. He had a No. 1 hit with 'Missing You'.

Waite appeared with Ringo Starr's All-Starr Band on bass and vocals in 2003 and is included on the album *Ringo Starr And His All-Starr Band Live – Vol 3* recorded at the Casino Ramo. John's tracks are 'Missing You' and 'When I See You Smile'.

He was to comment, 'I'm gonna go and play bass guitar with Ringo in the summer for a couple of months. I used to be the bass player in the Babys before I became the lead singer, so I'm looking forward to hanging out with Ringo and playing Ringo's songs and being the fifth Beatle, you know. They made the call, and it looks like it's a complete go.'

Walking After Midnight

A film with narration by Ringo. The film was completed in 1989, although Ringo didn't add his narration until January 1991.

Walters, Lu

A Liverpool singer and bass guitarist, who was a member of Rory Storm and the Hurricanes. Lu's real name was Walter Eymond, but Rory Storm (real name Alan Caldwell) decided to change the names of the members of his group to give them a Western flavour. Ritchie Starkey became Ringo Starr and Charles O'Brien became Ty Brien.

In 1963 Walters was to talk about Ringo in an article in *Mersey Beat*:

I met Ringo during the old skiffle days. He was appearing at the Mardi Gras with Rory Storm and was dressed in a long black

Teddy Boy suit. Later, I joined the group which was then known as
the Raving Texans and we played numerous dates around the
Liverpool area.

Ringo was not an exceptional drummer at the time, but as the
group progressed he improved to such an extent that we realised
he would be a very good drummer.

We had some good times when we made our first appearance at
Butlin's holiday camp. Ringo was the lazy one of the group. In the
mornings he used to sleep late, and if woken would be very bad-
tempered. The first signs of him waking took the form of one open
eye, which was staring round the chalet. Then it would be between
one hour and one-and-a-half hours before he'd stir properly. Then
he wouldn't speak for an hour or so. After that he'd revert to his
normal self.

He was the life and soul of any party we went to and was well
liked because of his sense of humour.

We had quite a laugh watching him take swimming lessons off
Ty. At one time he seemed to be doing fine until he realised that he
was out of his depth and in the twelve-footer. Then he just yelled
and vanished from sight. It ended when three of us dived in and
pulled him out – we had a good laugh about it afterwards.

Members of the group often went horse-riding, but Ringo only
joined us once. The horse bit him and he ended up walking back
to camp.

At that time he started to show some of his exceptional talent on
drums and he also started singing. One of the numbers was 'Alley
Oop' and the girls started to scream their applause. Ringo was
born as a singer!

Following the season at Butlin's, we left for Germany. The audiences there liked him, but they also used to make him angry by
asking if he had dyed the streak in his hair. 'It's natural!' he used
to scream back at them.

His popularity reached its peak when a girl became so excited
that she had to be forcibly carried out of the club shrieking 'Ringo!
Ringo!' at the top of her voice.

We then met Tony Sheridan, who joined in sessions with us, and
he thought very highly of Ringo's ability. Before we left, Tony asked
Ringo to join him, and he stayed in Germany for a few months.

On his return he rejoined the Hurricanes and we later returned
for another season at Butlin's. Ringo now had a regular vocal spot
in the group, and we all worked together as a team.

When Ringo left the group last year to join the Beatles, we felt
we had lost a vital part of the group.

Now, Ringo is still one of our closest friends and we are all
thrilled at his success, for now he is one of the most famous drummers in the country.

When the Hurricanes were appearing in Hamburg, bill-topping above the Beatles, their agent Allan Williams was impressed by Lu's voice and paid for a recording session with Ringo, George, John and Paul backing him.

Walters later became a psychiatric nurse before his retirement.

Was, Don

An American producer/keyboard player/bass guitarist, born Donald Fagenson in Detroit, Michigan, on 13 September 1952. He teamed up with David Weiss and the duo called themselves Was (Not Was). He later gained prominence as a producer and has worked with an astonishing array of artists including the Rolling Stones, Elton John, Marianne Faithfull, Willie Nelson, Bob Dylan, the B52's, Joe Cocker and Neil Diamond.

Don was one of the producers of the 1992 *Time Takes Time* album. He was to comment, 'The coolest thing about this project is watching Ringo play drums.'

He produced the tracks 'Weight Of The World', 'Don't Know A Thing About Love', 'I Don't Believe You', 'In A Heartbeat' and 'What Goes Around'. He also remixed the tracks produced by Phil Ramone and Peter Asher.

Webb, Cynthia

Los Angeles-born singer/songwriter Cynthia Webb was to marry Klaus Voormann in the early 1970s. Klaus was a close associate of each member of the Beatles and it was through her husband that she contributed background vocals to Ringo's song 'Call Me' on the *Goodnight Vienna* album.

Between 1974 and 1975 Ringo, Klaus and Lon and Derrek Van Eaton backed Cynthia on recordings of several of her own compositions, although the tracks remain unreleased. They are: 'Changing', 'Dream Baby', 'I Am Sorry', 'Let Go Of Love', 'Secret', 'Take Your Love' and 'Widow Blues'.

Cynthia and Klaus were divorced in the 1980s.

Webb, Jimmy

A singer/songwriter born in Elk City, Oklahoma, on 15 August 1946. He penned some major hits for various artists including 'By The Time I Get To Phoenix', 'Witchita Lineman', 'Galveston', 'Up Up And Away' and 'MacArthur Park'.

He decided to record his own songs on some solo albums during the 70s and recorded *Land's End* in London. Webb was to receive a contribution from Ringo via their mutual friend Harry Nilsson, who persuaded Ringo to participate in the sessions.

Webb recalled, 'I was thrilled with the sight of Ringo and his drum kit in the studio. I had first met the Beatles at Trident Studios when they were recording *The Beatles*.

Ringo told Webb that his drums had been packed away and it was some time since he had played them. The engineer at the studio felt that the drums needed tuning and spent a few hours with Ringo trying to get the right sound, which made the session stretch out for a lengthy time. Webb could see that Ringo wasn't too happy and took him outside for a chat to cheer him up. They then returned and Ringo played on the track 'Alice Blue Gown'. Webb was later to say that the track was the best on the album.

He was with Ringo and John Lennon a few months later in Los Angeles and Ringo told him that the incident over the tuning of his drum kit had unnerved him at the time and shaken his confidence.

Weekend Of A Champion

A documentary film directed by Roman Polanski about Formula One racing driver Jackie Stewart. Filmed in 1970 to celebrate Stewart winning the 29th Monte Carlo Grand Prix, Ringo appears in a scene showing Stewart and his friends at a celebratory party.

Weight Of The World

Ringo's 14th solo single was a track from the 1992 album *Time Takes Time*. Penned by Brian O'Doherty and Fred Velez, it is 3 minutes and 54 seconds in length. It was released on Private Music 115 392 on 4 May 1992 and reached No. 74 in the British charts. 'After All These Years' was on the flip. There was also a CD issued on Private Music 665 392 with the addition of 'Don't Be Cruel'. The track was produced by Don Was, engineered by Ed Cherney and remixed by Bob Clearmountain. Ringo was on lead vocals, drums and percussion, Mark Goldenberg on guitar, James 'Hutch' Hutchinson on bass, Benmont Tench on keyboards and Roger Manning and Andrew Sturmer on backing vocals.

Weiland, Scott

The former singer with Seattle-based grunge band the Stone Temple Pilots, who Ringo sang with on a track on the *Vertical Man* album. Weiland was later arrested on drugs charges, which caused Ringo to comment: 'He was vertical when he was on my record, but he is not vertical now.

'In the music business, you are allowed to drink, and you are up all night, and you are allowed to take drugs – it's part of it. But, you know, we must always remember that the highest suicide rate is among dentists.'

Weinberg, Max

An American musician, born on 13 April 1951. He became drummer with Bruce Springsteen's E Street Band. His 1984 book *The Big Beat* contained an interview with Ringo, and his series of CDs about drumming in 1994 included Ringo's 'Drumming Is My Madness' on Vol 3.

Weinberg made several guest appearances with the All-Starr Band At the Radio City Music Hall, New York, on 13 July 1995, where he drummed on 'No No Song' and 'With A Little Help From My Friends' and did the same at the Garden State Arts Center in Holmdel, New Jersey, a few days later on 18 July. Weinberg also guested at the Garden State Arts Center on 3 June 1997 and drummed on 'Photograph' and 'With A Little Help From My Friends'.

What Goes Around
A number from the 1992 *Time Takes Time* album, written by Richard Suchow. It was produced by Don Was and engineered by Ed Cherney and Rik Pekkonen. Ringo was on lead vocals, drums and percussion, Michael Landau on guitar, David Grisson on acoustic guitar, James 'Hutch' Hutchinson on bass, Benmont Tench on piano and Hammond B3, and Andrew Sturmer, Roger Manning and Andrew Gold on backing vocals. The number is 5 minutes and 51 seconds in length.

What Goes On
A track on the *Rubber Soul* album on which Ringo takes over on lead vocal. John Lennon was to comment, 'A very edgy song of mine. Ringo and Paul wrote a new middle-eight together when we recorded it.' The number became the first song for which Ringo received a songwriting credit.

Ringo was to say, 'I wish I could write songs like the others – and I've tried, but I just can't. I can get the words all right, but whenever I think of a tune and sing it to the others they always say, "Yeah, it sounds like such a thing," and when they point it out I see what they mean.'

The number is 2 minutes and 43 seconds in length.

What In The ... World
A track from the *Vertical Man* album, 3 minutes and 29 seconds in length, written by Starkey/Hudson/Grakal/Dudas.

Ringo provided lead vocals, drums and percussion, with Paul McCartney on bass and backing vocals, Joe Walsh on electric guitar, Steve Dudas on electric guitar and acoustic guitar, and Mike Hudson on electric guitar, acoustic guitar, percussion and backing vocals. Paul McCartney played bass and provided backing vocals. Producer Mark Hudson recorded it at Paul's home studio the Mill.

What Love Wants To Be
A track from the 2003 *Ringo Rama* album lasting 3 minutes and 3 seconds, with Van Dyke Parks playing accordion.

Whatinthewhatthe? Studios
Mark Hudson's studio in Santa Monica, California, situated above a Thai restaurant and a liquor store.

Mark recalled that in the 1950s and 1960s, before swearing became acceptable in films, people in the movies weren't allowed to say things like 'What the hell!' – they'd have to say 'What the . . .' and stop. One day he was watching a 1950s sci-fi film in which Martians had poisoned some cows, leaving punctures in their necks. A cop looks at one and says, 'What the . . .' The other cop looks and says, 'What in the what the . . .' Mark recalled, 'I'd never heard an addition to a "What the . . ." Whatinthewhatthe? I thought it the coolest thing I'd ever heard.' So he decided to call his studio that.

Discussing the recording of *Vertical Man* at the studio, he said, 'It was Ringo's request. I'm a garage-band guy. We were just going to demo the songs there, but he loved the vibe so much, he said, "I don't want to go any place else," so he brought his drums over – the same old silver-and-black Ringo kit, from *Ed Sullivan* and everywhere else. The guests added their contributions later. This means that the album has a very even feel to it and never loses its identity – in fact the album would still have been great without the Starr guests – something that couldn't be said about the previous Ringo albums.'

When You Wish Upon A Star
The Ringo track from the Disney album *Stay Awake*. It was issued as a promotional disc in Germany in October 1988 on A&M 871 170-7 with Aaron Neville's 'Mickey Mouse March' on the flip. The disc came with a copy of the edited version of the 'Stay Awake' track.

Where Did Our Love Go
A number originally penned by Motown's Eddie Holland, Lamont Dozier and Brian Holland, which was a million-seller for the Supremes and their first No. 1 hit in 1964.

Ringo's version was the final track on Side One of his 1978 album *Bad Boy*. It is 3 minutes and 14 seconds in length.

Whispering Grass (Don't Tell The Trees)
A number from the *Sentimental Journey* album, arranged by Ron Goodwin. It is 2 minutes and 35 seconds in length.

White Christmas
The ultimate Christmas standard, penned by Irving Berlin, which Ringo included, in reggae style, on his 1999 album *I Wanna Be Santa Claus*. Ringo was on lead vocals, drums and percussion, Armand Sabal-Lecco on bass, Steve Dudas on electric guitar, Jaydee Maness on pedal steel guitar, Jim Cox on B3 organ and synthesizer, Mark Hudson on percussion and backing vocals, and Timothy B. Schmit, Bill Hudson and Christina Rasch on backing vocals. It is 3 minutes and 14 seconds in length.

White, Andy

A session drummer who was employed by Ron Richards to play on the Beatles first single on 11 September 1962. British A&R men at the time often hired session drummers, because they were familiar with the sound required in the surrounds of a studio.

At the time White was 32 years old and had played with the Vic Lewis Orchestra.

When the Beatles arrived they saw that White had set up his drum kit and Ron Richards began the recording session. When George Martin turned up he told them, 'I'm giving you a very good drummer who's probably better than Ringo Starr, and that's who's going to play the drums.'

White performed on 'Love Me Do' and 'P.S. I Love You', and spent three hours in the studio, but received no royalties, just the usual session fee. In recent years he says the fee was £11 (although at the time he said he was paid less than £6). He recalls, 'That was about the rate they paid for a session back then, and it was actually pretty good money.'

Commenting on 'Love Me Do' he said, 'It didn't take very long after I learned the routines. They just put the light on and did two or three takes. Ringo tapped a tambourine and I did the drumming. I was paid a session fee and that was it, really. It couldn't be any other way, he was in the group and I was a decade older than them. It was just one session of the week.'

He also said, 'I was told later that when Ringo saw me setting up my kit he thought he was getting the bullet.'

There has been some confusion regarding the version of 'Love Me Do' that was released, and even Ringo thought that his own version wasn't used, recording another version himself in 1988 because it was 'the very first record that I didn't drum on'.

It actually took White eighteen takes to record while Ringo did it in only fifteen.

The first version of 'Love Me Do' had been recorded on 6 June 1962 when Pete Best was with the band – this was eventually included on the *Anthology 1* CD in 1995.

The second version, this time with Ringo, was recorded on 4 September 1962. Ron Richards, George Martin and even Paul McCartney seemed uncomfortable with Ringo's drumming on the session and for the next recording, 11 September, session drummer White had been hired, to the surprise and discomfort of Ringo.

The version by Andy White was included on the *Please Please Me* album and on the EP 'The Beatles Hits'. It was also on the reissue of the number in March 1976 when EMI Records were reissuing the entire Beatles catalogue.

Ringo's version was released as the A side of the Beatles debut EMI single on Parlophone R4949 on 5 October 1962.

At the time of the 'Love Me Do' recording White was married to Liverpool singer Lynn Cornell, who'd been a neighbour of Paul McCartney and a former member of the Vernons Girls.

White was later to join the BBC Radio Orchestra in Glasgow. He later moved to America, where he worked with a number of prominent artists including Louis Armstrong, Shirley Bassey, Marlene Dietrich and Chuck Berry.

By 1992 he'd settled in New York as a librarian, but worked part time as a drummer with the New York Police Band.

Who Needs A Heart

The opening track on the 1978 *Bad Boy* album, lasting 3 minutes and 47 seconds. The number was penned by Ringo and Vini Poncia.

Winter Wonderland

One of the numbers featured on Ringo's 1999 album *I Wanna Be Santa Claus*. The song, written by Richard B. Smith and Felix Bernard, was originally featured in the *Ziegfeld Follies* show in 1934. Ringo was on lead vocals, drums and percussion, Mark Hudson on bass, electric guitar and backing vocals, Steve Dudas and Bill Hudson on electric guitars, Jim Cox on Wurlitzer and piano and Gary Burr on backing vocals. It is 2 minutes and 55 seconds in length.

With A Little Help From My Friends (song)

The number that Ringo always uses as a final encore on his All-Starr Band tours and the one in which various guest artists join them on stage.

The song was written by Paul McCartney, with a little help from John Lennon, and Paul had used the working title 'Badfinger Boogie'. He was later to suggest the name Badfinger for a group Apple had signed up called the Iveys. He was to pen a number for Badfinger called 'Come And Get It' which became the theme tune to the Peter Sellers/Ringo Starr movie *The Magic Christian*.

The song was included on the *Sgt Pepper's Lonely Hearts Club Band* album. It was recorded at Abbey Road Studios on 29 March 1967. Ringo played drums and sang the lead vocal, Paul was on bass, piano and backing vocal, John was on backing vocal and George on tambourine.

Paul was to say, 'Ringo's got a great sentimental thing. He likes soul music and always has, though we didn't see that scene for a long while 'til he showed us. I suppose that's why we write these sort of songs for him, with sentimental things in them, like "With A Little Help From My Friends".'

With A Little Help From My Friends (television special)

A television special focusing on George Martin in which Ringo appeared and performed 'Octopus's Garden'. Due to a Musicians'

Union ruling regarding miming, the original track by the Beatles couldn't be used and Ringo had to re-record the number at Abbey Road Studios on 8 December 1969. He was videotaped performing the number in Studio Four at the television centre in Yorkshire on 14 December and Yorkshire Television broadcast the programme on 24 December.

Without Understanding

A track on the *Vertical Man* album, 4 minutes and 22 seconds in length, written by Starkey/Hudson/Dudas. Ringo provided lead vocal, drums, a plastic guitar solo, keyboard and percussion. Brian Wilson was on backing vocals, Mark Hudson on electric guitar, acoustic guitar, string synthesizer and backing vocals, Steve Dudas provided an electric guitar solo and was also on acoustic guitar, Jim Cox played B3 organ, Steve Gordon percussion, John Bergamo tabla, and Christian Phillippe Quilici provided an opera vocal. There was also a gospel choir on the track.

Wood, Ron

A musician born in London on 1 June 1947. His first group was the Birds, followed by the Jeff Beck Group and the Faces. When Rod Stewart left the Faces, Wood made his own solo album *I've Got My Own Album To Do* with contributions from George Harrison.

When Wood appeared on NBC TV's *Midnight Special* on 8 June 1979 Ringo played drums on 'Buried Alive', a number from Woods *Gimme Some Neck* album. Wood contributed to the numbers 'Giveaway' and 'Brandy' on Ringo's 1981 album *Stop And Smell The Roses*.

Since 1975 he has been a member of the Rolling Stones.

Wrack My Brain

A track from the *Stop And Smell The Roses* album that George Harrison originally wrote in 1974. George also produced the number for Ringo and played lead and acoustic guitars on the song. Apart from Ringo and George, the other musicians were Herbie Flowers on bass and tuba, Al Kooper on piano and electric guitar, and Ray Cooper on piano, percussion, synthesizer and lead guitar. George Harrison and Ray Cooper provided the backing vocals.

The number is 3 minutes and 26 seconds in length. It was issued in Britain on RCA 166 on 13 November 1981 and in America on Boardwalk NB7-11-130 on 27 October 1981 with 'Drumming Is My Madness' on the flip. It reached No. 38 in the American charts.

Write One For Me

A track from the 2003 *Ringo Rama* album, 3 minutes and 14 seconds in length. Ringo alternated between lead vocal and duetting with Willie Nelson.

Mark Hudson was in a writers' camp with Gary Burr of the Roundheads when Ringo called him and said, 'Write one for me.' Mark thought that he meant he wanted to write a song for him, but he said that 'Write One For Me' was the title of the song. The song tells the story of a boy who doesn't have the nerve to tell a girl that she's the right one for him. He doesn't know how to put his feelings into words, then meets someone in a bar and asks them to write his feelings for the girl down for him. It was Ringo's suggestion that they get Willie Nelson to sing it with him.

You Always Hurt The One You Love
This song from *Sentimental Journey* was penned by Allan Roberts and Doris Fisher and gave the Mills Brothers a four-week stay at the top of the charts in America in 1944. Johnny Dankworth arranged this version. Ringo recorded the basic track at De Lane Lea Studios on 25 February 1970 and overdubs were done at Morgan Studios on 6 March. It is 2 minutes and 18 seconds in length.

You And Me (Babe)
A track from the *Ringo* album, which was written for Ringo by George Harrison and Mal Evans. George also played electric guitar. It is 4 minutes and 31 seconds in length.

You Belong To Me
A number from the 1981 *Stop And Smell The Roses* album that was penned by George Harrison. George played lead and acoustic guitar and Al Kooper and Ray Cooper were on synthesizers. It is 2 minutes and 7 seconds in length.

You Don't Know Me At All
A track from *Ringo's Rotogravure*, written by Dave Jordan, 3 minutes and 14 seconds in length. Other musicians on the track include Lon Van Eaton on guitar, Cooker Lo Presti on bass guitar and John Jarvis on piano.

You Know
A track Ringo recorded in Los Angeles on 14 September 1991, produced by Steve Dorff. The number was used over the closing credits

of the film *Curly Sue*, which starred James Belushi, and was included on the soundtrack album, released in America on 23 November 1991 on Giant 9 24439-2 and in Britain on 6 January 1992 on Giant 7599 244392.

You're Sixteen

Ringo's third million-selling single, a track from the *Ringo* album. The number was written by Robert and Richard Sherman, and Johnny Burnette had a million-seller with his version.

On Ringo's recording, backing vocals were by Harry Nilsson, Nicky Hopkins played piano and Paul McCartney imitated a saxophone. It is 2 minutes and 45 seconds in length.

It was issued as a single in Britain on Apple R 5995 on 8 February 1974 with 'Devil Woman' on the flip and reached No. 4 in the British charts. It was issued in America on Apple 1870 on 3 December 1973 and became his second American chart-topper, selling over two million copies worldwide.

The number was also included on Ringo's 1975 *Blast From Your Past* album.

You've Got A Nice Way

A number penned by Steve Stills, which was recorded at Cherokee Recording Studios in North Hollywood on 19 December 1980 during the 'Can't Fight Lightning' (*Stop And Smell The Roses*) sessions. It was one of three numbers that Ringo had asked Stills to contribute.

Zappa, Frank

An American musician born in Baltimore, Maryland, on 21 December 1940. Zappa achieved success and notoriety with his band Mothers of Invention and in 1971 filmed *200 Motels* in Britain. This rock-band parody featured Ringo as both Frank Zappa and Larry the Dwarf.

Ringo's chauffeur Martin Lickert applied to appear in the film as a bass player in the Mothers of Invention.

Pictures of Ringo were featured in the soundtrack album booklet.

Zappa was diagnosed with prostate cancer and died on 4 December 1993. He was posthumously inducted into the Rock and Roll Hall of Fame in 1995

Zoom

A Jeff Lynne album on which Ringo and George made guest appearances. George played slide guitar on two tracks and Ringo drummed on 'Easy Money' and 'Moment In Paradise'.